DIVINATION, ORDER, AND THE *ZHOUYI*

Richard Gotshalk

University Press of America,® Inc.
Lanham • New York • Oxford

Copyright © 1999 by
University Press of America,® Inc.
4720 Boston Way
Lanham, Maryland 20706

12 Hid's Copse Rd.
Cumnor Hill, Oxford OX2 9JJ

Library of Congress Cataloging-in-Publication Data

Gotshalk, Richard.
Divination, order, and the Zhouyi / Richard Gotshalk.
p.   cm.
Includes bibliographical references and index.
1. I ching. 2. Divination—China. I. I ching. II. Title.
PL2464.Z7G67 1999   299'.5182—dc21   98-50879 CIP

ISBN 0-7618-1315-2 (cloth: alk. ppr.)

Contents

PREFACE

My earliest encounter with the *Zhouyi* touched me in a way that I did not understand, and did not pay much attention to either. For a budding philosopher in the Western tradition, it was like myth, something out of another world and to the rational mind not something to be taken seriously, except perhaps to understand what irrational impulses it appealed to. That was long ago, before the deepening of my experience and the slow clarification of what developed in it, of what seemed most revealing, most profoundly and forcefully disclosive. Over the years both myth and the *Zhouyi* grew on me. Vaguely it seemed that the latter might be important in the background of Chinese philosophy, a manifestation of the Zhou mentality in whose context the drive toward philosophical reflection arose and grew. But it was not clear how that might be, even as I sought to bring to light what fascinated me in the work. Especially was it unclear as long as the work seemed only a patchwork, a hodge-podge.

Works can fascinate, even though one has no clear notion of how or why. It is usually only in retrospect that one can gain much clarity concerning what was attracting one, and that is the case here. It has emerged after these many years-- over forty by now-- that what the work was touching on in me had to do with a sense of order, of the way the universe is coherent and we, as human agents placed in the midst of things here on earth, participate meaningfully in ongoing affairs. If we are patient enough with our own evolution, if we can learn to take part in a truly participatory fashion, the universe seems a much different affair than it does to observers who hold back, who take note in distant fashion, and who are impressed, indeed overwhelmed, by the "starry heavens", to allude to Kant. Would that they, like

Kant, found the moral evoked by the sublime!

In this searching out the nature of the *Zhouyi* and the divination it is suited to facilitate, I have had no mentors, yet have found help in numerous places along the way. Two places in particular, I mention here. Back in the mid-60's, Bob Henricks helped me enter into the Chinese language, and though he has never found anything of interest in the *Zhouyi* we have over the years shared an interest in Chinese thought (and food!), particularly in Lao-zi. He has also been my lookout, so to speak, bringing much to my attention (newly discovered manuscripts, scholarly writings) that he thought would interest me. I have never met Edward Shaughnessy, but my encounter with his doctoral thesis came at an auspicious time when my own sense of what was involved in divination and in the *Zhouyi* was well formed enough to find analyses, claims, and comments, of his fruitfully helping me on my path. However, and in no derogation to the two scholars, the closest thing I have had to a mentor on this matter of divination, has been a river and a creek, to mention the foreground, and more intimately and powerfully, an opening up of time's being as I fished in them and found a dark and mysterious presence indwelling closely our strange companionship. Time, it is, that is of the essence for understanding divination, but not the time of everyday life, or of physical science, or of biological evolution-- not even the time of history. Find the source and ground of all these, find the peculiar confluence of future and past in the deepening of presence, and one is on the way to understanding how the *Zhouyi* works and how it is that it does, indeed, form a significant marker on the way to the beginnings of Chinese philosophy.

Be patient with what you read here, it will take time-- and more than time-- for its meaning to come forward for you. Take divination seriously-- but not necessarily fortune-telling. For that distinction, and other matters that make the *Zhouyi* of inestimable worth as a work to study and use even in this world of ours today, read on. May your engagement with it prove fruitful to you over the years!

INTRODUCTION

In the late 9th century BC, toward the end of the Western Zhou era, someone composed a divination work which, in the historical records currently known to us, initially was referred to as *Zhouyi*. The meaning of the title is not altogether clear. "*Zhou*" is the name of the people among whom the sort of divination served by the work was used to help carry out important purposes in their governance of themselves and of the civilized and civilizing part of the world. "*Yi*" signifies "change" or "changes". But what do the two terms mean together?

Divination anticipates the future and expresses the sense that change lies at the heart of existence and makes the future uncertain to us in the present. Because there is something at stake in our lives and actions, it is important that we be able to venture into the future in our undertakings based on as assured an anticipation as we can manage. Presumably the *Zhouyi* was referred to under that title because it represented a distinctively Zhou way of seeking to anticipate the future, a way grounded in the Zhou sense of themselves and of the universe in which they found themselves. That way involved inquiry addressed to the Zhou ancestral spirits. Through a manipulation of yarrow-stalks in a religious ritual, response from those spirits was elicited, in the form of signs that point to the basic change-dynamic in the real world and therein to factors harbored in that reality and bearing in determining fashion on the matters being inquired about. Apprehension and understanding of those factors coming to attention under the guidance of those signs would be the basis both for forming an anticipation which would be securely grounded in the realities of the situation and for responsively shaping the inquirer's own taking part in the matters in question.

At least, that is the vein in which I understand the title of the work which is studied and translated in the following pages.

In Part I of this work I approach the *Zhouyi* in the following fashion.

The first step recalls salient points in the larger historical background for this work, with a focus on the political and cultural background and context. The exposition sets forth an understanding of who the Zhou were: at the start, when the Zhou assumed leadership in the civilized world and offered a vision of the Mandate of Heaven; during the continuation of that leadership, as it prospered, then declined and threatened to disintegrate; and finally, in those times of (as it turned out) temporary revival and renewal of the early Zhou commitment and vision, during which the *Zhouyi* was composed. This divination work was one expression of the renewed Zhou spirit in those late 9th century times.

The second step considers divination, with a focus on the stalk-divination tradition within which the *Zhouyi* stands and which it transforms. This involves us first in recalling the pre-*Zhouyi* stalk-divination tradition, so far as evidence allows us to see it; then we reflect upon divination in its address to change, and in particular, to change as human beings are caught up in this as agents effecting and affected by change. Then we consider how in general the *Zhouyi* reflects a transformation in the way change is addressed in the stalk-divination tradition, a transformation which enhanced the suitability of stalk-divination to play a role in a renewed Zhou rule.

The third step sets forth the features of the *Zhouyi* system of divination as conveyed in the written work, and then sketches out first the nature of the world reflected in the images drawn upon within the work, and second, reality as it is presupposed in the method of divination which uses those images as symbols to address change.

The fourth and final step addresses the relevance of this ancient divinatory work to us today, and in particular, its possible employment by a contemporary American reader. The *Zhouyi* was not originally a text to be read, but the written representation of a divination system to be used. Can it be used in a different historical setting, by persons outside the tradition in which its images and symbols had their origin and initial meaning?

Part II is a translation of the text and a brief commentary upon it. This is prefaced by a note concerning the text for the translation and in particular concerning features of the traditional and Mawangdui versions which seem to reflect modifications made in the original text in the course of its transmission over the centuries. The commentary is mainly concerned to point to those elements of order-- in the whole, in the immediate context of a hexagram, and within the hexagram itself-- which are immediately relevant for understanding the full meaning of each part of the work.

PART I
CONTEXT AND PERSPECTIVE

Chapter 1
Historical Background and Setting

Divination takes innumerable forms, but in general the divinatory act is oriented toward one of two types of starting-point.

In the one case, divination begins from events whose occurrence has a quality due to which those events are taken as signs-- as omens of something. At the most profound level, they have a numinous character, and are-- or at least, are taken as-- initiated by divine powers and form significant 'speech' chosen by those powers as medium for communicating with human beings. Divination in this form is the effort to interpret the disclosure of such signs, to determine the meaning of such speech.

In the other case, divination makes as its focus certain man-made happenings. Seeking guidance, human beings produce something, and regard what is produced as a significant sign, an intimation (say) or an omen. Such a humanly-produced sign is taken as 'speaking' on this occasion to matters one is inquiring about or proposing to do. In the measure in which the act of divination is religious and such as to draw the divine into play as participant in the act, that sign is taken as 'speech' from the divine, even though human action had a decisive part in 'producing' the sign. Divination in this case is the act of initiating the interplay in which such signs are selected, and the act of interpreting the meaning of those signs for the matters at issue.

At its most profound the divinatory act in both cases involves a working of divine powers as well as human, and focuses on an encounter with signs which are taken to voice those powers in their disclosing of something to human beings, and in particular, in their disclosing something futural.

The Chinese seem to have known many significant events and types of event, and also to have developed several types of humanly constructed and initiated divinatory system. Of the latter we know something from our earliest written records, for these often consist of pieces of shell or bone with inscriptions made in the course of conducting divination. These are the oracle bones and shells which come from the Shang dynasty and the predynastic Zhou times-- times before the middle of the 11th century B.C. Divination using turtle shells or ox bones involved a method of heating the medium to produce cracks, and a reading of the cracks as significant signs, as 'speech' which responded to questions or proposals in regard to which one sought light from ancestral spirits and divine powers.

The *Zhouyi* is a written work which sets forth elements of a different divinatory method and medium. In light of present evidence,[1] it is the work of an official attached to the royal Zhou court, and was composed by him toward the end of the 9th century BC. This work had a place in another tradition of divination which may even be longer than the bone/shell tradition. The first-order and concrete medium for this form of divination is a set of milfoil (yarrow) stalks. These are manipulated in order to select out the signs which voice the response of ancestral spirits and divine powers to queries or proposals. In their *Zhouyi* form, those signs are found in the language which accompanies certain abstract line-figures, which form the second-order and abstract medium in this divinatory process. The manipulation of the yarrow stalks selects out the line-figures or individual lines whose associated language is taken as the response to be interpreted. The basic signs are the images and representations of events and occurrences embodied in the language-elements associated with those line-figures or lines. Such signs are often accompanied by other verbal elements, which (among other things) interpret the bearing of the sign in various ways.[2]

Behind this work lies not only a long tradition of divinatory practice including both types of divination just mentioned, and presumably a long oral tradition handed down in the continuation over the centuries of such practice. Behind it also lies a larger historical movement and setting, and in particular, the Zhou conquest of the Shang and assumption of the Mandate of Heaven, in the mid-11th century BC. If we are to understand the *Zhouyi*, we need to recall aspects of this history and to place the use of both modes of divination in this basic setting, as practical instruments for the use of the rulers and their diviners.

A. The Shang, and shell/bone divination
by their rulers

Early in the 16th century BC, one people among those of the central and lower reaches and drainages of the Yellow River in north China seems to have become supreme. Known as the Shang or Yin, their dynasty lasted until, in the mid-11th century BC, it was overthrown in an uprising of the Zhou peoples, neighbors to the south and west.[3]

So far as we currently know, the Shang were the first literate people of Asia east of the Urals. The system of writing which is found on such archaeological remains as we have from the time is the initial known form of the Chinese still in use today. The remains which contain this script are of two main kinds. One is certain bones of animals (mostly oxen) and the shells of certain turtles. These shells and bones were media in the most important divination system of the Shang leaders. They represent most of the script we have from the Shang.[4] The other materials containing script are certain bronze vessels, on which signs of possession and offering are to be found as inscriptions.

The form of the Chinese script that is found in all these cases seems already a well-developed writing system, which presumably has a considerable previous development behind it. And the casting techniques and artistic conception involved in the bronze vessels likewise are advanced to a considerable degree. Thus there is likely to be a long history involved here, only the last phase of which is still accessible to us sufficiently to allow us to say much that is assured or definite about it.

In the culminating phase of Shang civilization, starting probably in the late 14th century, with the reign of King Wu Ding, the Shang knew themselves as a civilized center surrounded by peoples with lesser cultural achievement. Their civilization had an urban center, yet economically it was based mainly on an intensive village agriculture which took advantage of the climate, land and water conditions of the area, which were conducive to agriculture. It also involved considerable development of specialized craftsmanship, and an extensive enough trade that the term "Shang" became standard Chinese for "merchant".

Socially the civilization seems to have been stratified. At its bottom were the "multitudes", the mass of men who were the farmers who cultivated the fields of the King, of the other lords, and of the ruling powers generally. These lived in farming villages or on the outskirts of the urban areas. At much the same level, though some at least were apparently on a higher level, came the craftsmen. Those on the higher level were those mainly whose crafts were particularly valued by the highest class. At the apex of the social structure came the small group ("the hundred families") which constituted an aristocracy centered in the King and the royal family. From these upper clans were probably drawn most of the Shang officials as well.[5]

Two things about this civilization are of primary importance for our purpose.

First is its political ordering, in which the King ruled in a way that accorded a place to officials and functionaries as carrying out the King's charges and assisting in his affairs but apparently did not involve such delegation of authority as would be involved in a feudal system. The area governed was limited enough, the governing structure simple enough, the connection of the important subordinate figures close enough to the King, that a sense of unity could be maintained.

Significant in governance was the other matter of primary importance for our purpose, namely, the religious vision which animated the Shang leaders at least and through them the whole people. The vision was realized in the very structure of their domiciles, palaces, temples and tombs. Invariably they were square or oblong, and governed in orientation by the four cardinal directions and dominated in design by a persistent attempt at symmetry. This signified their being a microcosm, for the macrocosm was also square, with each of the four directions having its own deity, and the winds from these directions being the agents of these deities. Beyond these divine powers, were those manifest in the sun, moon, stars, earth, mountains, rivers, and the like.

But the primary divine powers involved in the worship of the Shang leaders were twofold.

On the one hand, were the spirits of their ancestors, as the superior ancestral powers among the dead. For the dead formed a hierarchy parallel to that of the living, and the more ancient the power the more powerful. These spirits had vast but relatively undefined powers, and in particular served as mediator between the King and the supreme divine power.

On the other hand, rising above all these divine powers was a deity whom the Shang characteristically called Lord (*di*) or Lord-on-High (*shang di*).[6]

Among the Shang, certainly in the royal family and aristocracy and probably more widely, sacrifice was commonly directed to the relevant ancestral spirits. Its sense was one of mutual sustenance between the living and the dead. For sacrifice would provide nourishment that would support the spirits in their being. Those spirits in turn would support the living line in the measure in which its members showed respect for the ancestors and would threaten it when the living neglected or did not respect them. Such spirits were the primary divine powers of immediate significance.

In the case of the King, whose royal ancestors became divine powers elevated to serve in the court of the highest divine power after death, his ancestors provided the mediating powers in his relation to Lord-on-High. For apparently there was no direct sacrifice made to the ultimate divine power, despite its being the all-powerful and controlling force within human affairs as well as in the order and happenings in the world at large. As supreme directive power in charge of all else, it was remote like the heavens through which it was mainly manifest. Communication with this power by living human beings was made by the King by way of the ancestral spirits of the royal line; they alone, themselves high deities, were worthy and able to mediate human communication with this power.

The divinatory medium through which the Shang King sought to gain information and guidance from such powers involved the use of certain bones and shells and the production of cracks in these by the application of heat. The sort of divination in question was not unique to the Shang; indeed long before the them it seems to have been important enough to have given rise to specialized groups of diviners. But there, as in the case of the Shang, it was closely connected with ancestor-worship.

What was distinctive in the Shang seems to have been three things: (1) they used not simply certain bones from cattle, but turtle shells as well; (2) they cut an orderly series of hollows or depressions into the bone or shell, so that the omen cracks were not free-form but structured, assuming specific shapes in specific places; (3) they incised the divination records into the bones and shells, using that script which has characterized the writing of China ever since.[7]

Since it was a religious sense that placed divination into an important place, the undertaking of divination was a religious ritual. After extensive physical and ritual preparation of the bones and shells to be used, the ritual involved posing questions, or charging the bones or shells with the matters concerning which information and guidance was sought, producing the cracks through the application of heat, and reading the disclosure of the cracks.

The matters placed into question in this ritual were varied, but since the King was the ultimate questioner they were matters he took to be of crucial import to himself as leader of the community.

Of matters that concerned the future, some related to proposed human initiative in the present. Thus the question could concern the advisability of undertaking certain actions in the current conditions, and the possibility of a successful issue of such actions; ritual of one sort or another, addressed to one or another divine power with one or another request or prayer being involved; or agricultural activities, or hunting expeditions, or excursions to inspect one or another region or to travel. Or... the question could concern whether divine assistance would be forthcoming (or divine approval) if certain activities were undertaken: building projects, military ventures, the forming of one alliance or another, the issuing of an order for someone to carry out a certain task.

But of the matters that concerned the future, some also related to affairs in which the initiative was beyond the King. Thus it might lie in the realm of nature (and that means, ultimately of the divine), for example: weather as this would affect agriculture, or as it might affect certain excursions or ritual activities, the issue of harvest, childbirth (in the timing, the sex of the child, the difficulty of the birth). Or the initiative might lie in the realm of man, for example: the arrival of tribute and its quantity and character. Or it might lie simply in the indefinite, for example, whether the King would suffer distress or trouble of some unspecified sort; included here were divinations concerning the ten-day period ahead, or the night-time period ahead, or the day ahead, with the question concerning the possibility of disaster.[8]

In the case of matters that concerned not the future but the present, there was divination to discover what ancestor or divine power was the source of an ominous dream, or of a specified illness, or what spirit was cursing the crops.

The divination procedures were undertaken mainly by the priests, but the reading of the significance of the cracks produced[9] was apparently the King's responsibility. Generally, it seems these were taken as disclosing the spiritual forces of the universe in such way as to allow determination of 'yes' or 'no', 'auspicious' or 'inauspicious' (with some degree possible here), although apparently the cracks could fail to give any intelligible response.[10]

Presumably, as with sacrifice so with divination: different Kings and their different priests took part in these religious rituals with a greater or lesser depth in spirituality, with greater or lesser profundity and self-consciousness, with clearer or vaguer understanding and idea of the nature and meaning of what was involved. And for that reason if for no other, what these rituals meant to each was likely to be somewhat different.

Our records are fragmentary, to say the least, and they are not supplemented directly by much helpful evidence from the period. From what evidence we have, however, it seems that we may trace "a gradual but certain development in the role of divination during the 250-odd years of the late Shang".[11]

The Shang oracle-bones which attest this development have been grouped and periodized. The earliest inscriptions indicate that the consultations were framed as questions, and were undertaken in a more or less *ad hoc* fashion, as responding to specific incidents or situations rather than taking place at regular intervals or set occasions. Another set of inscriptions, still belonging to the extended reign of Wu Ding (1324-1265), lacks interrogative phrases but includes what seem to be paired divinations, with declarative statements positive and negative being employed.

Shortly after Wu Ding, and to the end of the Shang dynasty, some dramatic changes appear in the inscription record. A reduced scope in the topics involved, fewer consultations, and the use of fewer shells in each consultation, go along with a focus of divination on the sacrifice cycle, the ten-day week and the night, and the hunt. The *ad hoc* quality of the early inscriptions is gone, and in its place is divination which takes place periodically and seems basically *pro forma*. In addition, instead of prognostications which could be either favorable or unfavorable, we find only favorable ones, and these are related to topics which are uniformly positive.

What seems indicated by these changes is twofold. First, divination through shells/bones, while once vital and brought into play in crucial times, over time lost that vitality and intimate connection with significant change. Second, concomitant with this routinization went a shift in the manner of address to the spirits. Inquiry which sought greater understanding and the resolution of doubts with the help of the spirits gave way to an address which is more like an attempt to sway the spirits to support an already decided upon course of action.[12]

B. The Zhou: at the beginning,
the Mandate of Heaven

1. The Zhou and the initial conquest

While the nucleus of the Shang civilization was confined to a relatively small area in north China, its influence radiated fairly widely in all directions. When the downfall of the dynasty came, two things connected with the outlying regions seem to have been important contributing factors. First was a long military involvement with some of the barbarian peoples to the south and east, which weakened the Shang militarily. Second was the rise of another and kindred civilization, the Zhou, in the Wei River basin south and west of the main Shang land.

The Zhou seem to have been members of a separate sub-culture from the Shang, who moved into the Wei River valley, in present-day Shaanxi province, about a century before the conquest of the Shang.[13] The leader who brought his people to settle there on the plain of Zhou, under Mount Qi, was the Ancient Duke Dan-fu. If the movement and settlement there were crucial steps in a building Zhou sense of themselves as a people with a future and with a culture on the rise, Shang connections and influence were also already part of Zhou life. The walled city which the Zhou laid out was built in the Shang manner. And Dan-fu himself was given the rank of Duke by the Shang King.[14] The importance of Dan-fu for the subsequent Zhou undertaking is reflected in his grandson's (King Wen's) retrospective reference to him as the "Great King" who was the first in the line of Zhou Kings.

The ambivalent pattern of Zhou-Shang relations that the sketchy indications of this early history exhibits, involving war and conflict and at the same time assimilation and attraction (at least from the side of the Zhou), was maintained until the conquest. For this "relatively unsophisticated but vigorous people",[15] expanding and evolving on the strength of some impetus internal to themselves as well as under some influence and challenge from the outside, enlarged its sphere of control and influence in a way which was basically hostile to the Shang.[16] Yet the thrust of expansion, while aggressive, continued to be hedged in by an acknowledgement of the Shang overlordship.[17]

Beyond the matter of political power and its balance and precise nature, there was an integration of elements of Shang culture and ways into the cultural evolution of the Zhou themselves. Something in the becoming of the Zhou made Shang ways attractive, made aspiration toward such culture as the Shang represented natural to the Zhou. Thus the Zhou learned writing from the Shang; given the closeness in native language of the two peoples, little alteration in the system was needed. Similarly for other elements: for example, the Shang use of tortoise shells in the divination process.

If the interconnection of Zhou and Shang had not already involved some intermarriage in the royal and aristocratic families, this happened with the son of the Great King. This son, King Ji,[18] took a wife who came from the Shang,[19] and their son, Ji Chang, was called King Wen when he became king.[20] Appropriate as such a name was to express his character and what it involved of attraction to the higher culture of the Shang civilization (it means "civilized king"), it was nonetheless an ironic name to this extent, that it was this King Wen who seems to have first formed the idea of the conquest of the Shang.

In sum: by the beginning of the 11th century, the Zhou were an evolving and expanding people whose leaders had become strongly drawn toward Shang civilization and were becoming civilized in directions that it pointed out to them. Eventually, in one of their leaders, King Wen, the idea of a Zhou conquest of the Shang was formed.

Such a conquest would be something different from the 'conquer or be conquered' military quests that might obtain within the Wei river basin itself. For it had to be something "carried out on a large scale, against peoples who probably had little desire and certainly had little ability to menace the tribesmen of the Wei valley, protected as they were by natural barriers. Such a conquest required the motivation of an idea, backed by vaulting ambition. The origins of this idea and this ambition were ascribed, and plausibly ascribed, to the father of the actual conqueror",[21] that is, to King Wen.

When it came, the conquest would not be that of a merely alien people over another alien culture, but it would also not be merely an internal uprising within a single cultural group. The Zhou were alien, 'barbarian', yet also increasingly steeped in important elements in the Shang which had been made their own. Thus as the Zhou assumed the role of leader of the civilized world, the old Shang culture was reinvigorated and renewed in many central elements, as well as drawn out in new directions through these new energies.[22] Throughout the whole a distinctively Zhou spirit and character is to be found.

King Wen died before he could carry out the project he had conceived, but he bequeathed it to his son. The latter, Ji Fa by name, came to be known as King Wu, meaning the "martial king". And that was as appropriate a name as in the case of King Wen. It was he who actually carried out the conquest.[23]

The timing of King Wu's attack may have reflected a number of variables: perhaps the exhaustion of the Shang from their military ventures, perhaps famine among the Wei River valley peoples, perhaps a number of other things.[24] In any case, in the 9th year of his reign,[25] he led an expedition of a number of allied peoples eastward, which disbanded before the Shang were engaged in battle, and in the 11th year, he undertook a second. This time he engaged the Shang, overcame them, took over their capital, and established the Zhou as the head of the "central states".

How this occurred, and the events in the first ten years of the dynasty, are absolutely crucial to the development of the Zhou dynasty, and to its eventual undoing.

2. The conquest consolidated

According to the extant accounts, when King Wu overcame the Shang forces and took over their capital, the Shang King had committed suicide but a son, Wu Geng, remained. King Wu established him at the head of the fallen dynasty, installing him as vassal there at Yin but placing him under the watchful eyes of two (or three; the accounts vary) of his own younger brothers. These brothers, he made Inspectors and enfeoffed in neighboring areas, so that they might guard against the possibility that the new vassal might try to lead a rebellion.

The rationale for making Wu Geng a vassal chief was apparently complex. The Zhou address to the Shang was not a repudiation of their tradition; quite the contrary, it included recognition of much that was important in it, and a general policy of continuing worthy elements in the Shang. Indeed, Zhou leaders over this century before the conquest honored earlier Shang rulers in their own sacrifices.[26] Thus, for one thing, maintaining a Shang leader, in a more appropriate figure than the recent one and in clear subordination to the Zhou, would help to make it clear that it was the unworthy conduct of the late Shang leader and not the Shang people themselves that had been the object of the Zhou aggression. For a second thing, such an act would enable continuation of the sacrifices to the Shang royal ancestors. That could not only avoid the vengeful anger of those spirits, which might be vented on the Zhou if the new dynasty had simply cut off the old altogether and stopped the sacrifices. For a third thing, the preservation of the Shang as a people expressed by such an act might lessen somewhat their resentment against the Zhou, and facilitate a relation that could make possible constructive Shang contribution to the ongoing Zhou endeavor.

Things seem to have gone well enough until, two years after the conquest, King Wu died. Then a combination of events raised trouble. There was restiveness among the previous subjects of the Shang peoples east of the Shang territory, and there was restiveness in the Zhou capital over the matter of succession. For the son of his which King Wu had designated his successor was quite young yet, and not likely to be able to rule with the forceful hand needed. There are conflicting accounts of the next events, but it is clear that two things happened. First, upon the enthroning of Song, the son of King Wu, one of the brothers of Wu, the second oldest still alive, Dan, the

Duke of Zhou, assumed the role of regent (whether by appointment or not, is unclear) so as to rule in the name of the new king (King Cheng). Second, the two brothers of King Wu who had been made Inspectors became disaffected to such an extent that one of them, Xian of Guan, the oldest remaining brother of King Wu, led a rebellion that was joined by the other, by the former Shang ruler's son, and by former Shang vassals and some barbarian neighbors.[27]

With these events, the third in the succession of extremely able Zhou leaders came to the fore. The turn of events threatened the continuation of the dynasty, and disintegration was prevented only by the decisive action of the Duke of Zhou. It was he who gave the Zhou dynasty its consolidation and set it underway as an enduring affair, by his renewal of the spirit and character of Kings Wen and Wu and his embodiment of this spirit in definite achievements and forms. A very remarkable man, with tremendous energy, intellect, and force of character, he acted immediately to draw back the kingdom into one piece and to establish it on its course once again.

His first step was to put down the rebellion; this he did, recapturing Yin, executing the Shang scion who had been earlier there, executing the brother who had been leader in the rebellion while exiling the other, and appointing another of King Wu's nine brothers, Feng of Kang, to be the Duke of Wei, a territory in the heart of former Shang land.

His next steps were to move farther east and to conquer the more outlying territories that had not been directly conquered before but that had been involved in the rebellion.

His last step was to see to the building of an eastern capital for the Zhou, at Luoyang in western Henan, to facilitate the control of the eastern parts of the Zhou kingdom. To this place, about 150 miles southwest of Yin, he transported a large number of the Shang people and officials, forcing them to build this new city and to live there under the watchful eyes of the Zhou officials. The Duke hoped this city would be the new capital for the Zhou, but this did not happen.

When King Cheng came to maturity, the Duke of Zhou returned the government into his hands (in 1035,[28] after seven years of regency, apparently). The regimes that followed the regency and represent the firmly established Zhou dynasty (those of Cheng and Kang) maintain Zhou royal power at its peak, from which it began a long slow decline. Eventually, at a low time and just before the series of events which led (in 771 BC) to the shifting of the capital eastward and the considerable lessening of Zhou power, we reach the time and conditions under which the *Zhouyi* was composed.

There are two things about this conquest and unification under Kings Wen, Wu, and the Duke of Zhou, that need emphasis if we are to understand properly the *Zhouyi* and see it as expressing a Zhou spirit.

First, this final unification involved the establishing of a feudal system of sorts on a rather large scale. The particular character of this system had a crucial role to play in the downfall of the Zhou dynasty.

Second, the conquest was animated in a consistent, genuine, and forceful fashion in all three of the leading figures, by a particular religious vision of the world, of man, and of human history.

3. The Mandate, and history

In certain documents that apparently date from these times or from quite close to them,[29] we find the Zhou leaders offering a distinctive and novel[30] perspective on the situation and events we have been recounting. Included in what is set forth is an indication of the animating vision of those leaders.[31] The heart of the vision can be formulated in one phrase: the Mandate of Heaven. What is Heaven? What is meant by its Mandate?

"Heaven" is the distinctive or primary Zhou name for the ultimate divine power, which is also referred to under the Shang names "Lord" and "Lord-on-High".[32] It is a power characterized through such epithets as "bright", "unpitying", "august", "majestic", "awe-ful"; but these characters, and the reference to its "aiding" or "threatening" in relation to humanity, all pertain to its nature and functioning in focus around one central thing.

Heaven is a power which, out of itself, is concerned for humankind to the extent of laying a claim on human effort. In that laying claim Heaven presupposes and affirms human initiative, the need and capacity for humanity to assume responsibility for its existence on earth, and the leeway to venture and to achieve in the give and take of active interplay with powers human and non-human, visible and invisible. But the claim has the force of directing human beings in their venturing toward an end, the elevation (refinement, civilizing) of their own existence on earth. This means that the divine power, Heaven, functions in a way that is purposeful, intentional, but also in a way congruent with the moral character of human action. It is up to humanity, in acknowledgement of this claim, to respond effectively or not, and thereby to enter into some sort of responsive interplay with the ultimately controlling divine power.[33]

This general statement needs careful understanding. Let me clarify it by approaching it from two different perspectives, first the political, and second the religious.

As to the first perspective, the political one: the claim of Heaven is on all human beings, but it is laid in a particular form and manner, which involve a particular constitution to human existence. The "all" of human beings consists of a diverse set of distinct groups, each ordered internally and involved in a way of life more or less different from that of other groups. This "all" does not function as a single whole through any institutions of collective self-direction. Governing is internal to each group, a self-governing, although a group may seek to subdue and to exercise rule over other groups. The claim of Heaven is laid on all in the form of a Mandate which is granted to a single ruler of one group, of that state (that kingdom) which stands on the civilized forefront of the whole human community. By this grant, that ruler is recognized by Heaven to be the one King who, as leader, is to govern not simply his own people but in principle all human beings, and to do this in such way as would foster the universal realization of the end in question, the elevation of human existence on earth. This Heaven-appointed ruler, this King, is to be Heaven's counterpart or match on earth, even the Son of Heaven, and thereby the human center from which is to radiate as well Heaven's urging of human beings toward a civilized mode of life. With this, the meaning of governance is profoundly altered. It has a function in regard to the community of all human beings, the collective existence of humanity on earth; and it has this function not in the mode of political authority and power simply, but in the mode of these spiritualized. For *this* governance is ordained toward a universal culturally refined realization of human life in the concrete.

Now the Mandate involves giving over into the keeping of the King, entrusting to his care, a responsibility and a task, whose general meaning is settled but the manner for whose realization in changing circumstances is the responsibility of the human recipient of the Mandate to find and define. That responsibility is to be carried out under a condition essential to the grant of the office of King. For in his concrete promotion of the broad end, in the use of his judgment and leeway for initiating and carrying through the action required for concrete achievement, the ruler must embody a certain morality. Service to the divine in working toward that end of elevated human existence requires exercise of judgment and decision-making that are suitable morally as well as apt to the realities of the world. Because the grant of standing as King is conditional upon the presence of a certain moral character in the ruler, it may be revoked if the exercise of the requisite freedom and judgment is sufficiently immoral and thus divergent from what is called for. But unless the King acts in a way that clearly attests his inability or unwillingness to reform himself, the Mandate is conceived to be inherited on his death, and to be retained by the new King only under the same moral conditions.

Effectively to be the counterpart of Heaven on earth, the King must have that moral character which embodies *de²* (德). This is not an easy term to translate in the present context without introducing misleading connotations through the English words chosen. In general, *de²* has (among others) meanings of "kindness", "favor", "benefit", and these remain as connotations when, in the present context, the term gains the sense of "virtue". Thus a somewhat clumsy translation of this term would be "kindly virtuous power". *De²* is a power that harbors justice, piety, wisdom, the solicitous concern to encourage and help the people toward peace and contentment, toward prosperity and the realization of such popular virtues as are relevant to the mass of human beings (those involved in family coherence, work and service to superiors, and the like).

The King is the leader and leading center, but only that; he cannot succeed in the appointed work unless he can call to his assistance persons able to extend his influence by their mediation. The virtue in his person and his direct functioning as ruler must be amplified, complemented, extended, by that in his ministers and officials; but equally, this virtue must be found in his vassals, in those who gain from him in turn their own mandates through which, as they exercise their own responsibility, the effectiveness of the virtuous power in the King is also enhanced throughout the relevant directions of governing action.

In short: the idea of the Mandate expands the scope of governing to embrace the collective existence of humanity on earth, gives to such governing a spiritual meaning and dimension, and requires of the one who is to be equal to the task involved a certain moral character and an extraordinary capacity for judgment in the concrete.

As to the second perspective, the religious one: sometime in the development of the Zhou-- from our records, it is in the time of King Wen-- the Zhou achieved a remarkable sort of religious transcendence.

In civilizations centered in religion, it is normal that what becomes celebrated as the controlling power of all is something held in mind through religious ceremony. The sense of origins, the sense of direction in life, are then usually tradition-bound, and that divine power acknowledged and worshiped as a people's source is also "its own" as something uniquely intimate to itself and concerned for itself.

Now so long as a people is alive and forceful, its tradition may itself evolve and change from out of its own energies and resources, and its sense of that source may evolve as well. This may happen directly, as a deepening appropriation and extension and transformation of elements already present in the tradition and experience of the people. Or it may happen indirectly, through the assimilation of other traditions, whether through influence from the outside or through integration of conquered peoples and their cultures into one's own. In any case, as a tradition itself changes through the vitality and energy involved in the people, the sense and conception of the ultimate divine power over against which it feels itself to be itself is apt to change as well.

What happened with the Zhou, however, was not simply evolution in this sense, a deepening sense of Heaven as intimately linked with itself. It was rather a spiritual transcendence in which the leadership (at least) came expressly to acknowledge that that divine power which the Zhou people themselves took as ultimate and which they conceived as Heaven, must be conceived to have been at work also among a people acknowledged to be alien to itself.

More, that power must be conceived to have supported the claim of that alien people (the Shang) to its superiority in preceding times and to its position of leadership in the civilized world.

Finally, that power must be conceived as only now having shifted its support to the rising Zhou people and having given as the central task for the Zhou not the conquering of that older and more cultured people but what this was only a means to, namely, the assumption of a role in the civilized world that that other people had previously had.[34]

The Mandate notion understands this shift to reflect an honoring primarily of the moral character of the Zhou leadership, but in a sense of morality that was not simply a traditional "Zhou" sense. Concomitant with, and integral to, the transcendence in the sense and conception of the divine, went a transcendence of any and all traditional versions of morality which were tied back to particular groups and traditions, the Zhou included. Internal to the divine according of kingly status to a ruler was both the sense that this power was reaching out to all human beings in this action, not just to some, and the sense that the governing center that was being called to mediate this reaching must embody a morality apt to that universal reach. This power which was their own as the one worshiped by them as ultimate and felt to have given them a divine mission, was discovered now as in reality everyone's, although not everyone recognized it as such; and more importantly here, it was seen as now, although not before now, selecting its leadership for a basic role, and as nonetheless also capable of rejecting that leadership and replacing it with other leadership in time. If they are a chosen people, it is part of the meaning of that choice that it may be revoked, that the ultimate divine power is not unconditionally committed to supporting the Zhou leaders in that status, that that power would not always be on their side no matter how they lived and acted. With their lapse in the needed effort and qualities, it might sponsor others while remaining precisely itself in that very being through which it is currently supportive of the Zhou.

Let me bring these political and religious perspectives together in a specific reference.

King Wen's formulation and promulgation of the notion of a Mandate of Heaven, with all that that involves, not only initiates and initially effects a novel and unique beginning within the Zhou tradition; it does this in such way as introduces a notion of history, through which the Zhou people and their traditions and past are placed and given a role in a much larger context temporally and culturally than otherwise. The venture of conquest over the Shang, continuing an already underway expansion of the Zhou in power and influence, was transformed-- as was that expansion-- into an element in a venture, new to the Zhou, to assume responsibility for an old function, which had a meaning for mankind at large.[35]

A fairly radical sense of history has emerged into conception here, although no word precisely comparable to "history" is to be found in these early writings. Put in general terms, the early Zhou leaders envision a distinctive interweaving of the divine and the human in a medium that embraces both, namely, history. The time of history extends indefinitely backward and forward from out of the pregnant richness of the decisive historical present, of the present as that time in which history is in the making and is being made.

History is possible because the ultimate divine power (Heaven) is concerned with, and is operative with regard to, the becoming of mankind collectively. This collective becoming, responsive to that concern and operation, harbors at its center a spiritualizing impetus, initiated and sustained in ongoing dialogue with the ultimate divine power. Such existence is meant to move somewhere, in a direction that is meaningful to human beings. The sustaining of the impetus and movement on the human side, while it is the initiative of a few, concerns the realization of a richness and fulness of life which, spiritual in its upper reaches at least, is to be communally realized and to include all human beings.

Now if the consolidation of mankind involved is basically spiritual, leadership in the sustaining of the impetus and the movement in question is nonetheless importantly political. The political center is formed by a King and his Kingdom, which constitute the concrete center for radiation of the spiritualizing impetus. Both the King and the Kingdom (the "central kingdom" at the heart of certain "central states") are to lead the way themselves and to foster the movement of others upon the way, so that an upsurge of mankind toward civilized existence may be realized in their persons and that realization may gradually spread toward the eventual inclusion (politically and otherwise) of all human beings in the one community of civilized existence under this ultimate divine power.

Neither King nor Kingdom is to be conceived in personal, group, or geographical terms, except as spirit is realized only concretely, in and through individual human beings living together and dwelling somewhere in some particular place on earth.[36] King and Kingdom are thus functional notions. Not only may the human beings who are King change, through death or through revolution, but likewise may the people in question as well as the particular ordering, organizing, patterning, institutionalizing of the people involved at any time. The functioning of one people and certain leaders for a while is essential, but the assumption of this role by any particular people and leaders is not. What is essential is only some leadership, and if not the recurrent renewal and purification of the leaders in their leadership function, then the need for the rise, somewhere, of new leaders and a new people fit to assume the essential role.[37]

This means that the Zhou leaders are conceiving themselves to be part of a collective spiritual movement sustained over time which essentially involves both discontinuity and continuity.

To the extent that such sustaining means the keeping alive of a relation to the divine through which a dissociation of the sustaining human center from any particular human being, group, and tradition, is possible, radical change in such centering is possible. In the Zhou case, the notion of the historical interweaving of human and divine was extended backward by the Zhou leaders even beyond the time when the Shang people and their Kings assumed these roles. And the prospect was held before themselves that, if they did not live up to the Mandate, the Zhou themselves might some day be replaced.

Yet as was likewise the case in the Zhou conquest of the Shang, history is understood to involve continuity. And in fact, in the case in question considerable continuation of Shang ways and the expanding of the Zhou tradition to include the Shang as now an important element of their own past was achieved. The realization of spirit and the political mediation of that radiating spiritual center are concrete, and this binds and limits the dissociation.

What is alone held fast to in this notion of history is this: the effective sustaining, in the course of changes and with the help of change as well as fixity, of the radiation of the divine summons from a divinely ordained human center, and the persistent functioning of this center to effectively support human beings, both within the current sphere of civilization and beyond, in their participation in the movement into fuller, more civilized, more refined, future existence. It is in the midst of such a movement that human beings now always find themselves, somewhere along the way of its unfolding. Given its character, there is accumulation in it, as well as a persistent direction into something never realized before. In those respects, as in the periodic shift in the mandate-bearer which occurs in function of a failure on the human side and not some divinely pre-determined allotment of a limited span, a sense of temporality is being realized which is distinctive, and which contrasts with that of periodic cycles such as the rhythm of the seasons, or of change in oscillation from one pole to another.

C. The Zhou: at the beginning, divination by their rulers

Given this vision of the Mandate of Heaven, and of history, lying at the heart of the Zhou establishment of themselves as leaders of the civilized world, what were the divinatory means by which such leaders would consult with their ancestral spirits and the divine powers? How were those means constituted, in keeping with this sense of the Mandate? And to anticipate a part of the story to which we will turn later, does this sense of the Mandate help us understand the character of the *Zhouyi*, whose composition in the 9th century B.C. occurred at a low time in the Zhou dynasty's capacity to live up to the Mandate?

In the parts of the *Documents* I have referred to above as conveying the early Zhou idea of the Mandate of Heaven, there is also some indication of how divination was used and thought of by the early Zhou rulers. In this case it is divination in the shell/bone form.

Such divination came into play in the acts of the King as King, not in his acts as an individual human being. Its employment involved a ritual process in which he participated. The divinatory effort was directed first and foremost toward royal actions and affairs as ordained toward an end which was not a merely personal end but was divinely-ordained, namely, that end which the Mandate established. For his fitting participation and for the efficacy of the ritual, it was important that the King be living up to the Mandate in his functioning as ruler.

What did that mean?

It meant his governing was grounded in his being, and more particularly, was animated by the Mandate-required moral character and aims and by genuine commitment to the securing of the mandated end, namely, the elevation of collective human existence to a "civilized" mode.

The Mandate was broad, and there would always be leeway involved in action under it in the concrete. If the King was effectively to live up to the Mandate and further the elevation on a collective level, he needed to exercise sharp judgment and choice based on insight. He needed to know the concrete world well, the better to be able to make the decisions and carry out the actions that would work to foster that end.

Fitting participation in the divinatory ritual, then, involved the presence in him of moral character and commitment to service of Heaven in his political actions. What the divinatory ritual offered was a means for receiving some guidance that would confirm and amplify, correct and modify, the knowledge, the know-how, whereby he was to be able to effectively promote Heaven's aim in the concrete.

Governing was an ongoing affair, and the King's action at any time was taking place in the middle of a work already underway. He was continuing something already started, and among the Zhou the effort started at least with King Wen. In this connection, the broad but relatively indeterminate Mandate was given some greater specificity, for the task (under the hands of King Wen and others since) had already been entered upon in one way rather than others. Actions had already been taken, directions of change had already been initiated. So the concrete action to be undertaken was not to be simply one that would promote the elevation of human life, but one that would do this in a way that continued, expanded, extended, the work of previous Kings, and achieved the civilizing of the human race in this cumulative way.

Yet even with the greater specificity given to the mandated efforts from the inheritance from the past, how the work was to be carried on in the particular situations and circumstances of the present-- in novel situations and circumstances, to some extent-- was something which each successive King had to judge and decide for himself. With regard to any such judgment there was always the question, not simply whether a particular effort was accordant with the Mandate and continued the work of predecessors, but whether it was apt to the current circumstances. Was it not only right as in keeping with the Mandate and the settled norms and directions, but also fitted to be successful because it was apt to the reality of today?

Divination entered in as a way of resolving some doubts about a proposed action (say) or about some future issue which was in doubt at the time. The doubt did not concern the moral, political, and tradition-honoring commitments involved in the ruling, but arose within these, and concerned whether the proposed action (say) was apt to present reality and thus would be supported by Heaven because it effectively furthered Heaven's aim.

How this might be so, is exhibited in the document entitled "The Great Announcement", which is contained in the *Book of Documents* in which we found the adumbration of the idea of the Mandate of Heaven. In this document, the Duke of Zhou is speaking at the time of his departure from the old capital in the west on his way east to quell the rebellion there. This undertaking is not something which any of his various officials feel is a good thing. But he himself feels the call to extend the Mandate his father and then his older brother had received, and feels committed to the undertaking not only as in keeping with that generally but as a relevant concrete step called for in the circumstances to achieve that.

In the course of his address, he speaks of using "the great precious tortoise shell" which King Wu had left him "to transmit to me Heaven's bright (intelligence)", and of giving it the charge to make disclosure to him on this matter. "All the tortoise oracles have been auspicious." He notes that his followers have remonstrated: "Why does not your Majesty go contrary to the divinations?" And he admits that the thought of the hardships ahead for him and his people affect him greatly. Yet he keeps urging himself not to let his distress overwhelm him, but to push ahead and bring to completion King Wu's work. "Yes, I, the little child, dare not disregard the Charge-and-Mandate of Lord-on-High. Heaven, blessing the serene[38] King, raised our small country of Zhou. The serene King simply divined and acted accordingly, and so was able calmly to receive this Mandate. Now Heaven having given such aid to the people, how much more should we divine and act accordingly!"

After enlarging on his sense of the need to go to the end with and to complete King Wu's work, and his sense that the task of living up to Heaven's Charge-and-Mandate is never easy, he says: "I ever think and say, Heaven in destroying Yin is like a farmer (weeding his fields), how dare I but complete the work on the fields? Heaven, after all, has shown its favor to my serene predecessor. How should I be all for the oracle of divination, and then dare not go and follow it, following the serene men[39] who point to boundless lands? How much the more, when the divinations are all favorable! Therefore will I grandly make this expedition in force with you to the east. Heaven's commands are not being mistaken, the indications given by the tortoise shell are all to this effect."

In this language, we find the Duke of Zhou acknowledging and cleaving to the Mandate and centering himself on following it out as he can discern how to do this. He has sought confirmation of his particular judgment about how best now to act on that commitment by using tortoise-shell divination, and has found the signs auspicious for the undertaking he is proposing to venture on. When he is urged to disregard those auspicious signs, he has recourse to the Mandate and the settled norms and directions, and then returns to the auspicious turtle-divinations as confiming his judgment that this particular venture was not only accordant with the Mandate, norms, and directions, but was something Heaven would also be supportive of because it would contribute to the end his actions were ordained to serve.

The Zhou leaders evidently knew shell/bone divination even before their conquest of the Shang. In an important archaeological discovery in 1977, a cache of 17,000 turtle-shell pieces was found in the Zhou ancestral temple at Qishan.[40] These come from the predynastic Zhou contemporaneous with the last Shang rulers, and the inscriptions show a marked contrast in the character of the divinatory spirit among the Zhou compared to the relatively lifeless and routine spirit among the Shang. As among the Shang at the time of Wu Ding, the inscriptions here seem to reflect divination as being undertaken on an *ad hoc* basis, in response to specific events. And they reflect as well the late Shang penchant for charges which are positive. But the meaning of this latter is colored by an express element in the ending of the Zhou inscriptions, namely, a prayer-phrase "we desire that", as if the divination was "a request that the future event concerned be allowed to happen".[41] This suggests a participative attitude, a recognition that things are not simply in one's own hands but will work out as they do in a way that involves divine powers. These powers are here being asked (but not in question form) to join in support of human judgment and desire, with the recognition that indeed they may not give their approval and support. Thus the address to those powers, through a proposal that is hopeful, takes form in the optative mood which reflects a commitment that can be withdrawn if the response is not supportive but which is hopeful of being supported.

At the same time as these inscribed shells show something of pre-dynastic Zhou divination in the shell/bone tradition, they also contain hints of the other tradition which will be the one most of concern to us. Several of the Qishan oracle-bones were inscribed with sets of numbers. Further study has revealed that in addition to occurring in Western Zhou inscriptions, such numerical symbols are also to be found on late Shang oracle-bones. These number-sets have been interpreted as "numerical predecessors of *Zhouyi* hexagrams" by Zhang Zhenglang.[42]

Such evidence has led Zhang Yachu and Liu Yu to further conclusions, to the effect that the two modes of divination not only go back at least to the reign of Shang King Wu Ding, but that they were often undertaken in conjunction with each other.[43]

If yarrow stalk divination in some form was a Shang practice and not exclusive to the Zhou,[44] it was among the latter that the practice achieved that development which issued, eventually, in the work we are concerned with, the *Zhouyi*. Since this work belongs to the later Zhou dynasty times, we need to take a final step in our preparations for considering it, by tracing briefly the historical movement and changes which lie between the Zhou beginning in the mid-11th century, and the late 9th century time when we think the *Zhouyi* was composed.

D. The Zhou: the continuation of the beginnings

The concrete outworking of the Zhou venture whose start we have been briefly considering, seems at first to have been extraordinarily successful viewed by almost any standard, including its own. The success of the venture depended first and foremost on excellence in leadership, and that meant, if the venture were to endure, excellence in a succession of Kings who were the offspring of a single family line. Birth would not be enough; what would be needed would be a coherence of spirit and an animating idealism which the King must personally embody and effectively radiate. Success of the venture also depended importantly on the availability of capable persons that these Kings could employ as supporting figures, as well as the development of effective ways of enlisting and employing them so as to further the venture.

As regards the human side, the Zhou were blessed for at least the first seventy years of the dynasty with capable leaders and a people who were able to be sufficiently motivated, sufficiently contented and cooperative, to keep alive the venture.[45] As regards the institutional side, the Zhou Kings and their supporting figures met the challenge not simply of ruling extensive domains and hostile people but also of sustaining and realizing the spirit in the act of governing, by developing a feudal structure for governance.[46] That is, the King sought to realize his leadership over the whole domain by delegating a limited authority and sovereignty to a variety of vassals while maintaining ultimate sovereignty, attending to affairs that concerned the whole, and keeping watch over his vassals' execution of their limited authority and sovereignty as this effected the whole.

During the initial times when the governing force was becoming structured, power was being dispersed yet held in ultimate tow to the center, and various means for appropriate governance were becoming developed and tried and discarded or refined, the Zhou leaders seem to have been able to find themselves caught up in the process of making history and serving the highest deity. The feeling of belonging in a joint effort of such magnitude was able to nerve all toward the best in themselves and to bind King, vassals, ministers, and people, into a relatively cohesive whole.

But spirit cannot be coerced. And clearly the unfolding drama involved such a welter of forces, such a multitude of possibilities, such a variety of individuals, that the effective preservation of such unity of spirit and such realization of political community in diversity was bound not simply to have its variable effectiveness in times and places but, seen in large, to have its initial surge eventually subside.[47]

According to its own sense of things,[48] as well as according to the traditional accounts that come from a much later time, the dominant reason for the dissipation of this initial surge lay in the decline in the excellence of the Kings.

This decline apparently began after Kings Wu, Cheng and Kang. Later tradition provides a common assessment of Kings Zhao and Mu, to the effect that in the first case "the royal way became diminished and defective" and in the second "the royal way declined and diminished".[49] But this kindred assessment obscures the significant differences in what happened in the two reigns. One might well expect, seventy years after the initial conquest and consolidation of rule, some weakening of the spirit, unless of course the sense of adventure could be sustained in further venturing. In the case of King Zhao, that venturing seems to have taken the form of an attempt to extend Zhou rule into southern China and to include Chu under that rule. Unfortunately, that venture resulted in his death and the considerable loss of military strength. Thus when King Mu came to the throne, the Zhou were at first involved in a withdrawal back toward the more secure capital area.[50] But it was the work-- and a successful one-- of King Mu to defend and then reassert Zhou supremacy in the larger area, and to extend it even to the place where Chu now sent tribute to the Zhou court.[51] If there was in his reign something more as well,[52] and if this was maintained in the time of King Gong, then the extension of the Zhou spirit in these kings sustained the dynasty at a fairly high level through the nearly eighty years they ruled, making the first one hundred fifty years of the dynasty fairly faithful to its beginning.

Problems for the continuation of the dynasty, posed first by the misadventure of King Zhao but resolved in great measure by King Mu, come forward seriously with the decline in quality in the next two generations of ruler after King Gong (roughly, 900-860).

When King Yì succeeded King Gong around the start of the 9th century, he proved to be inadequate to the task of rule, especially in the face of barbarian incursions. He failed to keep the regional lords in order,[53] and as Sima Qian reports in *Shiji*, "poets composed satires".[54] Under circumstances which are not spelled out in the records we have, King Yì moved from the capital Zongzhou to a place called Huaili: this seems to be an euphemistic way of saying he was exiled.[55] Apparently in his stead and at least until his death, an uncle of his (a younger brother of King Gong) ruled as a kind of substitute king, called King Xiao.

This break in succession pattern ended with the death both of King Yì and of King Xiao, and the ascent to the throne of King Yì's son, called King Yí. Sima Qian characterizes this by speaking of the regional lords "restoring" him; other bits of information suggest as well some kind of intrigue among parties of feudal lords and the royal family.[56]

The brief tenure of King Yí (he reigned for only eight years) seems to have continued in the pattern of intrigue, reflecting two things. For one, by this time in the development of the Zhou dynasty an aristocracy that was feeling its own distinctive status and interests had arisen and was able to make its presence effective, and even decisive, in royal affairs. For the second, the decline in the quality of Zhou ruler had reached such a place that only this intervention could sustain the dynasty; whether Zhou would survive would depend for a while on the quality of such supporting action by various feudal lords.

With the reign of the successor to King Yí in the middle of the 9th century, we find serious political disruption.

King Li, as he was known, succeeded in provoking a revolution that sent him into exile in 842, and for a while there was an interregnum when authority was exercised by a feudal lord, He, from the state of Gong.

But on Li's death and the coming of age of his son, the latter was installed as King Xuan (827-782). He proved to be far better as King than his father or any of the previous 9th century Zhou rulers, and he considerably increased the respect and allegiance of the feudal lords for the throne. This achievement took the shape of a revival of the spirit of the earliest Zhou leaders and an appeal to their example as to be lived up to in these new and very difficult times. But as it turned out, this was a last gasp, not a sign of the future.

The sense of foreboding that accompanied the prolonged and increasing failure of the Zhou line to sustain its ideals in its Kings and that anticipated Heaven's removal of the Mandate, may have been allayed somewhat in King Xuan's time, but the end was near. It came with the next King, You (781-771), who was slain eleven years after his accession. A disaster as a ruler, he provoked the enmity of one feudal ruler in particular. That ruler, seeking help among the barbarians whose resentments were no doubt long-standing, led a revolution which unseated King You and resulted in his death.

On his death, a peculiar and yet quite revealing thing happened. If the feudal lords who had come to the fore in this last century of the Zhou dynasty had gained such strength and independence as rendered them the effectively dominant powers, if the growing disrespect for the actual Zhou leaders had confirmed the growing sense in such lords of their own worth and capacity for self-sufficiency, nevertheless there was no new King Wen among them, to aspire to the Mandate in replacement of the Zhou as King Wen had in regard to the Shang.

Instead, the reverence for the early Zhou leaders and that vision that had animated them was strong enough that, rather than some new dynasty emerging, a number of these lords joined together to reinstate the old dynasty.[57] Moving the Zhou capital from the west to the east (at Luoyang) to distance it from the main barbarian threats, and diminishing Zhou political control to a very restricted domain so that overall political authority no longer remained in the hands of the Zhou King, these lords placed the son who would have been rightful heir on the throne, as King Ping. But all that was left to him as King was his functioning as the central religious power relating man back to Heaven. He would maintain the royal sacrifices. That was no little thing, for these sacrifices still formed an important reference point for the civilized Chinese world, making it aware in an express way of the spirit that still worked for its unity through the community of culture it had succeeded in engendering over the centuries. But despite the fact that the Mandate was also nominally left in Zhou hands, and the King was therefore also nominally political leader, significant political power was shifted, and not for over five hundred years was it to be re-established effectively in one center for the whole civilized Chinese world.

E. The Zhou: in the time of the composition
of the *Zhouyi*

The *Zhouyi* was composed in the reign of King Xuan. As the preceding review of the history of the Zhou dynasty has just made clear, that reign came after a seventy-five year period in which a decline in the quality of the Zhou rulers threatened the continuation of the reign. To understand the *Zhouyi* it is important to take a fuller look at these times within which its composition took place. For the proper perspective on those times, however, we need to look first at events and decisions taking place in King Li's reign. For these did much to establish the dynamic of forces and events which marked the initial years (at least) of King Xuan's reign. And for proper understanding of King Li's time, we need to remember its own historical context in at least this regard, that after the re-establishment by Kings Mu and Gong of the viability of the dynasty following on the disaster which included the death of King Zhao, the Zhou dynasty knew recurring problems in the functioning of its royal administration, and every 'solution' was at best temporary and at worst facilitated further decline.[58] With King Yì at the beginning of the ninth century we have ineptitude, exile, and his replacement by a brother of the previous King Gong, namely, Xiao. Upon the latter's death, we have King Yí, the son of King Yì, and with him, intrigue and deepening lack of respect from the feudal lords. It is after his fortunately short reign that we find his son, King Li, ascending the throne.

King Li was young when the responsibilities of rule became his.[59] Partly because of that youth he was initially guided and restrained by his elders, in particular, by Earl He of Gong.[60] But more than his youth made such restraint necessary. In historical records he appears as "a spoiled child"[61] who, once he can exercise power, does so in very immature fashion. He is re-called, for example, as taking pleasure in a certain Duke Yi of Rong, who embodied a love of "monopolizing benefits". That is, he was greedy. And a cognate sort of greed in King Li, reinforced by Duke Yi, seems to have been at least a part of what induced King Li to take the course of action that provoked rebellion and brought on his exile.[62]

A second side to the character of the young King seems also to have been important. He was prone stubbornly to believe in the rightness of his own judgment and in the folly of others. In his self-righteousness, he could not abide criticism which he would receive of what he was doing, even from high figures who would warrant his respect. As at the time of King Yì, there were satirists abroad who directed their satire against him. He sought to suppress such criticism, and is reported to have prided himself on having succeeded in this through his threats.[63]

A third factor likely to have been important in the conditions which led to rebellion was the weather. A series of years seems to have brought on severe drought, and undoubtedly this put a strain on the productive capacity of the land and also introduced an insecurity into the livelihoods, even into the continued existence, of all who depended on the land. As an agricultural people the Zhou knew nature as normally bountiful enough that, if human beings operated properly within it, they would be able to sustain themselves. And where unevenness in production due to differences in the land, in the weather, and in human action, led to hunger and the threat of starvation, it was the function of the Zhou King, if not also of lesser lords, to see to the spread of benefit (here, foodstuff) to all within the Zhou sphere of rule. But here, stress from such natural conditions seems to have been coincident with royal action which was heedless of its impacts on the land-dependent people affected.

We may perhaps understand the intensity of the reaction that built up in his subjects and finally exploded, then, if we see broad segments of the Zhou people as feeling oppressed by nature and man both, and feeling a misery-- including a sense of injustice at the King's violation of traditional ways-- that put them at the end of their rope. Apparently the uprising was indeed intense: growing from a fairly localized start around the capital, it spread widely in the heartland of the civilized Chinese world which nominally at least gave allegiance to the Zhou King. In the capital area angry hordes attacked the royal palace, wanting to slay King Li. He escaped, fleeing across the Yellow River. The crowds then wanted to kill his son; but this effort was foiled by Duke Hu of Shao,[64] to whose estate the youngster had fled and who, acting to preserve royal rule, deceitfully offered his own son to the crowd. The crowd slew the boy, thinking he was the King's son, and then set fire to King Li's palace residence and temple.

Into the place of the King stepped Earl He of Gong. Already a supervisor at the royal court, he had sought to help suppress the rebellion. But when the King fled, he assumed the role of a substitute king, to conduct the affairs of the kingdom. His actions over the fourteen years of his regency seem to have eased the situation, but not to have dissipated the rebellion altogether. On what basis, historical records do not disclose, but it seems that at a time near to the death of King Li and the accession of King Xuan (who would still be a minor), he sought to seize for himself the throne. But he was unsuccessful.

The situation which the young King Xuan was placed in when he ascended to the throne, was not enviable, despite what Earl He of Gong had achieved. Unrest still endured, and the loyalty of the feudal lords to the Zhou house was by no means assured. The King was still young enough to require supervision by the Dukes of Shao and Zhou during the first years of his rule. Duke Hu of Shao gathered the noble clans together at Chengzhou some time after the accession of the new King, seeking to strengthen and confirm the family bonds within the clan brotherhood and thus to hold the world centered in the Zhou King together in some fashion.

Fairly soon, however, the young King and/or his supervisors had to face head on the perilous political, economic, and social situation, and to restore the credibility, the legitimacy, and the effectiveness of the Zhou claim to be worthy of the Mandate of Heaven and thereby to lead the civilized world. The alternative was the complete breakdown of the long tradition, and then what?

Historical records characterize only in brief fashion what happened. Sima Qian says:[65] "When King Xuan ascended the throne, two ministers helped him overhaul the administration; he modeled himself on the ways left behind from Kings Wen, Wu, Cheng and Kang, and the feudal lords returned to Zong-zhou." And yet, in the end, as Creel[66] says: "Hsuan could not escape the troubles that increasingly beset the Chou, though he did try. He made strenuous efforts to keep the precariously subject barbarians under control, and established his relative, the Earl of Shen, in a state intended to serve as a buffer against the tribes of the south. As a result, the *Poetry* says, 'All of the Chou states rejoice, for warfare they have an excellent support; the greatly illustrious Earl of Shen, eldest uncle of the King, is a model in peace and war.' Nevertheless, Hsuan's military campaigns against the barbarians were by no means uniformly successful. The glorious days of Wen and Wu were not to return."

Overall, King Xuan's long reign is remembered as a time of the "revival" of the Zhou. Part of what that means has just been indicated, namely, that as ruler King Xuan took the early Zhou Kings as models, and renewed the spirit of early Zhou rule. In particular that seems to have involved an overhaul of the royal sacrificial system, which would be an important unifying factor in the exercise of the King's leadership. Enduring signs of this overhaul are to be found in the remains we have of two types of element in the sacrifical ritual, namely, the bronze vessels and the poetry that would be used in it. Together the evidence of these factors indicates that the revival involved two things at once: a recall of the spirit of the early Zhou, but a change in some of the institutions and elements that had up to then carried the tradition stemming from that beginning-point. Let us consider this matter in a bit more detail.

If we look to the development of bronze vessels within the Western Zhou tradition as a whole, and leave to one side the historical material provided by inscriptions,[67] what do we find of relevance for our understanding of the times of King Xuan?

In a recent work, *Western Zhou Ritual Bronzes from the Arthur M. Sackler Collections*, Jessica Rawson has sketched out a vision of the artistic development of ritual bronzes in the Western Zhou period which she relates in rough fashion to political development. Thus there are Early, Middle, and Late periods in the development of bronzes, and the latter period runs roughly from King Yí through to the end of the Western Zhou period.

Early Western Zhou bronze work-- that of the first seventy-five years of the Western Zhou period-- basically carries on Shang tradition in shape and ornament. But because that tradition itself was rather rich, both in time and in the provincial variations on the work produced at the metropolitan center, the Early Zhou bronze work showed a considerable variety of designs applied to a standard range of vessel shapes. There were some differences in the forms of vessel favored among the Zhou in contrast with the Shang: food vessels, for example, were favored over wine containers. And there were some striking divergences in ornament from the main Shang tradition. But what is most important for our purposes is the somewhat gradual trend toward rounded shapes and smooth surfaces, modifying the Shang heritage of angular containers and compartmented decoration.

In the Middle Western Zhou art work, some new motifs appear, further standard Shang vessels disappear, some novel types and shapes appear; and overall the time-- a hundred year period from King Mu through King Xiao-- is mainly a transitional one, in which in various limited ways the Zhou is more successfully breathing its own spirit into the bronze tradition. Preference for rounded contours and smooth surfaces is joined now with experimentation in patterns of ornamentation that ignore the division of mould sections which the Shang emphasized. Ornamentation becomes focused in pattern more than motif and thereby becomes more abstract and uninterrupted.

With Late Western Zhou, however, we find something fairly striking emerging, which also links closely with our concern here. It is as if the

ventures in which something Zhou and not Shang is finding its expression
are finally gathered up together and a new tradition is initiated. Early in Late
Western Zhou, our evidence shows a widespread and apparently conscious
consolidation of ritual bronze work. All of the major early types of wine
vessel become eliminated, and food vessels, including a number newly
invented in Middle Western Zhou, predominate in the prescribed ritual para-
phernalia for sacrifices to the ancestors. Gone are the highly articulated
vessel shapes and the compartmented compositions of the Shang. And de-
corative schemes dominate which in their encircling patterning and insistent
impression of movement are counter to those of the Shang.

Rawson occasionally puts her description of the stylistic phenomena into
a larger context. To her mind, what is expressed in the bronze changes and
features she notes is the emergence of a new ritual system as a result of a
deliberate policy and some centrally made decision expressing a reforming
spirit. The universalization and standardization which she notes manifest or
express two things of interest to us here. One is the appearance of a codified
system of nobility and rank; in the bronze tradition, this involves the wide
adoption in the Zhou metropolitan area of a local, western tradition of
matching vessels used as insignia of rank. The other is a three-sided mixture: (1) an abandonment of certain of the old-- for example, vessel-types
and shapes and ornamentations associated peculiarly with the Shang; (2) a
reclaiming of other aspects of the old-- for example, vessel types and features
which echo some early Western Zhou features discontinuous with the preceding middle Western Zhou tradition; and (3) an incorporation of ceramic
vessel-types into the bronze tradition, in particular, types which are provincial and western and point to a local source in the area of the pre-dynastic
and early dynastic Zhou. This three-sided mixture can be put as one: what
is involved is the consolidation of the Zhou in contrast with the Shang, both
through the reclaiming of certain early Zhou expressions within the bronze
tradition and through the introduction into the bronze tradition of Zhou
creations originating outside that tradition altogether.[68]

In sum: The bronze tradition as visible in the early part of Late Western
Zhou shows in its forms that some deliberate ritual reform was undertaken
at that time. The changes that become manifest there are (in Rawson's
words) "truly revolutionary". Overall, they express an attitude and outlook
in the religious (and thus political and social) life of the Zhou which suggests
a purifying and a recollecting of itself to its earlier roots. What precise
political and religious events, figures, and movements are finding their
expression in these changes, Rawson does not claim to know with assurance.
But she sees the artistic development as reflecting changed social needs, and

points to elements of the broader context in which she sees this ritual change, such as signs of altering land-tenure practices, as also reflecting altering social or class conditions.

The tradition of poetry gives us complementary indications of such a reform effort from another side of the ritual arena, and enables us to gain fuller insight into the spirit that animated that reform.

In his *Shijing yu Zhoudai shehui yanjiu* (*A Study of the 'Book of Poetry' and Zhou dynasty society*), Sun Zuoyun analyzes the *Book of Poetry* collection and suggests that in two of its four major parts (the *Da Ya* and the *Xiao Ya*), almost all of the poems included were composed in the time of Kings Li, Xuan, and You. In particular, more than half of the poems from the two *Ya*'s come from King Xuan's time: roughly, 65 of the 105 poems. Analysis of the content and probable function of those poems, together with a broader analysis of the political, social, and economic dimensions of the late Middle Western Zhou and the early Late Western Zhou periods, lead him to see this high proportion as expressing two things: one, the length of King Xuan's reign (46 years), and the other, the "revival" or "resurgence" for which King Xuan's reign is remembered in historical records.

If we take this claim by Sun as sound in its major thrust and take up the poetic record he points us into, we can amplify our understanding of the heart of the revival.

Among the 65 poems which Sun claims come from King Xuan's time, there are 10 from the *Da Ya* which seem to belong to sacrificial ritual.[69] In general, these recall from much later times the Zhou beginnings and the crucial figures in their past; they hearken back strongly to the leaders who founded the Zhou dynasty, and in particular, to the matter of the Mandate of Heaven.

Poem 245 traces the "birth" of the Zhou people back to Jiang Yuan who, through Lord-on-High, gave birth to Hou Ji (Lord Millet). The story of his marvellous birth and upbringing, his husbandry, his initiation of sacrifice, culminates in the claim that the Zhou carry on sacrifices initiated by him.

This sense of themselves as an agricultural people is complemented in Poems 250 and 237, which recall the early history of the evolution of this people and the emergence of an expanded sense of themselves. Poem 250 recalls Duke Liu, his mobilization of his people for a shift to a more suitable area of settlement, his discovery of that in a northern Shaan-xi area, and his construction of a capital there (Bin) and the settlement of the larger area. The orderly method of the proceeding in this whole venture reflects something of the far-sighted leadership and organizational genius which is to mark the Zhou dynasty, at least at its start. Poem 237 recalls "ancient Duke Dan-fu", the grandfather of King Wen and the leader who is recalled later as King Tai (Great King). It was he who led the Zhou to what became their traditional home at the foot of Mt. Qi; in the account of this settlement, we find clear indication of assimilation from the Shang, but also the beginnings of the dominance of the Zhou over their neighbors from their home on the Zhou plain under Mt. Qi in the Wei River valley.

In Poems 241, 235, and 236, we find sounded the themes which are most important for our concern. Poem 241 recalls the time of the Zhou people leading up to and including King Wen's receipt of the Mandate of Heaven and his initial exertion of Zhou hegemony over peoples in the immediate area. Poem 235 focuses on King Wen, but expressly brings the charge down through the generations to the present (presumably, the time of King Xuan): the Zhou hold the Mandate, but it is not forever.

> Should you not be thinking of your ancestors, and so
>   cultivate their virtues?
> Forever be a match for the Mandate, seek for yourself its
>   many blessings.
> When Yin had not yet lost its multitudes, it was able to
>   be a match for Lord-on-High;
> You ought to see yourself in the mirror of Yin, the great
>   Mandate is not easy (to keep)!
>
> The Mandate not being easy, do not make it cease in
>   your person!
> Display and make bright your just renown! The Lord of
>   Yu as well as Yin, both (received the Mandate) from
>   Heaven.
> But the actions of Heaven above are without sound,
>   without smell;
> You should model and pattern yourselves on King Wen,
>   and make the myriad states put their trust in you.

Poem 236 provides another account of the Mandate, focused initially on King Wen but ending with notice of King Wu and the oncoming of the battle in which the Zhou overcame the Shang. Here it is King Wen's virtue that is seen as significant:

> Now this King Wen, he was cautious and reverent,
> Shiningly he served Lord-on-High, and so he could hope
>   for many blessings.
> His virtue did not deflect, and so he received the states
>   of the four quarters.
>
> Heaven looked down on the world below, the (new)
>   holder of the Mandate had already arrived.

With mention of King Wen's wife giving birth to the future King Wu, the poem turns to him; at his birth ...

> (Heaven said), 'I shall protect and help and mandate you,
>   to march and attack the great Shang.'
>
> A solemn declaration was made at Mu Ye: 'It is we who
>   are rising! Lord-on-High looks down upon you, do not
>   let your heart be of two minds!'

Included in the set are Poems 240 and 243, which present the Zhou dynasty founders, especially King Wen, in features of character and conduct, attitude and achievement, meant for emulation by later Kings, including (presumably) King Xuan.

Poem 240 speaks as follows:

> (King Wen) was in accord with the princely leaders of
>   the clan,
> So that the spirits were never angry,
> The spirits were never grieved;
> He was a model to his chief bride,
> He extended this to his brothers older and younger,
> And thereby governed his family and state.
>
> Agreeable he was in the palace,
> And reverent in the ancestral temple,
> Greatly illustrious, he also looked down in care;
> Without indifference, he was also protective.
>
> His great energy was unquenchable,

His brilliance and greatness had no flaw;
He did not have to hear a thing first-hand before he
    made use of it,
He did not have to be spoken to in remonstration before
    he admitted something.

Thus as a grown man he had virtue,
Even as a child he had trained to become perfected;
That man of old was untiring!
Renowned and fine was that gentleman!

Poem 243 focuses upon later Kings as successors and (in their times)
counterparts to the three founding Kings (Wen, Wu and Cheng) who brought
the beginning of the dynasty to completion.

Following in footsteps here below are the Zhou,
Generation after generation of wise Kings;
The three (founding-) rulers are in Heaven,
And the King is their counterpart here in the capital.

The King who is counterpart in the capital,
He actively seeks the hereditary virtue,
Ever to be a match for the Mandate,
To achieve trustworthiness as a King.

Achieving trustworthiness as a King,
He is a pattern to the gentlemen-officers below,
Ever is he filial and thoughtful,
To be filial and thoughtful is his norm.

Lovable is this One Man,
Responsive is his compliant virtue;
Ever is he filial and thoughtful,
Brightly shining, he continues the task.

Brightly shining he comes and is permitted
To continue in his ancestors' footsteps;
Oh, may the years be myriad
During which he receives Heaven's blessings.

Receiving Heaven's blessings,
The four quarters come to wish him well.
Oh, may the years be myriad
During which his helpers are not far away.

Seen from the standpoint of young King Xuan, the thrust of the poems cited above is not simply to recall the significant ancestors of the past but also to summon him to fit himself to continue the work of the founders. Keeping the Mandate is always difficult, but it is possible, and to be aspired to. It is up to the young King to rise to this challenge, to show himself worthy of the succession and the awesome task he takes on in becoming King, in continuing the work begun by King Wen.

If the bronze and poetic traditions give us such pointers to a kind of revolution taking place in the early part of Late Western Zhou, and in particular, culminating in the reign of King Xuan, we find that the revolutionary spirit is traditional in this sense, that it would recall and revive the spirit and vision of the early Zhou leaders who founded the dynasty.

It is amidst the work of this revival, involving military, economic and a variety of political actions as well as the overhauling of ritual which has been our main focus in the preceding discussion, that the *Zhouyi* was composed. We might expect, then, that this work would also somehow express that revived spirit, both in its recall of something past and by its embodiment of the spirit in a form apt to the novel present and changed conditions of life in the time of King Xuan.

We have previously noted that the early Zhou leaders employed divination, in the forms both of shell-and-bone-divination and of stalk-divination, to aid in the decision-making and venturing through which they would live up to the Mandate of Heaven concretely. If stalk-divination were to be overhauled in the spirit of this revival-- if it were to undergo a comparable strengthening but modifying and consolidating of traditional elements to that found in the bronze and poetic traditions of the time-- what sort of affair would it become?

In the bronze tradition we noted more specifically that the 'revolution' consolidated an affinity for certain shapes and embracing patterns, a certain feel for movement and vitality, that had been increasingly manifesting itself in Zhou bronzework. We noted as well how this 'revolution' included bringing certain earlier ceramic models into the bronze tradition and giving them a place there in this new medium. Is it possible that, in the *Zhouyi*, a previous form or forms of stalk-divination may have been not simply maintained unchanged from the past but rather have been gathered up into a new medium (that of verbal images) and shaped for a more distinctively and fully Zhou functioning of the divinatory medium than ever before? Would this medium also more fully and purely express a Zhou sense and feel for life and change, for how a human being might best discern the play of 'rounded curves' and 'embracing pattern' in the dynamic of the present which harbors the future of ventures and risks that are of moment in the unfolding of history?

Something like that is what I think happened, and what makes the *Zhouyi* an incredibly rich and interesting work for our understanding.

Chapter 2
Change and Divination

In Chapter 1, our focus was the Zhou, and in particular, the character and evolution of the Zhou spirit and the Zhou dynastic rule. Having brought that account down to the time of the composition of the *Zhouyi*, we need now to turn to the matter of the employment of divination by the Zhou rulers in their attempt to carry out the Mandate of Heaven in the concrete world of change.

Life-- personal and collective-- is inherently an affair of change. In its temporality it involves movement into the unknown and the uncertain. Given our natures we develop a capacity to anticipate what that movement is bringing, and because something is at stake for us in our participation in that movement, we desire to anticipate well what is coming and aided by that to share effectively in securing what is at stake as we encounter and interact with what we do. The various forms of divination are devices for grounding and strengthening our capacity to anticipate. In this way they enlarge the resources which make it possible for us to participate well.

We have already noted that among the early Chinese rulers, both Shang and Zhou, two forms of divination provided vehicles through which such rulers approached ancestral spirits and divine powers seeking answers to questions or responses to proposals.

We have also noted, in regard to one of these forms (the use of shells or bones), that the cracks which were taken as significant signs were interpreted as having a disclosive meaning that was auspicious or inauspicious (or some variant of these), or else was a simple 'yes' or 'no'. We find numerous words connected with the use of this medium, from words inscribed on the shell or bone at the time of its use, to words from a time centuries later than King Xuan which record in a categorizing manual the interpretations which were eventually given to the variety of types of crack in a variety of types of inquiry. But all of these words belong only to the record of the inquiry or to the interpretative framework. There are no words which are themselves part of the medium.

As a result, the disclosure achieved through the sign and the interpretations which read it are both relatively limited, and depending on the question being asked or the proposal being tested, the disclosure is one suited for simple resolution of doubt and uncertainty about matters being inquired into or for simple determination of the presence (in degrees) or absence of support for a proposal.

The *Zhouyi* is a written work embodying elements of a divinatory method which uses yarrow stalks as the concrete or first-order medium for securing disclosive signs. Those signs are quite unlike cracks: they are images framed in language. Two questions arise here. First, is the utilization of language as sign-bearer inherent in stalk-divining, or is that something which reflects one way in which stalk-divining was developed, in contrast with other ways which may not utilize verbal images at all? Second, if it is not something inherent but distinctive, what was antecedent stalk-divination like, and how-- and why-- did this transformation arise?

A. Pre-*Zhouyi* stalk-divination

According to the discussion of the office of Grand Diviner in a Warring States work called *Zhou Li* (*Zhou Ritual*), that office-holder oversaw stalk-divination using the methods of the three *Yi*, namely, the *Lianshan*, the *Guizang*, and the *Zhouyi*. The implication is that there were (by then, at least) three 'books' in which a system of stalk-divination was presented. Of these three, only the last one still exists, although there are still some fragments that might have come from the other works as well as some that come from forgeries which were composed in the course of time and were passed off under the first two names.

In keeping with the tidy ways of later systematizers, the *Lianshan* is claimed to be a work from the Xia dynasty, the *Guizang* from the Yin-Shang, and the *Zhouyi*, of course, from the Zhou. But there is no evidence which makes such attributions plausible. Instead, all that is said about the *Lianshan* and *Guizang* makes it more plausible to take them as later imitations of the *Zhouyi*.[1] Were there in fact any genuine predecessor works to the *Zhouyi*, expressing its type of stalk-divining method using not simply line figures but also verbal-images? There is no trace of any in the historical evidence as we have it, making it appear that the *Zhouyi* is the first of a kind.

This does not mean, of course, that stalk-divination started with the *Zhouyi*. Quite the contrary, it was already an old tradition by the time of the composition of the *Zhouyi* in the late 9th century BC, and the author of the

Zhouyi presumably stood within and knew that tradition. As I noted earlier, recent study of unusual marks found on some Shang and Western Zhou bronzes, oracle bones/shells, even jade pieces and pottery moulds and jars, has led to the tentative conclusion that the marks are sets of numbers, commonly groups of three or six but sometimes in other size groupings. In a 1980 article,[2] Zhang Zhenglang recalls his earlier insights into these, and develops the connection which he drew between these number sets and the line-figures known to us through the *Zhouyi*. In the discussion which has evolved since then, Zhang Yachu and Liu Yu,[3] and Wang Ningsheng,[4] and others have explored different sides of this matter.

Wang suggests there was an early phase of stalk-divination in which, like various primitive forms of divination he cites, the diviner uses the stalks as a means for arriving at numbers whose significance lies in whether they are odd or even. He sees the two types of line (solid and broken) which are constituent elements in the *Zhouyi* hexagrams as simply ready representations, in line form, of this odd and even feature of numbers. One of these two is auspicious, the other inauspicious, and in the simplest cases that is the outcome of the divinatory process. But he notes a more complex form, in which divination on a matter is undertaken three times, generating three numbers. Using the two types of line to record and keep in mind the divination results as they emerge, the records of the sets-of-three would be sets of three lines, which if written as parallel lines, would be three-line figures. Since the possibilities of different combinations of odd and even in ordered sets of three numbers is eight, he sees in the trigrammatic representation of these sets-of-three-numbers the origin of the eight trigram figures which, traditionally, are claimed to have been the precursors in the development of stalk-divination of the six-line figures of the *Zhouyi*.

Wang's understanding of three-line figures as standing for sets of odd/even auspicious/ inauspicious numbers gives us one connection of numbers and line figures with stalk divination. It is simpler than, and rather different from, the connection which Zhang Zhenglang puzzles over. Collecting together 32 examples[5] of inscriptions from late Shang and early Zhou times and treating them as forming for preliminary analysis a single whole,[6] he considers what they show. In these examples, the number sets contain the numbers 1, 5, 6, 7, and 8, but not 2, 3, and 4, or any number higher than 8.[7] One needs to ask a series of questions here: If each number is the result of a manipulation of the stalks, what is the method (if there was only one) that produced such results? What is the significance of the range and diversity included, not simply from the perspective of how they were generated but also from the perspective of how such numbers would function in a divinatory vein?   If lines are used to represent numbers here, and there are only two types of line (solid and broken), why are there this many numbers, and why these specific ones? Is the significant difference between the numbers involved simply that of being even and being odd, or is there further significant difference among the even numbers and among the odd ones? If the sets containing these numbers have a divinatory meaning, what is that meaning? How do the auspicious and inauspicious enter into this matter? (For example, are odd numbers auspicious and even ones inauspicious, thus solid lines auspicious and broken ones inauspicious? What of the auspiciousness/inauspiciousness of a set of numbers/lines?) Are there any meanings associated with the numbers or number sets? with the lines or line sets used to represent the numbers?

Zhang addresses some of these questions. He explains the absence of 2, 3, and 4 from his collected sets as due mainly to a desire to avoid confusion produced by the old style writing. But avoiding confusion in the way he suggests-- any 2, 3, or 4 was lumped together and listed under the nearest odd or even number (1 or 6)-- means that in the divinatory use as he envisions it, what would be important would only be the character of the number as odd v.s. even, and not its own specific self. And yet, this can not be altogether so; for if it were, why were there more than two numbers, one to represent odd, one even?

What is on his mind becomes clear when he struggles to connect the use of several numbers with the creation of line-representations such as are found in the *Zhouyi*. There, according to the usual reading of the text, a solid line with a title including the number 9 and a broken line with a title including the number 6 are said to be "moving lines", in implicit[8] contrast with a solid line entitled with a 7 and a broken line entitled with an 8. These four numbers seem to signify that there are in functional reality, although not in the visible representation, two kinds of solid and two kinds of broken line, with different functions in the divinatory method.[9] If the number diversity is expressive of something like that, however, there is a puzzle: how are the five numbers he finds being used in his original sample related to the use of only four numbers in the *Zhouyi*? Zhang concedes that we do not yet know what method might have been used to generate the numbers in either case, nor the one used (in the materials he is analyzing) to create lines based on them. But presumably if we knew the method, we would also know why there were five numbers (and the particular five in question) and how they were being used as divinatory signs. Given the limitations in evidence, our best thought is that in general the numbers somehow reflect a method of manipulating a number of milfoil stalks; but why in some cases or at some times, there seem to have been five numbers generated and used while in other cases or times there were only four,[10] remains elusive.

Zhang Yachu and Liu Yu point also to examples of sets of three and six numbers in early materials, and make the same claim for them as signifying line figures, either trigrams or hexagrams. But they point to the early signs of stalk-divination (already visible by the time of Shang King Wu Ding), its widespread character (not restricted, it seems, to use by the King), its utilization already of six-number sets (thus the precursor of the hexagram), and its appearance on bones which also contain markings and inscriptions relating to shell/bone divination. As they interpret the evidence, the Shang were more advanced than the Zhou in both forms of divination, even at the time of the conquest. Other things catch their eye as well. For one, a very few oracle bones include inscriptions in which the number sets are "followed" by a *yue¹* (曰); the word or phrase following the *yue¹* (in two cases an indecipherable character, in a third a fragmented line) is claimed by them to be a hexagram name or statement.[11] For a second, they point to four bronzes on which (with what connection to the number sets, it is unclear) are found four or five parallel lines, some solid, some broken into three parts. While recognizing that these are not identical to the later *Zhouyi* line-figure representations, they note a similarity and point to these early figures as possible precursors of another type of divinatory system which is found otherwise only in Han dynasty times. Like Zhang Zhenglang, Zhang and Liu acknowledge not being able to determine what sort of method lies behind the generation of the numbers/ number sets; but they do make the interesting suggestion that perhaps there was more than one method for generating numbers lying behind the material.

The discussions just mentioned are interesting explorations which contribute to the inquiry into the character and early history of stalk-divination in early China. But they concern limited aspects of such divination, and at best barely touch on what is unique in the *Zhouyi*. Moreover, they exhibit two presumptions which need to be brought into question if we are going to incorporate their findings into a grasp of the *Zhouyi* in its distinctive character.

One presumption is that, in divination as a way to "probe the intentions of the spirits with the aid of the permutations of certain kinds of signs",[12] the important thing to be determined by the inquirer is whether the sign is auspicious or inauspicious as relates to the matter which is subject of the divination inquiry.[13] Then what differentiates stalk-divination from other forms, and what makes for different types of stalk-divination, lies within this horizon, in the manner and method whereby such determinations are arrived at.

The second presumption is that the *Zhouyi* is a work with such a focus. This view, implicitly shared by numerous students and scholars of the work, is reinforced by how later tradition is understood to have developed and conceived the sort of divination which uses the *Zhouyi*. In this view the image-language which forms the heart of the divination act and system in the *Zhouyi* becomes a secondary accompaniment with *little or no divinatory* function in its own right. Attention paid to such language is concerned with its value for dating the work, its content of historical or sociological data, its poetic elements, its various linguistic features. But studies of the language in those respects, valuable as it is in other regards, do nothing to make intelligible the role of language in the act of divination. Neither does making such language represent a collection of omens arbitrarily attached to the line figures.

To get to the heart of the *Zhouyi* one needs to be able to take divination seriously and to be willing to approach the work in a profoundly self-critical and historical vein.[14] History unfolds in the movement forward in time. If there is change as well as continuity in that movement, the retrospect of later times on earlier times may be (wittingly or unwittingly) constrained by later and relatively novel ways of thought which, rather than actually doing (or even seeking to do) justice to the earlier, may see it only from newly arrived at perspectives and see in it only what is precursor to itself. Examples of such readings of the past are commonplace: consider the way in which the dialogue form of Plato's writings is understood in our contemporary Western world, or how the notions of *logos* and *nous* in the classical Greek philosophers are read as "reason" in a very modern sense.

A sensitive understanding of the earlier can not simply ignore the later, of course, especially in the case of a continuing tradition. But neither can it be captive to the presumptions and preconceptions of the later (especially if these are newly emergent), nor to the later penchant for seeing the earlier only as leading to itself. It must be open to the earlier as itself, in its own making, moving into an unknown and uncertain future, as perhaps being creative in relation to anything past or present, but as also perhaps not being intended to lead to anything like the future which actually does come.

If the use of language as a sign-bearer was something distinctive to the *Zhouyi*, why did such a use arise? What does it contribute to the divinatory act? Does its use reflect a transformation in the divinatory act, in the very meaning of divination?

B. Divination and the direction of the *Zhouyi* transformation

In the discussion up to now, we have been proceeding under the assumption that we know sufficiently what divination is that we do not have to probe that matter itself but can simply attend to various forms of divination. But while it is appropriate to treat the *Zhouyi* as a work emerging within the stalk-divination tradition and holding elements of that mode of divination internal to its system, to grasp the distinctive character of that system and to understand the type of divination being undertaken through it we will have to take a step back and consider this matter of divination a bit more self-consciously and self-critically.

Just as the emergence of the Zhou spirit introduced something radically new in history, so the *Zhouyi*'s continuation of the stalk-divining tradition transformed that tradition in fundamental respects. As a result, neither can be understood simply by looking to their antecedents. Similarly, if our records from later times are genuine and accurate, not only did the Zhou dynasty in fact end-- although it continued in name-- with the end of the Western Zhou and the beginning of the Eastern Zhou periods; but the divinatory revolution which was accomplished in the *Zhouyi* was lost in its essential spirit not long after it began, even though in name and form the system of the *Zhouyi* was maintained, was refined and reunderstood, and came in time to inspire significant contributions to the reflective life of the Chinese throughout the Eastern Zhou period.

We can see in our records some traces of the original spirit and use of the method, which survived for a while. But for the most part the altered inventiveness of the Eastern Zhou mind recast the way of anticipating the future involved in the use of the *Zhouyi*. By the time philosophy arose in the late Springs-and-Autumns period, the *Zhouyi* was well on its way to becoming something rather different from what its author seems to have envisioned it as being-- not only different in the divinatory vein, but different as becoming turned into a wisdom book whose divinatory meaning was definitely secondary, if considered at all.

To make our step back, let us start with the pointer which Zhang Zhenglang provides to us when he speaks of divination as a technique for probing the intentions of the spirits. As we draw out and refine this idea, we will keep in mind the character of the revived Zhou spirit, and note how the transformation of stalk-divining which is embodied in the *Zhouyi* expresses that spirit and enables divination in that vein to become a more suitable instrument for the Zhou King's efforts to grasp the concrete circumstances of his governance and to find the best way to act on the renewed commitment to the Mandate of Heaven.

1. Divination: knowledge of the future?

Divination seems to offer a knowledge of the future, a seeing into it. But does it? What kind of knowing, seeing, is involved?

The future does not exist as fact at the time of any divinatory seeing into it, so the seeing can not amount to something like seeing present fact, even present fact at some distance-- what is currently happening in Shanghai, for example. It is even different from seeing past fact, which after all once was and so had a determinateness, traces of which may remain in the present and provide an inquirer clues as to what once was.

The seeing is *in advance of* the factuality of what is said to be seen, so that the seeing is a *fore-knowing* of what *will* be, even though it does not yet exist.

But is this what divination provides?

Zhang Zhenglang spoke of probing the "intentions of the spirits". Such intentions come into play because the very spirits which are being called upon to provide some response, are also being presumed to have some power to impact the ongoing of things. Within the ultimate governance of Heaven, the royal ancestral spirits in particular are such powers, whom the King is consulting through the various forms of divination. Those spirits are forces which are governed by Heaven but which also, in their closeness to this ultimately governing power, are able to be privy to such will as Heaven may have-- that expressed generally in the Mandate but more particularly in other ways. Now that is a will which respects human initiative, which indeed calls it (in the case of the King directly) to assume a certain responsible role in those affairs which Heaven ultimately governs.

Within this situation, what is at the center of the divination inquiry by a human party is something futural. What is asked for is some sign in the present which points the inquirer now into the future, in a way that discloses something about matters of the future about which that inquirer cares sufficiently to make inquiry of the spirits. In the royal case, it is matters relating to that Mandate in the execution of which he has the basic responsibility.

But what is being disclosed through such divination, through the response from the spirits and the interpretation by the human agent? If we speak of "intentions"-- whether of the spirits simply, or of Heaven beyond as well-- we are speaking of something which exists *in the present*, yet something which has meaning for the future, indeed something whose essential sense is futural in its import. We are speaking of what these powers are intending at present, as regards the matters at issue in the inquiry.

Let us postpone for a moment consideration of the assumptions that would have to go along with this: are we assuming, for example, that the intentions in question will not change, that the powers that have the intentions will be able to make good on them into the future, that human effort or other powers will have no significant bearing on the issue? Let us instead consider here: what is this anticipatory knowledge a knowledge of?

Zhang said: In divination we probe the intentions of the spirits "with the aid of the permutations of certain kinds of signs". If divination conveys or engenders a seeing into the future, it does this by operating by way of signs. It is the interpreting of these signs which brings the inquirer into such fore-knowing as is achieved with the help of those signs.

Such signs portend, they indicate and intimate, they point.

Commonly, they portend in the mode of the auspicious and the inauspicious. Does that not mean: they speak to a future being inquired about, but they do not speak directly about it-- how it will in fact be? Instead, they speak indirectly about that future, disclosing the '*how*' of those forces *at work in the present* whose working has a bearing on *how that future will be*. They disclose, more specifically, the *character* of that bearing on what is anticipated, what is wished for, what is being asked about. An auspicious sign is a sign which 'says': at the moment, matters bode well in regard to the matter at issue in the future in question; the unfolding of the present is currently working in a manner favorable to that future matter. An inauspicious sign 'says': at the moment, matters bode ill or badly in regard to the matter at issue in the future in question, the unfolding of the present is currently working in a manner unfavorable to that future matter. In both cases, the future in question will eventually come to pass out of the very present in which the portending sign exists, so that the sign is signifying something of futural import about its own concurrent matrix.

This is the level at which the shell/bone and the pre-*Zhouyi* forms of stalk-divination operate, so far as our present evidence can give us any assurance. It is also a level on which the method embodied in the *Zhouyi* can be made to operate, if its distinctive character and potential for disclosure is disregarded and it is treated as a method like those other methods-- more complex, perhaps, and with different features, but in essence, functional only for the same sort of disclosure.

But is any other disclosing possible?

So far, divination does nothing to disclose *what* in particular it is that will be happening in the future, what the specific events or happenings are which will be the case then and which will (or will not) include what inquiry is focused on. But might one not be also concerned to know 'what' that future will be in fact? Could this be a part of divination, to bring the inquirer into a knowing and more or less specific anticipation of what it is that the future will be like?

Let us go back to the spirits: If they-- and Heaven behind them-- are effective forces in the unfolding of the present into the future, what is the place of ourselves, the inquirers, in this matter of that unfolding present? Are the human beings of the present also participants, with an effective role as well? Or are we merely onlookers, so to speak, able perhaps to adapt to what will be but not participants in its coming to pass?

Let us consider: If one says that divination amounts to a seeing into what *will* happen, what *will be fact* at some future time, it becomes important to understand how the actual future is an outworking of the present. That some future will eventually be (and when it is, be present fact) is part of the nature of time and temporal existence. But on what basis does what will actually be come to happen and be such as it then is? How does the future (the will-be) in all its particularity arise from the present and take the determinate shape it then has, having this-character rather than that-character?

The reasons for the future being such as it will be lie in the present, both in what is actually so and in what is potentially so, in the possibilities latent in the present. For the actual future is an outworking of such a present.

There are two rather different alternatives for this outworking.

According to one alternative, the basis for the future being as it will be is such that, because of that basis, what-will-be will be and be as it is *no matter what anyone thinks or does*. That, of course, can not be something universal, since thinking and doing do seem to make a difference at least in some cases. But if that is what divinatory insight is into, something 'fated' to be so, something outside the being and the sphere of control of the inquirer, then the response of the inquirer based on his/her grasp of the insight can make no difference whatever to the outcome.

In that case foreknowledge of this might at best affect the inquirer's response in the present and his/her adaptation to the 'fated' outcome-- supposing that *this* response and adaptation themselves lie outside the 'will be no matter what', that the inquirer has some effective freedom and leeway to make such a response and adaptation. Divination then would provide cognitive insight into things beyond human control, and insight which is at best (in the context of its use) predictive in nature.

The other alternative is this: the coming to be of the future depends at least in part on responses which are free in the present and which mean that what-will-be is not something that will be and be as it then is regardless of what we do. Rather it will be this-or-that in a way that depends in some measure on ourselves, and in particular, upon the self of the inquirer when the latter is participant in the situation being inquired into.

Consider this role of the inquirer as participating agent more closely.

In a case where a person who is participating in something gains what purports to be anticipatory insight into what is to come, that very insight itself forms an added element in the shaping of what is actually to come. It could even be that, if that anticipation was of a future that depended on how that participant would act, such insight could evoke in the person the motivation to act differently from the way anticipated and thus to 'falsify' the 'prediction' of the determinate future in question. Divination would then, paradoxically, undermine itself as anticipation of what-will-be. For its very insight, as made known to a participant (and that is the point of the participant's employing divination, to come to know something), would alter that on which depends (to some indeterminate degree) how the future will come to be and be what it will be.[15]

Can divination nonetheless have a place and function in such a situation? If so, it would have to address a determinate future (the one into which inquiry is being made) in some other way than by anticipating it in the particularity it *will* have. It would have to be an art, then, whose fruit is something other than a predictive knowledge of what the future *in fact will be* like.

If there is such a type of divination, we would need to pose and answer two questions in order to characterize the type. First, what other type of seeing into the future can there be? And second, what other fruit of divination could there be if not knowledge of the future in that sense?

2. Divination: exploration of the futural side to the present?

Consider more fully this present in which inquiry is being made and which is the matrix for the making and becoming of the future which that inquiry concerns.

As we have already noted, that present is marked by the presence of operative (ancestral) spirits, as well as of the ultimate divine power. As to Heaven, it is steady and unchanging in its will, however incomprehensible the outworking of that will may be concretely at times to human beings. But as to the (royal ancestral) spirits, there is a more ambivalent sense: they should be aligned with Heaven, but as kin they may well act in more personal ways that mean one cannot count on their support, certainly not regardless.

In the case of Heaven and the spirits both, however, there is this, that if they are approached in an appropriate spirit, then one may count on a helpful response to one's query. Divination as we are concerned with it here is a ritual act; it is part of a religious outreach back to the relevant spirits and divine powers. If that outreach is genuine, if the participants are effectively devoted in this outreach, then the divinatory act has partners who would presumably provide a response apt to the spirit and the needs of the undertakers of that act. And because those partners are also effective powers in the bringing to pass of the future in the way it comes to pass, they might be expected to disclose their "intentions" to such inquirers.

But there are other participants effective in determining the future, making it depend in some measure on how they take part in its unfolding out of the present.

At the level of ongoing personal and collective life and of the happenings of nature, the present is marked not simply by finished fact, so to speak, something over and done with and about to pass into the past; it is also marked by *actual* forces *continuing* to be at work in it. In addition to such energies already at work and continuing to operate, however, the present is marked by two further things. One is a measure of novel possibility, potentiality, a limited opening to change, which resides in the actual beings who are at work in the present; the other is the element of freedom (where human beings are involved, at least), and with this, some measure of leeway. Even if how much leeway is present is never knowable, the presence of *some* leeway means that as the human being (say, an inquirer) freely acts differently, so the outcome of what he/she is participant in *might* be genuinely different *in dependence on* such acting.

As the matrix of the making and becoming of the future, then, the present has a dynamic whereby its own outworking into this-future rather than that-future is not simply a function of the past, and is also not simply a function of that past together with present fact. The particular future does indeed arise, and take on the character which it does, on the basis *in part* of the continued working of energies already at work in this-way rather than in that-way. There is continuity, and to that extent also, some basis for predictability, provided that this continuing involves a sameness to the way those energies are at work or an assured and knowable trend of change or variation. But *in part* the particular future arises and takes the specific character it does because, immanent in the forces at work, there is *also* novel possibility, and (where human beings are among the forces included) there is *also* a freedom which is effective even if within a scope that is indeterminate and might be minimal. I say "might be minimal" because Heaven and the ancestral spirits are also effective and ultimately governing partners in the arising of the future. How great the scope of effective control the human being exerts, is never known or knowable.

The dynamic of this matrix in which the future is in the making, then, while it may include some *predisposition* for one certain future to arise rather than another based on continuing energies and the way they operate, does *not* in principle *predetermine* such an eventuality as unavoidable, and certainly does not do this regardless of how human beings use their freedom.

In this matrix of the future, in this dynamic of the present on which depends the particular character of the future, the human being has a part which includes his/her desire to know and anticipate and to form his/her participation in the situation informed by such cognizance and anticipation. Divination expresses such a desire and seeks to assist its realization.

But if possibilities and potentiality, and freedom, are effective factors present in the dynamic along with the continuing tendencies of actualities and the more or less steady working of Heaven and ancestral spirits, divination can not give insight into the future as if its particularity were dependent *only* on continuing tendencies which are unaffected by how the inquirer acts. Neither can it disclose a future whose particularity is dependent in any measure on the activity of the agent to whom the disclosure is made. For in that case we have the real possibility of the fore-knowing agent undermining the validity of the claimed foreknowledge by deliberate effort.

The upshot here is this: divination adapted to the involvement of the diviner as agent in a situation whose issue includes what is being inquired into, can not (and would not be intended to) give insight into the particularity of the 'will be' that includes that issue. Its address to the future (the 'will be') is indirect, just as in the case of the auspicious and inauspicious. Its seeing is not a fore-seeing directed upon the 'will be' but an attending and discerning focused initially on the present *in its futural side*. That side is manifest in three facts: that any future issue being inquired into comes to be out of the present, that the coming to be determines itself through the actualities and potentialities of the present, and that whether this-future or that-future is given birth to depends on *how* the active beings in the present together define the actual ongoing movement into the future in their interaction with each other.

Divination adapted to the agency of the inquirer *in partnership with* Heaven and the ancestral spirits points into the future that is currently harbored in the dynamic of the present by pointing in appropriate fashion into the futural implications of the continuing energies-- divine and human-- actually at work in the present and of the range of possibility and potentiality immanent there as well. That is, it points into the shaping of the future which is currently underway *with* the agent's participation, and into the implications of that shaping, *as it is currently occurring* at the time of the divination, for the particular future being inquired into.

If the sign-pointers through which this divinatory directing of attention takes place are shaped to point to a structured dynamic which marks the way active forces in a situation are working together and the way potentiality and possibility indwell that situation and open up a more or less novel future for those forces, then the inquirer is pointed beyond the surface of affairs, to assess the complexity of the situation and to reach toward the essential coherence of the present as it relates to the future. The force of such pointers is to urge and support a many-sided exploration of the present in its futural implications, in search of what the spirits and the divine powers have-- presumably with some fuller understanding and with a concern for certain ends-- pointed the inquirer to. The issue of such exploration would (at its highest and best) be an intelligent anticipation of the future and one which would be superior to an anticipation not so guided and inspired.

3. The practical function of such divination

If the seeing which is achieved through such a form of divination is into the future in this fashion, if it amounts to a fuller discerning not only of the continuing energies in the present and their already-present futural implications but also of the possibilities and potentiality harbored in that very same present, to what end, for what purpose, would such seeing be needful, and such insight helpful?

Put succinctly, the function of divination of such a type as we are con-sidering now is to contribute to a more fully responsive functioning of the human being in the situations of action in which he/she is involved. By fostering a greater practical insight into the futural dimension of concrete reality, such divination enables the inquirer to adapt his/her participation in the coming to pass of the future and to make it more appropriate and effective in virtue of its being responsive to such more intelligent anticipation. In this way such divination enhances the capacity in a participating agent to take part more knowingly in that situation and to become more adequately responsive in helping shape the future on the strength of his/her response in the present. Such divination would be particularly suited as aid to a King charged with a Mandate whose execution in the concrete conditions of life is left to his responsibility and judgment-- subject to the directional and directive conditions laid down in the Mandate itself. For its shape would assist him in the needed concrete exploration of the conditions of his carrying out the Mandate, so that his execution of that responsibility could be more knowledgeable and be more effective because it would be more in keeping with the realities of that situation.

Such divination fosters greater insight *not* by *giving* the inquirer knowledge (of the future or of the present), but by providing a *guide* for the inquirer's active *attending* to the present. Under the guidance of a divine pointer (the sign), the inquirer is to seek practical insight into the situation at hand and can attain it with this help. But both this attainment and the effort are those of the human inquirer, and the use of this guidance is the inquirer's own as well. Similarly, the strengthening of the inquirer's capacities for responsive participation in things as he/she makes the effort and shares in the achievement of whatever is achieved is the inquirer-agent's own. What is given is a pointer; knowledge and strengthened capacity come only with human effort that interprets and uses such a pointer as its guide, employs the resources available to it in the circumstances, and explores the present in those facets of it relevant to the shape of the future that will come forth out of it.

4. The character of the divinatory sign

Consider, now, the manner of pointing which would function in this way, compatibly with the role of an inquirer as responsible agent complicit in the unfolding of the future. What manner of sign would form the appropriate occasion and guide for the attention and eventual insight in question?

Keep in mind that we are talking of a sign which does more than simply anticipate in the vein of the auspicious or inauspicious. We are talking of a sign which focuses attention and exploration on the futural side of the present, so as to deepen insight into what is coming in the unfolding of the pres-

ent and to enable the agent to be more sensitive and knowledgeable as a responsible participant in that unfolding.

Would a sign that functioned straightforwardly to hand over clear knowledge without such attention and exploration be apt to promote the responsible taking part that is called for? Would a sign which functioned indirectly
and obscurely, to hand over knowledge that could be appropriated only if
one could sift through the indirection and obscurity and grasp the knowledge
unadorned, be any more appropriate?

In neither case would such (open or obscure) transmission of knowledge
demand of human beings a development of their own capacities for concrete
insight. In the first case there is no earning of insight through the exercise
of capacities at all; one is simply given a fully-formed gift. In the second
case-- the deciphering of a clever puzzle-- such exercise as there is addresses
the sign (its complexity and obscurity) and its application within the horizon
of currently known reality, without requiring an exploration of reality itself
that would deepen insight into the concrete. But the enhancement of judgment in practical affairs above all requires first-hand exploration into reality
itself.

There is a type of sign, however, which would in principle be able to
function in an appropriate way, to point away from itself as if it were a repository of knowledge which had simply to be deciphered, and to point
attention into reality. That is a sign which is in principle enigmatic. Such a
sign would be a thing or event, or in the broadest sense, a reality, which is
intelligible in its own right as such, a recognizable entity but one which, in
this context, would be functioning as portent, as omen. When I speak of its
pointing as enigmatic, I mean: the pointing by which it points into the futural
dimension of the present is an intimating which intrinsically is not transparent in its disclosive meaning or bearing but inherently needs interpretation
for such meaning to become available.

Such a divinatory sign as I have in mind, however, would not be
enigmatic in the way, say, certain phenomena are puzzling or riddling to us
because of our ignorance. In the latter case we can remove the puzzling or
riddling character by appropriate inquiry and knowledge; the puzzling character is *only* relative, and relative to a certain condition in ourselves (ignorance) which we can change. But the enigmatic character of a divinatory sign
does not have this relativity and removability. Since that character belongs
to it as such, there is no interpretation which can 'unveil' its 'true meaning'.

Yet one might say: consider the case when we interpret a sign's pointing into a situation, and after exploring that situation, we think we have come to understand the sign's pointing-- what it is that is being anticipated in that sign. Suppose two alternatives: one, that what comes to be is indeed what we anticipated based on the sign, or two, that it is not but that, once we see what in fact came to pass, we can in retrospect see the sign as having been pointing to precisely that even though we could not see it at the time.

Can we not say in either case: *this* is what the sign *really meant*, *this* is what it was pointing into in its obscure way but which we can now lay out clearly? Would we not have deciphered the sign and eliminated its enigmatic character?

Not at all. It is *always appropriate* to return to the pointer itself and to read it otherwise. In particular, one can *always appropriately* read the situation under its guidance *more profoundly* and *sensitively*-- if one has the resources and capacity for this-- and can find the sign working effectively under a different interpretation. For a divinatory sign intrinsically 'means' in a *suggestive* fashion that inherently supports manifold ways of drawing out its meaning. There is *no one* meaning which may be drawn out of it which is *'the' 'true' meaning* of the sign. Rather, the enigmatic means in manifold fashion, and in a way that is meant to lure the sensitive interpreter to achieve a focused discovery and understanding of the situation. Yet however deeply discovery and understanding reach, they never exhaust the meaning of the sign-- even though the present resources of the interpreter may have reached a point of exhaustion in their capacity to find meaning in the sign.

The interpreting of a sign by which one draws out its meaning this-way or that-way for a situation and searches for what the sign is pointing to in the situation, is just that: an interpreting which appropriates the sign as pointer but does this by forming *one* interpretation *among others* of the meaning and import of the sign. To ask, "What is 'the' 'true' or 'real' meaning of the pointer?", is to presume that the divinatory sign 'means' in a univocal fashion, and that if one is able to decipher the 'true' meaning of the sign, then one has found 'the' 'true or correct' interpretation of the sign, that is, the correct reading of its true or real meaning. But that is to miss the point and mistake the character of the divinatory sign.

The function of the pointing of an enigmatic sign is to catalyze an exploration and insight into reality itself that goes beyond anything 'contained' in the sign itself and is as full and profound as the capacities of the explorer can produce. The effective richness of the sign is its power to command and guide the appropriate attention to the ongoing present, so that that present may be seen in its truth more accurately and complexly, more profoundly, and more adequately to the needs of the agent in question. The effective working of such a sign, however, depends on the effort and resources of the explorer being guided by it. The warranty of the sign-- that it is from the divine and thus is assured of being relevant in the effort to discern truth-- is this practical one, that under its guidance one may proceed relevantly in exploring the futural implications of the present. It is no guarantee, however, of success in discovering significant knowledge regardless of the effectiveness with which the inquirer probes the concrete situation.

Thus, rather than handing over knowledge-- straightforwardly or hiddenly-- to the inquirer, as if this were something contained in the sign itself, the enigmatic character of the sign allows it to *suggestively but relevantly guide* an inquirer's inquiry into the reality of the situation itself, the reality beyond the sign but to which it points. Supposing that it is received and responded on appropriately, such a sign would be able to galvanize attention and inquiry into that reality. The sign would speak in the imperative voice, so to speak, and say, 'Pay heed to the situation guided by this suggestive pointer into its encompassing or underlying dynamic, into its coherent change-character'. What any interpreter would find of reality in an exploration heedful to this command would depend upon that interpreter's own capacities and resources and on his/her way of utilizing these, among other things.

The inquiry which answers to this imperative, and the assessing and noticing which are part of the inquiring, are meant to have a clarifying function. That clarifying in turn is meant to enable one's active involvement and response in the situation to become more apt than otherwise, more suited to reality.

The more effective the clarifying of a sign's pointing and the more its suggestive richness informs attending and issues in relevant practical insight, the more reponsive our response in the situation can be in virtue of this taking to ourselves such signs and engaging in such sign-reading. The more this is so, the more such signs play their intended role in our activity, namely, to strengthen our capacity as active beings to live wittingly with reality and in particular to register and respond to the futural implications of the present and to anticipate the future which is being born out of the present in the continual onflow of time.

In keeping with the sense that the function of such divination is to serve the enhancement of our capacity for responsibility, the actual participation in divination itself strengthens this capacity by the demands which the enigmatic signs make upon us. Since they are irreducibly enigmatic in character we must interpret the divinatory signs for them to mean anything for us practically. But that act of interpretation is our own, a making-our-own of the meaning of the sign. That making-our-own is meant to make a difference in how we take part in things: it is to make possible a more sensitive response, say, as well as to strengthen our capacity for being sensitive.

Thus the interpreter (and anyone acting on the basis of an interpretation which he/she accepts) must take responsibility on him-/herself for whatever he/she has made of the sign. And because there is no 'one and only true meaning', we must always accept the possibility that our reading is more superficial than it could and should be, inadequate in one or another way by reason of our own inept or insensitive engagement with the sign. We have made less of its power to point us into reality and to facilitate our exploration and discovery of truth, than we could have.

The pointer is a catalyst for attention, but the attending is our own, and as it inflects action which is also our own, we not only become different but we act differently. And all this is so in a way such that we can not pass it off onto the signs-- for we did not act on them except under *our own interpretation* of them, for which the signs themselves are not responsible.

5. Divination in the distinctive *Zhouyi* form

Let me sum up, then, what I am suggesting, as it relates to the *Zhouyi*.

The introduction of the line images and the use of the hexagram title images as the essential medium of divination in the *Zhouyi* transformation of stalk-divination brings verbally-framed images from out of the familiar context of 9th century Zhou life forward to function as divinatory images, as symbolic pointers which are to guide the inquirer's attention to the futural dimension of the present. Through them, the spirits-- and Heaven, ultimately-- respond to the inquiry, and respond in keeping with the sense of human responsibility as a participant in the unfolding of the future.

The method presupposes the King as inquirer, a King responsive to the Mandate and one in need of resolving doubts or testing proposals that concern the concrete conditions under which he is exercising his responsibility in keeping with the Mandate. What was meant to issue from his employment of this divinatory technique was twofold. On the one hand, it was a thoughtful penetration of concrete situations in which his responsibility is to be exercised, thus recurrent insight into the concrete. On the other hand, it was a strengthening in himself of his capacity for judgment, for insight into the concrete; this in turn would enhance in a cumulative way his capacity for carrying out the Mandate in the concrete.

The signs which would function as guides in the divinatory situation are symbols of a dynamic holding in present reality. They are not mere examples of omens, extraneously attached to lines and line figures; nor are they records of omens from other situations or omens with historic standing, which have been attached to the lines to 'explain' or give some definite body to their auspicious or inauspicious character or to reflect that the selection of such lines has historically been often associated with the presence of such omens. If the images were any of these things, they would have no intrinsic function in the divinatory act; they would have no intrinsic disclosive significance but could be disregarded altogether without loss to the divinatory act. As it is, as symbols with the disclosive sort of pointing I have characterized above, they form the heart of the distinctive *Zhouyi* mode of divination-- even though the system embodied in that book can be used in other ways as well.

Chapter 3
Zhouyi: its divinatory system

If the *Zhouyi* is a vehicle for a divinatory inquiring which has the character sketched out above, what is its structure as such a vehicle and how do its elements function?[1]

The *Zhouyi* has survived for roughly 2800 years. But it has reached us today in two basic versions, which have some significant differences between them. One is the traditional form, handed down and recopied, and continually edited and re-edited, over the centuries. Variant readings have survived among the several versions of this form which still exist, but the differences among them are slight. The other is a form discovered in a 2nd century BC tomb excavated in 1973, which contained a manuscript copy of the text with (among other things) a quite different order to the parts than the traditional order.[2]

We will take up with the meaning and consequences of that and other differences in a moment. Since the work in both versions is composed of the same elements, we begin by taking note of these.

A. *Zhouyi*: elements of the system

1. The line figures

The first basic component of the *Zhouyi* system is a set of sixty-four abstract line figures, each composed of six lines which are normally drawn horizontally in parallel with each other. These hexagrams, as they are called in English, are made out of two types of line-element, a solid line and a broken line. Together the sixty-four figures exhaust the possibilities of combination of such lines with each other in a six-line figure.

We do not have from anywhere close to the 9th century BC any exposition of the method by which such figures were brought into play. All we do know, by inference from early sources, is that it was through some manipulation of milfoil stalks. Originally, this was part of a religious act whereby the Zhou King sought responses from his ancestral spirits (and from Heaven, beyond them) to inquiries concerned with the futural issue of something which was sufficiently clearly conceived that he could bring questions or proposals for action to bear on (some aspect of) it.[3]

These line figures are not the basic divinatory images in the *Zhouyi*. Rather, both as wholes and in their separate constituent lines, the line figures are meant basically to function as intermediary factors whose accompanying verbal images form the signs through which the ancestral spirits and divine powers respond to the questions or to the proposed courses of action that are posed in inquiry. The stalk-manipulation selects these image-signs only by selecting the line figure(s)/line(s).

Nonetheless, in this context of inquiry those abstract six-line figures seem also to have a symbolic sense and a secondary disclosive function. Inquiry is into something determinate within the whole, some determinate future that is to emerge out of the present in an interplay of factors, of forces and powers. Each six-line figure holds a multiplicity internal to itself; it is a unified many-ness, relatively rich but limited. In the attention-guiding function of the divinatory signs in this system, that many-ness signifies in a general and indeterminate way another many-ness in the real world, namely, the constellation of forces and powers which mark the actual world-situation within which the matter about which one is consulting the diviner is to be found.

That is, each set of six lines, as a unity of a limited multiplicity, points the inquirer toward the relevant concrete matrix of the future in question as a limited constellation of forces and powers whose operation is conditioning the issue of that matter. What is being symbolically intended through the line-figure itself is that determinate interplay of factors conditioning the movement into the future in which the actual issue of the matter in question will in fact be found.

The line-figures of themselves, while they thus symbolize a distinctive unified many-ness, do so indeterminately. They do not represent any fixed and absolute content,[4] but a relative one-- that constellation of forces *relative to* the matter at issue in the inquiry.[5]

2. The words

The second basic component is the verbal one, which includes the divinatory images that constitute the distinctive heart of the system. The verbal images-- harbored in the hexagram title-names, hexagram texts, and the line statements-- are associated with the line figures and are selected in the divinatory act by way of the selection of those figures. These verbal images provide the more determinate symbolic guide which the *Zhouyi* offers for the inquirer's attention to the real world, and in particular, to this real complex which the line figures only abstractly point to as indeed a *complex* of powers and forces. The verbal elements are not limited to such images, but are of several different sorts and are diverse in their nature and function.

Normatively, these verbal elements occur in a certain order in the exposition of each of the hexagrams in the *Zhouyi*. Viewed overall, the normative order is as follows: first, the title-name; second, the hexagram text; and third, the line statements of the six lines.

2a. The title-name

Each of the sixty-four hexagrams has a title-name.[6] In their own immediate reference and meaning, the title-names signify concrete elements in the life-world of the upper class of the 9th century BC. They have associations and connotations which are emphasized and slanted when the verbal elements linked with the lines of the figure with that name are taken into consideration.

These title-names have two roles.

One is the function of pointing to the theme of the hexagram as a whole, which is embodied in the series of its line images. The title does not need t name that theme nor to indicate it in any direct and obvious sense, in order to serve this pointing-out function. Yet its connection with that theme is intimate, if of varying forms.

The other role of the title-name is its own divinatory function. The title names certain matters, and the line images internal to the hexagram help to give fuller coloring and a slant upon the meaning of the title. When the stalk-manipulation selects the hexagram-whole, it determines the response to be the referent of this title-name, so far as this is taken *as symbol, as image* under which, as guide, the spirits are directing the attention of the inquirer to the real world.

That is, within the limited world-situation which holds the matter about which the inquirer is inquiring, there is a constellation of forces bearing on that matter and working in a way imaged by what that name stands for as it is used in the title of the hexagram. For example, the title-name of Hexagram 53 is "Advance"; a further determination of its meaning is provided by the lines, which tell the story of the wild swan returning to its home in the highlands. Through this complex image-- of the advance which is bodied forth in that story-- the dynamic of the situation which holds the matter at issue in a consultation is pointed to. The constellation of forces working to bring forth the future about which there is a question, has the dynamic, the change-structure, bodied forth in the advance of such a migrating-home of this bird.

When it is the hexagram as a whole that is selected through the stalk-manipulation, then, it is the image conveyed through the title-name that is to guide attention. The spirits and divine powers thus *intimate* a complex reality under this *image*, under a familiar part of the life-world of the inquirer taken as *image* for a working of multiple forces, for an overall *dynamic* which is present in the situation and which affects the issue that the inquirer wishes to know about in anticipation.

It is one of the difficulties in understanding the *Zhouyi* aptly in a historical reference, that the terms used as title-names and the images meant through them probably had a variety of associations and connotations that are difficult, even impossible, for us to recover today. We may suspect their presence, and may even conjecture it from a basis in the usage, say, of the *Book of Poetry*. But some of the feel of the words and the richness of the symbol, here and in the line images as well, is probably lost to us in almost every case.

2b. The hexagram text

Accompanying each hexagram as a whole, there is normally not only a title-name but also a set of further words having a variety of functions, only one of which is intimately connected with the image of the title-name. As a collective set, these verbal elements form the hexagram text (statement, judgment). They have different functions from the title-name and its image.

In standard form, the hexagram text consists of four parts, not all of which, however, are found in every such text. When they are all present, their order of presentation in the text is normatively as follows: first, the occasion responses; second, the action indicators; third, the specialized prognostications; fourth, the scene-setting images.

The first standard[7] part is a set of three characters, often with further modifiers, which function as a single (modified or unmodified) character and a two-character phrase. These represent a limited and specialized use of the *Zhouyi* system, which does not draw on its distinctive features but moves simply within the horizon of the auspicious and inauspicious. Here the system is made to function much like the pre-*Zhouyi* stalk-divination is likely to have done, or much like the bone-and-shell divination of the Shang and Zhou rulers. The single character ("sacrifice"), along with its modifier(s) ("grand", "minor"), is apt as a positive answer to a question on the specialized matter of whether an occasion calls for a sacrifice, and if so, at what level of grandeur. The paired characters ("beneficial divination") are apt as a positive answer to questions related to whether or not an occasion is auspicious for (say) a marriage, a significant military undertaking, or for holding a sacrifice, or .... Because of their character and use, I have called these elements "occasion responses".

The second part[8] is a set of phrases which do not address directly the future matter at issue in the inquiry, but do concern the futural implications of the present out of which the future will unfold. Within that present, the inquirer, as a participant in it (at the very least, as making the inquiry), is called to recognize something which it would be beneficial for him/her to do, or more strongly, to recognize that he/she is being enjoined to do or not to do something in that situation. These matters-- undertaking a risky major venture, consulting a figure of some authority, undertaking a trip, establishing feudal lords, taking up arms, engaging in litigation, undertaking to marry or to have someone married, taking someone captive, believing someone's words-- are addressed in an exhortatory, even imperative, vein to the inquirer. The horizon here is that of active participation, and of norms and values governing that. But the action has no inherent connection with the matter addressed through the image, and the presence of this part reflects another use of the *Zhouyi* than that involved in the image.[9] Because of their character, I have called these elements of the hexagram text "action indicators".

The third part[10] is another set of elements which are also not directly related to the question or proposal being addressed to the spirits through this mode of divination. This set focuses attention on the present as the inquirer is involved in it, and relates to it as something auspicious or inauspicious in this or that other specialized reference, quite regardless of what is at issue in the question or proposal. Thus these elements may speak to going, to travel, to security, to dwelling, to hardship, to major and minor affairs, to campaigning, to eating, to the use of animals in sacrifice, or more broadly, to animals, to noblemen or big men, to women; or they may speak to directions of the compass, or to time-periods or times. In each case, there are indications of the bearing on such matters of the situation involved in the inquiry. As with the second part, the presence of this part reflects another use of the *Zhouyi* than that involved in the image.[11] Because of their character, I have called these elements of the hexagram text "specialized prognostications".

The fourth part of the hexagram text[12] is not a divinatory element at all, but rather a complex scene-setting image or set of images whose function is to expand or refine the meaning of the title-name by indicating the context for the line images accompanying the component lines of the hexagram. It is present simply to help make intelligible the set of line images which embody the theme voiced in the title-name, and thus to help fix the meaning of any line image if and when it comes into play. Thus it is unlike all the other elements of the hexagram text, both in being intimately linked with the title-name, the theme and the line images, and in having no intrinsic divinatory function of its own. Because of their function, I have called these elements of the hexagram text "scene-setting images".

In general, the hexagram text is that area of the exposition of a hexagram which copyists used as a repository for phrases or lines which have become displaced or detached from context, or are duplicate or alternative forms. The conscientious copyist usually has placed them here rather than guessing and placing them where his guess surmised they should go.

2c. The line statements

After the hexagram text comes a verbal component which forms for each line its "line statement". These statements are set forth in order, from bottom to top. Normatively, each line statement is formed of four parts, but not every line has all four.

In addition, copying has introduced disorder into the setting forth of the components of the line statement in all of the versions of the text which we have. This is particularly the case in regard to the line titles, which seem to have been a later addition to the work and, in being added, to have been entered in the wrong place in numbers of cases. This has often led (say) to the grouping of phrases which in fact belong to different lines but which, as copied, are set forth as belonging to the same line.

Normatively, the order would be this: first, the line title; second, the line image; third, the action indicator; and fourth, the two forms of the prognostication element, the one relating to the bearing of the imaged dynamic on the matter at issue in the question, the other relating to its bearing on specialized factors not intrinsically connected with that matter.

To begin with, each line, whether solid or broken, has a title which includes two things.

One is a number which places the line in a serial ordering of the lines in the hexagram whole: there is a 'beginning', a 'top', and in between a 2, 3, 4, 5.[13] The numbering shows that the lines of the line figures are thought of as starting at the bottom, so that the line figure is formed by an ascending series of six lines.

But two, the title contains in each case another number: a 6 or a 9. If one looks to the line in the figure, then it turns out that the 6 is always associated with a broken line, the 9 with a solid line. These numbers apparently have a significance related to the way the individual lines are brought into play in the act of consultation. The two numbers are presumably arrived at by the manipulation of the milfoil stalks, and when that manipulation which engenders the line in the hexagram (say, Line 2) results in them (say, a 6 for Line 2), then the line is selected out as response to the inquirer-- in modification of that response provided by the hexagram as a whole, or in substitution for it.

However it may be with this latter alternative, in either case the hexagram is being treated not simply as itself (through its title-name) an image of the change-dynamic of a situation, but as harboring further images which, in function of the results of the manipulation, may operate in special cases to provide more complex images as responses to the inquiry being undertaken in the divinatory process.

After the title of the line comes the remainder of the verbal component associated with that line. As with the hexagram text, so with the line statements: in general, this component consists of parts not all of which appear in every line.

The first part of the verbal component that follows the line title is an image or set of images; I call it the "line image". Together with the title-name image this forms the distinctive feature of the *Zhouyi* mode of divination.[14] Within the line statement, it is this image which is to guide the inquirer's attention to the present and effort to understand the dynamic of the complex of forces which bear on the future about which inquiry is being made. But it is not an image in the sense of a picture; it is an image as embodying and exemplifying a disclosive meaning that points to a dynamic of change obtaining in the interplay of a constellation of diverse powers.[15] Under the guidance of this meaning-conveying image one is to attend to and seek to understand the forces that are at work in the situation as well as the way they are operating to bear on that issue. The image functions for the line like the title-name does for the hexagram as a whole when the latter is the response being given to one's inquiry.[16]

Take an example: "a cauldron overturned, its feet upturned". An everyday thing, a cauldron, in a certain state, that of being turned upside down so that its legs stick up, is here being conveyed verbally. In this context, that thing in that state is being pointed to as embodying a meaning, that is, as in its character symbolizing the dynamic, the forces at work and the way they are at work, in the situation of the matter about which inquiry is being made. As a divinatory image, the overturned cauldron is **not a picture** of that situation, those forces, or the issue they are at work bearing on. Rather, it **symbolizes** the dynamic and the forces, and thus provides a guide to the inquirer's attention to the situation of the matter about which he/she is asking: let us say, the undertaking he has ventured upon (a building project, perhaps) and whose issue he is concerned about. The line image here says: the forces at work in the situation of that venture are presently bearing on it and shaping its future in a way symbolized by this overturned cauldron with its upturned feet. The task of the inquirer is to attend to the situation guided by that symbolic image, to see in the concrete and in regard to that particular situation what such an image is pointing him/her to in the way of the actual character of the situation and the dynamic of change marking it.

In general, the line images represent modifications or particular expressions of the change-dynamic which is imaged in the title-name of the hexagram as a whole. They may be seen as indicating modifications through which the initial overall change-dynamic is itself transformed, to become of another character. But if one understands them in this way, the emphasis of the line image is nevertheless not on the initial dynamic or on the subsequent one, but upon that modification itself. In terms of the example just used, the emphasis is not on the dynamic imaged by the cauldron (Hexagram 50) or on that imaged by great blessings (Hexagram 14[17]), but upon that particular expression of the change-dynamic represented by the cauldron which is an overturned cauldron with its feet upturned (Hexagram 50/Line 1).

The second part of the verbal component that follows the line title[18] functions like the second verbal component in the hexagram text. I call both the "action indicator". It is formed by a set of phrases which do not address directly the future that is at issue, but address rather the situation out of which that future will arise. They speak to how the inquirer, as participant in that situation, might well act: in the example I just referred to, this part of that line reads, "it is beneficial to expel evil and to acquire a female bonds-maid along with her offspring". This pointer, whether taken straight-forwardly or taken in symbolic fashion, may or may not have any relevance to the particular matter addressed in the inquiry-- in the example, a building project. The verbal elements here are imperatives or are pointers to what is beneficial or not; in both cases, they point the inquirer into something which would have a beneficial bearing in that situation. But they do not necessarily or directly concern the specific matter in question in the inquiry which generated the response.

The third part of the verbal component following the line title[19] is a set of elements which speak within the horizon of the auspicious and inauspicious. They interpret the boding of the working of the forces symbolized in the line image. In the building-project example I have been using, the response which points to those forces under the image of an overturned cauldron also indicates that the bearing of the working of the forces so imaged is 'without harmful-mishap'.

I include under this component both words/phrases which concern the bearing of the imaged-forces on the matter at issue in the question (the "image prognostication"), and those which do not directly concern the specific matter involved (the "specialized prognostication"). There seem to be several strata of vocabulary introduced into the text here, with the basic terms being (in the case of the bearing on the matter at issue) that the divi-nation is 'auspicious' or 'ominous', or points to a 'threat' or a 'difficulty'; the other kind of bearing-disclosing phrase (not relating to the matter at issue) is represented by 'this is a beneficial divination for such-and-such a sort of thing'. But there are numerous other terms of each sort which are used to point to the bearing of the dynamic and the working of forces in the situation, ranging from 'without harmful-mishap' (as in the example I used above) to 'without anything beneficial', from 'troubles vanish' to 'without troubles', and so on.

B. *Zhouyi*: order of the hexagrams

1. In the Mawangdui version

I mentioned at the start of this section that the Mawangdui version and the traditional texts ordered the sixty-four figures differently. The Mawangdui ordering is a mechanical one formed according to the character of the two trigram constituents of each hexagram. It is indifferent to meaning, ignoring the linguistic elements altogether. The basis of that ordering is as follows.

To begin with, the eight trigrams are themselves ordered, beginning from the one with three solid lines, moving to ones with a single solid line and two broken lines, then to the one with three broken lines, and finally to the ones with a single broken line and two solid lines. In the case of the two single-double groups, the order is again mechanical: first comes the trigram with the single line on top, then the one with it in the middle, then the one with it on bottom. Exhibited visually, the order is this, reading from left to right:

☰   ☳   ☵   ☶   ☷   ☴   ☲   ☱

Next, using this order of trigram figures, the eight hexagrams whose upper[20] trigram is composed of three solid lines are placed first, then the eight hexagrams whose upper trigram is composed of the single solid line on top of the pair of broken lines; and so on until the series of trigrams is run through and all sixty-four are grouped into eight groups of eight.

Next, each set of eight hexagrams has as its own first hexagram that one in which the upper and lower trigrams are the same-- the double-trigram hexagrams. Internally, each set of eight has the same basic order, except that because of this type of beginning in each case, some difference in what follows has to ensue. The basic internal order is defined according to the lower trigram's character. In general, that order is this: three solid, three broken, one solid on top of two broken, one broken on top of two solid, one solid in the middle of two broken, one broken in the middle of two solid, one solid on the bottom under two broken, and one broken on the bottom under two solid. Exhibited visually, the order is this, reading from left to right:

☰   ☷   ☶   ☳   ☵   ☲   ☴   ☱

Because the first hexagram in each set of eight is the double-trigram hexagram, only in the first group does the first hexagram have as its lower trigram the first trigram-figure in this different ordering (namely, three solid lines). That is because such a trigram forms the double-trigram figure with which the first group can start. This first group has the following configuration and order, reading from left to right; the numbering is M = Mawangdui and T = traditional.

M-1	M-2	M-3	M-4	M-5	M-6	M-7	M-8
(T-1)	(T-12)	(T-33)	(T-10)	(T-6)	(T-13)	(T-25)	(T-44)

In the second group, the single-solid-over-two-broken trigram is the needed duplicate, so the second hexagram in this set has the single-solid-over-two-broken trigram on top of the one with three solid lines, the third has the same top with a three broken line bottom, and the fourth, since the single-solid-over-two-broken trigram has been used in the opening hexagram, is the single-broken-over-two-solid trigram.

M-9	M-10	M-11	M-12	M-13	M-14	M-15	M-16
(T-52)	(T-26)	(T-23)	(T-41)	(T-4)	(T-22)	(T-27)	(T-18)

A similar treatment takes place in each set of eight.

2. In the traditional versions

In contrast with this mechanical trigram-based ordering which is indifferent to the verbal content belonging with the figures, the ordering in the traditional text is meaning-determined.

The first feature of the order of the hexagrams is that the sixty-four are arranged into thirty-two pairs: 1 and 2 are paired, 3 and 4, and so on through all sixty-four. This pairing is achieved through the themes of the hexagrams, that is, by the verbal element by which each hexagram as a whole, and each line in it, gain definite significance. And yet, while pairing is achieved in each case, the type of pairing is rather different in different cases.

For example, the pairing may occur as it does in Hexagrams 1/2, because a single story runs through the 12 lines of the two figures and gives them a continuity. Or it may occur because in them a common theme is given different, even opposed, renderings, as in Hexagrams 9/10; the theme there is life as involving one in troubles, and the renderings relate to troubles as brought on mainly by the larger circumstances of life which make one victim (9), in contrast to troubles which one brings upon oneself by how one comports oneself (10). Or the pairing may occur because in the two hexagrams matters which are polar opposite are utilized as images, as in Hexagrams 37/38; the polarity there is that of inner and outer, of what concerns the household and family as the locus of the inner and what pertains to celestial phenomena observed in the most distant 'out there' of the physical world and related back to human life.

Depending on how fine the classificatory distinctions one would want to make, there are only a few-- or there are numerous-- *types* of pairing that occur, each with its own characteristic meaning-determined relation between the two pa⁻ ˒ ˄ hexagrams.

Each hexagram, while having the character it does as a set of divinatory images, is associated with a distinctive line figure. There is nothing which one can plausibly point to as the reason why any image-set should be associated with any particular line figure or constellation of six lines. But nonetheless, given an association, the line figures associated with any pair of hexagrams are themselves related, as line figures, in one of two types of relation.

The commonest relation is that of inversion. Given any particular line figure with its constellation of lines that is associated with any hexagram, the line figure associated with its pair hexagram is formed by inverting the first line figure so that the top line (say, a solid line) of the first is the bottom line of the second, etc. There are four cases in which this method of generation of one from the other would not in fact produce a different hexagram. These are the line figures associated with Hexagrams 1/2, 27/28, 29/30, and 61/62. In these cases, the method of generation of one line figure from its pair is simply to convert each of the lines of the first hexagram into its opposite (solid lines into broken, broken lines into solid).

In short: among the line figures associated with the hexagram pairs, there is a secondary or derivative pairing, which is visible when the whole six-line constellations are looked at and compared to each other as regards their constituent lines.

If there is a clear rationale for each pair, and a definite sense of order and connection between the two hexagrams of the pair based on meaning, is there any larger grouping and order, and a comparable definite sense of order and connection?

The answer is, Yes, but the analysis which justifies that answer is somewhat lengthy. So let me first anticipate its results, and then proceed to a fuller exposition of the order in the next sub-section.

The overall structure involves the grouping of the hexagrams as listed in the following diagram.

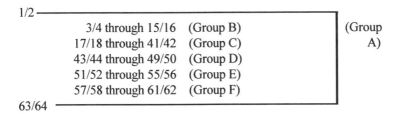

1/2
```
        3/4 through 15/16    (Group B)        (Group
        17/18 through 41/42  (Group C)         A)
        43/44 through 49/50  (Group D)
        51/52 through 55/56  (Group E)
        57/58 through 61/62  (Group F)
```
63/64

3. Exposition of the hexagram order

The beginning and end of the whole set of hexagram pairs provide us crucial clues to the order that gives structure and coherence to the thirty-two pairs of hexagrams.

Hexagrams 1/2 together delineate in a continuous chronicle the unfolding of a year in its seasonal rhythm, and within this, the unfolding of the basic human affair most closely integrated with (because dependent on) the seasons, the autumnal harvest of grain that sustains the Chinese of north China in the 9th century BC.

Hexagrams 63/64 address individual and collective ventures which involve major risk; together they place Chinese life of that time in the context of the collective venturing which defines the historical movement of human life on earth. That collective venturing is recalled in focus upon the leading political centers whose succession gives most meaning to 9th century life, namely, the Shang and the Zhou dynasties.

Through their own themes, these two pairs complement each other in such way that, taken together, they bring forward the encompassing context and matrix of 9th century BC Chinese life and life-ventures. I call this framing pair of pairs, Group A.

The thematic content and the associated line figures of the hexagrams at the beginning and end lead us to raise two questions.

One: Are we dealing here with a work whose divinatory images, while suitable for use in the type of divination we have sketched out earlier, are so ordered as *also* to adumbrate an encompassing vision of life? Is this adumbration, with whatever meaning-structure it may involve, itself the basis for the ordering of the hexagram pairs so that the series 1/2, 3/4, 5/6 and so on is what it is?

Two: In the case of hexagram pairs, we see an ordering in which meaning is determinative, and because of the association of image-sets with line figures, we also see a connected pairing whose principle has nothing to do with meaning but only with the constellation of constituent lines. Now if we look to the line figures associated with the beginning and ending pair of image-sets, the first pair is in each case composed of lines of only one type; the last pair is a set of figures whose component lines continually alternate between the two types of line. While both types of line-figure constellation are unique, if we look at the line constellations as each composed of two sets of three lines-- taking the lower and upper halves of each six line figure as themselves figures--, then we find that in the case of the first pair, there are six other hexagrams which have the same principle of order, that is, which are double-trigram hexagrams. Those companions are Hexagrams 29/30, 51/52 and 57/58. Exhibited visually:

1 and 2	29 and 30	51 and 52	57 and 58

These three latter sets appear as the fifteenth, twenty-sixth and twenty-ninth pair in the traditional order. If the first hexagram pair is a clue, then we might expect that those hexagram pairs, when looked at on the level of meaning, would also be foundational in an ordering of larger groups. Is that the case? Are they key ordering hexagrams in the overall structuring of the thirty-two pairs?[21]

a. Hexagrams 17/18 through 41/42: Group C

Let us begin our answer to the second question by taking up with the first double-trigram hexagram pair after the opening of the work, namely, Hexagrams 29/30.

Thematically, this pair-- entitled Pit and Mountain Spirit-- point us into divine powers which are manifest in the earth, and more specifically, the earth high above the surface of the plains and the earth below that surface. The images used in the lines of each of these two hexagrams focus the presence of such powers in certain definite ways, connected with hunting and warfare. As they fit within the framing pairs at the beginning and end of the work, they introduce a different side to earthly life than is found in the frame itself. Whereas earth was linked in the frame with the heavens as season-marking and season-inducing and was manifest primarily in the agricultural life of the community, here it is manifest in close connection with death, with hunting and with warfare. And the pair also recall a level of social existence which is more primitive than the agricultural but elements in which have endured on and been given a place in more advanced life nonetheless.

If this pair is an organizing principle for a group of hexagram-pairs, it will most likely be such by being the beginning or the ending of that group, or else by being the central pair in the group. While the scope of any grouping would be determined on the level of meaning, any ordering would also find an expression in the line figures, and the visible simplicity of those figures should allow us to pick up clues to it fairly readily.

Examination of the associated figures for hexagrams before and after Hexagrams 29/30 brings out a pattern related to the trigram-constituents of the hexagrams which suggests that Hexagrams 29/30 are the center of a fairly large grouping of hexagrams.

First: In all of the thirty-two pairings within the work as a whole, there are just six pairs in which the associated line figures of the two paired hexagrams are composed of four different trigrams. Two of those pairs (27/28 and 31/32) occur immediately around 29/30, two more (17/18 and 41/42) occur equidistantly before and after 29/30.[22] The four trigrams involved in both cases are the identical four, and are the four not involved in the pairing of the hexagram-pairs 1/2 and 63/64.[23]

Second: Scrutiny of the line figures and trigram relations of hexagram pairs which lie in between the outermost and innermost pairs of pairs, that is, scrutiny of the pairs from 19/20 to 25/26 and 31/32 to 39/40, shows a pairing of pairs which is sufficiently comparable to the pairing of 27/28 with 31/32 and 17/18 with 41/42, to suggest that the line figure relations of the hexagrams falling within this group may also be the visible expression of a meaning-grounded ordering of successively expanding brackets.[24]

The layout on the next page will help to visualize the line figure relations of all these hexagrams which form the group centered around Hexagrams 29 and 30 (I call it Group C).

GROUP C

27 and 28   31 and 32

25 and 26   33 and 34

23 and 24   35 and 36

29 and 30

21 and 22   37 and 38

19 and 20   39 and 40

17 and 18   41 and 42

    Is the suggestion of the line figure relations, that 17/18 to 41/42 is an ordered group centered on 29/30, confirmed when we look to the ordering itself, which is formed on the basis of the meanings embodied in the title-names and the line images?

    Seen thematically, the whole group draws for its themes and images primarily on various aspects of social life and action.

The outer pairs thematize the encompassing social order in fundamental aspects. The first pair (17/18) makes continuity in the social order its theme, using images expressing both the breakdown of such order and its continuity over generations through the family. The last pair (41/42) thematizes the poles of increase and decrease in the affairs central to the social order. In the one case it draws on sacrificial ritual and travel to point to different types of increase and decrease; in the other, it speaks to the founding of the Zhou dynasty, thus to the crucial event that formed the order of 9th century BC Chinese society. The two pairs link with each other thematically as pointing to complementary aspects of social existence and order, namely, continuity and its failure on the one hand, and change which brings increase or decrease on the other.

Within this embracing pair of pairs, do the themes and meanings which define the pairs also order them into pairs of pairs, in a way comparable to 17/18 and 41/42? A brief overview seems to provide an affirmative answer to this question. The pairs 19/20 and 39/40 are linked in a contrasting of two types of polarity important to the society: one involves the sense of higher and lower, the other involves movement as free or as obstructed. The pairs 21/22 and 37/38 are linked in a contrasting of two further forms of polarity important to the society: one involving the family in contrast with what is outside it, the other involving different forms of concealing and revealing that permeate relations throughout the order. The pairs 23/24 and 35/36 are linked, in the contrast of a movement involving a starting condition away from which or back to which one moves, with a movement that is aggressive, forward, and bounded by death. The pairs 25/26 and 33/34 are linked as contrasting realizations of the theme of injury and harm. The pairs 27/28 and 31/32 are linked as contrasting realizations of the theme of bounds-- in the one case bounds which function as norms or standards, in the other bounds which function as limits that can be abbreviated or extended.

It is important to keep in mind that this ordering is achieved by reference to themes. Themes are realized in variable ways. Not only are the variations intrinsically different from each other, but no theme is identical with any of its realizations. It can be, however, that the particular variations used in the realization of the theme of some hexagram may be important in their own right in the ordering; in Hexagram 42, for example, this seems the case in that it is the Zhou dynasty in particular that is defining for the social order being adumbrated, not just any dynasty. In contrast, it can be that the particular variations are simply one variant of a theme which is itself alone what is important; in Hexagram 41, for example, this seems the case,[25] since the types could be made visible in many different realizations.

In a pairing which is thematically based, the themes of each hexagram within the pair (as distinguished from the specific realizations involved in each case) are thought of as themselves connected in their own meaning. The character of that connection, and the character then of the unity of a pair, can differ considerably. Because the particularity of their own realizations is variable, the realizations of each theme may have no significant connection with each other in terms of their particularities, without this calling into question the genuineness of the connection of the two themes as themes. For example, the themes of Hexagram 21 (a covering which conceals something within itself) and of Hexagram 22 (a covering which displays) are in the one case realized in biting into meat/flesh and wearing stocks, and in the other case, in an event that is part of a marriage ceremony. The particularities have no connection with each other, but the themes are connected as themselves variations on the embracing theme of the interconnection of concealing and revealing.

Now if we extend this thought, we can think of two pairs of hexagrams, each of which pair is internally linked by the reference of their different themes to some embracing theme. We may think then of each of the embracing themes of these pairs as also linked by reference to an even more embracing theme. For example, the embracing theme of Hexagrams 21/22 (the interconnection of concealing and revealing) itself stands contrasted with the embracing theme linking Hexagrams 37/38 (inner and outer). What holds the two themes of the two pairs together is the embracing theme of polar opposition. Each expresses a different way in which the opposition of polarities is realized: one in which their contrast is achieved without setting them apart (what reveals at the same time also conceals), one in which their contrast sets them apart (what is within is not what is outside, the contrast is one of externality and exclusion).

The type of ordering effected in this Group, and in the other Groups as well, needs to be seen carefully in its own distinctive nature. In particular, in virtue of being thematic it is not classificatory in nature. The connection of theme and realization is rather different from that of (higher or lower) class and instance of the class.

For a diagram of this Group, its order, and its themes, see Diagram 1 (next page).

DIAGRAM 1: Group C

17 Pursuit Pair theme: continuity in the social order
18 Affairs

  19 Overseeing Pair theme: contrast of looking up to
  20 Contemplation the higher with overseeing the lower

    21 Biting through Pair theme: contrasting mixtures of
    22 Many-colored ornamentation concealing and revealing

      23 Flay and strip away Pair theme: moving away from or
      24 Turning back and returning back to a starting condition

        25 Pestilence Pair theme: an agricultural village beset
        26 Large Animals by plague or blessed by Heaven

          27 Cheeks and Jaws Pair theme: excess on a
          28 Going greatly beyond the norm grand scale

            29 Pit Pair theme: divine powers manifest in the
            30 Mountain spirit earth's higher and lower places

          31 Cutting off Pair theme: polarity relating to length
          32 Making endure/last

        33 Piglet Pair theme: a polarity relating to harm
        34 Great Harm

      35 Advance in attack Pair theme: a polarity relating
      36 Crying pheasant to aggressive action

    37 Family Pair theme: polarity of inner/outer
    38 Celestial Observation

  39 Hobbling Pair theme: a polarity concerning movement
  40 Liberation

41 Decrease Pair theme: opposite conditions/actions
42 Increase which involve each other intimately

b. Hexagrams 3/4 through 15/16: Group B

Between Hexagrams 1/2 and the beginning of Group C (17/18), there lies a group, 3/4 through 15/16, which has no double-trigram internal to itself to be an anchor to its order. Before passing on to the groups whose organization involves double-trigrams which are central to their order, let us consider this group, which I call Group B.

If we look to this set of hexagrams with the idea that it might be an organized group, we note first that it contains seven pairs, an odd number. If we take the focusing on a central hexagram as involved in the organizing here (as in Group C), given the odd number of pairs the central organizing hexagram pair here would be 9/10 (Small Pasture, and Shoes and Stepping).

This pair embodies in images from different situations a specific sense of our human life, namely, that our venturing and risking on earth under the heavens (the sense of the bracketing pair, 1/2 and 63/64) is unavoidably involved in troubles. But it speaks to troubles as, on the one hand, something which we can bring upon ourselves, or on the other hand, as something which are brought on mainly by the larger circumstances of life.

Given such a focus to the central pair, it is not surprising that the surrounding sets of pairs from 5/6 through 13/14 all develop their themes in ways that introduce aspects and facets of trouble in the form of a conflict/tension of forces. Indeed, the pairs 5/6 and 7/8 place trouble at the very heart of their imagery, being closely linked with each other thematically around conflict in military form.

Finally, this group is bounded by a pair of pairs (3/4 and 15/16) which introduce troubles in important ways, but which also focus on aspects of the non-human life forms (plant and animal), either as entered into the ceremonies of human life (marriage is the case in point) or as regarded in their own right. Fittingly for their appearance in this group, the wild, large and small, is included in the second pair as impinging on human life in threatening fashion. And this introduction of the wild is paired with an integrating of plant life into the human which (due to the set of images chosen) takes place on the background of a joining of human beings in marriage which is fraught with elements of force, pressure, coercion-- the savage in human beings, ritualized.

For a diagram of this group, its order and its themes, see Diagram 2 (next page).

DIAGRAM 2
Group B

3 Sprouts bunched together   Pair theme: marriage and the involvement
4 Dodder   of the non-human life forms in its rituals

   5 Pausing   Pair theme: a polarity of active conflict
   6 Open dispute   and of pauses in such conflict
   7 Army   Pair theme: the polarity of employing military force
   8 Supportively aiding   or of supportively aiding others

    9 Small pasture   Pair theme: a polarity concerning troubles
    10 Shoes and stepping   as endemic to human life

   11 Overflowing   Pair theme: a polarity concerning
   12 Obstruction   bounds and limits
   13 Gathering together of human beings   Pair theme: the story of
   14 Great blessings   a battle, victory, celebration and Heaven

15 Hamster   Pair theme: non-human life, in its own right but
16 Elephant   out of its independence impacting human life

c. Hexagrams 43/44 through 49/50: Group D

The other two sets of double-trigram hexagrams are Hexagrams 51/52 and 57/58. The line figures which express in their visual medium the pairing of hexagrams, suggest a different sort of organizing is at work here from that of any of the groups so far considered. Each pair of double-trigram hexagrams stands at the head of a group of three pairs. The first group is formed by 51/52 through 55/56 (I call it Group E), and the second by 57/58 through 61/62 (I call it Group F).

These meaning-organized groups are both structured in the same way and of the same size. Since these culminate the ordering of all sixty-four hexagrams in groups, and since the meanings involved seem to advance in an ordered movement which begins from the meaning-focus in the only group we have not yet noticed, namely, 43/44 through 49/50 (I call it Group D), let us consider this latter group first, and then return to these first two groups.

Group D contains an even number of sets and thus has no center pair as its organizing reference point. It also has no lead pair. Thus it differs in structure from Groups B, C, E, and F. Its ordering principle is also different from that of Group A, although thematically it correlates with this group quite closely.

Group D is composed of four sets of pairs, whose unity is effected in the pervasive reference of the pairs to contrasts which ultimately refer back to the conditions of a being who ventures under risk. As venturers we become engaged in flight or caught fast in entanglement or enclosure, weighed down in distress or drawn to rise upward in a sacrificial act, hedged in and distressed or restored to an earlier flow and functioning, caught up in change or stable but subject to troubling change.

If Group A points to the embracing context and matrix for the venturing of Chinese of the 9th century, Group D calls to mind those Chinese as active beings engaged in venturing there and-- because of factors without and within-- susceptible of becoming caught up in these differing conditions.

Structurally the unity of the set of eight pairs is made manifest in the line-figures as follows: each pair contains a common trigram appearing with a pair of further trigrams; this latter pair is the same pair in all four cases, but it is linked in each case with a different common trigram. The four common trigrams are the four which compose Hexagrams 1/2 and 63/64.

For a diagram of this group, its order and its themes, see Diagram 3 (next page).

DIAGRAM 3
Group D

43 Moving quickly   Theme: swift movement contrasted with forms
44 Bound together   of entanglement and enclosure

45 Weighed down in distress Theme: distress weighing one down
46 Rising up in ascent   contrasted with forms of ascent

47 Hedged in and distressed   Theme: distress from being hedged in
48 Well   contrasted with a well flowing again

49 A rawhide tanned and changed   Theme: change v.s. a stability
50 Cauldron   which is subject to troubling change

```
 43  and  44     45  and  46     47  and  48     49  and  50
 ▬▬  ▬▬▬▬     ▬▬  ▬▬     ▬▬  ▬▬     ▬▬  ▬▬
 ▬▬▬  ▬▬▬▬     ▬▬▬  ▬▬     ▬▬▬  ▬▬▬     ▬▬▬  ▬▬
 ▬▬▬  ▬▬     ▬▬▬  ▬▬     ▬▬  ▬▬     ▬▬  ▬▬▬
 ▬▬▬▬  ▬▬     ▬▬  ▬▬     ▬▬▬  ▬▬     ▬▬▬  ▬▬
```

The repeated trigrams are:

```
 ▬▬▬▬   ▬▬ ▬▬   ▬▬ ▬▬   ▬▬ ▬▬
 ▬▬▬▬   ▬▬ ▬▬   ▬▬ ▬▬   ▬▬▬▬
 ▬▬▬▬   ▬▬ ▬▬   ▬▬▬▬   ▬▬ ▬▬
```

The pair of further trigrams which appear in each set are:

```
 ▬▬ ▬▬   ▬▬▬▬
 ▬▬▬▬   ▬▬ ▬▬
```

d. Hexagrams 51/52 through 55/56: Group E

Group E is composed of six hexagrams; the structure to its order is that of a head pair of dual-trigram hexagrams followed by two further pairs. The unifying thematic here is the most intimate of connections of human beings out of their inwardness, that involved in the sexual relation between man and woman (husband and wife).

The leading pair contains a complementary reference to this matter of intimate connection: the first points to an ambivalent outward-presence (thunder, both intimidating and arousing) which links with spring and the sexual celebration in which spring is welcomed, and the second points to a staring, even a glaring, which embodies the distant, even hostile presence of one human being to another, the antithesis of the embracing and uniting presence represented in the first.

This leading pair is followed by a pair on marital relations (imaged in regard to a separation being closed in the course of a return home, contrasting with a marriage which ends in estrangement), and a pair eliciting some of the exploits (including sexual) of a royal figure.

Structurally, there is minimal manifestion of the coherence of this set in the associated line figures. The trigrams involved in the initial dual-trigram hexagrams do indeed appear in the other two pairs of this set, to that minimal extent linking them all together. But this appearance is with two other trigrams in the one case, and with a repeated trigram in the other.

For a diagram of this group, its order and its themes, see Diagram 4 (next page).

e. Hexagrams 57/58 through 61/62: Group F

Group F is also composed of six hexagrams, and the structure to its order is the same as that in Group E: a head pair of dual-trigram hexagrams followed by two further pairs. The unifying reference is an even more intimate connection, of human beings with the divine and not simply with each other.

The leading pair defines the character of the connection to involve from the human standpoint not simply a reverence (embodied in the act of offering sacrifice) but a sense of self which, while placing reverence toward the divine as essential, is instinct with an enjoyment of a life on earth that involves conflict, negotiation, but also leadership which brings about a harmonious connection of human beings with each other.

After this leading pair that draws its images from the religious and political sides of the Zhou King's role comes a pair contrasting the spurting lifeblood of a sacrificial victim in a royal sacrifice with the restraint essential to moral life, and then a pair contrasting loss and disconnection (related primarily to death) with that directly encountering and meeting each other (in contrast with passing by and missing each other) in which the living really live.

DIAGRAM 4
Group E

51 Thunder Theme: the contrast of spring thunder and
52 Glaring   sexual intimacy with hostile distance

   53 Advance   Theme: contrasting marital conditions
   54 Marrying Maiden   inwardly and outwardly

   55 Fulness   Theme: the story of Prince Hai's exploits,
   56 Traveler   sexual and otherwise

   51 and 52   53 and 54   55 and 56

The trigrams of the first two hexagrams ...

do appear in the other two pairs, but linked in one case with a repeated
trigram ... and in the other with two different trigrams.

Structurally, there is much the same sort of manifestion of this coherence in the visible figures as in the case of the Group E hexagrams.

For a diagram of this group, its order and its themes, see Diagram 5 (next page).

f. Order and vision in the hexagram pairs

The preceding exposition of the sixty-four hexagrams indicates that, on the level of meaning, the serial order is a structured one, first organized by pairs, then articulated into a set of six larger groups. This means that the *Zhouyi* is not simply a randomly put together set of line figures and images useful for divination. The two questions posed at the beginning of this section (Section 3) seem answered in the affirmative. On the one hand, the larger grouping, achieved on the basis of meaning, involves key hexagram pairs whose line figure accompaniments are double-trigram figures. On the other hand, not only did the author draw his title-names and images for the various figures from various areas of 9th century and earlier life in China, and thereby give us a glimpse into his world-- a world contemporary in much of its content to him, but with a historical presence integral to it as well. But he also ordered the image sets in such way that, when considered thematically, they adumbrate a coherent vision of life.

If we may briefly resume that vision, following the pointer of the grouping into six groups: human life on earth is caught up both in the seasonal rhythm and in the collective religious and political venturing which aspires to a civilized existence for human beings on earth. As an affair of venturing and risking, human life involves the dialectical interplay of effort and circumstance and the endemic possibility of troubles. It also involves divine powers beyond Heaven, powers which manifest themselves in earth's varied facets; in particular, it must cope with divine forces associated with darkness and threat. The venturing undertaken in a life so constituted implicates the living being in various inner conditions, dimensions, and forms of movement, change, and stability. Close to the heart of what is important in such the venturing is the most intimate condition and relation among human beings, the sexually-inflected connection of man and woman. But the life so lived has as its highest expression the reaching out to the divine and the reaching to include all other human beings simply as human. Within this reaching, life's involvement in sacrifice and in restraint, in death and in the encounter of the living with the living, are to be played out.

There is no reason to think the author of this divinatory work sought intentionally to draw images from *all* the aspects of life in that world, and thus

DIAGRAM 5
Group F

57 Laying out food offerings   Theme: complementary relation of
58 Pleasure   religious reverence and joy in human affairs

59 Spurting-and-spattering   Theme: contrast of spurting blood of
60 Restraint   a sacrificial victim with restraint within bounds

61 Bull's-eyeing the captives   Theme: life as mortal and as
62 Passing-by by a little   centered in connections

57 and 58   59 and 60   61 and 62

The trigrams of the first two hexagrams ...

do appear in the other two pairs, but linked in one case with a repeated
trigram ... and in the other with two different trigrams.

indirectly to give an encompassing or inclusive presentation of the world in which he lived. Nor is there any reason to think that the glimpse into various facets of his world, or the coherent ordering of the images which give us this glimpse at the same time as they function in divination, were either of them constructed systematically by an author working on a conceptual or philosophical level and embodying his philosophy in this divination work. Nonetheless, the work is clearly a product of a complex mind that has a coherent vision of life and the whole within which life is lived, that knows how to work in an orderly fashion, and that aspires in this work both to create an orderly medium of divination and to convey this coherent vision. And this in turn suggests that his sense of the universe, of the concrete world, was likely to have been that it also is an orderly place-- but orderly in a sense which fits with divination as a meaningful effort appropriate to reality as it is in truth, and not therefore orderly in just any sense.

Before we think more fully on this matter of the vision conveyed to us in the *Zhouyi*, we need to consider one final element of order entered into the work, that which is found within each hexagram, in its image sets.

C. *Zhouyi*: order within the hexagrams

In the preceding discussion we have focused on the hexagrams as manifesting an order in their relation to each other. But there is a complex and variable ordering within any hexagram-- and as in the previous case, one defined by the verbal elements involved.

Each hexagram is composed of lines/line statements which are thought of as ordered serially from bottom to top. When on the background of this pattern the images of the line-statements are taken together and considered in their placement, order, and content, we discover some type of coherence and development in every hexagram. Indeed, when we connect such order in one hexagram with that found in its pair, we find further forms of coherence and development. Depending on how the line images adumbrate the meaning of the title-name and gain further meaning both by their connection with each other and by their appearance in a hexagram with that title-name, the orderly connection displayed within a hexagram may be of very different sorts. But in every case it conditions the disclosive and prognosticatory force of the individual lines.

The full exposition of the order within a hexagram will be reserved for the commentary which accompanies the translation of the hexagrams. But as illustration of the varieties of type of coherence and development to be found within different hexagrams and within a pair, we may note that there are hexagram pairs in which a continuous story is being told, beginning with the first line of the first hexagram and ending with the top line of the second hexagram.[26] In one case that story-telling involves a narrative style which proceeds importantly by variations on a phrase which includes the title-names of the hexagrams involved;[27] in another case the story-telling has a more analytical cast, setting forth individual and dynastic venturing in a sort of counterpoint with each other.[28]

More common are hexagram pairs in which the lines of one hexagram tell one story, and the lines of the other either tell another separate story or form a set of variations setting forth a theme in various aspects.[29]

Occasionally[30] there is what amounts to an analytically-ordered setting forth of aspects of a matter; this can be linked with a story-telling in the other hexagram of the pair.

The story-telling is always elliptical and suggestive; it is on occasion historical.[31] But most often it is the exposition of a typical incident or occasion: for example, of a marriage-ritual,[32] or of a family caught up in the midst of war and drought.[33]

The variety of forms of coherence is considerable. Without too fine an analysis, one can identify twenty-five significantly different forms through which coherence in the lines of a hexagram is being achieved. On the other hand, one can understand the forms to be manifestations of two main ways of introducing coherence, one through a story-telling and the other through an analytical exposition of a theme.

The presentation of a story, or the setting forth of various aspects of a matter in a more analytical vein, or whatever other way in which coherence is achieved in a set of hexagram lines, is not an end in itself in the *Zhouyi*. As the presentations, expositions, and the like are intended to function, these are simply devices for developing images which can carry complex meanings and can function as guides for the attention of the inquirer to the concrete world. The selectiveness exercised, say, in the presentation of a story, the omission of much and the allusion to much, has made it difficult for interpreters of the work who are not steeped in the story-telling and poetic context and tradition to become alerted to the story-telling that is going on. All the more is there difficulty if divination in the *Zhouyi* method is not understood in keeping with the dramatic character of the universe, as the utilization of symbolic pointers into the reality-in-the-making character of the actuality one is involved with. But once one gets the hang of the way in which the hexagram lines are given meaning and are meant to function, and has regard for the use of language and the elliptical manner of presentation, then a coherence begins to show itself, within a hexagram and often within a hexagram pair, that is quite thought-provoking.

D. *Zhouyi*: its overall vision

Although the overall and pervasive order of this divination work has become marred and to some extent concealed by distortions introduced in its transmission and has disappeared from view because interpreters have forgotten the art of story-telling and lost the feel for how the lines express that art, such order does seem to be present in the text. Is there a coherent 'philosophy' being set forth in the work? No, not if one means by "philosophy" something in the way of disciplined conceptual thought, and if one means by "setting forth" something like a systematic exposition of that thought. Yet although this work is not philosophical in that sense, it does convey two things of great interest to lovers of wisdom. One is the glimpse into the world of the 9th century BC, caught in the image-content of the images being drawn on for their fruitfulness in a divinatory context. The other is the implicit sense of the universe in its coherence conveyed in the way in which the divinatory act works in the system of divination bodied forth in this work. A word about each matter.

1. The world conveyed in the images

The images used in this work are drawn from what we may conceive was the actual world of the author. Included in that world was not simply what was contemporary, but also the sense of the past as known in that time. While the images are introduced to serve a divinatory purpose, and while their ordering is used to give an added element of coherence to the medium of divination, nonetheless they and their ordering work together to adumbrate a vision, one that is broad and encompassing even if it is not thoroughgoing and complete. To a historian or a sociologist, the images offer a fascinating glimpse into a historical situation and culture, into a world seen from the perspective of the royal court; to a philosopher, they provide entry into a way of dwelling in the world that harbors a vision of the whole and of life's meaning which is worthy of consideration.

I have already given a brief indication of what the material tells us of the nature of the ninth century world, and of the vision of human life that is embodied in it. Here let me expand on that indication and do so without being tied down to its order of presentation in the hexagram groupings.

According to the images, the world is one in which human beings dwell on earth with a sense of Heaven as the ultimate divine power, the source of blessings and the source of a mandate for rule. Within the interplay of Heaven and what is on earth, two facets are companion to each other. One is the manifestation of heavenly forces seen in the seasonal rhythm and in celestial phenomena such as constellations and eclipses. The other is that, within the movement of this rhythm, human beings live closely tied to an agricultural pattern of activity, of planting and harvesting; they also live exposed to droughts and floods, incursions of pestilence and plague, and dependent on timely rains, all making the growing of foodstuff on which life depends subject to irregularity and uncertainty.

The persons most intimately tied up with carrying out the works which provide this necessary ingredient in life are one part of a larger social order. At the lowest end are slaves and bond-servants, and non-persons of one sort or another. Above these are the little men, and the officials, and the noble-men who are lords of domains of some size: all dependent upon the work of peasants but none themselves engaged directly in agricultural activities. This order is hierarchical in a particular way: it is oriented toward one King, who holds a Mandate from Heaven for his rule but who includes such noble lords as vassals whose authority in their own sphere is granted as a mandate from the King. Not only is the King served by royal ministers and by military men, but the lords and noblemen serve in turn as rulers with a mandate to open up their own lands (cultivate and claim to human use) and to maintain the family and clan (their own, but also that of others who serve them). Contrasted with this, the civilized world, we find other human beings living on earth but without such a structure, without the culture and drive toward civilization manifest in this world. These are barbarians, comparatively.

We catch glimpses of aspects of the domestic side to life in this world. It is realized in domains and estates, it involves families with traditions and inheritances, it has its crucial ceremonial elements such as marriage. But most of the images derive from the more public, political and religious, spheres of life. There is an elaborate religious system, for one thing, pointed to in references to the palace and the ancestral temple of the King, to the suburban altar and ceremonies conducted there, and to the "western hills" as locus of royal sacrifice. The ritual involved is in most cases sacrificial in nature. There are offerings made, of foodstuffs but particularly of animals and (quite often in the course of these images) of human beings, always captives taken in war. Elements in the preparation of animals for sacrifice-- flaying and dismembering-- play an important role in the images drawn on; libations, ceremonial cleansing, are further aspects of the ritual through which human beings reach out to divine powers-- the King to Heaven (God), lords and others beside the King to powers such as the Earth-spirit or Mountain-spirit.

There are other aspects to life enacted in the royal court-- and that is the perspective of the author of this work. There are pointers to some sort of legal system, to legal proceedings such as public denunciations, and to a variety of punishments in which offenders are subjected to devices such as stocks (feet) and cangues (neck), their foreheads are tattooed or their nose is cut off. The broadest reach effected in such life, however, is that enactment of the religious and the political in unison which is represented in the idea of a Mandate for rule devolving on the King from Heaven. Life is lived in that world within a sense of the past as holding a dynastic change: a shift from Shang to Zhou. The actual names and events introduced into the images seem to cluster around the late Shang and early Zhou: the earliest is a Shang ruler (Wuding), and then, among the pre-dynastic Zhou, Ji Li; close to the time of transition we find mention of Di Yi and Ji Zi among the Shang, and in the course of the transition, to the Lord of Kang and the Duke of Zhou, among the Zhou leaders. It would seem from the images that in the author's mind the continuation of the Zhou leadership in his own time is nothing assured but is something in doubt. Involved in this question of leadership are multitudes of questions about campaigning and war, fighting and taking captives. Yet closely linked as well is the sense that what is aspired to is a peace and harmony which can not be achieved by force.

In keeping with the sense of the military, yet deriving from an earlier time and serving some function of providing food as well as sport, is the hunting which is commonly alluded to. This is essentially a noble activity. It may involve the use of pits or wells, snares or nets, or bows and arrows. It involves a variety of game animals-- deer and fox-- but birds (pheasants, for example) and fish as well. Seen more broadly, the men of the time know of certain domestic animals-- oxen and horses, pigs and sheep and goats-- and of wilder animals-- not simply those hunted but also voles and hamsters, tigers and elephants, mountain goats and turtles, wild geese and cranes and hawks. They know also fruit and melons as important enough parts of ordinary life to serve as recognizable images in this divinatory work. And they know a life in which these-- at least, those which are part of the foodstuff of the lives of some people-- are prepared as food for human beings by being dried or by being cooked and served in a cauldron. This latter image, central to domestic life even of the King, seems to import a familiarity and a stability in counterpoint to the uncertainty and risk imaged in the "big river" whose crossing recurrently seems to come into focus as having to be risked at times.

Perhaps the overall sense of the world that comes through the images being used is that of rhythmic order. Life is ventured amidst an ongoing of affairs and events which harbors considerable risk and uncertainty for us individually and collectively, and yet some structure and dependability in the recurrent patterns. Probably the seasonal rhythm best expresses the combination of both of these facets, and that seems likely to be why the first hexagram pair focuses on that. In keeping with that is also the focus of the final hexagram pair, on crossing a river and (in its line imagery) on a crossing which is a matter of individual and of collective risking. Change is of the essence of life, and yet change is not mere ceaseless flux nor is all change for the best. It is with that essence that this work is suited to help us deal.

2. The universe presumed in the divinatory system

The divinatory system involved in the *Zhouyi* has a reach and function which go beyond the concerns of systems which focus on the matter of the auspicious/inauspicious, either in general or in specific references (marriage, war, etc.). Let me call these other systems types of fortune-telling. The distinctive work of the *Zhouyi* does not lie in fortune-telling; it lies in disciplining the mind of a participant agent to attend closely to reality and in particular to the implications of the present for the future, to the way in which the present harbors a future in virtue of the dynamic it contains.

Two things cooperate in the *Zhouyi* system to accomplish this distinctive work: one, the line figures, and two, the images or more broadly the linguistic elements.

The line figures (the sets of six lines) provide an abstract visualization of the situation in the real world which enfolds the matter that is the subject of inquiry and in which the inquirer, as agent, is included as in some measure and manner a participant. It visualizes that situation as a unity of a limited multiplicity, and one which has its own characteristic dynamic for change.

The distinctive work of the *Zhouyi* system is accomplished only when the line figures become taken up into the verbal domain, and there it is images conveyed in language which have the primary role. In the preceding section we have set forth the 'world' conveyed when the images which the author has employed to play a certain role in the act of divination are taken in their straightforward sense, somewhat as pictures. But when these images are used in divination, they are used symbolically, not as pictures; they body forth a meaning in the concrete, which is taken to symbolize the dynamic of a situation being inquired into.

How are these images brought into play, and brought forth so that there is some assurance that the image is relevant to the situation and matter being inquired into? Does this relevance mean that the world, reality itself, is constituted by a pervasive order, whose changes are all intelligible through sixty-four different change-types?

Let me consider these questions in order.

The verbal images are brought into play through a definite technique which invokes the images through the line figures which are their visual representative, so to speak. In our earliest glimpse that technique involved a use of yarrow stalks. How these were manipulated in those early times, however, we do not know with any assurance. But a question would arise about any type of use of yarrow stalks: what was important and crucial about the technique, what made it efficacious so that one could be assured that the selected image in its directive and disclosive power was really relevant to the situation of inquiry? If we explore that matter from within the tradition itself and ask how this act of divination was understood (or could have been understood) within the 'world' of the *Zhouyi*, we find that, in keeping with the early Zhou vision expressed in the *Book of Historical Documents* and reflected in the 'world' the *Zhouyi* draws its images from, the act of divination through this medium was understood as a religious one. More specifically, as it is found in the *Zhouyi*, it was an act important in the interplay of King with Heaven, through the royal ancestors.

An act of consultation which initiates an interplay and dialogue between human beings and ancestral spirits and ultimately Heaven must involve some common medium of communication. Although the divine and the spirits are conceived in ways that make them familiar through some anthropomorphizing-- and with the spirits, that is almost inescapable, since they are what endures in the spirit world of once living human beings--, it nonetheless remains that the chasm in status and nature which separates the parties in question precludes the sort of face to face conversation through human language (Chinese, here) that marks dialogue among living human beings. The medium then would have to mediate these very different parties over this chasm, using a vehicle intelligible to both parties and capable of effecting the needed communication so that each party could understand the other appropriately.

Let us consider religious ritual as expressing an acknowledgement of the divine which is instinct with the sense of special places where human beings are able to be more highly sensitized to emanations from the divine and the ancestral, and instinct also with special things and events as omens bearing meaning from the divine and ancestral to the human. In the case of the *Zhouyi* we have the creation of a sign system on the part of human beings, as part of an effort to reach out to the divine and ancestral. That sign system facilitates communication by drawing upon the life of the present that would be familiar in some fashion to the ancestral spirits whose own life on earth belonged to earlier phases of this same tradition in which the current way is placed and which it continues. It draws upon an experience and tradition which include interplay with the divine and ancestral in many forms, divination being one of them.

But this employment of the familiar put it to use in a certain function and context, in a dialogue about the future. In keeping with the different status of the parties (divine and human) to this dialogue and with the character of human being in particular, the use made the familiar into signs which are enigmatic pointers. We may see this use as attesting the same sense of divine and human that is involved in other aspects of the tradition, and in particular, in the vision of the relation embodied in the idea of the Mandate of Heaven. In that case, a demand is present but leeway is accorded to a responsible answering to that demand in the concrete. So here: the ancestral and divine do not respond to the human outreach by simply laying out information in return as 'answer' which authoritatively settles a question; they provide only a pointer, and demand of human beings an engagement with the situation under the guidance of this pointer. Human beings must put their minds to matters and utilize their own judgment to discern what the guiding image is pointing to.

Approaching the matter from this angle then, one may say in answer to the first question posed above: the relevance of the image selected as response to human inquiry is assured because the divine powers that have a cognizance of how things really are at the moment have a hand in the selection of this-image rather than that-image. For the technique for selecting the line-figure(s) and line(s) and thence the image(s) is a *religious act* in which the ancestral and divine are called forth into presence to function in the situation as immanent powers at work there. It is *not a merely mechanical or chance process* that is involved. Stated from a slightly different angle: if the selection technique is used in a merely mechanical fashion and without the religious dimension being effectively invoked, it is not being used as the *Zhouyi* calls for it to be used.

Does this relevance mean, then, that the universe itself is an orderly affair, whose order is captured in (say) the sixty-four symbols of change set forth in the hexagrams as distinctive wholes? No, it does not. Divination speaks symbolically, and speaks only to situations or *limited constellations within* the universe as a whole; in each case these situations are *relative to* questions being posed by inquirers and thereby to some matter at issue for human beings.

Thus, to begin with, it does not address the universe as a whole, which is not a situation or limited affair, let alone one relative to human beings. There is no reason to think that the intelligibility of that whole would be the same as that of any or all of its parts.

Secondly, thinking of various sets of realities which are so of themselves within the universe (for example, ecosystems) it is possible to conceive them as parts of an orderly world whose intelligibility involves a limited set of categories. But such systems are not relative to human beings and to matters at issue for them. And there is no reason to think that their intelligibility must coincide with that of situations holding matters at stake for human beings.

Finally, intelligibility and orderliness (intelligible order) may take varied forms. Not only may such forms differ in virtue of their relativity to different fields of reference; but they may differ in virtue of the character of the referring that articulates the intelligibility. These are very different kinds of referring, the symbolical kind marking the *Zhouyi* and the literal or classificatory kind marking (say) western science. The latter grasps things in terms of type. A type has instances which, as such, are identical or similar in character; the particularity and diversity of such instances is external to their being instances, simply an unessential fact. In contrast, the *Zhouyi* addresses the realities in situations through symbolic images. Such images are realizations of a common theme, and as realizations are variations on that theme; the particularities which distinguish the different variations are internal to their being realizations of the common theme. There is no reason to think that intelligibility achieved with the help of types and aiming at the coherence and logical self-consistency of a system must use the same terms, taken literally, as are involved in the intelligibility achieved with the help of symbols and aiming at the practical relevance and efficacy which assist responsible participation in affairs.[34]

What is implied if the divination system is suited to reality is that the order of the universe is such as holds human agents and those limited things which they encounter in their existence into a coming together which has sufficient intelligibility for human beings that this technique of symbolic guidance of attention can be a relevant one in the forming of their decisions and participation in the encounters which mark human existence. What place such 'coming together' itself has in the order of things within the universe, is a question, as are the appropriate terms in which to understand all these matters. Those terms might be rather different from those formed by the symbolic images; the latter might direct attention to matters whose own intelligibility as parts or participants in the universe is differently constituted and able to be articulated, say, through reflective concepts rather than practice-guiding symbolic images.

However that may be, some measure of orderliness within the whole is presupposed in the *Zhouyi* mode of divination-- one sufficient in type and extent to include human beings as agents who have a significant responsibility as participants in the unfolding of affairs on this earth, and to undergird the relevance of the symbolic images to the discernment of the change which is immanent in the unfolding of human affairs in interaction with things on earth. That unfolding, which involves divine and spiritual powers as well as human, forms itself with the help of a dialogue of partners in which this and other forms of divination have a role to play. The order and coherence of the universe, then, whatever else is involved, is one that includes us as (potentially) responsible participants.

Chapter 4
The relevance of this ancient divinatory work to us today

The *Zhouyi* was created in the 9th century BC in a Zhou world which is far distant in time and far different in its sense of life and the world from us and our time. It was intended to have a practical function for the Zhou King in that world. We live today in a quite different world, under a sense of things which does not encompass Heaven as a controlling divine power nor divination as a religious act addressed ultimately to that power. Can this work speak to us as something alive and functional for us in lives and circumstances so differently constituted from those of the Zhou?

That depends on the 'us' in question, both upon our experience of the world and upon the courage, honesty, and subtlety with which we address and understand the disclosures of experience.

The heart of the matter lies in time and in our relation to it. Seen in a historical reference time inherently separates the human beings who lived in the 9th century BC from those living now in the 20th century AD. And the separation, the distance, is not simply temporal. And yet ... for us as mortal and growing beings time also holds the possibility of discovering our condition as human beings to be one that is common. As we reflectively appropriate the meaning of such concrete discovery and gain some insight into that commonality, what about these matters of time, reality, and divination? Can we find grounds in our experience in this different and 'modern' world for taking divination in the *Zhouyi* form as a relevant act for us? even though we are not Zhou Kings, and do not act under acknowledgement of Heaven as a divine power?

This is not the place-- or time-- for launching into the extended discussion that could provide an intelligible and affirmative answer to such questions. All I would like to do now is to offer a few observations concerning this matter, and then provide an example of use of the *Zhouyi* divination system so that if a reader desired to test out that relevance first-hand, he/she would have a fairly definite idea of how to proceed.

Let me begin with two deceptively simple observations.

First, we are mortal, we will die one day, all of us. Second, the life we lead as mortals is an affair of growth, at the heart of which is an ongoing active participation in the world amidst which we find ourselves.

This matter of being active is not simple, and while taking it up within the horizon of our mortality and growth brings it into the appropriate perspective-- activity is always involvement by a mortal, and is the medium through which our growth as human beings takes place-- it does not remove the complexity of the matter. It does, however, enable us to highlight two further things.

First, in our involvement with the world around us we are continually drawing upon our potential, and the deciding through which we attend to things is continually fraught with possibilities, some pursued, many not. Second, both potential and possibility are futural aspects of the present, but neither are the "will be" that will emerge as time passes and our continuing involvement brings us into the present actuality of what before was still "not yet", still "in the future".

If we know our active involvement with what we encounter as involving us in a decision-making and an actualizing of potential and possibility, we also know that decision-making and actualizing as themselves conditioned by beings, by powers and forces, which enter into the concrete situation we are involved in. If we can then understand how this conditioned decision-making and actualizing, this conditioned involvement, could be an affair of responsibility, of responsible participation, then we would be in a position to consider whether, and if so, how, the *Zhouyi* divination system might be relevant to us today.

Let us assume, for the moment, that we have a sufficient preliminary idea of responsibility if we know it as a certain sort of ability to be responsive to reality in the way we bear ourselves actively and live our lives as human beings. How could *Zhouyi* divination be relevant to us as human beings, beings whose lives are intended to bring a growth in this capacity for responsibility? and be relevant to us whatever the concrete historical circumstances of our lives?

The *Zhouyi* presupposes activity, and in particular, a responsible participation in things, as the defining feature of our human existence. It recognizes our agency as situational, as one in which we are involved in a larger matrix of forces and powers and yet one in which we have some measure of leeway in the interaction, some degree to which the forming of our own participation in the situation is both dependent on us and can make a difference to how the interplay works out. Not that the human measure of human influence is taken to be always, or even often, decisive, only that it is there.

One may go further: the *Zhouyi* divinatory system is itself formed to stimulate human participation to develop in a particular way, one through which it becomes more knowing and grounded in reality than otherwise. That becoming-more-knowing-and-grounded will not necessarily make it more decisive for and controlling of what happens, but it will make it more apt humanly and more apt to the real dynamic of the situation in which the agent is involved.

In its own historical context, the *Zhouyi* was seen as relevant because founded in reality itself, but not simply in the reality of the human capacity for responsibility. It was founded more deeply in the reality of the universe as harboring Heaven as ultimate divine power, and in the possibility of an interplay between divine and human.

If in our own context, the latter foundation in Heaven seems no longer credible, is there any way in which we may urge the relevance of the method to ourselves?

At this point, there are two courses which we might take.

The first course is a reflective one. We could search out, and set forth, those reasons founded in reality that could warrant our thinking that the *Zhouyi* method can consistently function as an effective guide for attention. We could address and give answers to such questions as the following: How is it that a system of sixty-four figures, or of four hundred fifty statement-groups, could suffice as guide for attention in situations as varied and complex as we each and all encounter everyday? How is it that from among this limited range of images the technique of selecting the particular image(s) which is/are to guide attention can consistently choose a relevant image or images?

If the discoverable reasons which we find and set forth could enable us to see the answer to these questions, then even if those reasons are not exactly what the author of the *Zhouyi* had in mind, they could warrant us in paying attention to this work as something relevant to our taking part in the world.

Are there such reasons? One might find them in such an understanding of religious experience as discloses a divine ordering power which is cognate to the Heaven which the author of the *Zhouyi* takes as given. Then divination might assume its role as medium of a dialogue between human and divine, even if that divinity is not Heaven. Or, one might find them in an understanding of the human psyche as operating, deeply within, in terms of images, and as striving to order our experiences and their meaning in a way that utilizes images to focalize. Then one might claim that, even if the method of selecting is a matter of chance, how the images selected operate on our psyche, the resonances established, and the meanings that would emerge if we let the *Zhouyi* images strike deeply within us, would assure that we could make something of whatever came forward as selected image that enabled us to form a more apt anticipation than otherwise. In other words, there are reasons in the way in which what is otherwise chance could come to operate within our own psyche, that mean that the chance-selected images would have the relevance I am asking about.

In both these cases, one might be drawn to take up with this method of divination on the basis of some reflective assurance, held in advance of use of the method, that it is suited to work in virtue of its fit with reality.

One might also be drawn to see the method as relevant to us, simply by believing in the existence of such reasons without being able to provide an account that is satisfactorily convincing.

In this first course, *Zhouyi* divination is treated as made plausible in its connection with reality and its function for human inquirers on certain re-flectively discernible grounds, and on the basis of such antecedent reflective assurance it is deemed fit to be taken up with as relevant in principle.

The second course, in contrast, is a practical one which does not seek in advance to justify relevance and to invite participation in divination in de-pendence on such antecedent assurance. It is also one which appeals to something which is a strong part of ourselves already, our pride in our sci-ence and its experimental method. Is it not in keeping with that experimen-talism, that we venture-- without any presumed knowledge or belief in ad-vance, to the effect that the *Zhouyi* method *is* apt to reality-- to see for our-selves, in the most direct way possible?

If one proceeded in experimental fashion to test out the possible relevance of the method to us today, one would try it out in all honesty and without prejudgment, and determine on the basis of the issue of that experience whether use of the method of disciplining one's attentiveness and percep-tiveness under images had the sort of practical issue being claimed for it-- namely, the development of a more sensitive and subtle responsiveness through which to take part in life.[1]

Supposing that a person wanted sincerely to undertake this experiment and to make the sort of effort which the method calls to be made-- so far as he/she could--, how would such a person proceed?

We do not know with any assurance how the originator and early users of it proceeded, what method of manipulating yarrow stalks was involved. There is a later and complex method using yarrow stalks, and an even later but simpler method using three coins.[2] Either provides a mechanism for making a selection.

But keep in mind the initial limits of this approach: unless our willingness to engage with divination is itself responsive to presence in a religious vein, the open-mindedness with which we would be approaching the matter would presumably preclude something essential in the *Zhouyi* method, namely, the religious character of the act of consultation and the reality of the interplay of ourselves with our ancestral spirits and the ultimate divine power behind them. This religiousness and this interplay are not at our beck and call, so in a basic sense we are not undertaking *Zhouyi* divination in full keeping with its original meaning when we undertake the method open-mindedly.

Nonetheless, this course would provide an experimental test, provided we approached it in all seriousness and engaged ourselves with the requisite resourcefulness. And if nothing else, it would also facilitate both a better understanding of what was called for in the Zhou leaders and a fuller appreciation of how they engaged in things.

Let me here address those who would be willing to make this experiment, and more broadly, anyone who wishes better to understand the method first-hand by playing as much of the role of human inquirer seeking guidance from the divine as one can play on one's own initiative alone.

All starts with an inquiry, a question or a proposal, and to simplify matters, let us take the question form as what we pose.

The inquiry concerns a future, and one which is understood as being relative to things in the present, including the inquirer as participating agent in the situation in the present. That is, the future is understood as emerging in time from out of what is happening in the present.

When one selects a sign in the divination process and that sign is taken as the response which one is being given, such a sign-response symbolizes the dynamic of the situation in the present which holds the relevant forces on the strength of whose working the future will come to be in one form or another. The insight sought, then, is into the futural implications of the present, but the response to our inquiry is meant not to "give" us an "answer" about the future in abstraction from the present but to assist us in gaining insight into the prospects for that future given the character of the present.

More precisely, the sign-response is a guide for the inquirer's attention to the present in a prospective vein, and points under an image into the constitution of the dynamic of the present and into the implications of that dynamic for things happening in time ahead which will bear on the future being inquired into. In particular, the pointer is into that dynamic as it is constituted presently and prior to the (further) participation in the situation by an inquirer who has taken this pointer as guidance and who can adapt the direction of his/her energies accordingly.

Suppose that the technique used for identifying the sign(s) which form the pointer(s) to be interpreted, selects a single hexagram.

Interpretation of the meaning of this response would begin with the title-name as conveying an image of the dynamic that is relevant in the present for the coming to be of the future in question. "Relevant" does not mean "sufficient", it means what is determinative beyond whatever the inquirer as agent may subsequently bring to bear so as to influence the unfolding of the present into the future in question.

The second step in interpreting the sign would be to consider the hexagram text.

One part of this-- that which I have marked "H-O" in the presentation of the text-- you would ignore, since it is suited only for very specialized uses, relating to special occasions, and your question is not concerned with whether or not a situation is an appropriate one for sacrifice.

Normatively speaking, the second and third main parts of a hexagram text are elements-- an action indicator, and a prognosticatory word or phrase-- which do not directly speak to the matter at issue in the inquiry. So while attention is focused by the title-name image on the situation as concerns the future and the matter being inquired about, with these parts of the text additional matters relating to the situation and its futural import are conveyed. The second main part speaks in an imperative or advisory vein, and calls attention to things which it would be imperative or beneficial for the inquirer to do in the situation. I have labeled this part "H-A" in the presentation of the text, and would suggest taking its meaning in the following vein: "Given the character of the situation and the dynamic of the inclusive happening marking it, the inquirer will find that the time is one in which ...". The third main part of a hexagram text focuses on potential aspects of the situation including things which the inquirer as agent in the situation might do, and it speaks in a specialized reference[3] of something being auspicious/inauspicious. I have labeled this part "H-SP" in the presentation of the text, and would suggest taking its meaning in the following vein: "Given the evolutionary dynamic of the situation and of the forces working in the way the title-name images, the inquirer will find that in regard to such-and-such the time is ...".

The fourth part of a hexagram text does not come into play unless the pointer(s) selected in the divination process are not simply a hexagram whole but involve moving lines. I have labeled this part "H-SSI", that is, "scene-setting image", since it uses an image to refine the meaning of the title-name and to define the setting in which the lines will have their meaning.

Thus if the method of sign-selection results in a hexagram itself as the response, the basic procedure is fairly simple: attend to the situation relating to the matter at issue guided by the image of the title-name, and seek to discern the futural implications of the forces at work in that situation guided by the image.

Further steps in the consultation process would be called for if the technique which brings forward the relevant sign(s) introduces one or more lines as the focus instead of simply the hexagram itself. In those cases in which the hexagram text has a fourth part, its meaning comes into play here also, to help define the meaning of the line images. But it does not itself function as a divinatory sign.

In regard to any line(s) called into play, the act of interpretation would focus basically on the line image, but include as well the other elements where they are present.

That line image has its meaning as an expression of the hexagram as a whole, thus as one of six line images which develop the thematic to which the title-name points.

The interpretation of the meaning of the line image involves discerning how the situation holding the matter at issue looks when attended to focused by the dynamic of the image. As with the hexagram title-name image, it points to the dynamic of the present relevant for the coming to be of the future in question. I have labeled this part "L-I".

As with the title-name and hexagram text, so with the line statements: normatively there are other elements present beyond the line image. In this case, two-- action indicators, and special prognostication words or phrases-- are parallel to the second and third main elements of the hexagram text. These, I have labeled L-A and L-SP, respectively, and would understand in parallel vein. Thus, I would suggest taking the L-A element in the following vein: "Given the character of the situation and the dynamic of the inclusive happening marking it, the inquirer will find that the time is one in which ..."

it is imperative or beneficial for something to be done or occur. I would suggest taking the L-SP element in the following vein: "Given the character of the situation and the dynamic of the inclusive happening marking it, what is happening as imaged by the image is (auspicious, inauspicious, etc.) as related to (the specific type of matter which the prognostication concerns: e.g. travel or marriage or ...)".

Finally, there is another form of prognosticatory element present in many cases, one related to the matter at issue and the line image. I have labeled this element L-P, and would suggest taking its meaning in the following vein: "Given the character of the situation and the dynamic of the inclusive happening marking it, what is happening as imaged by the image portends ...".

In sum, when the selected sign includes not simply a hexagram but one or more line, the sign becomes more complex. Rather than relating simply to the overall dynamic that marks the futural dimension of the present situation, it points (through the line images) to modifications of that dynamic in the course of time. Attention is thus pointed more definitely into the course of the movement into the future, as the original overall dynamic (pointed to in the hexagram title-name) is modified.

An example will help clarify the above suggestions about how to carry through the divinatory act.

Take the case where I am consulting about a building project in which I am engaged.

The inquiry might be framed: "What is the future of the building project I am undertaking?" or "I am going to go ahead with the second phase of the project immediately: how would that be?"

Suppose that Hexagram 10 (Shoes-and-Stepping), with Line 1 as a moving line, is selected; this latter change makes Hexagram 10 change into Hexagram 6 (Open Dispute). Thus within the sense of the Shoes-and-Stepping hexagram, the focus is on a line whose image is "plain shoes" and whose prognostication is "going: without harmful mishap".

The lines of Hexagram 10 tell the story of an overconfident traveller who unwittingly brings trouble on himself. It talks, then, about a kind of movement on a path that inadvertently activates threats that the traveller meets along the way. The most obvious way-- but not necessarily the best-- to interpret and apply the title-name as symbol in the present case is to take it as pointing to my building venture as involving me in potential risks, and as pointing me (the traveller/venturer in this case) to attend to how I am proceeding, to the risk that I may be proceeding overconfidently, and so on. This pointing then is into the present, and into its futural implications as regards the matter at issue.

The line image that is the main guide is a simple pair of everyday shoes; they are artifacts, crafted articles, which enable a person to walk, to move. This image points more definitely to the situation of my building venture, and to the forces at work in it and shaping its future, and it places these in a specific light. What is the dynamic involved in the image, and how might the real situation be brought to light under the guidance of a sense of that dynamic?

The image points me as inquirer toward the complex of forces as holding one particular facet which is apparently crucial, namely, the 'shoes' or equipment with which the venture is to be carried out and completed. It is not simply physical things that are needed-- money and tools-- but also mental and emotional tools-- skill and knowledge, patience, and the like, things with which I need to be equipped and on the strength of which I am undertaking this venture. Are they more than 'everyday' in character, do I need something better? That is one matter that comes to attention. But the image is of the things themselves, simply them, and not any action or actual putting them to use; yet they are things meant for use, and indeed in the succeeding lines are put to use, so their pointing seems appropriately to include such a question.

As the image relates to my building venture, then, and my concern for insight into its future, it calls quickly to my mind two things about myself and the way I am engaged in that venture that need attention if I am to gain insight into the future of the venture: my possible obliviousness through overconfidence, and the resources with which I am venturing. Much more could be done to let the image be guide, but enough for a start.

Line 1 includes no specialized action-element, but it does have a specialized prognostication-element. It concerns "going". But what is that? Is it only travel in a literal sense, movement in space? Usually, such a specialized prognostication does not concern the matter at issue in the inquiry, but rather, concerns another aspect of the situation which is that related to the matter being inquired into. But in this case, if one takes it broadly so as to include the venturing which is the subject of inquiry, then it is something which can be taken to be relevant. The action-element then says: the dynamic of the situation, imaged by the matter of shoes-and-stepping and given the special dynamic imaged by a pair of plain shoes, holds no harmful mishap for the going (that is, venturing) which would take place within that dynamic. That is, there is nothing in the dynamic, and in particular, in the resources and equipment involved in the venturing, which definitely bodes ill at present for this as a going.

What I have just done does not involve a very profound interpretation, nor does it represent a very penetrating enactment of the method. But if this beginning is carried on further so as to reveal more fully and specifically how the situation of the building project, the possibilities latent in it, and the factors at work in my commitment to the project and my carrying it through, realize the title-name and line images, then it would serve as a model for an interpretative response. The ensuing anticipation of a futural outworking of a certain sort on my part could then be entered into the forming of my participation in the situation.

LOCATION KEY

In order to identify hexagrams from their constituent lines, I provide the following location key based on the constituent trigram figures.

	☰	☳	☵	☶	☷	☴	☲	☱
☰	**1**	34	5	26	11	9	14	43
☳	25	**51**	3	27	24	42	21	17
☵	6	40	**29**	4	7	59	64	47
☶	33	62	39	**52**	15	53	56	31
☷	12	16	8	23	**2**	20	35	45
☴	44	32	48	18	46	**57**	50	28
☲	13	55	63	22	36	37	**30**	49
☱	10	54	60	41	19	61	38	**58**

PART II
TEXT AND COMMENTARY

Prefatory Textual Note

The *Zhouyi* has been preserved over the centuries despite the fact that the original text of the work, as it came out of the hands of its author, no longer exists. That preservation has been accomplished mainly by the technique of hand copying onto perishable materials first the original text, and subsequently copies of copies. The act which enabled the work to survive brought modification into it, perhaps at times intentionally but probably mostly unintentionally. For copying is a human act which, while it may aim at perfect reproduction, is subject to failure in that aim in many ways.

We do not have a copy of the work which comes without further modification by copyists/editors from any time close to the time we think the work was composed (in the 9th century BC). The earliest datable copy which we presently have is the Mawangdui manuscript discovered in a tomb about twenty years ago. Because the conditions in the tomb enabled it to be preserved even though it was copied onto relatively perishable material , we have an unchanged version from the 2nd century BC, with only bits and pieces missing here and there because of damage to the material on which it was written. Other versions of the original text are represented by copies coming from much later times, which have been therefore subjected to the copying/recopying process many more times under many different conditions.

The early textual history of the *Zhouyi* is unknown. But even without a thorough text-critical study, a comparison of the Mawangdui version and some traditional versions indicates that what we currently have are representations of the original text which have considerable obvious differences and somewhat diverse lineages. No one has yet conducted the thorough text-critical work needed to reconstruct from present evidence the best text-- the closest to the original text. My efforts here are not offered as accomplishing it.

Rather, my aim has been to offer an understanding of the *Zhouyi* as a divination work composed in the late 9th century BC, and in order to do that, I felt I needed to provide a translation that would sufficiently convey the sense of the original work that that understanding makes sense. Such a translation requires a measure of text-critical work. If nothing else, the obvious major difference in the ordering of the hexagrams found in the Mawangdui version in comparison with traditional versions, required some decision, as did the presence of numerous variants in the different versions.

A less obvious but more fundamental reason for some text-criticism effort emerged as study of the work began to reveal the coherence of the whole and its parts, and the degree to which the work had apparently been thought together and been carefully set forth as an inclusive unity. There were what seemed like violations or breakdowns in the order that was emerging into view. If that is what they were, if they were not simply reflections of my still too limited grasp of the order, how did they enter into the text?

For example: why do the occasion response features not appear in some form in every hexagram text, instead of in only forty-eight? Why are there not line images in all the lines, instead of in only three-hundred seventy-eight of the three-hundred eighty-six lines? Why the proliferation of prognostication words, and the juxtaposition in some cases of different words leading in quite different directions, while in other lines there are no such words at all? Does the relatively great consistency with which prognostication words and action phrases are segregated, some being found almost always in hexagram texts but not in line statements, others in line statements but not in hexagram texts, indicate that originally there was in fact a functional difference felt between the types of word/phrase? Do some reflect an earlier usage, some a later? How understand the signs of inconsistency in distribution, then?

Important parts of an answer to these and other similar questions seemed likely to be found if I paid attention to how the text has been transmitted, and in particular, to how in that process it could have been distorted through errors, dislocations, and the like, occurring in the copying process.

To the extent that I approached the *Zhouyi* in a text-critical vein I was addressing a written text, and that means, a "unique complex and expression of ideas of an author or authors".[1]   But that text was available only in versions formed at least six centuries after the composition of the work. Because my concern was with the work in its original nature, I had to refer all of the available versions back to a source-- the original text from which these versions eventually came.

As we seek to reconstruct what any 'original text' was probably like, we already carry with us from the very start some notion of it, including some ideas of what it said and meant, how and why it was ordered as it was, and the like, as it came forth from the hand of its author. We cannot do otherwise; we cannot avoid giving it some definiteness in our minds if we are to think it at all. But we can be careful, be self-aware and self-critical, concerning *what* notion and ideas we initially operate with and *on what bases* they were formed. And perhaps more importantly, we can allow that notion and those ideas to change as we proceed, and can be self-aware to what degree and on what bases we do allow this.

In the case at hand-- the *Zhouyi*-- I was concerning myself with a work constructed to serve a practical function. Its parts were meant to be brought into play in a divinatory action, and their character-- the meaning of the language, the significance of diverse types of parts, and the like-- could be intelligible only to the extent that one could enter into and understand that action, and could grasp their role in it. But more profoundly, I was addressing a divinatory work composed in a certain social and historical context, to serve a function in that time. The nature and meaning of its original form-- its inclusion of both words and line figures, for example-- would reflect the author's working within that larger context and his creating something which would have a function in it.

In my notion of it, then, the original text of the *Zhouyi* which I could reach at best in an approximation through a text-critical working backward would be one which itself had such a context and matrix of its creation. Its structure, order and content, and the meaning of its form (and that includes its language), would be such as would be possible and appropriate for a work created under those conditions and meant to function in them.

Now that context was formed primarily by a way of life, a vision, a history. Satisfactory determination of the original text would require not only a sympathetic grasp of the act of divination, but an understanding of the Zhou and the early Zhou vision of the Mandate of Heaven, and attention to other such things as I have set forth in Part I. It was in the light of these that the work whose original text I wanted to recover could be appropriately grasped, and that the features and characteristics which the original text might exhibit could be most likely to be accurately discerned.

In short: what I found myself involved in was a two-sided effort. One side was the attempt to understand a divinatory work whose creation responded to a certain historical context and aimed at producing something functional within it; the other side was the attempt to engage in some measure of text-critical work and (given our current evidence) to work backward from later versions toward a reconstructed original text of that work which was sufficiently free of the distortions introduced in its transmission over the centuries as to enable us to see how the work was conceived originally.

As these two sides of my effort fruitfully played off against one another, I found an important aid to both sides in several studies of the text by four twentieth century scholars. I have drawn heavily upon them, both in regard to variants and the meaning of terms and phrases and in regard to fundamental features of the divination system; I have also found them helpful on the matter of understanding the context in which this work was created. The scholars, and their works, are:

> Gao Heng *Zhouyi gu-jing jin-zhu*
> Li Jing-chi *Zhouyi tong-yi* (also *Zhouyi tan-yuan*)
> Shaughnessy, Edward Louis *The Composition of the 'Zhouyi'*
> Kunst, Richard Alan *The Original 'Yijing': a text, phonetic transcription, translation, and indexes, with sample glosses*

In the end I arrived at the text which is translated in Part II by working with three versions currently available to us. I started from two versions of the traditional form of the text, using that version presented in Gao Heng's *Zhouyi gu-jing jin-zhu* as my primary one but drawing also on the one used in the Harvard-Yenching Institute Sinological Index Series (Supplement No. 10, *A Concordance to the Yi Ching*). In addition, I took into close account the Mawangdui text as presented in the *Wen Wu* article entitled "*Mawangdui bo-shu 'liu-shi-si gua' shi-wen*"; and after Edward Shaughnessy's *I Ching: the Classic of Changes* came out, I drew on his transcription of the Mawangdui text.

I did not take the Mawangdui version as the basic version, despite the fact that it seems to be much earlier than any others known to us. Priority in time does not by itself establish authority. There is much about the copying which created that particular version which we do not know: its reason, the function which that copy was to serve, the copyist(s) involved, the version or versions from which the copy was made, the care that was expected to be taken in making the copy faithful, and so on. But we do know from study of the manuscript that there are good reasons in the copy itself for questioning the reliability and authority of that version in comparison with other versions. Not only is there clear evidence of sloppiness in copy work, but the ordering of the hexagrams is definitely a derivative one not representative of the original text. Even so, there is much light shed on the traditional versions by the contrasts with the Mawangdui version. Thus I have used all three versions to establish the text I translate in Part II.

To reach back toward the original text from the versions which we have, we need to take two types of initial step. One is to note the differences of the various versions of the text, including the Mawangdui. The other is to note certain possibilities implicit in the shared method of transmission which can account both for some variations in the versions and for some shared errors, mistakes, or other features. The fruit of such initial steps would be the identification of modifications that the original text has undergone in its transmission.

In the Textual Notes placed after each hexagram I have recorded the editing which starts from such identification and seeks to restore the text to a form closer to the original.

In general, when looked at in terms of how they came about, the modifications to the original *Zhouyi* text which have become regarded eventually as part of that original text fall into three general types. Some are deliberately introduced modifications. Others have been introduced in virtue of copying mistakes. Still others have been introduced due to a misunderstanding of the manner of prior copying and a mistaking of the status and meaning of what initially were simply accompanying or additional elements which a prior copyist/editor wished to mark and retain.

In what follows I enumerate the specific types of modification I have found and indicate (where I can) how they might have come to be introduced. In some cases I point to further questions which their introduction raises.

First: There is an obvious difference between the Mawangdui and the traditional versions in the order in which the sixty-four hexagrams are presented. If the *Zhouyi* has the coherence which I have been pointing to, the Mawangdui text's order represents a derivative one.

The order of the Mawangdui version is not a result of a copy error but of a deliberate act. Why would anyone intentionally copy the text in such a different order from the original one? One can conjecture to possible uses of such an ordering: for example, it would be useful for enabling someone readily to find a certain line-figure and from that to attend to the meanings.

The mechanical line-figure ordering could be functioning something like an indexing device.

But however it may be with usefulness, and whoever it was that initially copied the text in that order (probably not the copyist of the Mawangdui version), the fact that the text was copied in a different overall order indicates a willingness to depart from the original text that may not be limited to this one modification. That raises further questions.

If the copying could make such a radical change as that relating to the order of the whole, could it also make other order-changes, say, in the order in which the elements in a hexagram text or in a line statement were written? changes which might reflect on the part of the persons for whom the copying was occurring a greater interest in the prognosticatory elements in contrast with the images, so that the former could be put at the start of the line rather than at the end?[2] Could such liberties be similarly felt to be quite acceptable to make, especially in a 'practical' text? And yet, in the course of making such 'convenience of use' or similar changes, could certain characteristic types of error have crept in-- error, say, concerning line-division, where one line ends and the next one begins?

Second: Continuing to consider the matter of order in the text, there is another feature, this time of all the versions of the text I am considering, which has modified the original text and introduced a certain amount of disorder into it, even though its insertion was meant to mark in explicit fashion an element of order. This is the line titles, consisting of a character for the line in its position in the serial order of lines (beginning, 2, 3, 4, 5, and top), and a '9' or a '6' for the "moving" character of the line. It seems likely that something like moving lines was a part of the original text. But the way of marking those lines by the numbers 9 and 6, which does not appear in the earliest references we have to the *Zhouyi* in use (in the *Zuozhuan* and *Guoyu*), seems likely to have been a late addition[3] to the original text.

When that addition was made-- again, deliberately and not in virtue of some copy error--, it was done in a somewhat sloppy fashion. A significant number of cases of faulty division between successive lines turn upon the placement (that is, misplacement) of these line titles. The consequent displacement of phrases from their original context and connections due to such uncorrected mistakes obscures the original content of the line statements as well as their orderliness (internally, and in series). This makes the text be jumbled in ways that it originally was not.

Third: A further feature reflecting sloppy copy work, found in the line titles only of the Mawangdui text, is the presence of certain copy errors which can not be reasonably understood as anything other than simple mistakes. In the titles of certain lines the numbers which designate the line as a "moving line" have been miswritten: as in Hexagram 5, Line 5, for example, where a '6' is written instead of a '9'. The nature of the correlation of number with type of line otherwise adhered to in the text makes clear this is a simple copy error, a carelessness which was not noticed and corrected. Such a mistake occurs in several places:[4] in all there are eleven such uncorrected errors.

That the Mawangdui text contains so many such mistakes suggests not simply that the copying was somewhat careless, but also that if there was a method for proof-reading it was not one which succeeded in correcting all the mistakes.

It is true that in these cases, mistakes relate to the copying of what are the most formal and repetitive elements of the text, and thus relate to those elements into the copying of which inattention and carelessness might most readily creep. But the uncorrected presence of such errors does not reassure one about the accuracy of the copying throughout.

Fourth: Another feature of all the versions of the *Zhouyi* I am considering can be occasion for mistakes in copying that obscure not only the structure of the text but also its content. The work is not a continuous essay or narrative; it is composed of short sections, themselves formed mainly of short sentences or phrases which often do not have obvious continuity. It would be easy to omit brief phrases or lines, and not to notice any disruption in sense-- for example, prognostication words could readily drop out without their disappearance being a cause for question. That this in fact happened seems likely in several cases.[5]

It would also be readily possible, in the case of some hexagrams whose structure is that of a variation on a phrase, to repeat a line (or the start of a line) mistakenly and thereby throw off the connection of line and line number. The Mawangdui text gives evidence of one such occurrence, when it is compared to the traditional texts.[6]

More broadly, dislocation of passages could readily occur, since the continuity of the text is not obvious and there is little in the way of context which would help place something, once detached, back in its proper place.

Fifth: Looking now to features relating mainly to content and not order and structure, in all the versions I consider we find modifications in the form of variants, and characteristic errors, which are grounded in certain features of the Chinese language and the evolution of its writing.

Among those features are the use of loan-characters,[7] and also the addition in the written language of radicals or classifiers to protographs in the earlier language so as to acknowledge or make distinctions in the later language and to provide separate characters for different meanings which were in earlier time represented by one and the same character.[8] The variants introduced on these bases are not errors so long as the usage in question is properly understood. Unfortunately, not only may they be misunderstood, but they may in turn become occasion for editorial 'corrections' which do disort the original text.

Depending on whether the copying took place from a written text or from an oral recitation of a text, further confusion is possible related to the sounding and the writing of words in Chinese.

To choose an example in English, we could write 'sea' for 'see', and even without context a reader would register a difference; but if one were only a listener and did not notice a basis in the auditory context which clearly made the one word/meaning appropriate and the other inappropriate, that could bring about a characteristic mistake for a listener and (if he was copying) for a copyist. And if some other reader later happened on the text with the mis-written word, he could take it as the proper word, and seek to emend other parts of the text to make the passage make sense. Error could then be compounded.

Or again, to make up something like a parallel, if there were two words "sea-level" and "see-level" and if "level" was the protograph while "sea" and "see" were classifiers added later to distinguish the two kinds of level, then a copyist could copy "sea-level" as "see-level"; put more broadly, a copyist could copy a character with one classifier for a character with another, the two having perhaps no meaning in common but having a similar look, and such miscopying could be fostered all the more if the sound of the two characters was identical or very similar. All of these factors are the occasion for mistakes to creep into the text in the copying.[9]

Sixth: There are features of both the Mawangdui and traditional versions which suggest that at some time in the transmission of the text one or more versions were created by copying from several other versions and by incorporating variant elements from these different sources. This resulted in characteristic additions to the original text which, so long as this manner of copying and transmitting was understood, created no confusion. But subsequent misunderstanding of the status of these additions led to regarding the results of editing/copying actions as parts of the original text. Thus certain characteristic modifications to what was taken to be the text were introduced.

For example, there seem to be alternative versions of the same line retained in the text, although not marked as such. Some of these occur in what is purportedly the same line (they are listed after the line-number as if they were one).[10] But there are cases when the alternative seems to have been saved in the hexagram text section-- as if, in analogy to the way we use the bottom of a printed page as the place for footnotes, the copyist/editor used this section as the locus for retaining material that has become detached from its proper place in the text and that the person wants to keep because it is relevant but does not want simply to guess the place of and perhaps misplace.[11] When the fact and meaning of this retention of alternatives, and of the way such retaining is accomplished, becomes missed, the text becomes complicated in ways that do not belong to it originally.

Seventh: There are features of both the Mawangdui and the traditional versions which suggest that among the antecedents to these later versions is to be found at least one text which had a commentary or commentary-notes included in it. At some time those notes-- a comment, a definition, a statement-- became mistakenly entered into the text as if they were an integral part of it, when in fact they were simply accompanying commentary or editorial notes.[12] Indeed, there seems to be one phrase in the later versions which reads like a copyist-note to himself, bracketing a whole section of the text for some reason;[13] but it has become treated as part of the text itself.

Eighth: Finally, there is a feature of the Mawangdui and traditional versions which seems to reflect contrasting responses by different copyists to a difficulty . In the traditional versions, either not being able to read a part of a phrase or not having it in the text from which he is copying, the copyist nonetheless made clear that 'something' was being said after the verb by putting a '*zhi*' there.[14] In contrast, the Mawangdui version lacks the *zhi*', and represents what you would have had if the copyist had copied only what was clear and had done nothing to note the omission of what was unclear.

The text which lies behind the following translation is what was generated after I made the emendations and corrections needed to address such matters as I have just enumerated.

In the presentation of the translation, the parts in bold-face type are ones which directly convey something in the original Chinese. Where the type is plain, there is nothing directly corresponding to it in the Chinese. The superscript letters refer to textual notes which I place at the end of the hexagram, while the superscript numbers refer to notes which are placed together at the end of the book, in the section entitled "Notes".

The translation is of a divinatory text which is not meant to be read as an essay might be, from start to finish, but is meant to be consulted now in one place, now in another, depending upon what sign or signs are selected. In the commentary, I presume that the discussion in Part I will be kept in mind, so that the manner of consulting and the function of the parts does not need continuous repetition along with the translation. The main burden of the commentary in each case is to point to the order and meaning of the set of images in each hexagram. But because of the importance of understanding each hexagram in its place in the whole and in its pairing with another hexagram, I have started the commentary on the first hexagram in each pair with a pointer to the relevant part of the overall order and to the specific connection of the hexagram with its pair, and have referred a reader back to those comments at the beginning of the commentary on the second hexagram. For a reader who proceeds straight through in essay-reading fashion, this will create a certain repetitiousness; for for one who is consulting the text in the divination process, it should serve a very important purpose.

HEXAGRAM 1

VIGOROUSLY ACTIVE

HEXAGRAM TEXT:
  (The occasion calls for a) **grand sacrifice.**
  A beneficial divination. [H-O]

LINES:
9 at the beginning:
  A submerged dragon. [L-I]
    Do not act![1] [L-A]

9 at LINE 2:
  See a dragon in the fields. [L-I]
    Beneficial to see the big man.[2] [L-A]

9 at LINE 3:
  **A nobleman, vigorously active throughout the day, is on the alert at
  night, as if there was some threat.** [L-I]
    Without harmful mishap. [L-P]

9 at LINE 4:
  Some (dragons) **frolicking in the depths.**[a] [L-I]
    Without harmful mishap. [L-P]

9 at LINE 5:
  Flying dragons in the heavens. [L-I]
    Beneficial to see the big man. [L-A]

9 on top:
  A throated dragon. [L-I]
    Have troubles. [L-P]

9's throughout:
  See a group of dragons without heads. [L-I]
    Auspicious. [L-P]

****

COMMENTARY

In the overall structure of the *Zhouyi*, Hexagrams 1 and 2 are paired with each other, as are Hexagrams 63 and 64. These two sets of pairs form a bracket around the whole work, and utilize images which recall the embracing temporal and historical frame of human life.

In their pairing Hexagrams 1 and 2 are linked in such way that through the imagery of their twelve lines they delineate the unfolding of time in an agriculture-dependent mode of life in north China. Knowing time as a seasonal rhythm based in the workings of the heavens, the civilized human beings who are the subject of these images fit their earthly lives into such a temporal movement and rhythm, and venture to provide sustenance for themselves in that context.

The present hexagram uses the image of a dragon in five of its six lines. Part of the meaning of this image-- the primordial part-- presupposes the dragon as a kind of living being, a presence marked by energy and connected closely with water and the heavens above. As these lines invoke this figure as image, the dragon is the active energy particularly associated with the vitality living things that grow and flourish according to the seasonal rhythm.

But there is another part of the meaning involved in the use of that imagery in these lines: the dragon is also a different sort of celestial phenomenon. It is a constellation with the shape of a dragon, whose place in the sky differs in the course of the year. On this point, Shaughnessy[3] suggests that the images portray "the disposition of the celestial dragon at various times in the course of the year, from his 'submergence' under the eastern horizon during the winter, through his spring appearance just above that horizon, to his full extension across the sky in summer, and finally, to his head-first descent beneath the western horizon at the eastern equinox". In the seasonal rhythm of north China, the times of year being represented are the winter solstice (Line 1), early March (Line 2), late April/middle May (Line 4), summer solstice i.e. late June (Line 5), and mid-August (Line 6 and the extra line). This period of the appearance of the dragon in the night sky coincides with the agricultural growing season in north China.

The images involving the dragon in this hexagram can, and do, carry a twofold meaning because the two essential things can be correlated: on the one hand, the variation in the course of the year in the location and kind of presence of the dragon constellation, and on the other, the manner and stage of the working of this active energy in the life-rhythm of things on earth. Dragon imagery formed in some reference to the various appearances of the constellation in the night sky during the year is also formed so as to convey the various conditions of the working of this vital energy at those different times in the seasonal rhythm.

One image, that in Line 3, does not involve the dragon. It focuses instead on human activity. Given the place in the series at which it is introduced, it would be located seasonally in the time between early March and late April/mid-May. Since the latter represents the beginning of the growing season, human activity enters on the image-scene at the time when the land would be being prepared and planted.

The dragon, the dragon-constellation in the night sky, and the nobleman, are parts of the natural and human world known to the author of the *Zhouyi*, and parts which he uses as divinatory images in this set of lines. Using these images he adumbrates in the series of lines the theme of the hexagram and what is meant in its title-name (*qian²*: 乾).

Thus in Line 1 the dragon image has an implicit reference to winter, when the dragon-constellation is hidden below the horizon; it holds as part of its meaning, thus, the dormancy or latency of the natural energies in the life-world at that time of year. Such latency of vigorous activity is not the same as its total absence.

In Line 2 the dragon image has an implicit reference to early March, when the dragon-constellation has first appeared above the horizon; it holds as part of its meaning, thus, the first appearance of the natural energies in the life-world at that time of year. The ground is thawing, life is beginning to stir. More specifically, vigorous activity is present in its first visible signs, and is present in the situation as in a limited and humanly-ordered place for growing things (a field in contrast e.g. with the wilds).

In Line 3 the image drawn on is not the dragon, thus the natural energies in the life-world at some time of year, but the nobleman, the preeminent human agent in the seasonal agricultural life. Because of its location in the series of images, the seasonal reference which this image bears with it is the time between early March and late April/mid-May, when the active human role of preparing the ground and planting the seed is to take place. Thus the image is of vigorous activity that is both continuous and daily, but also vigilant, alert to threat and to the risky nature of the venturing. In particular, it seems plausible to take the wariness and danger referred to in the line-image as pointing (say) to the vigilant landowner's characteristic apprehensiveness about changes in the weather conditions during this crucial time of pre-paratory work.[4]

In Line 4 the dragon image has an implicit reference to late-April/mid-May, when the dragon-constellation has its whole body above the horizon, with only its tail still hidden; it holds as part of its meaning, thus, the natural energies in the life-world as now well activated, the growing season as well-begun. And yet the life-prospering energy is not yet full-bodied. The watery depths are, indeed, a natural place for a dragon to be, and the 'frolicking' reflects the dragon's being at home in that place. But even those depths do not allow that activity full scope; put in terms of the imagery (some dragons, in the watery depths), that activity is increasing but is less manifest and visi-ble there than when in the sky.

In Line 5 the dragon image has an implicit reference to summer solstice (late June), when the entire dragon-constellation is displayed in the night sky; it holds as part of its meaning, thus, the natural energies in the life-world as now fully flourishing at the peak of the growing season. Just as the heavens are the most natural and most visible place for dragons functioning in full fashion, so plant life is flourishing in its full form and is ready to begin maturing in its fruit.

In Line 6 the dragon image has an implicit reference to mid-August, when the dragon-constellation is about to sink out of sight, its horns and head now below the western horizon and its 'neck' just at the horizon;[5] it holds as part of its meaning, thus, that shift in the flourishing of the natural energies in the life-world wherein the energies of growth decline and give way to energy de-voted to ripening the fruit. The plants are no longer getting bigger and beginning to put out fruit, but are now ripening and the filled-out heads are drooping. This is also a time of great vulnerability, and thus anxiety, on the part of the farmer.[6]

****

◆ TEXTUAL NOTES ◆

a. In the traditional and the Mawangdui texts the *huo*[4] (或) at the start of the line has only implicit reference to dragons. For discussion on the varied interpretations of the meaning of this character in this line, see Kunst (*OY*, 146-7, 408, 409-10), and Shaughnessy (*CZ*, 344, also 266 and 271).

HEXAGRAM 2

RESPONSIVELY RECEPTIVE

HEXAGRAM TEXT:[a]
  (The occasion calls for a) **grand sacrifice.** [H-O]
    **Beneficial to the south and west: one will gain friends; but in the
    north and east, one will lose friends.**[b]
    Beneficial female-horse divination.
    As a security divination, auspicious. [H-SP]

LINES:
6 at the beginning:
  Tread on hoarfrost, hard ice is arriving. [L-I]

6 at LINE 2:
  Inspecting the borderlands[c], very much not common practice. [L-I]
    Nothing is not beneficial. [L-P]

6 at LINE 3:[d]
  Cherishing the beautiful patterned display. [L-I]
    As a divination, acceptable. [L-P]

6 at LINE 4:[e]
  Bound-and-tied sack(s). [L-I]

6 at LINE 5:[f]
  Yellow skirt(s). [L-I]
    Highly auspicious. [L-P]

6 on top:
  Dragons fighting in the wilds, their blood black and yellow. [L-I]

6's throughout:
    A beneficial long-term divination. [L-SP]

****

COMMENTARY

For the place of Hexagram 2 in the overall structure of the *Zhouyi*, and for the meaning of its pairing with Hexagram 1, see the first two paragraphs of the Commentary on Hexagram 1.

In its first five lines, the present hexagram uses as images events in human affairs at the end of the agricultural season, the time of harvest and storage before winter sets in. The imagery sets forth the human register of these times, the human participation in them. No common image is used, such as the dragon of Hexagram 1; but that particular image does recur, in Line 6 here, when the harvest celebration is over and one is at the end of the 'living season'. The time in question is the tenth month, the beginning of winter, the 'dead' season. In this way the calendrical setting forth of the year started in Hexagram 1 is brought to a conclusion.

The images used here are memorable aspects of the two months of the harvest-culmination of the growing season, the stage for which was set in Hexagram 1. These aspects crystallize feelings in something like the way still-life painting arrests attention and enables a wealth of meaning to emerge for the onlooker, particularly one whose life is steeped in the rhythms in question and harbors a memory of immemorial traditions.

Thus Line 1 evokes the time shortly after the autumn equinox, when signs of the change of season appear and expectancy concerning harvest is evoked. At the time of the completion of the growing season, the sensitivity of human beings involved in agriculture is attuned to the signs of change of season, and in particular, to the coming of the cold which ends the growing season. Hoarfrost and hard ice are harbingers of harvest time.

Line 2 speaks of another thing which responsiveness to change in this near-harvest time calls to mind. This is the time when the King and the overseers of the land venture forth into the countryside to inspect the lands where the crops are growing and to assess the coming harvest throughout the distant reaches of the Kingdom. This is not an everyday affair, but a special venture, bearing with it the mixture of feelings associated with the harvest drawing near-- something crucial in the lives of a people intimately dependent on the harvest year to year.

Line 3 evokes what is seen by those who venture in the way pointed to in Line 2, namely, the lovely patterned display of fields and maturing crops ready for harvest; and it speaks of how those things are seen, namely, in a cherishing, a glad and grateful love and remembrance of an immemorial landscape.[7] The image, then, is of the marvelous and moving display of the earth under cultivation and about to deliver its yield.

Line 4 conveys the harvest-done sense evoked by tied-off sacks of grain. The work is finished, the food-stuff secured, the harvest successfully a-chieved, and this is one of the typical sights etched in one's mind in con-nection with this accomplishment. With the harvest secured, life on into the next year is safeguarded so far as concerns basic food-stuff.

Line 5 conveys the further step in the unfolding sensitivity in this con-cluding time in the agricultural calendar, namely, that in which, having viewed the grain secure in its bound sacks, one is drawn to ritual celebration of the harvest's completion. The "yellow skirts" are an auspicious symbol pregnant with such associations.

Line 6 takes us beyond harvest and places these human-centered acts and sensitivities related to harvest back into the larger seasonal rhythm which passes on into winter. With this line, we have the recurrence of the dragon-image from Hexagram 1, because the timing of the 'dragons fighting in the wilds' is that of the winter solstice-- a time when the forces of autumnal life struggle against the deadening force of winter. The celestial phenomena, and the mythical stories, that may lie behind this image-- relating to the master of the rains, the Yellow Emperor, the dark woman named 'Drought', etc. (the beginning of winter is the end of the rainy season [autumn] in north China)-- are set forth by Shaughnessy (*CZ*, 279-86). The import is life's (temporarily, cyclically) unsuccessful struggle against winter's onset and its own dormancy, once the season of harvest has passed.

All of the significant moments of the harvest season are parts of a world known to the author of the *Zhouyi*, and parts which he uses as divinatory images in this set of lines. Taking the harvest-related images and connecting the series back with the unfolding calendar begun in Hexagram 1 by use in Line 6 of an image from the natural world ('fighting dragons'), the author of the *Zhouyi* adumbrates the theme of the hexagram and what is meant in its title-name (*kun[1]*: 坤).

****

◆ TEXTUAL NOTES ◆

a. The Hexagram Text in its traditional and Mawangdui renderings includes the following image (according to one possible translation): "A nobleman, having a place to go, at first lost his way but then gained his host." It seems to be intrusive between two *li'* phrases, and not to make much sense in its present place. At first glance this image does not seem to have a function in the Hexagram Text. If it had an accompanying prognostication element, one could take it as a displaced line which has been 'stored' here just to retain it. Without such an element, it could function as a scene-setting image which sets the stage for the set of images in the lines of the hexagram: a kind of pointer to the slant, the reference and the coherence, of the lines, which usually tell a story. But if that is its purpose, it is not easy to see how it serves that function. And yet, especially if it is the vigorously-active noble-man of Hexagram 1, Line 3 who is involved, could the image be manifesting something like a Daoist sensitivity? Lao-zi, in traditional Chapter 26 of the *Dao De Jing*, speaks as follows: "The heavy is the root of the light, the still is the lord of the busy. For this reason the Sage, throughout the day, travels unseparated from his 'covered heavy'. Even though the view is magnificent, he dwells at ease, dispassionately transcendent." Is the image of the noble-man in the Text here, that of the traveller who, even though he has some-where definite to go, is so responsively receptive that he may become ab-sorbed in his sensitivity to that amidst which he is moving and may lose track of where he is going? Yet while he can be drawn off course by his re-sponsiveness to things, he has nonetheless the capacity also to regain course and reach the end-point at which he is received by his host. If this is the point of the image-- that being receptive is not being passive or inert but involves a receiving and welcoming of things, that being responsively recept-ive is not being closed in on oneself but being sensitive to and affected by and prone initially to following out what is received from beyond-- then the later association of this hexagram title with being obedient, being devoted, would be a natural evolution of the initial sense. [One translation which would strengthen this sense would be: "The nobleman, having a place to go, at first became confused but then gained (self-) mastery."]

b. The grammar of this set of phrases in the Hexagram Text is a bit puzzling and is treated differently by different scholars. Shaughnessy (*CZ*, 267) translates: "Beneficial to the southwest to get a friend, to the northeast to lose a friend." That or some variation ("beneficial to gain friends in the south and west, and to lose friends in the north and east") has the virtue of also making good sense *prima facie* in the historical setting of early Zhou. But does that still hold in the 9th century or later? Gao (*Zhouyi gujing jinzhu*, 6: later cited as *ZGJ*) claims the "*li'*" (利: "beneficial") is a gloss relating to the prior phrase (about the nobleman's having a place to go). Kunst (*OY*, 243) trans-lates more like the way I do: "Favorable to the west and south-- one will find a friend. To the east and north he will lose a friend."

c. For this meaning of the phrase *zhi² fang¹* (直方), see Shaughnessy (*CZ*, 346n140).

d. Line 3 contains a phrase which seems to be an editorial comment or a note from a commentary on the text, and not a functional part of the text itself. It reads: "At times service to the King has a termination without any completion." It reminds and warns: promising as things are, they may not work out. Crop-growing to furnish food for the royal court is a serving of the King. A similar phrase is also found in Hexagram 6, Line 3.

e. Line 4 contains a phrase which, like the phrase in Line 3, seems to be an editorial comment, perhaps even a note from a commentary on the text, and not a functional part of the text itself. It reads: "Without blame or praise." It may be that this comment belongs with the one in Line 3, and has only mistakenly been detached and located here; if so, then it would relate to the lack of completion marking the work undertaken in service to the King, even when it has been carried through to the end. If it belongs here, it relates to the achievement of a successful harvest.

f. The first five lines begin with rhyme-couplets. Kunst (*OY*, 78-79) suggests that these may be formulae which are "abbreviated short-hand references, 'keys', to folk-songs in the oral tradition, known at least to the diviners, if not to clients as well. Furthermore, the variation among these omen-images from line text to line text in one hexagram may result from their function as a catalogue of those variations which occurred in incremental repetition from stanza to stanza in the songs." Even without accepting this proposal, one may allow that the images, especially as rhymed, may be intended to bring back more to mind than is apparent from the two characters themselves. In the divination context these associated meanings would be part of the sign and thus directive for attention as the sign is interpreted and the world is attended to guided by the image. But we have little idea of what such complicit meanings might be.

HEXAGRAM 3

SPROUTS BUNCHED TOGETHER

HEXAGRAM TEXT:
(The occasion calls for a) **grand sacrifice.**
A beneficial divination. [H-O]
Do not act to have a place to go.
Beneficial to establish feudal lords. [H-A]

LINES:
9 at the beginning:
Pillars and posts, rock-like in their firmness and stability.[a] [L-I]
Beneficial to establish feudal-lords. [L-A]
Beneficial dwelling-divination. [L-SP]

6 at LINE 2:[b]
Teams of four horses circling round, 'they are not bandits, it is a marriage match'. [L-I]
As a maiden-divination: there is no betrothal, ten years and then a betrothal. [L-SP]

6 at LINE 3:
They approached[c] **the deer without a gamekeeper, but the deer entered into the middle of the forest; the nobleman regarded seizing the opportunity**[d] **to be not as good as letting it go.** [L-I]
Going is difficult. [L-SP]

6 at LINE 4:
Teams of four horses circling round, 'they are demanding a marriage match'. [L-I]
To go is auspicious, there is nothing which is not beneficial. [L-SP]

9 at LINE 5:
Collect and bunch the fat meat. [L-I]
As a divination on minor things, auspicious; as a divination on

major things, ominous. [L-SP]

6 on top:
Teams of four horses circling round, silently they weep blood in unceasing flows. [L-I]

****

COMMENTARY

In the overall structure of the *Zhouyi*, Hexagrams 3 and 4 are paired with each other and belong in a group of pairs which is centered around Hexagrams 9 and 10. This latter pair concerns the involvement of human life in troubles, and the various pairs which belong to this group all develop their themes in ways connected with this matter of troubles.

Hexagrams 3 and 4 belong together in terms of a certain shared reference to marriage. Both concern preludes to this act and its initiation of a life together that will produce the next generation of human beings. The one set of lines tells the story of the securing through force of the (young) woman who is to become wife through the ceremony; this prelude involves the infliction of troubles on one family, in order that the future of another-- in the form of its next generation-- may be safeguarded. The other set of lines tells the story of the actions through which a non-human natural life form (in one of its forms called the 'royal maiden') is ritualistically secured and prepared for a function in the marriage ceremony; this prelude gives an integral role to plant life in the ceremony that authorizes the act that is to continue human life on earth.

These two hexagrams thus thematically refer to ritual preparations for the beginning of a human life together that will continue such life through the production of the next generation. Contrasting as they are-- involving (for example) a reaching out to pluck, in one case, the bride from her home and in the other, the vines from their habitat-- the connectedness of the pair as contrasting preludes to marriage is underlined by the fact that the title-names of both hexagrams refer to plant life. Is there more? Does Hexagram 4, in its focus on preparation for a marriage ceremony, point to that ceremony which the plundering horsemen of Hexagram 3 will perform once arrived home? That would make for a thread of continuity between the two hexagram accounts, even if not in the form of a single continuing story. In any case, both extend the sense, adumbrated already in Hexagrams 1 and 2, that human life is interwoven with elements in a larger framework: there, heaven and earth and the rhythms of the seasons, here, other life forms with which humans share this earth.[8]

The present hexagram, in its series of lines, tells a story: a type-story with a series of type-events, not a historically specific account of any definite occurrence. The series has a pattern of alternation. Lines 2, 4, and 6 all begin with the same 4-character phrase and each has a different follow-up phrase; the repeated phrase itself conveys a circling movement, while the follow-up phrases advance the story. The circling horsemen are not bandits but seek a marriage match (Line 2), indeed they demand it (Line 4), and they eventually leave behind weeping families after their demands are answered (Line 6). Lines 1, 3, and 5 provide the starting point and further articulations in the movement of the story, and introduce other life-forms besides the horses.[9] In the sweep of the story, but not of course in each and every line-image taken separately, the set of lines clarifies the meaning of the hexagram's title-name, the "sprouts bunched together".

Put briefly, the story unfolds as follows: there was once a manor with rock-solid pillars and posts, sign of a stable and flourishing estate. One day, a crowd of horsemen rode up and circled the manor: they were bride-seekers, though that was not clear at first. While camping and negotiating, their noble leader was tempted by, yet eschewed, the opportunity to go deer hunting in the nearby woods. Perhaps the difficulties being encountered in face of the secure estate they had approached and the possibility of further difficulties ahead, made such diversion and food-gathering tempting; but without a guide, he might get lost and the going might be difficult. Finally, when it became clear that these intruders would not go away without brides, the estate-holders submitted to these demands, and fat meat was collected for a ceremony to solemnize the event. Then the horsemen departed, taking their bunch of captive-brides ('young sprouts'), and leaving the estate-holders weeping blood and tears over their loss.

To this story each line contributes in its own way.

The image of Line 1 points to the setting for the story to come: it is a manor whose rock-solid pillars and posts suggest the well built structure of a well established family. Symbolizing the estate whole of which they are parts, these pillars and posts symbolize also the power of estate members to offer firm resistance against any intruders if it should come to that. As first, this image establishes the stable reference-point around which the circling movement of Lines 2, 4, and 6 takes place and from which the circling riders eventually pluck the bride(s) in the course of the story.

The image of Line 2 introduces drama and action, yet with a kind of circling movement that recurs in Lines 4 and 6 and that helps give a tone of pause, of pressure and siege, as well as a pulsation, to the story. The crowd of horsemen who one day rode up and circled this stable and flourishing estate introduce pressure: they wanted women for marriage and not (as it might first have seemed likely) goods and wealth as booty.

The image of Line 3 relates to an undertaking that would digress from the main course of action which the images present. Internally, it conveys the mixture of an opportunity for something exciting (a hunting opportunity), the possibility that following it out will bring difficulty, and the decision to let the tempting opportunity pass by. Placed between the two circling-images in Lines 2 and 4, it suggest that the main action extends over a significant period of time.

In Line 4 the image, repeating yet advancing slightly that of Line 2, brings focus back again on what lies at the center of the circling movement, namely, the potential bride(s). The seeking is now more insistent, the circling exerts a more demanding pressure.

In Line 5, the image reflects the concession to this build-up of pressure: the bride-giving is agreed to, and some sort of festal or ritual occasion is being prepared, to solemnize the giving and make the plundering something more than a mere act of violence. The image-- of rich meat being collected and bunched together, in preparation for the feast-- is of a consummation, or the makings of a consummation. But as the prognostication indicates, while this image points to something auspicious as relating to what is minor (the food), there is another side to it. As concerns what is major (in the case of the image, the loss of their daughters), it is ominous. That is, the forces working together in the way imaged are ambivalent in the issue which they harbor: it depends on whether the matter is looked at on its deeper side, or on its more superficial side.

In Line 6, the image provides the final turn to the story: the circling horsemen are about to leave, taking the women they had come for, and the family/families which they are leaving behind weep(s) over what has happened. As in most of the lines in this hexagram, this image is a complex one, with an intricate dynamic of circling and stability, gain and loss, all centering on the culminating phase of the action adumbrated in the six lines, namely, the forced removal of their daughters from their family circle for the purposes of marriage.

The primitive custom drawn on in this story for its images, that of plunder-marriage, was known as part of the past in the late Western Zhou world of the author of these lines.[10] The story presents the prelude to a human beginning-together, along with its attendant circumstances, and does this through an account which refers to numerous elements of the non-human. The title-name, with its reference to 'sprouting', not only draws attention to these many subordinate non-human-life elements in the story. But when taken metaphorically, it points both to the young women ('sprouts') taken for marriage and (indirectly) to the 'sprouting' implicit in the human beginning whose prelude (in one form) is being told.

****

◆ TEXTUAL NOTES ◆

a. The two characters which compose the line-image in Line 1 could be read as loan-characters; the resultant phrase could be "encircling wall". See Gao (*ZGJ*, 13) for a suggestion to this effect. But the contrast in movement-imagery provided by taking *huan²* (桓) as "pillar, post" (see Karlgren *Glosses on the Book of Odes*, Gloss 1188) and *pan²* (磐) as "stable, firm; a rock", makes for a reading more suited to the context.

b. In Line 2 the traditional and Mawangdui versions have an additional four character phrase (*zhun¹ ru² zhan¹ ru²* [屯 如 邅 如]: "going without advancing, turning round and round"). In it, *zhun¹* (collect) is a protograph or loan for *zhun¹* (迍 : unable to get on), thus is given a meaning which reflects later interpretation; and the phrase is simply a kind of definition phrase, to clarify the meaning of the characters which I have translated as "circling round". It is presumably the work of a later editor-commentator, which has become mistakenly entered into the text of the work itself.[11]

c. In Line 3, Gao interprets *ji²* (即) somewhat more actively, as "follow, pursue, chase".

d. In Line 3, I read *ji¹* (幾: almost) as protograph or loan for *ji¹* (機: opportune, opportunity). Kunst retains the shorter form and translates: "nobles would almost do better to abandon the chase"; this provides a somewhat similar meaning.

HEXAGRAM 4

DODDER

HEXAGRAM TEXT:[a]
(The occasion calls for a) **sacrifice.**
A beneficial divination. [H-O]

LINES:
6 at the beginning:
 Discover and dislodge[12] the dodder. [L-I]
  **Beneficial to act to punish others, to act to remove[b] manacles due
  to which going is difficult.** [L-A]

9 at LINE 2:
 Carry[c] the dodder wrapped in one's arms. [L-I]
  **Auspicious to bring in a wife; auspicious for a son to manage the
  family/household.** [L-A]

6 at LINE 3:
  **Do not act to marry[d] a woman, she will see a 'metal'-husband, not
   one of flesh and blood.[13]** [L-A]
  Without anything that is beneficial. [L-P]

6 at LINE 4:
 Bundle[e] the dodder. [L-I]
  Difficulty. [L-P]

6 at LINE 5:
 Rejuvenate the dodder. [L-I]
  Auspicious. [L-P]

9 on top:
 Beat the dodder. [L-I]
  Not beneficial to be a bandit, beneficial to ward off bandits.
  [L-A]

****

COMMENTARY

For the place of Hexagram 4 in the overall structure of the *Zhouyi*, and for the meaning of its pairing with Hexagram 3, see the first three paragraphs of the Commentary on Hexagram 3.

The present hexagram, in its series of lines, is a set of variations on a two-character phrase which includes the title-name; that series is also ordered so as to point to the stages of a single inclusive action, namely, the gathering and preparing of the dodder plant for a marriage ceremony. That plant is a vine, also called the 'maiden creeper' (and in its big form, 'royal maiden'). Although the preparatory stage of the integration of this vine into the human ceremony is achieved in the course of the lines, the images center more on the step-by-step human actions by which this takes place. We reach out to include the plant, and we prepare it for its role in a ceremony which is to initiate a life together and to usher in the potential prolongation of human life through the generations.

The inclusion proceeds step by step, starting with the discovery and dislodging of the plant from the place in which it grows naturally, from its natural setting and connections, and the picking which begins the integration of this one form of non-human life (a plant) into the ongoing of human life (Line 1).

The next step is the carrying of the dodder wrapped in one's arms back to the place where one will treat and prepare it for its function. The dynamic here is of the transfer of something natural from its own sphere into the human sphere, accomplished with a certain gentle and intimate embrace.

The third step-- although we can not know it precisely since the line has lost its image-- would presumably be an action somewhere between the carrying of Line 2 and the bundling of Line 4. From the other elements of the line, it would seem likely that that would be an action of selection, of picking out the best of the plants that one had brought back, before bundling them.[14]

The fourth step, after the carrying back and (presumably) a selecting out of the best, is a bundling of the better plants, in preparation for an act of immersion (to clean and purify the plants).

The fifth step is a 'making youthful', a 'rejuvenating', of the bundled plants, such as would occur by means of a dipping of the bundles into water; such an act cleans and purifies but also revives and rejuvenates for a while.

The final step in the act of integration is a beating of the bundles of rejuvenated plants. Presumably this is a way of obtaining the juice from the plants, for use in the ceremony.

****

◆ TEXTUAL NOTES ◆

a. The Hexagram Text in the traditional and Mawangdui versions contains an additional phrase, which reads as follows: "It is not I who seek out the youthful and foolish, it is they who seek me out; on the first divination, I report the result, but on the second and third I am annoyed, and when annoyed I do not report the result." This is an intrusive commentary phrase, something like a diviner's note-- an extraneous comment which has been placed with this hexagram because it includes the title-name of the hexagram. Yet in its use in this comment, that title-name is used with a different meaning ("foolish") than in its use as the title ("dodder"). Perhaps more revealingly, it reflects a reading of the meaning of this hexagram from a much later tradition which has lost touch with the earlier meaning. The comment seems to express the annoyance of the diviner at being requested to make and interpret second and third divinations on the same matter, as if the inquirer did not want to hear what the first divination said but wanted to keep on trying until he got the sort of divinatory result he wanted to hear.

b. In Line 1, I read *tuo¹* (脫) here for *shuo¹* (說), but *tuo¹* (挩) would also be acceptable.

c. In Line 2, I read *bao⁴* (抱) for *bao¹* (包).

d. In Line 3, I read *qu³* (娶) for *qu³* (取).

e. In Line 4, I read *kun³* (捆) for *kun⁴* (困).

HEXAGRAM 5

PAUSING

HEXAGRAM TEXT:
   (The occasion calls for a) **sacrifice.** [H-O]
      Beneficial to cross the big river. [H-A]

LINES:
9 at the beginning:
   Pausing in wait at the suburban altar. [L-I]
      Beneficial to employ the *heng*-**ritual.**[15] [L-A]
      Without harmful mishap. [L-P]

9 at LINE 2:
   **Pausing in face of [OR: amidst] sand; have a minor verbal
   altercation.** [L-I]
      In the end, auspicious. [L-P]

9 at LINE 3:
   **Pausing in face of [OR: amidst] mud; that brings about the arrival
   of bandits.** [L-I]

6 at LINE 4:
   Pausing amidst blood, having come forth from their caves. [L-I]

9 at LINE 5:[a]
   **Pausing in front of food and drink, having re-entered their caves;
   there are uninvited guests: three persons come, they give them
   respect.** [L-I]
      In the end, auspicious. [L-P]

6 on top:[a]
   Pausing amidst captives and glory. [L-I]
      As a divination, auspicious. [L-P]

****

COMMENTARY

In the overall structure of the *Zhouyi*, Hexagrams 5 and 6 are paired with each other and belong in a group of pairs which is centered around Hexagrams 9 and 10. This latter pair concerns the involvement of human life in troubles, and the various pairs which belong to this group all develop their themes in ways connected with this matter of troubles.

Thematically Hexagrams 5 and 6 develop the polar contrast of active conflict and pauses in such conflict. Thus Hexagram 5, while it unfolds the story of some sort of conflict in progress, nonetheless focuses on various types of pausing over or in front of, of temporarily halting or stopping or waiting, which occur in the course of that conflict. In contrast, Hexagram 6 unfolds the story of an ongoing struggle between a feudal lord and vassal. In the course of the story-telling, various facets of the disputing, of the being in conflict, are elicited and form the images of the lines.

In its series of lines, the present hexagram sets forth pausing as occurring 'at' some place or 'amidst' something. Implicitly the lines narrate a conflict, while explicitly they set forth, line by line, different typical kinds of pausing that would occur in the course of a conflict.

The start is with a pause at the suburban altar, presumably to pray for the cessation of hostilities, or else for continued peace, for the aversion of a seemingly imminent conflict (Line 1). In this context, it would seem plausible that the *heng*-ritual would be (say) for stabilizing any cessation in strife, any peace-- the current one prior to hostilities, or any halt in hostilities once war has broken out.

This is followed (in Lines 2 and 3) by pauses in face of hard conditions (sand and mud) that make successful engagement in battle difficult, pauses signifying a being mired down that occasions frustration, tension, and other forms of aggression (banditry, for example) than the one in question. Sand is land difficult to move over, easy to get bogged down in, at the very least sufficient to slow down progress; as the second part of the image in Line 2 suggests, the resultant situation is one of some tension such as might provoke a minor verbal altercation-- one readily surmounted, to judge from the prognostication. Mud, likewise, is a difficult and frustrating condition for movement; in correlation with the graver extreme it represents compared to sand, the second part of the image of Line 3 points to the arrival of bandits to carry out their depredations on the stalled party.

Then come two pauses of another sort. Line 4 points to a pause after the fighting has erupted (or revived) and then been brought to some halt again: a pause amidst the bloodshed of battle. One party has come forth from its homes and/or hiding places (namely, some caves), to survey the carnage and presumably to mourn the dead. Line 5 points to a pause in front of food and drink. Apparently hostilities have ceased for the moment, and that has allowed the one party to draw back into their cave-homes for food and drink. There they find themselves approached by uninvited guests, from the enemy presumably-- perhaps a deputation to talk of peace or an 'arrangement'. The hosts show them respect.

Finally, there is a pause amidst captives and glory, the battle presumably being won and the occasion being some victory celebration (Line 6).

****

◆ TEXTUAL NOTES ◆

a. In the traditional text, there are some dislocations and at least one copy error. The title-name has been mistakenly collapsed with the same character used as the first word in a phrase that follows; and that phrase itself has been displaced from Line 6. In place of the original Line 6, the last part of Line 5 has come to be taken as Line 6. I have emended the text in the Hexagram Text and in Lines 5 and 6, to bring it back to its original form. That has meant the following changes. First, I have transferred xu^1 $(you^3=)$ yu^2 $(fu^2=)$ fu^2 $guang^1$ (需 [有 =] 于 [孚 =] 俘光) and $zhen^1$ ji^2 (貞吉) from the Hexagram Text to Line 6, and taken the remainder as the whole of the Hexagram Text. [I read fu^2 (俘) instead of fu^2 (孚) everywhere in the text, including here.] Next, I have added to traditional Line 5 all the image-language that belonged to traditional Line 6, which had become detached from its place when original Line 6 became displaced into the Hexagram Text. Finally, the two 'auspicious' prognostications of the traditional Lines 5 and 6 seem likely to represent what belonged to the original lines; and since the 'auspicious in the end' fits the original Line 5, I have kept it in Line 5 and treated the 'as a divination, auspicious' as belonging to original Line 6 (something supported by its appearance in the HT with the displaced Line 6 line-image).

HEXAGRAM 6

OPEN DISPUTE

HEXAGRAM TEXT:[a]
(The occasion calls for a) **grand sacrifice.** [H-O]
Beneficial to see the big man.
Not beneficial to cross the big river. [H-A]

LINES:
6 at the beginning:
He does not prolong his service, there is a petty verbal altercation.
[L-I]
In the end, auspicious. [L-P]

9 at LINE 2:
Not winning out in the public denunciation, he returns home and
flees; for his villagers, three-hundred households of them, there is no
calamity. [L-I]

6 at LINE 3:[b]
He eats old catch[c]. [L-I]
As a divination, danger, but in the end, auspicious. [L-P]

9 at LINE 4:
Although not winning out in the public denunciation, he (eventually)
returns and follows the mandate/command (of the feudal lord); **but**
things go from bad to worse. [L-I]
As a security-divination, auspicious. [L-SP]

9 at LINE 5:
There are captives[16], they are frightened.[d] [L-I]
Auspicious for the mid-stage (short-run), ominous for the end-
stage (long-run). [L-P]

9 on top:

Someone bestows[e] on him a leather belt, but by the end of the morning it has been taken away from him three times. [L-I]

****

COMMENTARY

For the place of Hexagram 6 in the overall structure of the *Zhouyi*, and for the meaning of its pairing with Hexagram 5, see the first two paragraphs of the Commentary on Hexagram 5.

In its series of lines the present hexagram tells a type-story, as contrasted with a historically determinate account. The story concerns a many-sided conflict centered in an open dispute between a feudal lord and one of his vassals.

The story begins (Line 1) with a reference to the vassal's decision not to prolong his service to his lord; this led to (or the decision was occasioned by or was made in the midst of) a minor verbal altercation. (Why such an action might be auspicious, can be seen from the characterization of the feudal lord from whom this vassal is seeking to detach himself: see the top line of the hexagram, for example. Freeing himself from subjection to such a lord would seem plausibly an act which would be auspicious when looked at far-sightedly.)

The decision leads (Line 2) to an open public dispute, a public accusation and denunciation presumably brought by the lord against the vassal. Losing that dispute, the vassal returned home and fled, leaving behind three-hundred households of townsmen who nonetheless suffer no calamity through the events.

While on flight, he came into such dire straits as to have to eat 'old catch', that is, game taken in some earlier hunting expedition, in contrast with fresh meat (Line 3).

In the end, the recalcitrant vassal returned, submitted to the lord, and accepted a mandate again, so that he once again followed the commands coming from the feudal lord, as well as assumed his own role as vassal with villagers to deal with. But things went from bad to worse, even though he had a certain security back (Line 4).

In the deteriorating situation, there was some sort of battle, between whom and whom is not said, but I presume it was not between lord and vassal but some other action in which the vassal was supposed to be helping out his lord. In the course of things, prisoners are taken. All this was at first good for the vassal; but the captives are fearful, and in the long run fear does not make for loyalty. To make captive slaves be loyal requires a more positive approach, winning their allegiance through kindness and other such actions.[17] Thus the prognostication.

Finally, while someone (presumably his lord) did bestow on him a "leather belt", in recognition of his part in the victory, this was a temporary and swiftly withdrawn recognition and honor, the bestowal no sooner done than it was revoked (Line 6).

****

◆ TEXTUAL NOTES ◆

a. In the traditional and Mawangdui versions, the initial portion of the original Hexagram Text and the whole of original Line 5 have been displaced, exchanged with each other. I have restored the order, and eliminated the duplication in title-name at the start of the Hexagram Text that results from the exchange. [Presumably, the title-name was filled in again, after the original displacement, resulting in this duplication when the original order is restored.] I have also restored $heng^1$ (亨) for ji^2 (吉), the latter being substituted for the former when the exchange took place (as appropriate for a line statement in contrast with a hexagram text); that substitution also reflects a later reading of $heng^1$ as 'successful, auspicious'.

b. In the traditional and Mawangdui versions Line 3 contains a phrase ("At times, pursuing royal service lacks fulfilling-completion") which does not seem to be a functional part of the text itself. As with the similar phrase of Hexagram 2/ Line 3, it seems more like an editorial comment or a note from a commentary on the text, which has by mistake become part of the text itself.

c. I read here de^2 (得: 'catch') for de^2 (德: 'virtue'). There is a common sort of loan function relating to these two characters, so that the one is written for the other with some frequency.

d. I read zhi^4 (怓) for zhi^4 (窒), as Kunst does, and take zhi^4 ti^4 (怓 惕) as meaning "frightened".

e. I read ci^4 (賜) for xi^2 (錫). It is also the Mawangdui reading here.

HEXAGRAM 7

ARMY

HEXAGRAM TEXT:
As a divination concerning big[a] men: auspicious, without harmful mishap. [H-SP]

LINES:
6 at the beginning:
The army goes forth with pitch-pipes, not secretively-and-hiddenly[b].
[L-I]
   Ominous. [L-P]

9 at LINE 2:
In the midst of the army, the King bestowed[c] command three times.
[L-I]
   Auspicious, without harmful mishap. [L-P]

6 at LINE 3:
The army now carting corpses. [L-I]
   Ominous. [L-P]

6 at LINE 4:
The army encamps on the left. [L-I]
   Without harmful mishap. [L-P]

6 at LINE 5:[d]
In the hunt they have game. [L-I]
   It is beneficial to shackle and interrogate[e]. [L-A]
   Without harmful mishap. [L-P]

6 on top:
The great lord has a mandate: open the country, maintain the family.
[L-I]
   Little men should not act. [L-A]

****

COMMENTARY

In the overall structure of the *Zhouyi*, Hexagrams 7 and 8 are paired with each other and belong in a group of pairs which is centered around Hexagrams 9 and 10. This latter pair concerns the involvement of human life in troubles, and the various pairs which belong to this group all develop their themes in ways connected with this matter of troubles.

Hexagram 7 is a type-story concerning the functioning of an army, and Hexagram 8 is a set of variations on the theme of providing aid and support.[18] The thematic relation of the two hexagrams is complementary, focused on ways of bringing people together, willingly in a supportive vein or by force The complementary thematic relation of the two hexagrams is strengthened by some details which show how much the two are being thought together.

For one thing, the top line of the first hexagram and the bottom line of the second introduce an aspect of the theme of the other hexagram into each, and through this interweaving readily lead the first into the second figure. For 'Army' ends with 'opens country, gives continuity to the household', thus setting the stage for the kind of alternative supportively-aiding activity which the other hexagram portrays; while 'Supportively Aid' begins with 'taking prisoners' and its reference back to military affairs.

For a second, the single solid line in each figure is the only one with express reference to the King (although 7/6, with its reference to a "great lord", does this under another name); and the actions involved in each case, point to the contrast of the two hexagrams: the King appointing commanders in his army, and the King acting toward villagers in kindly fashion-- even in forgiving fashion, if we think that the villagers may have had some hand in the failure.

In its lines the present hexagram sketches out the type-story of a military campaign, of the army in action. The start (Line 1) is with the troops going forth in orderly fashion, openly and not secretively, toward a place of battle.

Next commanders are named (Line 2). This is another facet of order, the King's appointing of commanders for the three major segments of the military force mobilized by him. Traditionally, these three were called the left, the right, and the center. It is a crucial part in the preparation for battle.

While the battle itself is not separately set forth, it is implicit in the imagery of Line 3, which addresses another facet of order: after a battle has been fought, the army removes the corpses from the battlefield. This carting of corpses signifies that the battle was costly, but not necessarily that it was lost.

In the follow-up effort to maintain control and keep peace and order in the area in which military action had taken place, the troops encamp on the left, that is, in a semi-permanent garrison for securing the peace (Line 4).

Another possibility opens up in the peace that arises after the battle: as part of the post-campaign ritual the leaders at least may return to the hunt, which was not only a recreation but also a training exercise (Line 5). In this case, it is a hunt in which the hunters find game.

Finally (Line 6), as the climax to the victorious campaign described in the previous lines, the great lord or King, having been granted a mandate to rule by Heaven, is commanded to open up and found countries and to maintain and sustain families. The final line thus points to the higher purposes which use of an army is to serve, while the previous five lines have focused on various forms of orderliness displayed in the working of the army and its leaders, in that functioning which enables a great lord to engage in action to support those purposes.[19]

****

◆ TEXTUAL NOTES ◆

a. I follow the common emendation of *zhang⁴* (丈) by *da⁴* (大). 'Big men' would include those men who would likely be at the head of an army, be leaders in it.

b. I read *zang⁴* (藏) for *zang¹* (臧) here, also (following the Mawangdui reading) *bu⁴* (不) for *fou³* (否).

c. As in Hexagram 6/Line 6, I read *ci⁴* (賜) for *xi²* (錫).

d. In the traditional and Mawangdui versions, there is a phrase in Line 5 which reads: "While older sons lead the army, younger sons cart the corpses: a divination that is ominous." This is a commentary note that has intruded into the text, and done so at the wrong place; the note concerns Line 3.

e. Emendations of *yan²* (言) by Shaughnessy (*CZ*, 41, using a character meaning "prisoners") and Qu Wanli (reading *xun⁴* [訊]: "interrogate" [see Kunst, *OY*, 212]) are also worth considering.

HEXAGRAM 8

SUPPORTIVELY AID

HEXAGRAM TEXT:[a]
(The occasion calls for a) **grand sacrifice.** [H-O]
As a long-term divination, without harmful mishap. [H-SP]
**The unsettled border-states come,[20] the last man suffers
harmful mishap.** [H-SSI]

LINES:
6 at the beginning:[b]
Take captives, supportively aid them. [L-I]
Without harmful mishap. [L-P]

6 at LINE 2:
Supportively aid those on the inside. [L-I]
As a divination, auspicious. [L-P]

6 at LINE 3:
Supportively aid the non-persons. [L-I]
Ominous.[c] [L-P]

6 at LINE 4:
Supportively aid those on the outside. [L-I]
As a divination, auspicious. [L-P]

9 at LINE 5:
**Illustrious supportive aid: the King, employing three game-chasers,
lost the game in front of him; the villagers are not frightened.** [L-I]
Auspicious. [L-P]

6 on top:
Supportively aid those who are 'head'-less.[21] [L-I]
Ominous. [L-P]

****

COMMENTARY

For the place of Hexagram 8 in the overall structure of the *Zhouyi*, and for the meaning of its pairing with Hexagram 7, see the first four paragraphs of the Commentary on Hexagram 7.

The lines of the present hexagram are variations on a theme. They set forth various types of supportive aid, with a focus on who is being aided. But their exposition takes place on the background of a scene-setting image in the Hexagram Text, which reports a context of unsettled border-region conditions in which parties come to the royal court to seek aid and support. In particular, the context is such that if one is not from the start in on the honoring-- and the deal-making at the royal court which such conditions invite-- but arrives late on the scene, such late arrival is likely to have detrimental consequences for one.[22]

The initial pointer is into such aid to prisoners as expresses the sort of kindness spoken of elsewhere in which one seeks to change the attitude of the captives, to gain their allegiance or at least cooperativeness by the kind of treatment which one accords to them (Line 1).

Alliance can also be formed with, and supportive aid given to, those on the inside-- and given the context provided by the Hexagram Text image, that would mean here, those on the inside at the royal court (Line 2).

Between these two extremes, there are others: for example, those who in terms of the political and social structure are non-persons, are 'nobodies' who 'do not count'. Here as in the case of the captives in Line 1, support is directed to persons who have no recognized power or standing.

In contrast there are others who are 'somebodies' but are not insiders at court (Line 4). Such persons may still be within the state, but they might also be persons from other states.

Before passing to a final focus for supportive aid, Line 5 addresses this matter of supportive aid from a slightly different perspective. The line image here sets forth an incident which attests a drawing close in support which is genuinely illustrious, a shining example.[23] The incident seems to be a ritual-ized hunting action in which the game is chased from three sides; that which flees the chasers toward the King is allowed to go free, and only that which turns away from him and runs is shot. The respectful restraint and recognition of limits expressed in this ritual act, when embodied in the King's governance, is what makes it possible for the villagers not to be afraid of such a King.

Finally, Line 6 addresses a type of supportive aid which links with the types imaged in Lines 1 and 3, with their concern for those who are less well situated. Here it concerns the unorganized masses who have no leader, no head or chief. (Or, the expression may refer to barbarians who, lacking the structure which the Chinese thought belonged to civilized life, had no 'chiefs'.)

From the range of types set forth in the lines, one may see the supportive aid being adumbrated as closely related to court life and power, to standing within a hierarchical order, to the positioning of persons to be 'powers' in a country. But what seems most significant in the outwardly-different referents of such aid is not so much their own proper standing and the differing character of the relation and attitude that might be expected in correlation with that; for a "supportive aid" which is a "drawing close in support", with the sense not simply of support and aid but also of a measure of intimacy and closeness, is somewhat different from that which is a "drawing close in alliance", an "allying oneself with ... and supporting and aiding those with whom one is allied". Instead, what is most striking is the inclusive quality of the relation and the character of the attitude involved. These seem essentially the expression of the strong-- the leader allying himself with one or another of lesser strength and position. But in every case, they represent a rather different working of strength than the use of force (as in an army), and one that is essential if there is to be cohesion in a state, continuity in a family, and the like.

****

◆ TEXTUAL NOTES ◆

a. In the traditional and the Mawangdui texts, a commentary note has intruded into the Hexagram Text. The note consists of a two character phrase ("original divination") followed by *yuan²* (元). It points out that originally the *ji²* (吉), which I take to be a copy error or an equivalent-replacement for *heng¹* (亨), was preceded by a *yuan²*. That is, the original reading was *yuan² heng¹*, later modified to *yuan² ji²*. I have excised the comment and read the introductory phrase as *yuan² heng¹*.

b. In the traditional and Mawangdui versions, there is an alternative form of Line 1 retained as if it were simply a further element in the line. It reads: "Take captives, fill the earthen-vessels: eventually come to have extraordinary concern/worry. Auspicious." Whether the prognostication elements belonging to each version of the image were kept properly with each version when the two were placed in the same line, might be questioned; the "auspicious" makes better sense in relation to the line, and the "without harmful mishap" in relation to the alternative version.

c. For this *xiong¹* (凶), see Li (*Zhouyi tanyuan*, 160: later cited as *ZTan*), Ding (*Du Yi Hui-tong*, 192), and Gao (*ZGJ*, 32).

HEXAGRAM 9

SMALL PASTURE

HEXAGRAM TEXT:
(The occasion calls for a) **sacrifice.** [H-O]
Extremely cloudy but no rain comes from our western out-skirts.[a] [H-SSI]

LINES:
9 at the beginning:
Returning from the paths,[1] **what's blameworthy in that?** [L-I]
Auspicious. [L-P]

9 at LINE 2:
Returning leading (the ox and cart). [L-I]
Auspicious. [L-P]

9 AT LINE 3:
The cart casts off[b] **its spokes**[c]**, the man and wife quarrel.** [L-I]

6 at LINE 4:
Have captives, blood goes far forth[d]**.** [L-I]
Without harmful mishap. [L-P]

9 at LINE 5:
Offer as sacrificial victims captives who are tightly trussed up[e]**; riches**[f] **because of the neighbors.** [L-I]

9 on top:
After it rains, and the rain stops, they still get[g] **to plant**[h]**.** [L-I]
As a woman divination, danger.
When the moon is almost full, it is ominous for the nobleman to attack. [L-SP]

****

COMMENTARY

In its overall structure the *Zhouyi* begins (Hexagrams 1 and 2) with the seasonal rhythm and life in an agriculture-dependent mode fitting itself into that rhythm, and ends (Hexagrams 63 and 64) with life placed within the matrix of the collective political/historical venturing which the Mandate of Heaven and the Shang and Zhou leadership of human life on earth provides.

Within these brackets, the thirty remaining hexagram pairs are grouped into five sets, the first of which (3/4 through 15/16) centers on Hexagrams 9 and 10. This pair make as theme that our human life-- this venturing and risking on earth under the heavens-- endemically becomes involved in troubles, in troubled situations.

Hexagrams 9 and 10 point to this involvement as exhibiting two complementary types: in one case (Hexagram 9), the troubles are brought on mainly by the larger circumstances of life (drought, war); in the other case (Hexagram 10), the troubles are brought upon one mainly by oneself, by how one comports oneself. Yet in both cases, what is involved is a dialectical interplay of a human being's own venturings and the forces of the larger matrix of that being's life. Given that something is at stake in life, threat and danger (from within and from without) unavoidably trouble our participation in that interplay.

The title-name of the present hexagram points to the situation under the image of a "small pasture", and the scene-setting image refines that imagery: it is such a pasture at a time of drought. The dense clouds coming from the west promise rain, but nothing has come of it. In such a time, conditions are not providing much support for human beings, at best they represent small nurture; whatever is possible through our own efforts is limited by such conditions.

The lines tell a story of such a time: it is a time of war also, and these conditions-- war and drought-- are the setting for a domestic conflict that reflects the tensions of the time, until finally... the war is won with the help of neighbors, and the drought breaks in time to plant a crop. The focus is on our being caught up and beset by forces beyond our own control, and yet... in this case... upon our being eventually freed also by powers beyond ourselves individually, so that we may safely do the planting that is central to continuing life on earth in the seasonal rhythm.

The image of Line 1 concerns a farming family caught up in the normal rhythms of an agricultural existence. The start of the story is with the recurrent activity of coming back along the old pathways that lead from field to home, that is, with everyday activity continuing to be carried out despite the difficult (drought) conditions. What is blameworthy in that?

The image in Line 2 develops the matter of everyday existence and its patterns further; this time, on the return, someone is leading the animals drawing the cart-- pulling, dragging them. Presumably conditions are getting worse, to the point where the animals are becoming reluctant to move; and yet work goes on, and difficulties are being overcome.

The image of Line 3 moves from patterns to a specific incident. Evidently one day, into the persistent effort to maintain the everyday patterns intrudes an accident: the cart becomes disabled; and this sets man and wife to glaring at each other eyeball to eyeball, so to speak, the strain of the effort to persist despite conditions and obstacles erupting into a quarrel on this occasion of a breakdown of the cart.

The image of Line 4 addresses another element of the context, which makes manifest another stressful condition (beyond the drought) which might make the arising of the quarrel more intelligible. What has been happening has been taking place in a wartime situation, one of quarreling on a large scale. Prisoners are taken, and blood spurts forth for some distance. Perhaps under the drought conditions it is enemies that have attacked seeking to steal food, but have been defeated in a bloody fight.

The image in Line 5 addresses further the wartime context of the story; this time, prisoners (presumably some of those taken in the bloody fight) are offered in the ritual celebrating victory. Because of crucial help from neighbors, this aspect of the stress has been dealt with, and the upshot of the matter has been booty and perhaps other forms of riches also.

Finally the image in Line 6 points to a change in the other condition which encompassed the domestic quarrel, namely, the drought. The rains come and bring relief from drought, but they also stop in time for planting to take place.

****

◆ TEXTUAL NOTES ◆

a. The scene-setting image in the Hexagram Text is repeated in Hexagram 62/Line 5, where it is an intrusion.

b. I read *tuo¹* (脫) here for *shuo¹* (說); *tuo¹* (挩) would also be acceptable.

c. An alternative reading here would be *fu²* (輹), meaning "axle-braces".

Ding Shou-chang (*Du Yi Hui-tong*, 200) argues for this variant as the correct character. It is what occurs in the same phrase in Hexagram 26, Line 1 and Hexagram 34, Line 4.

d. Much the same phrase is found as a definition of the title-name (spurting, spattering) in Hexagram 59, Line 6. I read *ti*[4] (惕) as loan for *ti*[4] (呬).

e. This phrase appears alone in Hexagram 61, Line 5.

f. Li (*ZTong*, 23) treats *fu*[4] (富) as a loan for *fu*[2] (福) (presumably meaning "blessed").

g. Reading *de*[2] (得) for *de*[2] (德). There is a common sort of loan function relating to these two characters, so that the one is written for the other with some frequency.

h. Reading *zai*[1] (栽) for *zai*[4] (載).

HEXAGRAM 10

SHOES AND STEPPING

HEXAGRAM TEXT:[a]
(The occasion calls for a) **sacrifice.**
A beneficial divination.[b] [H-O]

LINES:
9 at the beginning:
Plain 'steppers' (i.e. shoes). [L-I]
As to going, it is without harmful mishap. [L-SP]

9 at LINE 2:[c]
Step on the way confidently[d]. [L-I]
As a prisoner divination, auspicious. [L-SP]

6 at LINE 3:[e]
Step on a tiger's tail, it bites the person. [L-I]
Ominous. [L-P]

9 at LINE 4:[a]
**Step on a tiger's tail, the person looks panicky, the tiger does not bite
the person.** [L-I]
In the end, auspicious. [L-P]

9 at LINE 5:
Split-open[f] **'steppers'** (i.e. shoes). [L-I]
A divination of danger. [L-P]

9 on top:
Watching his step, keeping an eye on the omens. [L-I]
For the return home, greatly auspicious. [L-SP]

****

COMMENTARY

For the place of Hexagram 10 in the overall structure of the *Zhouyi*, and for the meaning of its pairing with Hexagram 9, see the first three paragraphs of the Commentary on Hexagram 9.

The lines of the present hexagram unfold another type of story than the one found in the pair-hexagram (9). Again, it is in general terms but this time in ways allowed by the varying meaning of the title-name (both 'shoes' and 'step on', the nominal and verbal meaning of the character). This set sketches our condition as venturers on the road, and in particular: we are venturers with a confidence and attentiveness/inattentiveness by which we bring danger upon ourselves unwittingly, and... providing we escape... with a capacity to learn such that we come through such experience chastened, more cautious and vigilant, at least for a while.

The story put briefly: putting on our plain travel shoes (Line 1), we start off confidently, stepping along boldly and straightforwardly (Line 2), and as it turns out, rather obliviously. For along the way, we unwittingly step into a dangerous situation. One possibility is that we are devoured by it (Line 3); the other is that we recognize the danger in time and, while terrified, we manage to escape (Line 4), our shoes split open but our lives intact (Line 5). But with split open shoes, we can not run; after our escape, we watch our step and keep an eye out for any signs, any omens (Line 6).

****

◆ TEXTUAL NOTES ◆

a. In this hexagram there are signs of dislocation, as well as of commentary being taken as text. The Hexagram Text contains a displaced line-statement ("Step on the tiger's tail, it does not bite the man"); this probably belongs as an alternative version of Line 4, being the correlative opposite of Line 3.[2] I have combined it with what is Line 4 in the traditional and Mawangdui versions. This combining enables the prognostication phrase in traditional Line 4 to have good sense: the 'does not bite' gives the reason why the 'step on the tiger's tail, the person looks panicky' is 'in the end, auspicious'. After the 'storing' of alternative Line 4 in the Hexagram Text occurred, the title-name of the hexagram and the first character of the line-statement became collapsed into one. I have reinstated the separate title-name when I have returned the displaced line-statement to its proper line.

b. I add the *li⁴ zhen¹* (利貞), following the variant cited by Ding Shou-chang (*Du-yi Hui-tong*, 204).

c. In Line 3 of the traditional and the Mawangdui versions, there is the following phrase: "The sight-impaired are able³ to see, the lame are able to walk." This is a displaced editorial/commentary note which actually belongs with Line 2, although due to faulty line-division it is presently found in Line 3. It interprets first of all the line-image: the traveler who is 'blinded' by the obliviousness of his confidence, is like the sight-impaired and the lame, who are held back by their limitations, yet are able to see and walk. Presumably, as regards the L-SP, the fact that the sight-impaired and the lame, while confined by their limitations (like a prisoner, who is confined in his mobility), are nonetheless able to see and walk, is a good sign for prisoners, concerning their release.

d. Li (*ZTong*, 24) also does not take the binome *tan³-tan³* (坦坦) to refer to the "road", and understands it to mean "a heart broadminded and magnanimous"; but Kunst and Gao relate the binome to the road, as "flat and level" (Gao) or "flat and smooth" (Kunst).

e. In Line 3 of the traditional and Mawangdui versions, there is another phrase: "Military men act for the 'big lord'". It seems more like an editorial/commentary note which has intruded by accident into the text. What its meaning and function in its proper setting would be, is not clear; here it seems to suggest one interpretation of the line image, to the effect that it is through military men that the 'tiger'-'big lord' 'bites' those who 'step on his tail'.

f. I read the *guai⁴* (夬) as a protograph or loan for *jue²* (决).

HEXAGRAM 11

OVERFLOWING

HEXAGRAM TEXT:
(The occasion calls for a) **sacrifice.** [H-O]
Auspicious for the big-and-great coming and the small-and-petty going. [H-SP]

LINES:
9 at the beginning:
Pull the mao-grass and madder up root and all, using their stems. [L-I]
Auspicious for going on a campaign.[a] [L-SP]

9 at LINE 2:[b]
A gourd[c], hollow, useful for fording the river. [L-I]

9 at LINE 3:
Without the flatland, there is no slope; without a going, there is no return. [L-I]
Do not worry, there will be a capture, and as to food, there will be blessing. [L-A]
As a hardship divination, without harmful mishap. [L-SP]

6 at LINE 4:
Flit-flitting: not rich on account of his neighbor, not on guard against and because of that, captured-and-plundered. [L-I]

6 at LINE 5:
Emperor Yi gave his daughter in marriage, as a result there was happiness. [L-I]
Greatly auspicious. [L-P]

6 on top:
The city-wall falls back[d] into the moat. [L-I]

Do not use troops, announce commands from the town. [L-A]
As a divination, difficulty. [L-P]

****

COMMENTARY

In the overall structure of the *Zhouyi*, Hexagrams 11 and 12 are paired with each other and belong in a group of pairs which is centered around Hexagrams 9 and 10. This latter pair concerns the involvement of human life in troubles, and the various pairs which belong to this group all develop their themes in ways connected with this matter of troubles.

Hexagrams 11 and 12 are linked in a subtle fashion that is obscured to some extent by some textual dislocation. That pairing is given a specific direction in the Hexagram Texts, with phrases that are almost a mirror image of each other. They read: 'the small-and-petty goes, the big-and-great comes' and 'the big-and-great goes, the small-and-petty comes'. To define the pairing, however, there is no continuous account of something, indeed no story-telling at all; and there is no set of variations on a theme by way of a word or phrase-- nothing that obvious. Instead, the themes of all the lines of Hexagram 11 are an elevation in some form; those of all lines of Hexagram 12 but the first are an obstruction, a limitation, of some sort, while the first is a line common to the two hexagrams, a line which in Hexagram 11 is meaningful in reference to the elevating involved and in Hexagram 12 is meaningful by reference to the obstruction (of the ground) involved.

The connections reinforced by this presence of a common line which has somewhat different emphases in its different contexts, are further reinforced by the way the top lines in each case lead into the opposite hexagram thematically. For the 'collapsed obstruction' in Hexagram 12 prepares a re-turn to the overflowing of Hexagram 11; while the 'falling of the city-wall back into the moat' in the top line of Hexagram 11 prepares for the grass-pulling which starts Hexagram 12. In this way a circle is formed between the two hexagrams with their complementary themes.

Internally the present hexagram is a series of variations on an image which is not marked by any one name: the image of elevation. Thus the 'overflowing' is given meaning through

    a. An elevation achieved by force (uprooting a plant, despite the resist-ance of roots in the ground) (Line 1);

    b. An elevation achieved by floating on water, using a hollow gourd as float-device for helping one to ford a river (Line 2);

   c. An elevation envisioned through climbing a rise (hills as elevated land masses presuppose flatlands, as returning presupposes going) (Line 3);

   d. An elevation achieved in a flying (the "flit-flitting", relating literally to such creatures as birds, bees, butterflies, and the like, relates metaphorically to human beings, signifying a flightiness, an inattentiveness in someone flitting here and there, and more specifically to the remainder of the image, an incautiousness which gave his neighbor an opportunity to plunder him) (Line 4);

   e. An inward elevation imaged in the Shang ruler, Di Yi, giving his daughter in marriage to King Wen, leader of the Zhou. That was a high point in his and her life, but more to the point here, the attendant happiness was the height of good feeling.[4]

   f. Then an elevating which goes too far, the upward movement being extended beyond the point of stability: the high wall falling back and collapsing into the moat. The 'up' tumbles 'down', not only recalling the theme of Line 3 (the polarity of height and level ground) but also making a transition possible to 'obstruction'-- starting from the ground again, as Line 1 of Hexagram 12 does.

****

◆ TEXTUAL NOTES ◆

a. In Line 1 of Hexagram 12, the same line-image appears, followed by the same prognostication words, except that *zhen[1]* (貞) has replaced the *zheng[1]* (征) found in Hexagram 11. Should the reading here be *zhen[1]*?

b. In Line 2, there is a doublet (five-character rhyming lines) which has become part of the traditional text, but which does not seem to relate to the context. I treat it as an intrusive editorial/commentary note, whose lack of proper context makes it impossible to tell with any assurance what is actually being said. Quite different translations are possible, of which one is: "He did not go far, but left behind friends who perished; he got a reward en route."

c. I read *pao[2]* (匏) for *bao[1]* (包).

d. Gao reads *fu[4]* (復) as *fu[4]* (覆), bringing out more fully the "collapse, topple, overturn, fall flat" sense involved in the image.

HEXAGRAM 12

OBSTRUCTION

HEXAGRAM TEXT:[a]
 (The occasion calls for a) **sacrifice.** [H-O]
  Not a beneficial nobleman divination: the big-and-great goes, the small-and-petty comes. [H-SP]

LINES:
6 at the beginning:
 Pull the mao-grass and madder up root and all, using their stems. [L-I]
  As a divination, auspicious.[b] [L-P]

6 at LINE 2:
 Wrap a steam-meat offering.[5][c] [L-I]
  Auspicious for a little man, but not for a big man.[6] [L-SP]

6 at LINE 3:
 Wrap a prepared-food offering [OR: a wrapped prepared-food offering].[7] [L-I]

9 at LINE 4:
 Holding a mandate, he finds happiness in ploughed fields and *lia*-birds.[d] [L-I]
  Without harmful mishap. [L-P]

9 at LINE 5:
 Cessation of obstruction. 'About to perish, about to perish: tie to a bushy mulberry'.[e] [L-I]
  For the big man, auspicious. [L-SP]

9 on top:[f]
 Collapsed[g] obstruction. [L-I]

****

COMMENTARY

For the place of Hexagram 12 in the overall structure of the *Zhouyi*, and for the meaning of its pairing with Hexagram 11, see the first three paragraphs of the Commentary on Hexagram 11.

In its own internal structure, the present hexagram has two parallel phrases in Lines 2-3 and again in Lines 5-6. Line 1 is the same here as in Hexagram 11. Looked at more closely, the structure (1, 2-3, 4, 5-6) plays off against Hexagram 11.

The common line, which in Hexagram 11 is utilized as relating to the 'up' theme (pulling up), is here taken in relation to the obstacle, the hindrance, the obstruction which is represented in the plants holding to the ground through their roots. If the obstruction to one pulling on the grass and madder can be readily overcome, it is nonetheless an obstruction.

Lines 2-3 contrast in particular with Line 2 of Hexagram 11 (concerning the gourd): the wrapping/enclosing here is in keeping with the obstruction theme, and the content enclosed contrasts with the empty/hollow character of the gourd which allows it to float. In both cases in the present hexagram, 'the petty or small at work obstructing' is understood in a positive vein: the wrapper encloses the small thing (steamed-meat, offering) and prevents it from falling apart.

Line 4, with its 'holding a mandate', fulfills the obstruction theme in two ways. A command or mandate represents not simply power and authority, but involves settled conditions and terms, thus limitation and constraint upon power and authority. However small or petty the limit may seem, it is essential and allows the power to be exercised while being subject to critique on grounds of legitimacy. Thus it is fitted to obstruct simply arbitrary action. But more fundamental for the imagery of this line as realizing the title-name of the hexagram, is the vision of happiness at the level of the lesser, the small or petty. Holding power is a matter of a higher order than agri-culture. The image-- of someone holding a mandate/command but finding his happiness in ploughed fields and *lia*-birds-- places weight on the lesser over the greater. At the same time as this realizes the situation of ob-struction, in which the petty or small takes precedence over the great or big, it provides a contrast with Line 4 of Hexagram 11 in the condition being intimated: the happiness of ploughed fields and lia-birds vs. the suffering of one plundered by one's neighbor.

Lines 5-6 alone contain express use of the term 'obstruction' (*pi³*: 否). In both Hexagrams, Line 5 represents a high-point: in Hexagram 11, it is a King giving his daughter in marriage, while in 12 here, it is the cessation of obstruction, swept away in a turmoil that is auspicious for a great man.[8] In both, Line 6 prepares for the opposite Hexagram: the collapse of the city-wall in Hexagram 11, and the collapsed obstruction in the present one.

****

◆ TEXTUAL NOTES ◆

a. The original Hexagram Text's *heng¹* (亨) has been displaced and duplicated (found at the end of Lines 1 and 2), and an intrusive phrase (*fou³* [or, *pi³*] *zhi¹ fei³ ren²*: 否之匪人) is found in its place. I have restored the *heng¹*, retained the *pi³* as the title-name of the hexagram, and excised the *zhi¹ fei³ ren²*.

b. In Line 1 of Hexagram 11, the same line-image appears, followed by the same prognostication words, except that *zheng¹* (征) has replaced the *zhen¹* (貞) found here (12). Should the reading here also be *zheng¹*?

c. I read *cheng²* (承) as *cheng²* (脀).

d. In Line 4 it might be that the "without harmful mishap" is not a pro-gnostication phrase at all, but that the line means: "while holding a mandate without harmful mishap, he finds happiness in ploughed fields and *lia*-birds". That is, while having a position of authority and command and hav-ing nothing go wrong would seem to be the epitome of happiness for a ruler, he finds instead that his happiness lies elsewhere. The image of ploughed fields and birds is one of those still-life images that evokes a whole sphere of existence through a condensed image. It is, nonetheless, in the terms and values of the order of Zhou existence, a lesser level.

e. As in Line 4, so in Line 5: the structure of the line in the traditional and Mawangdui versions suggests that the second image in each case might be a later addition-- at least in Line 5, a rhyming couplet which is likely to be a poetic reference or allusion which some commentator makes. The fact that the same pattern occurs in Line 6 (see the following note) except that the initial image is not followed by a prognostication word, adds strength to the suggestion. That means that the last five lines originally would each have had a two-character line-image; only the first line, which is the one shared with Hexagram 11, would then have had a different pattern.

f. In Line 6 of the traditional and Mawangdui versions, there is a phrase ("At first an obstruction, then happiness") which I have excised. It seems like an editorial note or explanatory phrase from a later commentary which has intruded into the text. It explains the text-phrase in terms of the later meaning of the title-name of the pair Hexagram, namely, "happiness" (originally, the title means "overflowing"). This adds to the sense that Hexagrams 11 and 12 are connected, especially as it can pick up the element of happiness in 11/5; but it seems not part of the original text.

g. If one followed the Mawangdui text, which reads *qing³* (頃) for *qing¹* (傾), the meaning would presumably be "momentary obstruction".

HEXAGRAM 13

GATHERING TOGETHER
OF HUMAN BEINGS

HEXAGRAM TEXT:[a]
  (The occasion calls for a) **sacrifice.** [H-O]
    Beneficial to cross the big river. [H-A]
    A beneficial nobleman divination. [H-SP]

LINES:
9 at the beginning:
  Gather people together at the gate. [L-I]
    Without harmful mishap. [L-P]

6 at LINE 2:
  Gather people together at the ancestral temple. [L-I]
    Difficulty. [L-P]

9 at LINE 3:
  Ambushing troops lying hidden in the thick high weeds, climbing the high hills: three years, not succeed. [L-I]

9 at LINE 4:
  (The defenders) astride the city wall, (the enemy) not able to storm it. [L-I]
    Auspicious. [L-P]

9 at LINE 5:
  The people, gathered together, at first wept and wailed, but then afterward they laughed-and-smiled. The big armies were able to meet each other. [L-I]

9 on top:
  Gather people together at the suburban altar. [L-I]
    Without troubles. [L-P]

****

COMMENTARY

In the overall structure of the *Zhouyi*, Hexagrams 13 and 14 are paired with each other and belong in a group of pairs which is centered around Hexagrams 9 and 10. This latter pair concerns the involvement of human life in troubles, and the various pairs which belong to this group all develop their themes in ways connected with this matter of troubles.

Much as in Hexagrams 1 and 2, Hexagrams 13 and 14 are paired by forming a continuous story. This one focuses on a battle (preparations, the battle itself, victory) and a victory celebration (pointed to in the first hexagram, developed in the second).

In the present hexagram the story begins with the people drawing together at the royal gates (Line 1). Presumably the gathering is preparatory to sending out the army into battle, thus for the announcing of what is going to happen and for the exhorting.[9]

In the next step, the people draw together again, this time at the royal ancestral temple (Line 2). Presumably preparation is moving ahead, and this gathering is a matter of consulting with and receiving the direction and support of the ruler's ancestors: would the forefathers have the ruler and people go to battle?

As it turns out, the fighting which was lying ahead in the first two lines, was not a single decisive battle, but a series of ambushes and ascents onto high ground. For 'three years' (= a significant time) something like guerilla warfare takes place, involving a standoff in which nothing was resolved, no one prevailed (Line 3).

Eventually, the drama comes to a decisive stage: the enemy is now closing in on the city, the indecisive fighting is about to be ended (Line 4). The image can be construed differently (there is no explicit subject), but it seems to speak of defenders sitting astride the city wall and preventing the enemy from storming it and bringing the downfall of the city. [It could be that the enemy has mounted the wall but is unable to carry its attack over the wall into the city.]

The decisive event is conveyed in an image that is hard to understand. Apparently the populace is inside and is anticipating being overwhelmed by forces gathered for an attack. But then something happens and the attack is lifted, and the dispute is apparently settled. It seems that an ally intervened or more likely, that royal forces arrived from a distance (Line 5).

The phase of the story told in this set of lines ends (Line 6) in the gathering together of people at the suburban altar, in celebration of the victory (or at least, the rescue from defeat).[10]

****

◆ TEXTUAL NOTES ◆

a. In the traditional and Mawangdui versions of the text, the title-name has been collapsed with the beginning of another phrase, namely, "Gather people together in the wilds." I restore the separate title-name. That phrase seems to be an alternative version of Line 1, 'stored' in the Hexagram Text.

HEXAGRAM 14

GREAT BLESSINGS[a]

HEXAGRAM TEXT:
(The occasion calls for a) **grand sacrifice.** [H-O]

LINES:
9 at the beginning:
There's no calamity[11] in not exchanging injuries. [L-I]
As a hardship divination[b], without harmful mishap. [L-SP]

9 at LINE 2:
A big cart for transporting. [L-I]
As for having a place to go, that is without harmful mishap. [L-SP]

9 at LINE 3:
The Duke acts to make an offering[c] to the Son of Heaven, little men are not capable of that. [L-I]

9 at LINE 4:
It was not the *peng*-sacrifice.[12] [d] [L-I]
Without harmful mishap. [L-P]

6 at LINE 5:
Their captives are tied up crosswise and look terrified. [L-I]
Auspicious. [L-P]

9 on top:
From Heaven, blessings to him/them. [L-I]
Auspicious, nothing is not beneficial. [L-P]

****

COMMENTARY

For the place of Hexagram 14 in the overall structure of the *Zhouyi*, and for the meaning of its pairing with Hexagram 13, see the first two paragraphs of the Commentary on Hexagram 13.

The lines of this hexagram conclude the story of the battle-events by speaking of the enjoyment of the blessings whose coming is mediated by a ritual offering made to the ancestral spirits. Focusing on the celebration which is the reason for the gathering together at the suburban altars (13/6), this phase of the story account starts with preliminary affairs: the victors see no harm in not exchanging injury (14/1) and use a big cart[13] to transport the offerings (14/2). Then comes the sacrifice: it is made by the Duke, to the Son of Heaven (14/3); but it is not the *peng*-sacrifice, made at the side of the temple gate (14/4); it is rather one involving human sacrifice (14/5). It ends with the benefits coming from Heaven, blessings to the King and to the people (14/6).

****

◆ TEXTUAL NOTES ◆

a. I read *you⁴* (祐) for *you³* (有) here, for reasons which Shaughnessy (*CZ*, 254-5) sets forth well.

b. I read *zhen¹* (貞) for *ze²* (則) here, the latter being a copy error and the former maintaining the main pattern of the use of *jian¹* (艱) in the *Zhouyi* (see Hexagram 11/Line 3, for example).

c. I emend *heng¹* (亨) to *xiang³* (享), simply to make the usage consistent (the former appears in the Hexagram Texts, the latter in the Line Statements). There is no change of meaning involved.

d. An alternative reading of the line, when taken in the context of the series of lines, could be: "It was not the case that he was arrogant." See Liu Dajun (*Zhouyi gailun*, 263-4) for the meanings of 彭 that could support such an interpretation.

HEXAGRAM 15

HAMSTER[a]

HEXAGRAM TEXT:
(The occasion calls for a) **sacrifice.** [H-O]
Auspicious for a nobleman to act to cross the big river.[b]
[H-A]

LINES:
6 at the beginning:[b]
'Crunch, crunch' (sound of the hamster gnawing on something).[c] [L-I]

6 at LINE 2:
A calling hamster. [L-I]
As a divination, auspicious. [L-P]

9 at LINE 3:
A hamster hard at work. [L-I]
As to things having an end for the nobleman, it is auspicious, nothing is not beneficial.[d] [L-SP]

6 at LINE 4:
A hamster rending and tearing open. [L-I]

6 at LINE 5:
Not rich, due to a neighbor. [L-I]
Beneficial to act to invade and attack. [L-A]
Nothing is not beneficial. [L-P]

6 on top:
A darkness-(bringing)[e] hamster. [L-I]
Beneficial to act to mobilize armies and to attack cities and countries. [L-A]

****

COMMENTARY

In the overall structure of the *Zhouyi*, Hexagrams 15 and 16 are paired with each other and belong in a group of pairs which is centered around Hexagrams 9 and 10. This latter pair concerns the involvement of human life in troubles, and the various pairs which belong to this group all develop their themes in ways connected with this matter of troubles.

The linking of Hexagrams 15 and 16 is manifest in the very title-names they bear, the names of animals, one a large animal, one a small one. These are wild animals, not domesticated ones, which are attended to as troubling human life.[14]

The linking of Hexagram 15 with 16, beyond the complementary title-names and the story in each case of how the animal in question brings troubles to human beings, seems strengthened by the beginnings and endings of each. Line 1 of Hexagram 15 is the rodent-sound, Line 2 refers to a calling hamster"; Line 1 of Hexagram 16 is a "calling elephant". Line 6 of Hexagram 15, in the traditional text a duplicate of "calling (*ming²*: 鳴) hamster", probably should be instead the same *ming²* (冥) as that used to characterize the elephant in Line 6 of Hexagram 16.

In its structure, the present hexagram holds a series of 2-character phrases in five of the six lines (only Line 5 lacks this), with the title-name found in four of the phrases (the fifth represents the sound of the animal). The series seems to point, in a very elliptical fashion, to the unfolding of an event, that of rodents invading and eating foodstuff. The precise kind of rodent in question-- a hamster, for lack of a better English term-- and its associations in the ancient Chinese mind, are unclear.

The beginning of the story is the crunching noise which is the first sign of the rodent's presence: perhaps not the crunch of an eating, but of a gnawing to get through an obstacle (in a granary, for example) (Line 1).

This is followed by a further sign of the rodent's presence: the sound of hamsters calling to each other (Line 2).

Soon the rodents are working hard, laboring away (presumably, in seeking to get at the grain in its storage place, but perhaps, in eating the stored-up foodstuffs) (Line 3).

In the next line, that laboring has become a rending something, tearing it open-- and in the context, that seems most likely to mean, they are gnawing away at the sacks of stored grain (Line 4).

The next line breaks the unfolding of the story of the rodent invasion by introducing a human counterpart to what the story is addressing in the rodent-images. Its image is of the attack by a neighbor which deprives the person of his riches (Line 5).

In the final line, the focus returns to the invading rodents, and the image calls forward the darkness which is particularly associated with the other world, with hell under one or another name among many peoples (Hades among the Greeks, for example) (Line 6). What the rodent invasion does, by robbing human beings of the food needed to sustain them, is to impact the survival of the persons in question; and that sense of the matter, seen from the point of view of the conqueror however, is confirmed in the action-phrase.

****

◆ TEXTUAL NOTES ◆

a. I read $qian^3$ (鼸) for $qian^1$ (謙) here and throughout the hexagram lines.

b. In the traditional and Mawangdui versions (the latter except for a lacuna covering one character) there is a phrase which seems to reflect a copy error, a mistaken duplication of Line 3 ("The nobleman has an end") when the phrase actually to be copied here was another one with the same start, namely, "The nobleman acts to cross the big river: auspicious". The proper Hexagram Text phrase is currently found in Line 1 (I have restored it here); the copy error is likely to have been made before that displacement occurred.

c. I read $qian^1$ (嗛) here for $qian^1$ (謙).

d. In the traditional and Mawangdui versions, this phrase (wu^2 bu^4 li^4: "nothing is not beneficial") has been separated from Line 3 and placed at the beginning of Line 4 as a result of faulty line-division. I have restored it to Line 3. The combination ji^2 wu^2 bu^4 li^4 (吉无不利) appears elsewhere: see Hexagram 3/Line 4; Hexagram 19/Line 2; Hexagram 50/Line 6.

e. In the traditional and Mawangdui versions, we find the unlikely repetition of the two-character phrase of Line 2 here in Line 6. I have emended $ming^2$ (鳴) to read $ming^2$ (冥), in parallel with Line 6 of the pair-hexagram (16). It is a term which means "darkness", but in particular, that of the underworld, of Hades; so it is closely connected with the other world, with death. That seems appropriate in virtue of the acts of the hamster set forth in the lines: they amount to robbing human beings of the food needed for survival.

HEXAGRAM 16

ELEPHANT[a]

HEXAGRAM TEXT:
   Beneficial for establishing lords and mobilizing armies.
   [H-A]

LINES:
6 at the beginning:
   A trumpeting elephant. [L-I]
      Ominous. [L-P]

6 at LINE 2:
   Bordered round[15] by rock, (the attack) will not last a day. [L-I]
      As a divination, auspicious. [L-P]

6 at LINE 3:
   A staring elephant: in trouble, walking slowly. [L-I]
      Have troubles. [L-P]

9 at LINE 4:
   A roaming[b] elephant. [L-I]

6 at LINE 5:
   Have a big catch. [L-I]
      Don't be hesitant, why not store up the cowries?[c] [L-A]
      **As a divination concerning disease: it will be long-lasting but not
         fatal.** [L-SP]

6 on top:
   Elephant of darkness, the city wall[d] collapses. [L-I]
      Without harmful mishap. [L-P]

****

COMMENTARY

For the place of Hexagram 16 in the overall structure of the *Zhouyi*, and for the meaning of its pairing with Hexagram 15, see the first three paragraphs of the Commentary on Hexagram 15.

In its structure, the present hexagram has two-character phrases which involve the name-title in Lines 1, 3, 4, and 6. Lines 2 and 5, in contrast, focus on the situation from another side. Together the six lines seem to tell a story in elliptical fashion.

The beginning is with a trumpeting elephant, a threatening figure-- angry, perhaps, since the prognostication points to a foreboding as marking the meaning of the image here (Line 1).

One is protected from this threat by defenses firm as a rock, which will not give in throughout the day (Line 2).

In the face of these, thwarted by one's secure place of refuge, the elephant stares or glares at one; but it is in trouble, and walking slowly-- presumably frustrated and worn down, perhaps injured, in any case unsuccessful in venting its anger (Line 3).

Thus the angry and frustrated elephant begins to roam (Line 4).

With the elephant wandering off and relieving the threat, the line image shifts here (as it did in the parallel place in Hexagram 15) to a human counterpart-image, that of a successful hunt (Line 5).

But the story ends with the return of the elephant, this time as a darkness-(bringing) elephant. As the accompanying "city-wall collapses" indicates, this return should indicate something somewhat calamitous, and yet nothing in particular is indicated and the prognostication is "without harmful-mishap" (Line 6).

This seems to be the story being intimated in the series of lines as giving meaning to the title-name of the hexagram as a whole, but the interpretation of those lines is anything but clear and straightforward.

****

◆ TEXTUAL NOTES ◆

a. Here and throughout the hexagram, I read *yu⁴* (豫) as *xiang⁴* (象), to make clear that the meaning is "elephant".

b. I read *you²* (由) as *you²* (游), as does Gao.

c. I read the *zan¹* (簪) as *zan³* (攢), following a suggestion from the discussion of Gao Heng (*ZGJ*, 61). In the traditional and the Mawangdui texts, the L-I and the L-A phrase are found in Line 4, due to a mistaken line-division. I have restored them to Line 5, as the proper image and action elements of that Line.

d. I read *cheng²* (成) as *cheng²* (城).

HEXAGRAM 17

PURSUIT

HEXAGRAM TEXT:[a]
(The occasion calls for a) **grand sacrifice.**
A beneficial divination. [H-O]

LINES:
9 at the beginning:[b]
There is a change for the worse among officials. [L-I]
As a divination, difficulty[c]**.** [L-P]

6 at LINE 2:
Bind the children, but lose the grown men. [L-I]

6 at LINE 3:[d]
In the pursuit, there is an attempt to capture. [L-I]
Beneficial dwelling-divination. [L-SP]

9 at LINE 4:[e]
In the pursuit, there is a capture. [L-I]
As a divination, ominous. [L-P]

9 at LINE 5:
Capture at Jia.[f] [L-I]
Auspicious. [L-P]

6 on top:
They grasp and bind them, then follow and hold them fast; the King
employs himself offering sacrifice[g] **in the western hills.** [L-I]
Without harmful mishap. [L-P][a]

****

COMMENTARY

In the overall structure of the *Zhouyi*, Hexagrams 17 and 18 are paired with each other and belong in a group of pairs which is centered around Hexagrams 29 and 30. This latter pair concerns divine powers manifest in the earth's higher and lower places, and the various pairs which belong to this group all develop themes which relate to earthly life under Heaven, particularly in its social aspects and in the general features of its being a temporal (mortal) affair.

Hexagrams 17 and 18 are linked in their focus upon continuity in the social order. The story told in 17 relates to a time of disorder and to the epitome of its disorderliness and discontinuity, namely, the flight of slaves. In a five-line series of variations on a phrase, 18 addresses the matter of social continuity in the form of attending to inherited affairs, and this, with a warning about elevating the family/clan form under the idea that it is a nobler affair than serving kings and lords.

The link of the two hexagrams is underlined by the echo of their top lines. In 17 (Pursuit), the lines end with the King asserting order and continuity in the face of disorder and discontinuity (in an act of sacrifice, presumably to Heaven); in 18 (Affairs), there is the contrary sort of ending, where after focus on the continuing of the family/clan traditional affairs, there is the vision of the ominousness of a noble virtuous power[1] which does not serve kings and lords but (presumably, given the theme of the set of lines) focuses on the family/clan as its horizon. The sense of disorder/discontinuity expressed in Hexagram 17 can come from just such a limited focus, however 'virtuous' it may be in that sphere, since the basic conditions of life require realization of such power at the highest and embracing point in the human order, namely, in the King who is Heaven's manifestation on earth.

The present hexagram develops the story of a flight and recapture of slaves in a time of disorder.[2] Within the turn for the worse of political life at the level of officialdom (Line 1), apparently the slaves are threatening to flee, and while the younger ones are secured in bonds the adults escape (Line 2). There is pursuit (Line 3) and attempt to capture, then success in capture (Line 4)-- apparently at Jia (Line 5). Finally, the slaves (some at least) are made part of the king's act of sacrifice in the western hills. At least that much of order is enacted.

****

◆ TEXTUAL NOTES ◆

a. I omit a *wu² jiu⁴* (无咎) which has been displaced from some Line Statement and 'stored' in the Hexagram Text. The common interchanging between HT and Line 6, together with the absence of a prognostication phrase in the latter, suggests it might be Line 6.

b. Line 1 contains an extraneous phrase ("To go forth and make exchanges, has merit", or "in the outside world, making exchanges has merit") which seems like a commentary note that has strayed into the text. It probably belongs with the other commentary note, in Line 4, which speaks of "reciprocal agreements among families and states for the return of run-away slaves" (Shaughnessy, *CZ*, 234).

c. The traditional reading of *ji²* (吉: "auspicious") is a copy error for *lin⁴* (吝: "difficulty").

d. In the traditional and Mawangdui versions, Line 3 starts with a phrase ("Bind the grown men, lose the children") which belongs with Line 2 but is found in Line 3 as a result of a faulty line-break. It is an alternative version of Line 2, with a reversal of the parties who are bound and those who escape.

e. In the traditional and Mawangdui versions, Line 4 has an extraneous phrase ("Have a capture on the road because of a covenant; what harm is there in that?") which has mistakenly been made part of the text. It is a commentary note, recalling reciprocal agreements among families and states for the return of run-away slaves. Shaughnessy (*CZ*, 233) discusses this line with the idea that the phrase is a part of the line, but nonetheless he recognizes the appropriate emendation of *meng²* (盟) for *ming²* (明) and the appropriate meaning of the phrase *you³ fu²* (有俘) (here, "there is a captive", whereas elsewhere, "to offer a captive in sacrifice").

f. Or one may read the line as Kunst does (*OY*, 273): "Captives at the *jia¹*-celebration." The latter is a ritual celebration involving human sacrifice.

g. I read *heng¹* (亨) here as *xiang³* (享), as the appropriate character in the Line Statements. Shaughnessy (*CZ*, 337) notes: "Reading *xiang* ... for *heng* ... on the basis of a comparison with 'Yi' (42/6) .... The close graphic and etymological relationship between these two words has led to their confusion here, as well as in 'Dayou' (14/3) and 'Sheng' (46/4)."

HEXAGRAM 18

AFFAIRS[a]

HEXAGRAM TEXT:
(The occasion calls for a) **grand sacrifice.** [H-O]
Beneficial to cross the big river: for three days before and three days after a *jia*-stem day.[3] [H-A]

LINES:
6 at the beginning:
Attending to inherited paternal affairs. [L-I]
Have son and deceased father without blame; danger, but in the end auspicious. [L-SP]

9 at LINE 2:
Attending to inherited maternal affairs. [L-I]
As a divination, not acceptable. [L-P]

9 at LINE 3:
Attending to inherited paternal affairs. [L-I]
Have minor troubles, without great harmful mishap. [L-P]

6 at LINE 4:
Making inherited paternal affairs flourish abundantly. [L-I]
As to going to visit, difficulty. [L-SP]

6 at LINE 5:
Attending to inherited paternal affairs. [L-I]
Employ the *yu*-sacrifice-and-incantation[b]. [L-A]

9 on top:
Not serving kings and lords, noble still his service.[c] [L-I]
Ominous.[d] [L-P]

****

COMMENTARY

For the place of Hexagram 18 in the overall structure of the *Zhouyi*, and
for the meaning of its pairing with Hexagram 17, see the first three paragraphs of the Commentary on Hexagram 17.

The lines of the present hexagram form a set of five variations on a
phrase, with a final twist in Line 6. They concern continuity, inheritance,
keeping the line and the affairs of the line going.
    The first variation is with such effort made on the side of the father and
father's clan and made in conditions of danger not due to son or deceased-
father. The second involves family affairs on the maternal side, attending to
which is nothing acceptable. The third returns to focus on affairs on the father's side, this time with minor troubles but no great mishap; the fourth concerns making the affairs on the father's side flourish, and a fifth concerns
attending to such affairs as involving employing a certain incantation-sacri-
fice.
    In contrast with this set of variations, the hexagram ends with a vision of
a noble virtuous-power which is not realized in serving kings and lords-- and
at the same time, a sense of the ominousness of this. Given the theme of the
hexagram whole in which this line appears, this seems to reflect concern for
social continuity which is threatened if the diversion of such concern and
power to clan and family affairs gains the upper hand. Such a diversion is
indeed characteristic of the forces which led to the disintegration of the Zhou
dynasty.

****

◆ TEXTUAL NOTES ◆

a. The title-name in the traditional and the Mawangdui versions of the text
is a loan word for *gu¹* (故: "affairs, old affairs").

b. I believe Kunst is right (*OY*, 275) in translating: "Use the *yu* incantation-
sacrifice." What is meant is a religious affair and not simply "praise" or
"eulogy". Li (*ZTong*, 38-39) interprets *yu¹* (譽) as "praise", and sees Lines
1, 3, 4 and 5 forming a kind of progression: Line 1 speaks of a continuation
of one's father's affairs with no problems (if there is something bad, it ends
in something good), Line 3 of a continuing that involves a small problem but
nothing major, Line 4 of an enlarging (but with problems), and Line 5 of a

continuing which is successful and wins praise.

c. The Mawangdui text reads *de²* (德: virtuous-power) for *shi⁴* (事: service) here, and suggests an alternative rendering of the line: "Noble and esteemed his virtuous-power."

d. The traditional text lacks this character (*xiong¹*: 凶), but I follow the Mawangdui text which includes it

HEXAGRAM 19

OVERSEEING

HEXAGRAM TEXT:
(The occasion calls for a) **grand sacrifice.**
A beneficial divination. [H-O]
Ominous up until the eighth month. [H-SP]

LINES:
9 at the beginning:
An overseeing that unites. [L-I]
As a divination, auspicious. [L-P]

9 at LINE 2:
A responsive[a] overseeing. [L-I]
Auspicious, nothing not beneficial. [L-P]

6 at LINE 3:
An overseeing which pinches-and-clamps-down.[b] [L-I]
Lacking anything beneficial; after grieving over it, without harmful mishap. [L-P]

6 at LINE 4:
Sincere-and-trustworthy[c] overseeing. [L-I]
Without harmful mishap. [L-P]

6 at LINE 5:
Knowledgeable (wise, skillful) overseeing. [L-I]
Auspicious for a Great Lord's sacrifice to the soil spirit. [L-SP]

6 on top:
Overseeing that is generous. [L-I]
Auspicious, without harmful mishap. [L-P]

****

COMMENTARY

In the overall structure of the *Zhouyi*, Hexagrams 19 and 20 are paired with each other and belong in a group of pairs which is centered around Hexagrams 29 and 30. This latter pair concerns divine powers manifest in the earth's higher and lower places, and the various pairs which belong to this group all develop themes which relate to earthly life under Heaven, particularly in its social aspects and in the general features of its being a temporal (mortal) affair.

Hexagrams 19 and 20 are linked in terms of a looking: of the higher looking down upon the lower, in an overseeing (relating to the political order, governing), and of the lower looking up to the higher, in a contemplating (relating to the religious aspects of life, the symbols, the elements of sacrificial ritual, etc.).

The present hexagram develops as a set of variations on a theme, grouped in two sets of three by sound pattern. Within each of these sets there is a grouping of two-then-one, and between the two sets of three, the third in each (Lines 3 and 6) play off against each other. All the variations concern the character of the overseeing: one that unites, one that is responsive, but then one that is restrictive and emphasizes control from above; one that is sincere-and-trustworthy, one that is skillful, and one that is generous. There seems no clear ordering of sense in the grouping, but all play on the differentiation of higher (ruler) and lower and speak to the way the higher looks down upon and oversees the lower. The variations indicate a range of kinds of overseeing.

****

◆ TEXTUAL NOTES ◆

a. In the traditional and Mawangdui texts, the character here (咸) is the same as that in Line 1. Lines 4 and 5 show a rhyme-connection between different characters, and while this might be anticipated also to be the case here, we have instead an identity in the characters involved. This repetition of identical character rather than writing of a second but rhyming character seems likely to represent a copy error; accordingly, I emend the second occurrence of *xian²* to *gan³* (感: the same character with an added heart-radical element). Li (*ZTong*, 40) emends the first occurrence instead of the second, interpreting the first as using the persuasive moral example of one's own person (*gan³* as *gan³ hua¹*: 感化) and the second as using a gentle moderateness (*xian²* as *wen¹ he²*: 溫和).

b. I read *qian²* (拑) for *gan¹* (甘) here. Such a reading (of 'clamping down' for 'sweet and agreeable') makes much more sense of the prognostication element present here. See Gao's discussion (*ZGJ*, 71-72) for supporting considerations.

c. The *zhi¹* (至 : utmost) of the traditional texts, while it can make sense, does not seem as appropriate as it might be, to pair with 'knowledgeable, wise, skillful'. I follow Gao, who emends to *zhi²* (質 : sincere and trustworthy).

HEXAGRAM 20

CONTEMPLATION

HEXAGRAM TEXT:
Hands washed but no animal offering yet, have captives the likes of big-headed⁴ persons. [H-SSI]

6 at the beginning:
Youthful contemplation. [L-I]
Without harmful mishap for the little man, difficulty for the nobleman. [L-SP]

6 at LINE 2:
Contemplate by guardedly stealing a glance. [L-I]
As a female divination, beneficial. [L-SP]

6 at LINE 3:
Contemplate our clansᵃ advancing and withdrawing. [L-I]

6 at LINE 4:
Contemplate our country's shining light. [L-I]
Beneficial to act to be guest to the King. [L-A]

9 at LINE 5:
Contemplate *our* sacrificial animalsᵇ. [L-I]
For a nobleman, without harmful mishap. [L-SP]

9 on top:
Contemplate *their* sacrificial animals.ᵇ [L-I]
For a nobleman, without harmful mishap. [L-SP]

****

COMMENTARY

For the place of Hexagram 20 in the overall structure of the *Zhouyi*, and for the meaning of its pairing with Hexagram 19, see the first two paragraphs of the Commentary on Hexagram 19.

The present hexagram develops as a set of variations on a theme grouped in three sets of two. The Hexagram Text sets the lines in the context of a sacrificial ceremony, so that the contemplation involved has a religious cast. The image is of a time in the ritual, after one act and before another, and in a ritual which apparently will involve human sacrifice. The religious cast fits well with a looking up, since it involves looking up to something higher in the form not only of divine powers but also of the King as the higher authority representing Heaven on earth.

The first two lines involve contemplating of different sorts: a youthful one marked by wide-eyed innocence, and a guarded on-the-sly one, more the stealing of a glance than the innocent open-eyed gazing at something. If one keeps in mind the sense of decorum and modesty which is to mark the participation of women in public in the society involved, then the connection of a guarded glancing and the beneficial character of what is imaged in this line-image becomes more intelligible.

The next two involve contemplating different figures involved in the ceremony: the various clans, and the king. There is the advancing and drawing back of the clans taking part in the sacrificial ceremony (Line 3); and there is contemplation of the King (or, taking the phrase to be "contemplate our country's splendor-and-brilliance", it would be the court and court members that are the focus of attention. The action-element might suggest that the former is the preferable reading.)

The final two involve contemplating the sacrificial animals involved: ours vs. theirs.

As with Hexagram 19, hierarchical differentiation seems involved, but in this case things are envisioned from the standpoint of the lower looking upward.

$$\text{***********************}$$

◆ TEXTUAL NOTES ◆

a. Here, I read the *sheng¹* (生) of the traditional and Mawangdui versions as the protograph for *xing⁴* (姓: clan), given the ritual context and the linking of this line's image with that of Line 4. In contrast, the *sheng¹* of Lines 5 and 6 seems to mean *sheng¹* (牲: sacrificial animal).

b. Reading *sheng¹* (牲) for its proto-graph *sheng¹* (生), which is what is found in the traditional and Mawangdui version.

HEXAGRAM 21

BITING THROUGH

HEXAGRAM TEXT:
   (The occasion calls for a) **sacrifice.** [H-O]
   Beneficial for acting to bring suit. [H-A]

LINES:
9 at the beginning:
   Wearing stocks on his feet, obliterating his toes. [L-I]
   Without harmful mishap. [L-P]

6 at LINE 2:
   Biting into flesh, obliterating one's nose. [L-I]
   Without harmful mishap. [L-P]

6 at LINE 3:
   Biting into dried meat, encountering poison. [L-I]
   Petty difficulty, without harmful mishap. [L-P]

9 at LINE 4:
   Biting into dried meat that still has bone in it, getting a metal arrow(head). [L-I]
   Auspicious. [L-P]
   Beneficial hardship divination.[a] [L-SP]

6 at LINE 5:
   Biting into dried meat, getting yellow metal. [L-I]
   As a divination, danger, without harmful mishap. [L-P]

9 on top:
   Bearing[b] **a cangue (around his neck), obliterating his ears.** [L-I]
   Ominous. [L-P]

****

COMMENTARY

In the overall structure of the *Zhouyi*, Hexagrams 21 and 22 are paired with each other and belong in a group of pairs which is centered around Hexagrams 29 and 30. This latter pair concerns divine powers manifest in the earth's higher and lower places, and the various pairs which belong to this group all develop themes which relate to earthly life under Heaven, particularly in its social aspects and in the general features of its being a temporal (mortal) affair.

Hexagrams 21 and 22 are linked as polar in their concerns: 21 (Biting Through) concerns a covering which conceals something within itself; 22 (Many-colored Ornamentation) concerns a covering which displays, an adorning which relates to the surface and in particular to a festive appearance.

The present hexagram holds images (Lines 1 and 6) which relate to stocks borne on the feet or a cangue worn around one's neck (and this focus on punishment is underlined in the Hexagram Text's characterization of the hexagram as auspicious to use for engaging in litigation). Such obstacles, introduced in punishment for something one has done, are self-brought-on and obliterate part of oneself. .

But the heart of the figure, Lines 2-5, all begin with "bite"; because they involve biting into and through flesh/meat of some sort, they answer more explicitly to the title. No story seems to be involved, but the two types of image (in Lines 1,6; and in Lines 2-5) are connected through the "obliterating" found in Lines 1, 2, and 6. Line 2 involves a biting into flesh which goes so deeply into it that the biter's nose becomes hidden, covered up. Line 3 involves a biting into dried meat which, while it does not encounter anything hard which resists the biting, happens on poison there-- thus on something whose impact back on oneself is potentially injurious. Line 4 involves a slightly different type of dried meat and discovery within it of a metal arrow(head)-- something hard and valuable. Finally, Line 5 involves a biting which again discovers something hard and valuable-- a piece of bronze, perhaps, or of gold.

Overall, the six lines connect as speaking to various forms of concealment, covering, and discovering; in particular, if one notes the emphasis lent by the title-name, they speak to some forms in which one can bite into what covers and can discover something, for better or worse.

****

◆ TEXTUAL NOTES ◆

a. The Mawangdui text omits the *li⁴* (利), but I keep it, since the phrase also appears in 26/3.

b. I read *he⁴* (荷) for *he²* (何).

HEXAGRAM 22

MANY-COLORED ADORNMENT

HEXAGRAM TEXT:
(The occasion calls for a) **sacrifice.** [H-O]
   Slightly beneficial to have a place to go. [H-A]

LINES:
9 at the beginning:
   Adorning their feet with many colors, they reject the carriage and walk. [L-I]

6 at LINE 2:
   Festively adorning their beards.[a] [L-I]

9 at LINE 3:
   Festively adorned and glossy wet in appearance. [L-I]
      As a long-term divination, auspicious. [L-SP]

6 at LINE 4:
   Festively adorned in appearance, and as if fluttering (in the breezes)[b], white horses as if flying along: they are not bandits, it is a marriage-match. [L-I]

6 at LINE 5:
   Festively adorned they go to the hill-garden, the bundles of silk are scanty.[c] [L-I]
      Difficulty, in the end auspicious. [L-P]

9 on top:
   Making white the festively adorned [OR: making the festively adorned be plain]. [L-I]
      Without harmful mishap. [L-P]

****

COMMENTARY

For the place of Hexagram 22 in the overall structure of the *Zhouyi*, and for the meaning of its pairing with Hexagram 21, see the first two paragraphs of the Commentary on Hexagram 21.

The present hexagram tells a story through its variations on a theme: the story of an event in the series of events that culminate in the marriage ceremony.[5]

It begins with the husband-to-be's family setting out to the house of the bride-to-be. Two lines refer to this setting out. In Line 1, the young within the bridegroom-to-be's family gaily adorn their feet and, rejecting riding in the cart, they walk to the bride's family's house.[6] In a complementary image in Line 2, the older men within the bridegroom-to-be's family gaily adorn their beards and presumably also become part of the party of family members going to the bride's family's home.

Next comes two lines referring to the procession en route. Line 3 points to the festively adorned, some of whom are also glossy wet-- presumably the walkers, whose walking has brought forth perspiration, so that their appearance has this added feature.[7] Line 4 points to the festively adorned in another form, horses on which some of the party are riding: themselves white, with silvery and shaggy look, they also are festively adorned. The riders are part of a marriage party, not bandits or thieves.

Finally, two lines referring to the end of the journey. Line 5 brings the party described in the first four lines to the hill-garden where the reception is to take place. But it also points to what they have brought: bundled silks, but only a scanty few. With this we get the first hint of anything amiss in the situation. Line 6 describes the acceptance of those gifts, but does the image point to a fulfillment (despite the sparse gifts), with "white" being like the white of Western weddings, an appropriate color? Or does it point to the finishing of the act, but with "plain" or "white" (signifying the absence of color, of the many-colored) corresponding with the "scanty bundles of silk" and marking a kind of plainness that has become entered into the affair?

****

◆ TEXTUAL NOTES ◆

a. Taking *xu¹* (須) in the sense of *xu¹* (鬚).

b. I read *po²* (旙) as *fan²* (幡), the latter presumably pointing to the fluttering or waving clothing on the riders of the fast-moving horses. [The *bai²* (白) immediately following may have influenced the writing of *fan²* (幡) as *po²* (旙).] Li (*ZTong*, 46) takes *po²* (旙) as a loan for *fan²* (燔) (the reading of one of the traditional versions of the text); it means "burning, flaming". Then taking *han⁴* (翰) according to one commentary's note ("raised head high and upward-looking"), thinking of that as the posture of a speeding horse, and noting its association with "flying" in one poem (263) in the *Book of Poetry*, he characterizes this line as follows: "running the path, the sun shining like a fire burning, the bridegroom and the small youngsters riding white horses flying along. This group of people is a marriage-party, it is not bandits coming."

c. Taking *can²-can²* (戔戔) as *can²-can²* (殘殘).

HEXAGRAM 23

FLAY AND STRIP AWAY

HEXAGRAM TEXT:
   Not beneficial to have a place to go. [H-A]

LINES:
6 at the beginning:
   Flay the ewe[a] starting with the feet. [L-I]
      As an exorcism divination, ominous. [L-SP]

6 at LINE 2:
   Flay the ewe starting with the knee-cap[b]. [L-I]
      As an exorcism divination, ominous. [L-SP]

6 at LINE 3:
   Flay ...[c] [L-I]
      Without harmful mishap. [L-P]

6 at LINE 4:
   Flay the ewe starting with the shoulder[d]. [L-I]
      Ominous. [L-P]

6 at LINE 5:
   Strings of fish for food[e], palace people are favored. [L-I]
      Nothing not beneficial. [L-P]

9 on top:
   Large fruit not eaten. The nobleman gains a chariot, the little man flays-and-strips his hut. [L-I]

****

COMMENTARY

In the overall structure of the *Zhouyi*, Hexagrams 23 and 24 are paired with each other and belong in a group of pairs which is centered around Hexagrams 29 and 30. This latter pair concerns divine powers manifest in the earth's higher and lower places, and the various pairs which belong to this group all develop themes which relate to earthly life under Heaven, particularly in its social aspects and in the general features of its being a temporal (mortal) affair.

Hexagrams 23 and 24 are linked as addressing complementary movements: the flaying which strips away the original skin, is posed over against the turning back which returns to the start and thus restores an original condition, takes one back to one's original place.

The present hexagram develops the phases in an act of flaying a ewe, whether in preparation for an act of sacrifice, or simply for food, is not clear. The series of images start the act of flaying with the feet (Line 1), progress to the knee-cap (Line 2) and to some part of the ewe's body between the knee-cap and the shoulder (the image in Line 3 is missing), and ends with the shoulder (Line 4).

Whether the flaying is preparatory to an act of sacrifice or simply to using the meat as food, the lines delineating it give way to two concluding lines that relate to an occasion for partaking of food, on which presumably (although this is not said) the eating of the ewe-meat was central whereas the things which these two lines point to were subordinate or secondary. Line 5 mentions strings of fish which were eaten, while Line 6 features some large fruits which were not eaten. Accompanying the eating-imagery in each case is further imagery: in Line 5, it is palace people (they are favored), while in Line 6, it is a contrast of noblemen with petty-men (the former as gaining a chariot, the latter as flaying-and-stripping their huts). It is not clear how all of these images are to be understood and connected.

****

◆ TEXTUAL NOTES ◆

a. Here and elsewhere in this set of lines, I read *zang¹* (牂) for *chuang²* (牀).

b. I read *bian¹* (辡) as loan for *bin¹* (髕).

c. The text here has an indefinite pronoun ('it, them') following the "flay". The general pattern in Lines 1-4 suggests this is probably something like an editorial marker to indicate that an undecipherable phrase came after the verb. Such a marker could have been used instead of the editor/copyist simply guessing and writing something. It seems very unlikely to be part of the original text.

d. I read *bo²* (髆) for *fu²* (膚).

e. I read *shi²* (食) for *yi³* (以), following the Mawangdui text.

HEXAGRAM 24

TURNING BACK AND RETURNING

HEXAGRAM TEXT:
(The occasion calls for a) **sacrifice.** [H-O]
Beneficial to have a place to go. [H-A]
Going forth and re-entering without haste, friends come without harmful mishap; they turn around and go back on their way, seven days for the coming and going back. [H-SSI]

9 at the beginning:
Return from not far away. [L-I]
Without great trouble[a], greatly auspicious. [L-P]

6 at LINE 2:
Rest and turn back. [L-I]
Auspicious. [L-P]

6 at LINE 3:
Turn back and return from the riverbank.[b] [L-I]
Danger, without harmful mishap. [L-P]

6 at LINE 4:
Mid-course, turn back alone. [L-I]

6 at LINE 5:
Turn back and return *en masse*. [L-I]
Without troubles. [L-P]

6 on top:
Lose the way, turn back and return.[c] [L-I]
Ominous. [L-P]

****

COMMENTARY

For the place of Hexagram 24 in the overall structure of the *Zhouyi*, and for the meaning of its pairing with Hexagram 23, see the first three paragraphs of the Commentary on Hexagram 23.

The Hexagram Text includes a scene setting image which sets the context for the lines, even though they do not tell a story. It is an image of a leisurely visiting by friends, in which they come and then go back home without incident. To the extent that it functions as a scene setting image, the turning back and returning to where one was before in the lines are a six-fold variation on (the latter part of) such visiting trips.

The first variation, which seems paired with the final variation, is a turning back from a point not distant from where one started-- a turning back which, in its contrast with the final variation did not get far enough to get lost before the turning back and returning to the start took place.

The next two lines seem paired. In isolation, Line 2 could signify several things: stop-and-rest and turn back; cease turning back; be happy and turn back; or even, happy return. In this context, however, as linked with Line 3 and a turning back which reflects a journeying cut short by a dangerous obstacle, the first meaning seems most appropriate. The image then points to a return from an excursion which reached a natural end and resting point before the journeyer(s) turned back. In isolation again, Line 3 could have several meanings, but in contrast with its pair (Line 2), the line image represents a turning back which is occasioned by a dangerous obstacle-- a riverbank. The journeying has been prematurely brought to a halt and forced to turn back in the face of a dangerous obstacle.

The next two images seem also paired in their contrast. Line 4 images a solitary person turning back in mid-journey, while Line 5 speaks of a return *en masse* of a group of persons.

Finally, and as paired with the image of Line 1, Line 6 speaks of turning back after having lost one's way, and thus of a journeying which presumably has gone a good distance before the turning back in question.

There is no story here, or systematic unfolding of character or type. Instead there is a variation on a theme, with some linking of lines through contrasting images. In each case, after some beginning, there is a turning back and return to one's original place-- a restoring, of sorts.

****

◆ TEXTUAL NOTES ◆

a. Or, reading *qi²* (衹) instead of *zhi¹* (祗): "without harm and trouble".

b. This phrase could also be translated: "Hurriedly turn back and return". But then it would lose its meaning-link with Line 2.

c. In the traditional and Mawangdui versions, this line also holds this: "Have a disastrous calamity. Act to mobilize the troops, in the end have great defeat because of the country's ruler. Ominous. Up to 10 years, not able to go on a campaign." This passage is an intrusion from a commentary, which initially interprets the prognostication, then applies the line-image and its prognostication to a particular case (namely, to mobilization of the army). When so applied, then the line-image is ominous; in the end, the country will suffer a great defeat because of the country's ruler, and for up to ten years it will not be able to go on a campaign.

HEXAGRAM 25

PESTILENCE[a]

HEXAGRAM TEXT:[b]
(The occasion calls for a) **grand sacrifice.**
A beneficial divination. [H-O]
Not beneficial to have a place to go. [H-A]

LINES:
9 at the beginning:
A pestilence is current and circulating.[c] [L-I]
Have calamity, without anything beneficial. [L-P]

6 at LINE 2:
Not plant and harvest, not break new ground and till old fields.
[L-I]
It is beneficial to have a place to go.[d] [L-A]

6 at LINE 3:
The disastrous impact of the pestilence: someone fastens it to an ox,
a traveler acquires the villagers' disaster. [L-I]

9 at LINE 4:
A divination of `acceptable'. Without harmful mishap. [L-P]

9 at LINE 5:
The illness due to the pestilence. [L-I]
Do not treat with medicine! [L-A]
Will have joy (= cure)! [L-P]

9 on top:
The pestilence goes.[c] [L-I]
Auspicious. [L-P]

****

COMMENTARY

In the overall structure of the *Zhouyi*, Hexagrams 25 and 26 are paired with each other and belong in a group of pairs which is centered around Hexagrams 29 and 30. This latter pair concerns divine powers manifest in the earth's higher and lower places, and the various pairs which belong to this group all develop themes which relate to earthly life under Heaven, particularly in its social aspects and in the general features of its being a temporal (mortal) affair.

Hexagrams 25 and 26 are linked in the contrast of what they portray as happening in an agricultural village and life. Both hexagrams tell a story-- a type-story, not a historical event; and they do so (particularly Hexagram 26) in an allusive way, not in a detailed setting forth of events. The lines of Hexagram 25 tell of an agricultural village beset by plague (from nature, Heaven-sent); the lines of Hexagram 26 tell of agricultural life blessed by relief from banditry/war and by flourishing animal husbandry (both Heaven-sent blessings).

Once the first and last lines of the present hexagram are restored to proper order, the six lines tell the story of the calamitous coming of a pestilence to an agricultural village.[1] It comes (Line 1), it goes (Line 6), and no reason is discerned in this visitation. But its presence disrupts the regular agricultural rhythms[2] (Line 2). After a scapegoat ritual is attempted in order to get out from under the disastrous impact of the pestilence (Line 3), something else happens (what, is unclear, since the image of Line 4 is missing); whatever further effort at protection against the pestilence is involved, it is to good effect, but still not enough to remove the pestilence. It is only after a pestilence-induced illness spreads (an illness which has a cure, but not through medical treatment) (Line 5) that the pestilence finally departs, apparently of its own accord just as was its coming.

****

◆ TEXTUAL NOTES ◆

a. Following Waley ("The Book of Changes", 131-32) and Shaughnessy (*CZ*, 196-201 and 139), I understand the title-name here to be the name of "some type of plague-like affliction" (Shaughnessy, *CZ*, 139). For the sake of intelligibility I have not used the name but the kind of thing it is as the title-name in English: thus, "pestilence". In the subsequent tradition, how-

ever, the title was understood quite otherwise; taking *wang⁴* (妄) as a loan for
wang⁴ (望), it became "the unexpected", or taking the *wang⁴* (妄) as 'wild-
ness, madness', it was understood as "innocence", "simplicity and sincerity",
or in the double negative, "lacking in recklessness and insincerity".

b. In the traditional and Mawangdui versions, this Text includes another
phrase: "If not correct, then have calamity." This is an intrusive commentary
note which has become taken as text. It is an explanation of the meaning of
the title-name understood as in later times, not in its naming a pestilence but
in its standing for a lack of recklessness and insincerity, a kind of measuring
up to standards of rectitude and sobriety.

c. Lines 1 and 6 have become exchanged in the copying process, so that the
traditional and Mawangdui texts have what I have in Line 1 as Line 6 and
what I have in Line 6 as Line 1. I have restored the order so that Line 1
speaks of the arrival and onset of the pestilence, and Line 6 of its departure.
I also follow the Mawangdui version and restore a *zhi¹* (之) to the phrase in
Line 1 (traditional Line 6); it may have been omitted at some time in the
thought that this Line should have a parallel structure to Line 6 (traditional
Line 1).

d. I follow the Mawangdui version in omitting the "then" of the traditional
text.

HEXAGRAM 26

LARGE ANIMALS

HEXAGRAM TEXT:
A beneficial divination. [H-O]
Beneficial to cross the big river. [H-A]
Auspicious for not eating at home. [H-SP]

LINES:
9 at the beginning:[a]
The cart casts off its axle-support[b]**.** [L-I]
Have danger, beneficial to sacrifice.[c] [L-A]

9 at LINE 2:[a]
Go so far as to form a chariot-barrier for protection. [L-I]
Beneficial to have a place to go. [L-A]

9 at LINE 3:[a]
Good horses, pursuit .[3] [L-I]
A beneficial hardship-divination. [L-SP]

6 at LINE 4:
The horn-protecting thwart of a young ox. [L-I]
Greatly auspicious. [L-P]

6 at LINE 5:
A gelded pig's fangs. [L-I]
Auspicious. [L-P]

9 on top:
Receive[d] **Heaven's blessings**[e]**.** [L-I]
Auspicious.[f] [L-P]

****

COMMENTARY

For the place of Hexagram 26 in the overall structure of the *Zhouyi*, and for the meaning of its pairing with Hexagram 25, see the first three paragraphs of the Commentary on Hexagram 25.

Once the images are distributed through the first three lines in the present hexagram, the six lines tell the story of Heaven's blessings.

The beginning is with a brief incident whose exposition occupies the first three lines. Line 1 begins that exposition, with the image of travelers whose chariot(s) burst the axle-supports or axle-bindings, resulting in temporary immobilization. Line 2, presupposing the immobilization and resultant vulnerability, points to actions taken to protect against what would be a common threat to travelers of the time, bandits. The chariots are used to form a protective barrier. Then Line 3 speaks of the arrival of help on good horses, and the pursuit of the attackers (bandits, say) whose coming had been the provocation for the defensive use of the chariots.

This forms the background for the next two lines, which address the prospering agricultural life to which the travelers have been enabled safely to return. Together their images point to a flourishing animal husbandry (in keeping with the title-name of the hexagram). Line 4 images the device which protects the horns of a young ox while they are growing; Line 5 images a gelded pig which is flourishing, its vigor pointed to through its fangs.

The image of the final line attests that in their rescue from attackers, and in the flourishing livestock they find on their safe return, the persons involved have been receiving Heaven's blessings.

****

◆ TEXTUAL NOTES ◆

a. In the traditional and the Mawangdui texts, Line 3 has two images, and Line 1 none; if one takes this as reflecting a copy error and moves the image of Line 2 to Line 1 and one of the images of Line 3 to Line 2, the text will resume a normal form, and a story will begin to emerge, told through the lines of this hexagram.

b. Or: "bursts its axle-bindings". See Textual Notes b and c, Hexagram 9, for variants in the comparable phrase there (Line 3); I read *tuo¹ fu⁴* (脫輹).
c. I read *si⁴* (祀) for *ji³* (己). The traditional and Mawangdui readings would

translate: "beneficial to self".

d. I read *he⁴* (荷) for *he²* (何).

e. I read *hu¹* (祜) for *qu²* (衢); Gao reads *xiu¹* (休), with the same meaning ("blessings").

f. I read *ji²* (吉) for *heng¹* (亨), to keep the distinction between the latter (whose characteristic use is in the Hexagram Texts) and the former (used almost exclusively in the Line Statements). There is no difference in meaning here.

HEXAGRAM 27

CHEEKS AND JAWS

HEXAGRAM TEXT:
> Beneficial to cross the big river. [H-A]
> As a dwelling-divination, auspicious.[a] [H-SP]

LINES:
9 at the beginning:
> Set aside your own numinous turtle, contemplate our hanging cheeks and jaws. [L-I]
>> Ominous. [L-P]

6 at LINE 2:
> Full cheeks and jaws: scrape a shin[b] on the cheeks of the (grave-) mound. [L-I]
>> Ominous for campaigning. [L-SP]

6 at LINE 3:
> Offending[c] cheeks and jaws. [L-I]
>> For ten years, do not use. [L-A]
>> As a divination, ominous, without anything beneficial.   [L-P]

6 at LINE 4:
> Full cheeks and jaws: a tiger looking around intently-and-longingly[d], its desire far-reaching[e]. [L-I]
>> Auspicious. Without harmful mishap. [L-P]

6 at LINE 5:
> Compliant cheeks and jaws. [L-I]
>> Danger. [L-P]

9 on top:
> Contemplate the cheeks and jaws (of others), seek by one's own effort to fill one's mouth. [L-I]

As a divination, auspicious. [L-P]

****

COMMENTARY

In the overall structure of the *Zhouyi*, Hexagrams 27 and 28 are paired with each other and belong in a group of pairs which is centered around Hexagrams 29 and 30. This latter pair concerns divine powers manifest in the earth's higher and lower places, and the various pairs which belong to this group all develop themes which relate to earthly life under Heaven, particularly in its social aspects and in the general features of its being a temporal (mortal) affair.

Hexagrams 27 and 28 are linked as giving different expression to a common theme-- excess, in particular, excess on a grand scale. In Hexagram 27 (Cheeks and jaws), it is set forth in contrast with deficiency, and develops by reference to the contrast of the haves vs. the have-nots, and the attitudes of both. In Hexagram 28 (Going greatly beyond the norm), it is set forth in contrast with a norm, and develops by reference to the contrast of either too much or too little, to a pushing beyond the norm in this way or in the opposite way.

After restoration of some textual dislocation, the present hexagram forms a set of variations on a theme, in which Lines 1 and 6, 2 and 4, and 3 and 5, are linked with each other. The title-name of this hexagram-- cheeks and jaws-- refers to that part of the face and countenance in two connections: one, eating, and the other, looks as manifesting one's feelings and attitude. In both cases, throughout the lines the reference to eating and to looks has as its horizon the matter of 'having' (in particular, of 'having enough and more than enough') and of attitudes based upon this. Thus the lines address the matter of great excess through images of the cheeks-and-jaws either as locus of fulness/emptiness or as manifestation of an attitude.

Lines 1 and 6 are counterparts: in the one case a person is called upon to set aside his own fine food and note the lack of food of others, and in the other the contemplation of the full mouth of others inspires an effort to fill one's own mouth through one's own efforts. Where there is need to set aside preoccupation with the fine goods of life in one's own case and to attend to the needs of others, as in the first case, the prognostication is 'ominous' both because of the disparity of 'have vs. have not' attested in the image and because of the prior heedlessness implied in the very need to enjoin such attention when it is of the essence for the King to care for the people. Such heed-lessness does not bode well for the future. (Recall, here, the recent history of Zhou Kings prior to King Xuan, especially the latter's father, King Li.) Where there is inspiration by the fulness of others to seek a comparable full-ness for oneself, the linkage with Line 1 suggests that the fullness aspired to here is not one which need make one oblivious to the needs of others.

Within the poles defined in Lines 1 and 6, the four intervening lines have two different types of linkage. In the one case, there are two further line-pairs: Lines 2 and 4, and Lines 3 and 5. In the other case, Lines 2 and 3 go with Line 1, and Lines 4 and 5 go with Line 6; in this latter connection of the lines, the first three go together because their images symbolize a having which is arrogant and oblivious, while the last three lines go together because their images symbolize a having which is worthy of emulation and increase.

Taking these four interior lines one by one:

Line 2 has two images: the first, of someone well-fed and (if we recall Line 1) with the attitude that often goes with that, of arrogance and of ob-liviousness to others; the second, of that person scraping a shin on a mound (the word is often used for a grave-mound, which would give the image even greater poignancy and point). This same initial image is found in Line 4 also, but followed up there differently. Together, the images suggest a cer-tain obliviousness to oneself as well as to others.

The image in Line 3, that of an offending set to the jaw which gives the countenance an offensive character, seems in the context of the hexagram pair and its theme to express an attitude of those who have enough and more than enough-- a kind of arrogance which might take offense at any perceived challenge and become offensive in the response. Such an attitude is nothing to be acted upon, but is something ominous in its import. (Again recall here the character of King Li, in the very recent background for the author of the *Zhouyi.*)

Like Line 2, Line 4 has two images: the first, of someone well-fed; the second, of a tiger looking around intently, its desire reaching out in the dis-tance beyond what is directly present. If Line 2 gets its sense for the meaning of "full" from Line 1 so that it there expresses the attitude that often goes with full cheeks, one of arrogance and of obliviousness to others, Line 4 seems to get its sense for the meaning of the introductory phrase from Line 6, where the fullness has the character of a fulfillment which is desirable and able to inspire emulation by others. Here, that fulness is nothing to rest satisfied with but is worthy of expansion; but as the tiger-image suggests, such expansion may require concentrated effort. (Recall, here, the repeated exhortations in the *Book of Historical Documents* to the King, to remember the grand unfinished work and to labor at it, not simply be content with an enjoyment of things as they are.)

Finally, the image in Line 5, a compliant and inoffensive countenance and set of the cheeks and jaws, seems in the context of the set of lines here to attest to the opposite attitude to that expressed in Line 3. It concerns someone who 'has', indeed, but (as the good King in relation to the people) who is giving and generous, compliant with the Mandate that involves being ready to minister to the people's needs. Yet there is danger in this, if it be taken as a sign of weakness-- as it might, in the increasingly harsh age of late Western Zhou.

****

◆ TEXTUAL NOTES ◆

a. Some textual displacement and exchange are evident in this Hexagram. To restore the text, I have transferred an image and accompanying prognostication, which occur in the Hexagram Text of the traditional and the Mawangdui texts, to Line 6, to form the line-image and prognostication there. A part of traditional Line 6 (and its counterpart in Line 5) have in turn been transferred here, to serve as the action-element: the phrases ("it is beneficial to cross the big river" and "it's not acceptable to cross the big river") never occur in the lines except in these two cases. I have also excised in traditional Line 5 a two-character repetition of a phrase in Line 2 (fu^2 $jing^1$: 拂脛: see Note b. below), and have assigned the other elements of traditional Line 6 (you^2 yi^2; li^4: 由頤厲) to Line 5. The ji^2 (吉) of the traditional Line 6 remains as part of the restored line.

b. I read $jing^1$ (脛) for $jing^4$ (經).

c. I read fu^2 (咈) for fu^2 (拂).

d. I read dan^1-dan^1 (眈眈) for dan^1-dan^1 (耽耽).

e. I read you^1-you^1 (悠悠) for zhu^2-zhu^2 (逐逐)

HEXAGRAM 28

GOING GREATLY BEYOND THE NORM

HEXAGRAM TEXT:[a]
(The occasion calls for a) **sacrifice.** [H-O]
  Beneficial to have a place to go. [H-A]

LINES:
6 at the beginning:
  An offering-mat made using white cogon-grass. [L-I]
    Without harmful mishap. [L-P]

9 at LINE 2:
  The withered willow bears shoots, the 'old man' gets his maiden wife.
  [L-I]
    Nothing is not beneficial. [L-P]

9 at LINE 3:
  The ridge-pole sags[b]**.** [L-I]
    Ominous. [L-P]

9 at LINE 4:
  The ridge-pole bulges upward. [L-I]
    Auspicious, but have difficulty of another kind. [L-P]

9 at LINE 5:
  The withered willow bears flowers, the 'old maid' gets her young husband. [L-I]
    No blame, no praise. [L-P]

6 on top:
  Cross over the river-ford, immerse-and-obliterate the crown of one's head. [L-I]
    Ominous, but without harmful mishap.[c] [L-P]

****

COMMENTARY

For the place of Hexagram 28 in the overall structure of the *Zhouyi*, and for the meaning of its pairing with Hexagram 27, see the first three paragraphs of the Commentary on Hexagram 27.

The present hexagram is composed of paired lines (3/4, 2/5, 1/6) which express deviations from the norm like 'too much vs. too little'.

The outer lines (1 and 6) concern crucial transitions in human life. Line 1 images a transition from the human world to the divine world. Its image is the offering-mat used in ritual as the medium for the passage of offerings to the spirits; in this case, the use of this kind of grass for making that mat goes to an extreme in the expression of respect.[4] Line 6, by contrast, concerns the dangerous passage from one part of the human world to another. It is the image of fording a river, in which the venturer gets in over his head and gets wet to the very top-- an extreme of a different sort.

The image in the case of Lines 3 and 4 is the ridge-pole. The norm for the ridge-pole to carry out its function well is the straight ridge-pole. The deviations are its bulging up and its sagging downward. The latter is threatening because of the likelihood of its breaking; in the former case the ridge-pole may still be able to carry out is function with such an upward bend to it, but the bulge may bring other problems with it.

The image in the case of Lines 2 and 5 is marriage. The norm here is persons close to the same age. The deviations are combinations of young and old in the different sexes: an older man (beyond the norm) taking a maiden wife (Line 2), or an older woman (beyond the norm) gaining a young man for husband (Line 5). While both cases are greatly beyond the norm, a different judgment is given in each case. For while the introductory images in both cases-- the withered willow bearing shoots (Line 2) and the withered willow bearing flowers (Line 5)-- point to both marriages as potentially productive, the prognostications differ: for the older man/younger woman, "nothing not beneficial", but for the older woman/younger man, only "no blame, no praise".

****

◆ TEXTUAL NOTES ◆

a. Included in the traditional and Mawangdui versions of the Hexagram Text here is a two-character phrase (棟撓: *dong⁴ nao²* : "Ridge-pole sags") which I have excised. It is an editorial note recording the correct reading of the phrase in Line 3: it is 'sags' rather than 'bends' (a difference in the classifier-element of the character). Its occurrence here suggests that the Hexagram Text area was used as repository for notes which relate to Line Statements as well as to the Hexagram Text itself.

b. I read *nao²* (撓) for *nao⁴* (橈), in keeping with the misplaced commentary note referred to in a. above.

c. The conjunction of "ominous" and "without harmful mishap" here can be understood as I have done in the text, but it is a rather uneasy conjunction. Other instances of several prognostication words occurring together have a similar uneasy feeling to them, enough to suggest to some editors and commentators that these words represent a collection of the record of different versions of the text. As a mere collection, they are not to be read together; indeed, the collector did not want to decide which was 'right' but simply collected what was said. Gao (*ZGJ*, 98) claims the *wu² jiu⁴* (无咎) here is a gloss. See his discussion of this and other like cases, starting from a passage in the *Hanshu* which claims that some early versions of the text lacked *wu² jiu⁴* and *hui³ wang²* (悔亡) in certain places.

HEXAGRAM 29

PIT[a]

HEXAGRAM TEXT:[a]
  The occasion calls for a sacrifice. [H-O]
  Traveling has its rewards[b]. [H-SP]

LINES:
6 at the beginning:[a]
  Double pit, entry into a pitfall. [L-I]
    Have captives, bind their hearts. [L-A]
    Ominous. [L-P]

9 at LINE 2:
  The pit has a steep drop-off. [L-I]
    Seek small catch. [L-A]

6 at LINE 3:
  Arrive at this pit, the pit is steep and deep[c], enter into the pitfall.
  [L-I]
    Do not act! [L-A]

6 at LINE 4:
  Wine in the flask, tureens in two's: use earthen vessels. Bring them
  bound through the window. [L-I]
    In the end, without harmful mishap. [L-P]

9 at LINE 5:
  The pit's not full, the Earth-spirit[d] is already appeased. [L-I]
    Without harmful mishap. [L-P]

6 on top:
  Tie using two-strand black cord and three-strand braid, put in the
  thickly-growing thorns; three years, no catch. [L-I]
    Ominous. [L-P]

****

COMMENTARY

In its overall structure the *Zhouyi* begins (Hexagrams 1 and 2) with the seasonal rhythm and life in an agriculture-dependent mode fitting itself into that rhythm, and ends (Hexagrams 63 and 64) with life placed within the matrix of the collective political/historical venturing which the Mandate of Heaven and the Shang and Zhou leadership of human life on earth provides.

Within these brackets, the thirty remaining hexagram pairs are grouped into five sets, the first of which (3/4 through 15/16) centers on Hexagrams 9 and 10. This pair makes as theme something which might well be brought home to the author in his times, that our human life-- this venturing and risking on earth under the heavens-- endemically becomes involved in troubles, in troubled situations.

In terms of this overall structure of the set of sixty-four hexagrams, Hexagrams 29 and 30 are the central and organizing pair in the next group of pairs (17/18 through 41/42).

Basically, Hexagrams 29 and 30 involve two contrasting modifications of the earth, one (the mountains and hills) rising up above the rest of the earth's surface, and one (various types of pit) descending down into the earth's surface. In each case there is a divine power intimately associated with the modification and significant for human life on earth under heaven. One is the earth-spirit, the other is a mountain-spirit. Both forces are associated primarily with darkness, threats, and the more questionable side of the presence of earth in human life-- in contrast with that presence, and its link with heaven, as adumbrated in Hexagrams 1/2. And as the ending of the line-sets in both hexagrams indicates (both end on a note of disappointment), these powerful manifestations of earth are somewhat inscrutable and not dependable in their support. Finally, in both Hexagrams 29 and 30 the images are drawn from the aspects of life relating to hunting and the involvement in warfare (something closely linked with hunting).[5]

Hexagram 29 relates to pits which originally were hunting pits but eventually gained other uses. The first three lines speak of elements of hunting and their function; the second three lines speak to a ritual use of the pits, seeking to ensure hunting success.

Line 1 images a pit constructed as a hunting tool, holding a pit within the pit so that whatever enters into the first pit enters into a (further) pitfall. Line 2 images a pit with steep sides; again it is a hunting device, but if it accumulates water and becomes a fish pond, the hunting in question could be for fish. Finally, Line 3 puts the images in the first two lines to work, so to speak, by offering a generalized action in which the factors imaged before come into play. Something, arriving at the steep-sided and deep pit, enters into the pitfall: the trap works!

Line 4 begins the imaging of the ritual function of such pits. The ritual, addressed to the Earth-spirit accessible through pits, is an effort to appease that spirit and to assure successful hunting. The initial allusion to the cere-mony itself in Line 4 by reference to certain features of it-- the wine and earthen vessels, and the removal of the bound prisoners through the window of the enclosing structure in which they were being held-- is completed in Line 5, with the image of sacrificed prisoners being stacked in the hunting-pit. Now in the case in question, even before the pit is full there are signs that the Earth-spirit is appeased. And yet, Line 6, addressing an after-step to this act of sacrifice-- the remaining prisoners, tied with special cord, are put into a thorn-thicket-- concludes: "there was no catch for three years". Apparently the ritual appeasement of the Earth-spirit was not sufficient, or at least, it did not immediately lead to hunting success.

****

◆ TEXTUAL NOTES ◆

a. In the traditional and the Mawangdui texts the Hexagram Text starts off with what seems like an alternative Line 1, which more directly anticipates the sacrificial elements of Lines 4-6 than does the traditional Line 1. The title-name for the Hexagram has mistakenly been collapsed with the begin-ning of this alternative Line 1, which starts with the title-name modified by a "double". I treat the simple character as the title-name. I also transfer the alternative Line 1 to Line 1, integrating it with what is there so as to intr-oduce an action-element in this Line. That element might also be translated: "offer captives in sacrifice to bind the hearts (of others)". An alternative way of treating the text: given the focus in the second half of the set of lines on sacrifice, and the presence of a phrase concerning captives in alternative Line 1, it seems plausible to see this alternative Line as in fact forming Line 3, with its introduction of the ritual theme being prepared for by delineation of the other (hunting) functions of the pit. Thus: Line 1 would set forth one feature of the pit important for its hunting function: "the pit is a double-pit with steep sides". Then Line 2 would put that pit to one of its common uses: "seeking a small catch, make them come to the pit, the pit is steep and deep, they enter into the pit-fall". Then in Line 3 comes the sacrificial use, related to hunting still: "offer captives in sacrifice to bind the heart (of the Earth Spirit)"

b. I read *shang⁴* (尚) as *shang³* (賞).

c. I read *zhen³* (枕) as *chen²* (沈).

d. I read *qi²* (祇) for *zhi¹* (祇).

HEXAGRAM 30

MOUNTAIN-SPIRIT[a]

HEXAGRAM TEXT:
(The occasion calls for a) **sacrifice.**
A beneficial divination. [H-O]
   For raising cattle, auspicious. [H-SP]

LINES:
9 at the beginning:
   Stepping hesitantly, in respect for them. [L-I]
   Without harmful mishap. [L-P]

6 at LINE 2:
   Yellow mountain-spirit. [L-I]
   Greatly auspicious. [L-P]

9 at LINE 3:
   **The sunset mountain-spirit: if you do not drum on pots and sing,
   there will be a great 'alas' from the elders.** [L-I]
   Ominous. [L-P]

9 at LINE 4:
   **Sudden-like is its coming, the likes of fire-burning, the likes of
   something acting in a death-like way, in a discard-like way.** [L-I]

6 at LINE 5:
   (This brings) **forth tears flowing-like, grief alas-like.** [L-I]
   Difficulty.[b] [L-P]

9 on top:
   **The King acts to go forth on a campaign, he has a celebration and
   cuts off heads, but his catch is not the enemy chief.**[c] [L-I]
   Without harmful mishap. [L-P]

****

COMMENTARY

For the place of Hexagram 30 in the overall structure of the *Zhouyi*, and for the meaning of its pairing with Hexagram 29, see the first four paragraphs of the Commentary on Hexagram 29.

Hexagram 30 relates to a numinous presence from out of the mountains, a mountain-spirit which is religiously ambivalent but apparently is predominantly threatening. The lines do not tell a simple story, but they do set forth an account of an incident and of possible responses and meanings for it.

The situation, as initially characterized, is a wartime one in which one steps hesitantly, in respect for the enemy (and for the spirits as well, presumably) (Line 1). The incident is the arrival of the mountain-spirit upon the scene at this time when the people are in a wary, hesitant mood-- presumably as being on the verge of a battle. The mountain-spirit is an ambivalent presence. Thus Lines 2 and 3 set forth alternatives. The first is that the arriving mountain-spirit is yellow; not only is yellow an auspicious color but it is the color of earth, and a yellow mountain-spirit (the spirit of one part of the earth) would carry with it the supportive attitude of earth as a whole. Thus such arrival would be a very favorable affair. The other alternative is that, coming at sunset, its presence is a threatening one, and that if one does not drum the earthen vessel and sing (to ward it off and/or to appease it), then the great-elders will know an 'alas', grief (Line 3).

The next two lines set forth what would happen if it were not favorable and were not warded off in this way. In its grief-bringing presence it would be a suddenly-arriving power, flaring up like a fire, and acting in the manner of a death-bringing power which rejects and casts aside (Line 4). In consequence of such a manifestation, tears will come forth flowing-wise, and grieving express itself 'alas'-wise (Line 5).

The final line (Line 6) brings attention back to the military situation at hand: in the setting defined by the mountain-spirit as an effective presence, if the King goes forth to campaign, he may be victorious in one sense, and hold a celebration and cut off heads. But the catch of his successful campaign will not be what he set out to catch, the enemy chief. Presumably that means it will be something of a pyrrhic victory.

****

◆ TEXTUAL NOTES ◆

a. Here and in the lines of the hexagram, I read this *li²* (離) as *li²* (离). The more complex version of the simpler character could, of course, be a loan character standing for it, but this emendation brings out the meaning more unambiguously.

b. I read the *ji²* (吉) in the traditional and Mawangdui versions as a copy-error for *lin⁴* (吝).

c. Shaughnessy (*CZ*, 298) takes *huo⁴ chou³* (獲醜: to bag [i.e. capture] a chief) as the "formulaic expression of military victory" found also in certain *Shijing* poems that date to the reign of King Xuan. He also claims (22, 292, 298) that Jia is a place name (as in Hexagram 17/Line 5) and would thus translate: "The king herewith goes out to campaign at Jia: he cuts off heads and bags their leader." [He also reads *fei³* (匪) as loan for *bi³* (彼) in this passage.] For his sense of the historical background involved here, see 145-46: "it is not unlikely that the 'king' referred to here is in fact King Xuan and that the campaign was against the Xianyun...".

HEXAGRAM 31

CUTTING OFF

HEXAGRAM TEXT:[a]
(The occasion calls for a) **sacrifice.**
A beneficial divination. [H-O]

LINES:
6 at the beginning:
  Cut off the (big) toe. [L-I]

6 at LINE 2:[b]
  Cut off the lower leg (= calf). [L-I]
    Ominous. [L-P]

9 at LINE 3:
  Cut off the thigh, grasp the bone-marrow[c]**.** [L-I]
    Difficulty.[d] [L-P]

9 at LINE 4:[e]
  As a divination, auspicious, troubles vanish. [L-P]

9 at LINE 5:
  Cut off the spinal flesh. [L-I]
    Without troubles. [L-P]

6 on top:
  Cut off the cheeks and jowls. [L-I]
    Difficulty.[f] [L-P]

****

COMMENTARY

In the overall structure of the *Zhouyi*, Hexagrams 31 and 32 are paired with each other and belong in a group of pairs which is centered around Hexagrams 29 and 30. This latter pair concerns divine powers manifest in the earth's higher and lower places, and the various pairs which belong to this group all develop themes which relate to earthly life under Heaven, particularly in its social aspects and in the general features of its being a temporal (mortal) affair.

Like Hexagrams 27 and 28, which link with each other around the theme of excess, in particular, excess on a grand scale, Hexagrams 31 and 32 link with each other around the theme of length. But they set forth the theme in different ways. 31 involves cutting off, thus a shortening and lessening in size and length; the term, as a noun, means "dismemberment", and the lines take up with cutting up a ritual sacrificial animal by severing this or that part. 32 involves making endure and last, extending and stabilizing; the term, as a noun, means "enduring, endurance".

The present hexagram has an ordered structure, with a series of images (only Line 4 lacks an image) that shows the act of dismembering represented in the title-name moving in ascending fashion on the body of the creature being dismembered.[6] Beginning with the toes (Line 1), and moving to the lower leg (Line 2), then the thigh (Line 3),[7] and then the spinal flesh on the back (Line 5), the series ends with an area of the face (Line 6). There is a missing image in Line 4, which from its place in the series would seem likely to be the waist; barring that, the series is complete from bottom to top and shows an order comparable to that of the lines of Hexagram 52.

****

◆ TEXTUAL NOTES ◆

a. In the course of the tradition of interpretation this hexagram became read according to a different sense of its title-name, namely, "to influence, to stimulate" (including "to woo"). In the traditional and Mawangdui versions, the Hexagram Text contains a prognostication-item ("For taking a maiden as wife, auspicious.") which seems to be a later addition reflecting that sort of interpretation of the meaning of the whole line-figure.

b. In the traditional and Mawangdui versions this line has a prognostication element ("Auspicious for dwelling.") added later when the meaning of the title-name was no longer taken as "cutting off".

c. I read *sui²* (隨) as *sui³* (髓).

d. I follow the Mawangdui version in omitting the *wang³* (往) present in the traditional texts. It presumably crept in under the influence of the *sui²* (隨), thus probably represents a later addition.

e. In the traditional and Mawangdui versions, this Line contains a phrase ("(In the) unsettled/unsettling coming and going, a friend follows your thoughts.") which is an intrusion from a commentary. Without the image, however, it is difficult to see why it occurs here, and under what sense of the meaning of the title-name it seemed relevant.

f. I emend *she²* (舌: 'tongue') to read *lin⁴* (吝: 'difficulty'). It would be an easy copy error to make, especially given that the copyist would be thinking of the face. Gao (*ZGJ*, 110) and Shaughnessy (*CZ*, 327) emend to *ji²* (吉), but the latter adds: "But, as Gao himself notes in a later study..., it would be very difficult under any circumstances to construe an injury to the face as being auspicious."

HEXAGRAM 32

MAKE ENDURE AND LAST

HEXAGRAM TEXT:
   (The occasion calls for a) **sacrifice.**[a]
   A beneficial divination. [H-O]
      Beneficial to have a place to go. [H-A]

LINES:
6 at the beginning:
   The dredging is continual-and-everlasting. [L-I]
      As a divination, ominous, without anything beneficial. [L-P]

9 at LINE 2:
   Troubles vanish. [L-P]

9 at LINE 3:
   Not make the catch[b] **last, someone presents him with prepared flavorful food.** [L-I]
      As a divination, difficulty. [L-P]

9 at LINE 4:
   Hunting, there is no game. [L-I]

6 at LINE 5:
   Make the catch[b] **last.** [L-I]
      As a divination, auspicious for a wife, ominous for a husband.
      [L-SP]

6 on top:
   The quaking is continual-and-everlasting. [L-I]
      Ominous. [L-P]

                    ****

COMMENTARY

For the place of Hexagram 32 in the overall structure of the *Zhouyi*, and for the meaning of its pairing with Hexagram 31, see the first two paragraphs of the Commentary on Hexagram 31.

The present hexagram may have an ordered structure, with Lines 1 and 6, 2 and 4, 3 and 5, being linked. But the absence of an image in Line 2 makes it impossible to tell for sure. At best one can surmise: given that Lines 3, 4, and 5 concern hunting, and that 3 and 5 begin with parallel phrases about making the catch last, it is likely that Line 2 concerned hunting and if it were parallel with Line 4 as 5 is with 3, then it would concern the catching of game and would read: 'hunt, have game'. Only Line 4 contains an additional image-phrase. Offered in the hunting context of the four interior lines including the first phrase of this line, it addresses the matter of not being able to make last such catch as one has had on the expedition. The embarrassing alternative: someone has provided food of a different sort-- delicacies, prepared and flavorful food, not game.

In contrast with Lines 2-5, Lines 1 and 6 do not seem to concern hunting and the sort of "lasting" which is involved in making the catch last. But they do echo each other in form, involving 2-character phrases, the second character in each case being *heng²* (恆), the title-name. In these phrases *heng²* apparently functions in a verbal rather than a nominal fashion grammatically. In Line 1, the image refers to the activity of cleaning out and deepening streams or wells; such activity needs to be done, but perpetual dredging is eventually counterproductive. In Line 6, the image seems to refer to a quaking and shaking, of the sort that might be involved e.g. in an earthquake or tremor; is the perpetual quaking that of a long series of fore-shocks and after-shocks? In any case, what the images share is a sense to *heng²* as a 'lasting'. This, together with the "making last" of Lines 3 and 5, underlines the contrast of the meaning of the Hexagram as a whole with that of Hexagram 31, whose pointer into a 'cutting off' would cut short any lasting.

****

◆ TEXTUAL NOTES ◆

a. I have excised an intrusive and non-functional *wu² jiu⁴* (无咎).

b. I read *de²* (得) for *de²* (德); each is a common loan for the other.

HEXAGRAM 33

PIGLET[a]

HEXAGRAM TEXT:[b]
(The occasion calls for a) **minor sacrifice.**
A beneficial divination. [H-O]

LINES:
6 at the beginning:
The piglet's tail. [L-I]
Do not act to have a place to go. [L-A]
Danger. [L-P]

6 at LINE 2:
Tether[c] it using yellow-ox rawhide, none is capable of escaping[d] from it. [L-I]

9 at LINE 3:
A trussed-up piglet. [L-I]
Have illness, danger; to keep the male and female servants is auspicious. [L-SP]

9 at LINE 4:
A fine piglet. [L-I]
Auspicious for a nobleman, not for a little man. [L-SP]

9 at LINE 5:
An excellent piglet .[1] [L-I]
As a divination, auspicious. [L-P]

9 on top:
A fat piglet. [L-I]
Nothing not beneficial. [L-P]

****

COMMENTARY

In the overall structure of the *Zhouyi*, Hexagrams 33 and 34 are paired with each other and belong in a group of pairs which is centered around Hexagrams 29 and 30. This latter pair concerns divine powers manifest in the earth's higher and lower places, and the various pairs which belong to this group all develop themes which relate to earthly life under Heaven, particularly in its social aspects and in the general features of its being a temporal (mortal) affair.

Hexagrams 33 and 34 are linked in their contrasting reference to harm. Hexagram 33 speaks to the kind of innocent harmlessness that is embodied in a little pig and which suits the piglet for use in religious sacrifice (an act of submissiveness to the divine); Hexagram 34 speaks to the contrasting kind of infliction of harm, especially intentionally through aggressive action, which has no single image-focus but is expressed in a variety of human and animal actions and sufferings.

The present hexagram lacks the title-name only in Line 2; in all the other five lines, the title-name appears in a 2-character phrase which in each case is the line image-- thus a kind of variation on a theme. There is no story-telling, and yet ....

The beginning focuses on the piglet's tail; it is not said, but was it cut off, as part of the raising that would properly fatten and fit it?

The image in Line 2-- unlike the rest in not being a two-character phrase containing the title-name-- is of a tethering, presumably of the pigs which are being raised and fattened to serve eventually as sacrificial animals.

The last four lines (in the figure, incidentally, they are all solid-lines) seem to speak to the so-prepared-and-raised piglet as readied for the sacrifice: it is trussed up (Line 3), and then commented on as to its suitability for use as a sacrificial offering (fine, excellent, fat: Lines 4-6).

Although the lines make no explicit reference to sacrifice or ritual, that seems the plausible context. When related to its counterpart in the pair with which the present pair is linked (Hexagram 26: Large Animals), the piglet may be seen as one of Heaven's blessings as well as a creature fit for sacrifice and the act of giving *to* Heaven.

****

◆ TEXTUAL NOTES ◆

a. Here and throughout the lines of this hexagram, I read the *dun⁴* (遯) of the traditional and the Mawangdui versions as *tun²* (豚).

b. I read the text as *xiao³ heng¹ li⁴ zhen¹* (小亨利貞), and take the reversal of the first two characters in the traditional and the Mawangdui versions (*heng¹ xiao³*) to be a copy error. See Hexagram 63 for the same emendation. These are the only two cases where the *li⁴ zhen¹* phrase is modified in the traditional version of the Hexagram Texts, whereas *heng¹* is commonly modified (12 times by *yuan²*, 2 by *xiao³* in addition to the two in question here). In the Mawangdui version of Hexagram 58 we also find *heng¹ xiao³ li⁴ zhen¹*, although the traditional text has no *xiao³* at all. [This reversal might also be called for in Hexagram 22, which reads *heng¹ xiao³ li⁴ you³ you¹ wang³* (亨小利有攸往). Reversal here would make both phrases fit normal patterns, instead of just one.]

c. I read *zhi²* (執) as *zhi²* (繫).

d. I read *shuo¹* (說) as *tuo¹* (脫); another possible reading is *tuo¹* (挩).

HEXAGRAM 34

GREAT HARM[a]

HEXAGRAM TEXT:
 A beneficial divination. [H-O]

LINES:
9 at the beginning:
 Harm to the foot.[b] [L-I]
  Ominous for going on a campaign. [L-SP]

9 at LINE 2:
 Take captives.[c] [L-I]
  As a divination, auspicious. [L-P]

9 at LINE 3:
 The ram butts the fence, entangles[d] **his horns.** [L-I]
  If the little man acts (in this situation), **injury** (will ensue);[2] **if the
   nobleman acts, it will not.** [L-A]
  As a divination, danger. [L-P]

9 at LINE 4:[e]
 The fence splits open, (the ram) does not get entangled.[d] [L-I]
  As a divination, auspicious, troubles vanish. [L-P]

6 at LINE 5:
 He lost his sheep at Yi.[3] [L-I]
  Without troubles. [L-P]

6 on top:[f]
 **The ram butts the fence, and is not able to draw back or to push
  through.** [L-I]
  Without anything beneficial. [L-P]

****

COMMENTARY

For the place of Hexagram 34 in the overall structure of the *Zhouyi*, and for the meaning of its pairing with Hexagram 33, see the first three paragraphs of the Commentary on Hexagram 33.

The present hexagram lacks the title-name in half its lines, and when one examines the collection of images in the six lines there is no immediately obvious coherence and rationale. But in each case the image is of some sort of aggressive act, and with it some sort of harm or injury. Rather than tell a story, the lines offer variations on a theme.

The first two lines focus on human beings. Line 1 concerns the feet (or perhaps, the toes), and injury to them. Line 2 focuses on an aggressive act indeed (taking captives), but along with Line 5 it lacks an explicit element of physical harm.

The final four lines in the hexagram all concern sheep, and in two of the cases explicitly but in a third implicitly, rams. Through this imagery, the theme of aggressive action, with harm to others but also some kind of difficulty for the perpetrator of the aggression, is sounded continually.

Thus in Line 3, a ram butts a fence and suffers as a result-- becoming entangled, or weakening his horns (depending on which meaning of the term one uses). Line 4 has a different issue to the ram's butting the fence: the fence splits open and he does not entangle himself in it.

Line 5 seems to be an allusion to the story of Yin Prince Hai, although it might be to other incidents involving other people.[4] It seems to link with the image in Line 2, at least as not involving explicit reference to physical harm but involving an aggressive act that could entail harm (and in the case of the incident with Prince Hai, did-- he lost his life).

Finally the image in Line 6, continuing the 'ram'-imagery of 3 and 4, also links with Line 1 through the immobilization which each involves: the ram butts the fence and is not able to draw back or to push through.

****

◆ TEXTUAL NOTES ◆

a. Here and throughout the lines of this hexagram, I read the *zhuang*[4] (壯) of the traditional and Mawangdui texts as a loan for *qiang*[1] (戕).

b. For an alternative line-image that has become displaced but should appear with this line, see Textual Note e. below.

c. This phrase, as a result of faulty line-division, appears at the end of Line 1 in the traditional and Mawangdui versions. I put it back here, as the image for Line 2.

d. I follow Gao in taking *lei²* (贏) here as loan for *lei²* (纍), but the original reading (meaning "weakens") provides a workable meaning.

e. In the traditional and Mawangdui versions there is a phrase ("Harm to the axle-support of the big carriage") which echoes Line 1 (in form and in its content-- an injury to a lower part) and which is out of place here in Line 4. It seems to be an alternative line for Line 1, which for some reason has become displaced in the text.

f. In the traditional and Mawangdui versions there is a phrase ("As a hardship divination, auspicious.") which seems displaced from elsewhere, so I have bracketed it. If it would be considered part of the text, I would also emend the *ze²* (則) to *zhen¹* (貞) here as in 14/1, to conform to all the other occurrences of *jian¹* (艱) which are in a technical phrase as a qualifier to "divination".

HEXAGRAM 35

ADVANCE IN ATTACK[a]

HEXAGRAM TEXT:
The lord of Kang[5] acted, he was bestowed[b] horses great in number, one day three victories[c]. [H-SSI]

LINES:
6 at the beginning:[d]
Aggressively advancing and destroying. [L-I]
As a divination, auspicious, troubles[e] vanish. [L-P]

6 at LINE 2:
Aggressively advancing and surrounding and compelling to surrender[f]. [L-I]
Accept this great blessing from the King's mother(s). [L-A]
As a divination, auspicious. [L-P]

6 at LINE 3:
The masses (= troops?) assent and have confidence. [L-I]
Troubles vanish. [L-P]

9 at LINE 4:
Aggressively advancing like voles. [L-I]
As a divination, danger. [L-P]

6 at LINE 5:
As to loss or gain, do not worry! [L-A]
Troubles vanish; as to going, it is auspicious, with nothing not beneficial. [L-P, and L-SP]

9 on top:
Aggressively advancing his horns. [L-I]
Act to attack towns. [L-A]
Auspicious, without harmful mishap; as a danger-divination[g],

difficulty. [L-P, and L-SP]

****

COMMENTARY

In the overall structure of the *Zhouyi*, Hexagrams 35 and 36 are paired with each other and belong in a group of pairs which is centered around Hexagrams 29 and 30. This latter pair concerns divine powers manifest in the earth's higher and lower places, and the various pairs which belong to this group all develop themes which relate to earthly life under Heaven, particularly in its social aspects and in the general features of its being a temporal (mortal) affair.

Hexagrams 35 and 36 are linked as polar opposites, in that the one speaks of aggressive advance and attack, the other (given the inflection provided by the lines) of suffering wounds from an aggressive attack. Both proceed by a story telling in the first five lines, which is epitomized in the last line of the hexagram.

In very elliptical fashion the present hexagram tells a story of the sort of thing which the scene-setting image in the Hexagram Text alludes to. It is the story of three victories in a day: the first in an aggressive advance-and-destroy kind of attack which is destructive (Line 1), a second in an advance-and-surround kind of attack which ends with subjugation (Line 2), then following reassurance that the masses are still supportive (or, troops still have confidence) (Line 3), finally, a third vole-like advance in attack (Line 4). The culminating image, which should appear in Line 5, is missing, but the accompanying elements in the line suggest that it would have been celebratory in character. All this is epitomized in a final animal image, 'aggressively advancing its horns' (Line 6).

****

◆ TEXTUAL NOTES ◆

a. Gao (*ZGJ*, 120-21) is right in understanding the *jin⁴* (晉) here as having an "invade" meaning, as if the original character were *jian³* (戩).

b. I read *ci⁴* (賜) for *xi¹* (錫).

c. I read *jie²* (捷) for *jie¹* (接).

d. In the traditional and Mawangdui versions, there is another phrase ("Captives are abundant, without harmful mishap.") which is something like a commentary interpretation of how the line could be auspicious and have troubles vanish. That is because there are abundant captives taken, and there is no harmful mishap in the course of the invasion and subduing.

e. I restore the omitted *hui³* (悔), following the Mawangdui version.

f. I read *chou²* (愁) as *qiu²* (遒).

g. The extensive set of prognostication words is puzzling, but makes sense if (taking the traditional and Mawangdui versions) *li⁴* (厲) is read with *zhen¹* (貞), treating *ji² wu² jiu⁴* (吉无咎) as an intrusive whole misplaced between *li⁴* and *zhen¹* in the course of copying.

HEXAGRAM 36

CALLING PHEASANT[a]

HEXAGRAM TEXT:
A beneficial divination.[b] [H-O]
Beneficial hardship-divination. [H-SP]

LINES:
9 at the beginning:[c]
A calling pheasant going in flight, drooping its left[d] wing; a nobleman
going on a journey, not eating for three days. [L-I]

6 at LINE 2:[e]
A calling pheasant wounded in the left thigh; (the nobleman) has a
place to go, his host has words (for him). [L-I]

9 at LINE 3:[e]
A calling pheasant, wounded in the southern hunt; (the nobleman)
got the big chief. [L-I]
Act to geld horses, (they will be) healthy. [L-A]
Auspicious. [L-P]

6 at LINE 4:[f]
A calling pheasant, wounded[g] in the left belly: (the arrow) gets the
calling pheasant's heart. [L-I]
As an illness divination, unsatisfactory. [L-SP]

6 at LINE 5:
Going forth out the courtyard and gate[h], Ji Zi reached the calling
pheasant. [L-I]

6 on top:
Neither light nor dark, it first ascended to the heavens, then entered
into the earth. [L-I]

****

COMMENTARY

For the place of Hexagram 36 in the overall structure of the *Zhouyi*, and for the meaning of its pairing with Hexagram 35, see the first two paragraphs of the Commentary on Hexagram 35.

The present hexagram tells the story of a calling pheasant, whose calling seems a crying out in pain. At the same time, in its first three lines it tells a second story, this time of a nobleman. The calling pheasant and nobleman are each underway on a journey, each suffering some debilitating condition.

The pheasant, its left wing drooping in flight (Line 1), has been wounded, but not in the wing itself, rather in the left thigh (Line 2). This wound was inflicted by some party who was part of a southern hunting expedition and royal tour (Line 3). In the accompanying human drama, a nobleman, going on a journey, had not eaten for three days (Line 1); and yet, while the nobleman's journey successfully leads him to a place where he is received, he receives words from his host there-- words of advice, perhaps, words which may amount to an argument even (the phrase could have that sense) (Line 2). In any case, he has a success to his credit: he "got" the "big chief".[6]

The wound in the left thigh of the pheasant has worked its way into the left belly and on through to the heart (Line 4), presumably bringing the bird near to death. At this point Ji Zi, the uncle of the Shang King Zhou,[7] is imaged as venturing forth from a courtyard and arriving at the calling pheasant (Line 5): presumably an act of compassion quite in keeping with the character of that historical figure, but it might be interpreted quite otherwise. The story ends with a final observation on a bird's life: at first, an ascent into the heavens, but in the end, entry into the earth (Line 6). That is: in its life, it belonged to the world of light, ascending into the heavens in flight, but upon death, it came to belong to the world of darkness, descending into the earth.

****

◆ TEXTUAL NOTES ◆

a. The title-name in the traditional and Mawangdui versions is composed of two loan-words the proper reading of which is *ming² zhi⁴* (鳴雉), "calling pheasant". Gao and Kunst read this in like fashion. See Shaughnessy (*CZ*, 221-27) and Li (*ZTong*, 71-72) for discussions of the title-name components as loan words.

b. This phrase is a part of Line 5 in the traditional and Mawangdui versions, but it is out of place there and seems to have been displaced from here.

c. Included in the traditional and Mawangdui versions of Line 1 is a phrase ("[The nobleman] has somewhere to go, his host has words (for him)") which does not seem to belong. The line image in that line is a rhymed couplet; these seven characters fall outside the couplet both in rhyme and in meaning. The intrusive phrase seems to have come from Line 2, due to a faulty line-division which is repeated (in parallel fashion) in the next several Lines. The phrase represents the second of a set of three human counterpart-action images in the first three lines; these offer a story of human actions that sounds over against the story of the pheasant. The human story-line reads: a noble went on a journey, and for several days went without food; he finally arrived at a place where he was hosted, with further stages to go, and as he left his host had words for him (of warning or advice, presumably); on his further journeying, he attacked and 'bagged' the 'great chief'. Shaughnessy (*CZ*, 226-7) suggests that the "southern expedition" is a reference to the disastrous campaign of King Zhao in which he died; and for the connection with this hexagram's imagery, he refers to the "Heavenly Questions" chapter in the *Chuci* (*Songs of the South*), and to a rhetorical question there which he translates: "Lord Zhao did much travelling. He went to the South Land. What did it profit him to meet that white pheasant?"

d. I follow the Mawangdui version in having zuo^3 (左) here.

e. As part of a series of faulty line-divisions the L-A and L-P phrases in Line 3 were mistakenly made part of Line 2 in the traditional and Mawangdui versions. I have restored the text.

f. As part of a series of faulty line-divisions the L-SP phrase in Line 4 was mistakenly made part of Line 3 in the traditional and Mawangdui versions. I have restored the text.

g. I follow the Mawangdui version here, starting the line with ($ming^2$=) $ming^2$ (yi^2=) zhi^4 yi^2 (鳴 雉 夷) instead of the traditional text's ru^4 (入) .

h. As part of a series of faulty line-divisions, the traditional and Mawangdui versions mistakenly placed this phrase in Line 4.

HEXAGRAM 37

FAMILY

HEXAGRAM TEXT:
A beneficial female-divination. [H-SP]

LINES:
9 at the beginning:
Barricade his own house. [L-I]
Troubles vanish. [L-P]

6 at LINE 2:
Lacking in (outward) achievements, but inside, provisions. [L-I]
As a divination, auspicious. [L-P]

9 at LINE 3:
The men of the house moan and groan, while the wife and children giggle and laugh. [L-I]
(For the men of the family), **troubles and danger;** (for the wife and children), **auspicious, but in the end, difficulty.**[8] [L-SP]

6 at LINE 4:
Prosperous family. [L-I]
Greatly auspicious. [L-P]

9 at LINE 5:
The King proceeds to and arrives at his own house. [L-I]
Do not worry! [L-A]
Auspicious. [L-P]

9 on top:
Have captives who have the appearance of persons terrified. [L-I]
In the end, auspicious. [L-P]

****

COMMENTARY

In the overall structure of the *Zhouyi*, Hexagrams 37 and 38 are paired with each other and belong in a group of pairs which is centered around Hexagrams 29 and 30. This latter pair concerns divine powers manifest in the earth's higher and lower places, and the various pairs which belong to this group all develop themes which relate to earthly life under Heaven, particularly in its social aspects and in the general features of its being a temporal (mortal) affair.

Hexagrams 37 and 38 are linked in focus on a polarity of inner and outer: the family and family life, within, and the observation of the celestial phenomena and connection of these with human life, without. The pairing is furthered because the human affairs with which the celestial observations are linked seem to be a series of events leading to a marriage, thus to the forming of a new family and family life.

The present hexagram unfolds as a delineation of household and family in various major aspects. It does not tell a story, nor simply sound variations on a theme; but it draws for imagery on the different sides to this aspect of life.[9]

The beginning in the delineation of the houshold and family in its various major aspects is with the home as a safe haven from the outside world, protected by bars on the gates. The division of outer and inner involved here is then built on in two different realizations of the family that might occupy such a household.

One is found in Lines 2 and 3: Line 2 points to a realization in which the lack of (outward) achievements by family members goes together with success inwardly (the provision of food). Line 3 points stereotypically to the family members in such a case: those concerned with the outward are moaning and groaning, those with the inward are giggling and laughing.

The other is found in Line 4: an integrated family unit which knows both inward and outward success. The family here is a prosperous one (or, with a different reading: a blessed or Heaven-blessed family).

Line 5 points to the household as a center of religious worship, taking the royal household as model. The King arrives at the family-estate to worship at the family shrine.[10]

Finally, Line 6 introduces one further side to the household: the slaves, who are primarily captives taken in raids and war.

****

HEXAGRAM 38

CELESTIAL OBSERVATION

HEXAGRAM TEXT:
> **Auspicious in regard to minor affairs.** [H-SP]

LINES:
9 at the beginning:
> **Lose horses, do not pursue, they return of themselves.** [L-I]
> **Troubles vanish. No harm in going to visit wicked people.** [L-P, and L-SP]

9 at LINE 2:
> **Meet the 'main man'[11] in the village-lane.** [L-I]
> **Without harmful mishap.** [L-P]

6 at LINE 3:
> **See a cart being pulled, its ox being dragged, and a man tattoed on the forehead and his nose cut off.** [L-I]
> **Have an end without a beginning.** [L-P]

9 at LINE 4:
> **Observe the fox[a], meet the primary man.** [L-I]
> **Without harmful mishap. For exchanging prisoners, danger.** [L-P, and L-SP]

6 at LINE 5:
> **Ascend[b] to the ancestral temple, eat flesh.** [L-I]
> **Troubles vanish. As to going, what is the harm?** [L-P, L-SP]

9 on top:
> **Observing the fox, see the pig shouldering mud, one cart carrying ghosts, a bow first drawn and then released[c]; it is not bandits, it is a marriage-match.** [L-I]
> **As to going, it is auspicious if one encounters rain.** [L-SP]

****

COMMENTARY

For the place of Hexagram 38 in the overall structure of the *Zhouyi*, and for the meaning of its pairing with Hexagram 37, see the first three paragraphs of the Commentary on Hexagram 37.

The present hexagram unfolds in a counterpoint between a series of celestial observations[12] and a series of human actions/events-- a counterpoint of allusions which can be woven into a story of events leading to a wedding.

The story begins with a celestial marker of the time: it is when the 'Heavenly Horses' become 'lost', that is, when the constellation of that name disappears from sight, as it regularly does for a while, only regularly to reappear later (Line 1).[13]

That is the time of the first in a series of human events which lead to a wedding. Someone meets with a certain 'main man' on a village lane (or in an alley) (Line 2); this is the the initiation of a marriage arrangement.

Then at a time marked by a certain further celestial event, a second step in the human story takes place (Line 3). The celestial event involves the lunar-lodges of Carted Ghosts and Led Ox, with the latter being a constellation which sets at the time of the rising of the former and which is thus able to be seen as 'pulling' the former; the former is traditionally the Eye of the Sky which presides over the inspection of miscreants. The human step at this time: a third party appears on the scene, a man branded as a criminal in punishment for things done. The line provides no hint of who this is or how he is related to the persons meeting in Line 2-- is this the husband-to-be? Has he suffered punishment, does that call into question the continuation of the commitment which came out of the meeting? Is there to be an end, here, to what has not yet really gotten started?

Next (Line 4), at a time marked by the observation of a fox-constellation (of Sirius), a third step in the human story occurs. Someone meets the 'primary man', that is, presumably the man who is to decide whether the marriage is to be carried through on.

There is then (Line 5) a ceremony and ceremonial feast: ascent to the ancestral temple, sacrifice at the ancestral shrine, the eating of flesh. Presumably the decision has been to go ahead with the marriage, and the ceremony relates to the coming wedding.

Finally (Line 6), we have arrived at a time when observing the fox-constellation also involves seeing other celestial phenomena and natural phenomena; that is, seeing Sirius, one also sees the Heavenly Swine, whose first appearance is at the beginning of the rainy season when the pigs are turned out into the harvested fields, and also sees the bow and arrow of Archer Yi. These sightings set the date in August. Part of the ritual for the wedding held then involves a large horse-riding party (see Hexagram 22/Line 4) which can be mistaken for a band of bandits.

****

◆ TEXTUAL NOTES ◆

a. In this line and Line 6, I read *gu¹* (孤) as *hu²* (狐). As Shaughnessy notes (*CZ*, 217), the "fox" intends Sirius which, properly, is called *lang²* ("wolf"); but "the intra-genus variation would be appropriate here for the sake of rhyme".

b. I read *deng¹* (登) for *jue²* (厥), following the Mawangdui version of the text.

c. In this line as in Line 4, I read *gu¹* (孤) as *hu²* (狐). I also read *shuo¹* (說) as *tuo¹* (脫).

HEXAGRAM 39

HOBBLING

HEXAGRAM TEXT:[a]
  Beneficial to see the big man. [H-A]
  **Beneficial to the west and south, not beneficial to the east and
    north. [H-SP]**

LINES:
6 at the beginning:
  He goes hobbling, and comes praised-and-honored. [L-I]

6 at LINE 2:
  **The King and his ministers hobble and bobble along, it is not the case
    that they are themselves[14] the cause of this. [L-I]**

9 at LINE 3:
  He goes hobbling and comes wobbling.[15] [L-I]

6 at LINE 4:
  He goes hobbling and comes transported in a carriage. [L-I]

9 at LINE 5:
  Hobbling greatly, friends come. [L-I]

6 on top:
  He goes hobbling and comes eminent. [L-I]
  As a divination, auspicious.[a] [L-P]

****

COMMENTARY

In the overall structure of the *Zhouyi*, Hexagrams 39 and 40 are paired
with each other and belong in a group of pairs which is centered around

Hexagrams 29 and 30. This latter pair concerns divine powers manifest in the earth's higher and lower places, and the various pairs which belong to this group all develop themes which relate to earthly life under Heaven, particularly in its social aspects and in the general features of its being a temporal (mortal) affair.

Hexagrams 39 and 40 are linked in focus on the contrast of a set of contrasts. Hexagram 39 centers on the contrast of a hobbling (hindered, crippled, hobbled) advance vs. a fluent and successful advance. Hexagram 40 centers on the contrast of a capture and being captured and prevented from moving freely vs. a freeing and having freedom to function and move. The contrast of these two sets of contrast centers on what is at issue in both sets, namely, movement which becomes impeded and then released to be more fluent. They represent alternative ways in which this common theme may be construed: in the one case, the constraint belongs to the moving party, in the other it comes from without and impinges on that party.

The present hexagram develops as a set of variations on a theme, in which four of the six lines are exact parallels while the other two include the title-name as a crucial part of their phrasing. There is no story, or significance to the order, except certain lines seem linked.

Both Line 1 and Line 6 posit a change in condition over time, implying release from a deficient or restricted condition and the achievement (how, it is not said) of a condition worthy of praise and honor (1) or a condition of eminence (6).

Lines 3 and 4 are parallel in structure, but contrast in content. In Line 3, the image is of a deficient or restricted condition which does not change over time-- or if anything, gets worse. In Line 4, the image is of a difference in earlier and later conditions, but not necessarily a transformation: the hobbler has succeeded in finding a way to be 'carted', but has not necessarily transcended his original condition.

Lines 2 and 5 are left, and share this, that in them the hobbling in question is not seen in the perspective of a going and coming. Instead, in the first case, it is seen in regard to the matter of responsibility: the hobbling is seen as something the person is not responsible for. Circumstance, say, accounts for it. In the second case, it is seen in an interpersonal perspective: regardless of responsibility, the hobbler needs assistance, and in this case, friends come to help the person, who is hobbling greatly.

****

◆ TEXTUAL NOTES ◆

a. In the traditional and Mawangdui versions there is a phrase in the Hexagram Text ("Beneficial to see the big man; as a divination, auspicious") and one in Line 6 ("Auspicious; beneficial to see the big man.") which seem to be the same phrase-set mistakenly duplicated. Because the *ji²* (吉) makes good sense in Line 6, and is an appropriate prognostication word for a Line Statement, I have left it there and excised it in the Hexagram Text. Similarly, because the *li⁴ jian⁴ da⁴ ren²* (利見大人) is an appropriate action-element for a Hexagram Text, I have left it there and excised it in Line 6. Copy errors involving the Hexagram Text and Line 6 seem rather common, even more common than those involving the Text and Line 1. This must reflect something about the manner of copying and/or the text(s) from which the copy was being made (for example, what the copyist had to do to take the text[s] he was copying from and to give the copy he was making the order which it has). Of course the exact stage in the copying/recopying of the text when such miscopying took place can not be discerned in our present state of knowledge.

HEXAGRAM 40

LIBERATION

HEXAGRAM TEXT:
> Beneficial in regard to west and south.
> Without a place to go, his coming and returning is auspicious;
>   have a place to go, early morning is auspicious. [H-SP]

LINES:
6 at the beginning:
> Without harmful mishap. [L-P]

9 at LINE 2:
> In hunting, catch three fox, get yellow arrowheads. [L-I]
> As a divination, auspicious. [L-P]

6 at LINE 3:
> Backpacking and riding at the same time, brings the arrival of
> bandits. [L-I]
> Difficulty. [L-P]

9 at LINE 4:
> "(We are going to) 'liberate' your thumbs": (so the bandits say in
> threat. But ...) friends arrive and capture them. [L-I]

6 at LINE 5:
> The nobleman is liberated, he offers in sacrifice some of the little men
> who are captives. [L-I]
> Auspicious. [L-P]

6 on top:
> The Duke, employing himself shooting at a hawk on the top of the
> high wall, hits it. [L-I]
> Nothing is not beneficial. [L-P]

****

COMMENTARY

For the place of Hexagram 40 in the overall structure of the *Zhouyi*, and for the meaning of its pairing with Hexagram 39, see the first three paragraphs of the Commentary on Hexagram 39.

The present hexagram develops as a story of a successful hunting foray (Line 2[16]) on which "three fox" were caught, but something else was gained as well, namely, some "yellow arrowheads" (most likely bronze: but in any case, symbolic of wealth).

On the return trip home (Line 3), the party attracts bandits. For riders who are also carrying things on their back are suspicious to potential bandits: they must have things of value that they do not want to let get any distance from them. And that indeed brings on the bandits to see.

As the bandits were threatening to cut off the thumbs of the leader(s) of the hunting party, friends arrive and capture the bandits (Line 4).

After his friends have liberated the nobleman, he offers a human sacrifice using some of the captives (Line 5).

The incident ends with the Duke (presumably the nobleman in question), restored to his old freedom, celebrating it by shooting a hawk on top of a high wall (Line 6). If the hawk is the bandits (who prey on travelers) and the shooting/hitting is the successful rescue (more precisely, the capture and sacrifice of the bandits), then the image epitomizes what has just happened to him.

****

HEXAGRAM 41

DECREASE AND DIMINISH

HEXAGRAM TEXT:
A beneficial divination.[a] [H-O]
Beneficial to have a place to go. [H-A]

LINES:
9 at the beginning:[a]
As for sacrificial services[b]: he makes them go quickly, he decreases the libations. [L-I]
Without harmful mishap. [L-P]

9 at LINE 2:[a]
He does not diminish them but increases them. [L-I]
Ominous for campaigning. [L-SP]

6 at LINE 3:
When three people travel, they decrease by one; when one person travels, he acquires friends. [L-I]

6 at LINE 4:
Decrease the illness, bring about quickly having a cure. [L-I]
Without harmful mishap. [L-P]

6 at LINE 5:[a]
Offer captives in sacrifice, diminish their number. [L-I]
Greatly auspicious, without harmful mishap: an acceptable divination. [L-P]

9 on top:[c]
He does not diminish their number but increases it. [L-I]
Beneficial to acquire a bond-servant without a family. [L-A]
Without harmful mishap, auspicious as a divination. [L-P]

****

COMMENTARY

In the overall structure of the *Zhouyi*, Hexagrams 41 and 42 are paired with each other and belong in a group of pairs which is centered around Hexagrams 29 and 30. This latter pair concerns divine powers manifest in the earth's higher and lower places, and the various pairs which belong to this group all develop themes which relate to earthly life under Heaven, particularly in its social aspects and in the general features of its being a temporal (mortal) affair.

Hexagrams 41 and 42 are linked as constrasting affairs (increase and decrease) which nonetheless involve each other in intimate fashion.

The present hexagram develops through three two-line groups. Each group involves a contrast which is vehicle for bringing forward different types of diminution.

The first pair takes up with a single sphere of concern, the conduct of sacrificial services, and suggests: one may diminish the libations and thus speed up the performance of the services (Line 1), or one may instead increase the libations (Line 2). As exhibited in this one sphere, diminution and increase relate to the temporal sense of one and the same performance, and they issue in opposite conditions (a shorter or a longer service).

The second pair takes up two different spheres of concern, one that of travellers and the other, that of disease; and in those different spheres it points to quite different relations of diminution and increase to a common and normative condition. In the case of travellers, there is a gravitation toward pairing: if "three's a crowd", the solitary also attracts a companion. Here increase and decrease are centered on a norm and middle ground (a pair of travelers) which can be reached by opposite actions from different directions: diminution from three, or increase from one (Line 3). But in the case of disease, we find no such norm in the middle. It is diminution of disease which makes for a speedy cure (Line 4); increase of disease, however, does not bring on the normative condition of health.

Finally, in the last pair of lines, the sphere of concern is a single one again, the taking and holding of prisoners and the offering of them in sacrificial ritual. On the one hand, one may diminish their number, presumably by the sacrificial act itself (Line 5); on the other, one may augment their number rather than diminishing it, presumably by further capture achieved in the spirit-supported action to whose success the sacrifice contributed (Line

6).

Throughout the three pairs of lines, the link of increase and decrease is maintained, but the character of this link is shown to vary. And more to the point of the constrast and connection of Hexagrams 41 and 42: this set of lines is about both increase and decrease (but mainly decrease) in some general and dispersed reference, while Hexagram 42 is about them both (but mainly increase) in a historical reference.[1]

****

◆ TEXTUAL NOTES ◆

a. There is some textual dislocation here, involving two different exchanges or transfers. To begin with, the first eight characters in the Text in the traditional and Mawangdui versions have been displaced to here from Line 5, where the first part of Hexagram 42/ Line 2[2] is presently to be found. I have excised this repetition from Hexagram 42, and restored the original Line 5 by transferring the Hexagram Text phrase and adding the phrase (*sun³ zhi¹*: 損之) which makes it parallel in pattern to Line 1 (just as lines 2 and 6 are parallel, and are even identical in their line-image). At the same time, the original occasion-response characters belonging to the Hexagram Text have also been displaced, to Line 2; I have restored them here. Finally, I have treated *he² zhi¹ yong⁴ er⁴ gui³ ke³ yong⁴ xiang³* (曷之用二簋可用享: "What is to be used for them (= the libations)? Two tureens: they are acceptable to use in sacrificing.") as an intrusive editorial/commentary phrase which concerns the matter of libations and properly belongs with the image in Line 1.

b. I read *si⁴* (祀) here for *si⁴* (巳), taking the latter as loan for the former.

c. In the traditional and Mawangdui versions, there is a phrase here ("Beneficial to have a place to go.") which does not normally appear in the Line Statements but which seems in fact simply to be the Hexagram Text phrase mistakenly repeated in Line 6. [The mistake seems likely to be a copy error, in the form of the inadvertent completion of the *li⁴* (利) phrase incorrectly, following the Hexagram Text phrase instead of the appropriate one.] I have omitted it here, but kept the phrase in the Hexagram Text.

HEXAGRAM 42

INCREASE AND BENEFIT

HEXAGRAM TEXT:
  Beneficial to have a place to go.
  Beneficial to cross the big river. [H-A]

LINES:

9 at the beginning:[a]
  Someone makes a beneficial gift to him of 10-cowrie[3] turtles, he is not able to resist. [L-I]
    Beneficial to act to make a grand construction.[4] [L-A]
    Greatly auspicious, without harmful mishap. [L-P]

6 at LINE 2:
  The King employs himself making sacrifice to the Lord. [L-I]
    Auspicious; as a long-term divination, auspicious. [L-P, and L-SP]

6 at LINE 3:
  Increase and aid it (= the big work of founding the dynasty?) **using labor**[b]**-service.** [L-I]
    Without harmful mishap. [L-P]

6 at LINE 4:[c]
  Take captives, Zhong-hang[5] **announces (the results of a divination), the Duke uses the jade-tablet**[6] **and complies, thinking it beneficial to act to make the Yin**[d] **move their country.** [L-I]

9 at LINE 5:
  Take captives, make their hearts be kindly.[e] [L-I]
    Do not ask! [L-A]
    Greatly auspicious. [L-P]

9 on top:
>   **No one comes to their aid, some strike-and-beat them.** [L-I]
>   **Establish-and-make-upright your own hearts, do not perform the**
>   ***heng*-perpetuation rite!** [L-A]
>   **Ominous.** [L-P]

****

COMMENTARY

For the place of Hexagram 42 in the overall structure of the *Zhouyi*, and for the meaning of its pairing with Hexagram 41, see the first three paragraphs of the Commentary on Hexagram 41.

The present hexagram speaks in story-fashion of the founding of the Zhou dynasty.

It begins (Line 1) with an irresistible gift (presumably to King Wu) of some valuable turtles, which is itself a good sign for undertaking a great work, presumably the founding of the dynasty.

Then (Line 2) King Wu makes sacrifice to the Lord-- presumably in connection with the conquest of the Shang, as celebration of its successful issue. Part of the sacrifice would involve divination and perhaps some use of the turtles mentioned as received in Line 1.

In Line 3, King Wu (or is it the Duke of Zhou now?) seeks to augment his successful conquest, by efforts of construction and building, in which he employs his people and others.

But what follows (Line 4) indicates further conflict has arisen. After the death of King Wu, the Duke of Zhou took charge and oversaw to a successful conclusion the conflict which ensued when one of the Duke's brothers led the Shang remnant and some eastern countries in rebellion. In this action which secured the founding of the dynasty, prisoners were taken, and the Duke's diviner interpreted a divination (presumably about the matter of what to do with the Shang people who had risen in rebellion). Guided by this, the Duke conducted a sacrifice involving some of the prisoners, and acted then to move the Shang peoples out of their homeland and to settle them closer to where he could keep his eye on them.

Line 5 points to the the further actions of the Duke of Zhou: in regard to the captives he had taken and had transported (amounting to the core of the Shang people), he sought to reconcile them to their new (but secondary) place within the new (Zhou) order of things, and thus to make their hearts kindly toward their Zhou masters, if possible.

Line 6, however, points to difficulty. There is a mixed response to the Shang on the part of the Zhou. No one else seeks to act in this aiding and benefiting way toward these new subjects; indeed some even attack and strike them and thereby aggravate the situation. The difference in response is important; in it, the enduring of the dynasty is at stake. Thinking that a perpetuation-rite will assure that endurance, instead of the capacity to stand settled within and to act out of kindliness of heart, is indeed something ominous for the future of the dynasty.

****

◆ TEXTUAL NOTES ◆

a. In the traditional and the Mawangdui versions this line has no line-image, due to a copy error which mistakenly divides the lines so that the line-image belonging here comes at the start of Line 2. I have restored the proper division.

b. I follow the Mawangdui version, reading *gong¹* (工) for *xiong¹* (凶).

c. In the traditional and the Mawangdui versions one rendering of this line appears at the end of Line 3, and another as Line 4. I treat these as alternative versions of the same line (of Line 4), with both being saved for their slight differences. I have united the two to form this version of Line 4.

d. I take *yi¹* (依) as *yin¹* (殷).

e. In the traditional and the Mawangdui texts, there are two versions of the line-image of this line, with a slight difference between them, kept as if together they form Line 5. One says "make their hearts be kindly" (有孚惠心: *you³ fu² hui⁴ xin¹*), the other "make our catch be kindly" (有孚惠我得: *you³ fu² hui⁴ wo³ de²*, reading *de²* [得] for *de²* [德]). I retain the first version and treat the second as a preserved alternative.

HEXAGRAM 43

MOVING QUICKLY[a]

HEXAGRAM TEXT:
Not beneficial to take up arms; beneficial to have a place to go. [H-A]

Make a presentation at the royal court; the captives cry out; there is danger, it is reported from the town.[b] [H-SSI]

LINES:
9 at the beginning:
Injury[c] to the front of his toes, he can go but not win[7]. [L-I]
There is a harmful mishap. [L-P]

9 at LINE 2:
Caution, outcries, fighting at night[d]. [L-I]
Do not worry! [L-A]

9 at LINE 3:[e]
The nobleman, traveling alone and going lickety-split, encounters rain; he's like one of those people who, on getting wet, get angry. [L-I]
Without harmful mishap. [L-P]

9 at LINE 4:
The skin on his buttocks has been worn off, his traveling is hard-going[f], he pulls along his sheep. [L-I]
Listen to what is said, but do not believe. [L-A]
Troubles vanish. [L-P]

9 at LINE 5:
Mountain goats[g] hopping[g] lickety-split down the middle of the road. [L-I]
Without harmful mishap. [L-P]

6 on top:
  Without outcry, an injury to the cheek-bones[h]. [L-I]
  In the end, it is ominous. [L-P]

****

COMMENTARY

In its overall structure the *Zhouyi* begins (Hexagrams 1 and 2) with the seasonal rhythm and life in an agriculture-dependent mode fitting itself into that rhythm, and ends (Hexagrams 63 and 64) with life placed within the matrix of the collective political/historical venturing which the Mandate of Heaven and the Shang and Zhou leadership of human life on earth provides.

Within these brackets, the thirty remaining hexagram pairs are grouped into five sets, the first of which (3/4 through 15/16) centers on Hexagrams 9 and 10. This pair make as theme that our human life-- this venturing and risking on earth under the heavens-- endemically becomes involved in troubles, in troubled situations. A subsequent group (17/18 through 41/42) centers on Hexagrams 29 and 30. This pair concerns divine powers manifest in the earth's higher and lower places, and the various pairs which belong to this group all develop themes which relate to earthly life under Heaven, particularly in its social aspects and in the general features of its being a temporal (mortal) affair.

The next set of hexagram pairs (43/44 through 49/50) has no central or organizing pair; its coherence is found in the common reference of all four pairs back to conditions of a being whose life is an active affair involving risk. In the venturing involved, such a being's efforts are caught up in various polar conditions.

Hexagrams 43 (Moving quickly) and 44 (Bound together) are linked in focus on the thematic contrast of the movement of flight vs. something caught fast in an entanglement/enclosure.

The present hexagram tells a tragi-comic story, set in wartime. In the Hexagram Text the scene is set: it is a time of conflict, prisoners have been taken and brought to the royal court (for interrogation? for trial?), and at the same time news of a threat comes from beyond (a town nearby, apparently).

The story-telling begins with a characterization of the 'hero' of our story: he is nobleman who has been injured in the foot, and while he can move he can not move with the speed and agility needed if he is to engage in victorious combat (Line 1).

The threat of approaching enemy forces has been voiced, and in an atmosphere of wariness and caution, there are outcries: night-fighting has broken out (Line 2).

The nobleman, injured though he is, flees lickety-split from the scene of battle, but on his flight he encounters rain and gets angry at being bogged down (Line 3).

By this time, the flesh on his buttocks being worn off from the hard riding, he is finding the going hard in the rain and mud, and is having to drag along his sheep-- it seems they are balky in the conditions. (Line 4).

Then (Line 5) an ironic contrast: out of the gray come some mountain goats going along lickety-split down the middle of the road! It seems they are fleeing also, ahead of the oncoming army behind them, and are thus a harbinger of the approaching enemy.

The story ends (Line 6) when, without outcry, he suffers injury to his face: the enemy has caught up with the fleeing nobleman.

****

◆ TEXTUAL NOTES ◆

a. The title-name in the traditional and the Mawangdui versions is *guai⁴* (夬); this is a loan and the primitive graph for *jue²* (趹), the real title-name. See the meanings of the graphs in Lines 3 and 5, for example.

b. By reading *yang²* (揚) as meaning a "military dance", Li refines this image. Beginning with the joyous affair of "dancing a military dance at the royal court," he sees the image proceeding to the intrusion of someone crying out in warning: "The enemy is coming to attack!" From the city the command is transmitted: "Going forth in attack is not a favorable thing, we must assume battle-stations and wait." (See Li (*ZTong*, 85).) This dramatic shift in situation, mood, and attitude then forms the background for understanding the series of line-images.

c. I read *zhuang⁴* (壯) as *qiang¹* (戕).

d. I take *mo⁴* (莫) as a loan and the primitive graph for *mu⁴* (暮).

e. In the traditional and Mawangdui versions, the first four characters are the last part of Line 6 displaced; the imagery, its lack of sense here and its appropriateness there, and the coincidence of prognostication elements, all support this. I have restored the characters to their original place.

f. I read *zi¹-ju¹* (赵趄) for *ci⁴-qie³* (次且).

g. I read *huan²* (萈) for *xian¹* (莧), and *lu⁴* (蹼) for *lu⁴* (陸).

h. This last phrase, found in Line 3 of the traditional and Mawangdui versions, belongs here, as a counterpart in the imagery with Line 1 (injury to feet vs. injury to cheek-bones).

HEXAGRAM 44

BOUND TOGETHER[a]

HEXAGRAM TEXT:

[Current versions retain nothing of what was originally in this Text.][b]

LINES:
6 at the beginning:[c]
  Bound to a metal spindle. [L-I]
    As a divination, auspicious. [L-P]

9 at LINE 2:[c]
  An emaciated pig, captured, plants its feet and balks at moving.[8] [L-I]
    Ominous in regard to having a place to go and visit. [L-SP]

9 at LINE 3:[c]
  The bundle holds fish. [L-I]
    It is not beneficial to be a guest. [L-A]
    Without harmful mishap. [L-P]

9 at LINE 4:
  The bundle is without fish. [L-I]
    Ominous for campaigning.[d] [L-SP]

9 at LINE 5:
  Using purple willow to wrap melons: a cherished pattern, something fallen from Heaven. [L-I]

9 on top:
  Entangle[a] its horns.[9] [L-I]
    Difficulty, (but) without harmful mishap. [L-P]

****

COMMENTARY

For the place of Hexagram 44 in the overall structure of the *Zhouyi*, and for the meaning of its pairing with Hexagram 43, see the first four paragraphs of the Commentary on Hexagram 43.

The present hexagram unfolds in its lines a set of variations on a theme of enclosure and entanglement. Once the textual displacement is corrected, the images group the lines: the first two use binding images, the next three wrapping or enclosing images, and the final line uses an entanglement image.[10] All are expressions of something binding and holding something else fast.

The beginning (Line 1) is with something bound to a metal spindle. This binding establishes a connection, and while restricting movement, also gives it an anchor-point that is constructive (as in spinning yarn).

The companion binding image (Line 2) relates to an emaciated pig which has been captured and (so it seems) bound fast-- either by a hobbling rope, or in some other way which allows it to resist by planting its feet in the ground and balking at moving despite the pull of the rope. Here the binding involves opposed forces working at odds with each other.

The first of the set of three wrapping or enclosing images (Line 3) is of bundles which contain fish. Here the enclosing wrapper is serving its function and holds an actual content.

The second image of this set (Line 4) is the opposite of the first: bundles without fish. Here the enclosing is not serving its function.

The third image of this set (Line 5) involves a wrapping that is made of purple willows and that holds melons, not fish. The image is of something which is meaningful as a cherished familiar pattern, one that seems Heaven-sent.

The final line (Line 6) shifts once more the character of the binding and holding fast which this set of lines images. Here the image is of an animal (presumably, a ram) entangling its horns in something, becoming entangled and bound. In addition to its function within this Hexagram, such imagery facilitates the connection of this Hexagram with its companion, to the extent that the sheep being dragged, the mountain goats going lickety-split down the road, and the ram becoming entangled and immobilized, recall each other.

****

◆ TEXTUAL NOTES ◆

a. The title-name in the traditional and Mawangdui versions is *gou*[4] (姤); it is a loan for *gou*[4] (構), whose basic sense is that of "intertwine, interlacery, trellis-work, connect, cross" (see Karlgren, *Grammata Serica Recensa*, 109g). This latter is also the reading in Line 6.

b. In the traditional and Mawangdui versions, the Hexagram Text contains an action element: "The woman is injured, do not act to fetch (marry) a woman." [I read *zhuang*[4] (壯) here as *qiang*[1] (戕), as in Hexagram 34, and thus translate "injured".] This phrase has been added at some later time in the course of the handing down of the text, when the title-name was read not as a loan character but as having the meaning it has in its own right, namely, the pairing of male and female.

c. Some textual displacement has occurred here, affecting the first three lines. What appears in the traditional and Mawangdui versions as Line 1 is a combination of original Lines 1 and 2, what appears in those versions as Line 2 is original Line 3, and what appears as Line 3 in those versions is a copy error that has introduced a repetition of Hexagram 43/Line 4 (in the main) into this place. The latter is intelligible to the extent that, because Hexagrams 43 and 44 are pairs created out of each other by reversal in their line pattern, the 'same' line is involved. I have omitted traditional Line 3 altogether (it belongs in Hexagram 43), and have restored the original lines, moving traditional Line 2 to Line 3 instead and placing the second part of Line 1 as Line 2. [In traditional Line 1, I have divided the first 6 characters from the last 10, to make the best sense of both line-images and their accompanying prognostications.] See Hexagram 41/Line 5 for a similar situation, relating to its 'same'-line counterpart (Hexagram 42/Line 2). These errors presumably reflect something about the copying process, and probably something about the way in which the text was written out, before the traditional line-titles were introduced.

d. I follow the Mawangdui version, reading *zheng*[1] ([正=] 征) instead of *qi*[3] (起).

HEXAGRAM 45

WEIGHED DOWN IN DISTRESS[a]

HEXAGRAM TEXT:[b]
(The occasion calls for a) **sacrifice.**
A beneficial divination. [H-O]
  Beneficial to see the big man; beneficial to have a place to go. [H-A]
  Auspicious to use big sacrifical animals. [H-SP]
    The King proceeds to and enters his own temple. [H-SSI]

LINES:
6 at the beginning:
  Offer captives in sacrifice; no end, then disorder and distress; their cries and cajoling[c] become smiles-and-laughs. [L-I]
    Do not worry! [L-A]
    Going is without harmful mishap. [L-SP]

6 at LINE 2:
  If one has captives, then it is beneficial to employ the *yue*[f]**-sacrifice.**[11] [L-A]
  Auspicious in extended fashion, without harmful mishap. [L-P]

6 at LINE 3:
  Distress-wise, sighing-wise [i.e. having the appearance of someone sighing and being weighed down in distress]. [L-I]
    Without anything beneficial; going is without harmful mishap but with minor difficulty. [L-P, and L-SP]

9 at LINE 4:[d]
  Distress weighing down those holding ranks. [L-I]
    Greatly auspicious, without harmful mishap. [L-P]

9 at LINE 5:
   There are no captives. [L-I]
   As an extremely long-term divination, troubles vanish.ᵉ
   [L-SP]

6 on top:
   Sighing and sobbing, weeping and sniffling. [L-I]
   Without harmful mishap. [L-P]

****

COMMENTARY

In its overall structure the *Zhouyi* begins (Hexagrams 1 and 2) with the
seasonal rhythm and life in an agriculture-dependent mode fitting itself into
that rhythm, and ends (Hexagrams 63 and 64) with life placed within the
matrix of the collective political/historical venturing which the Mandate of
Heaven and the Shang and Zhou leadership of human life on earth provides.

Within these brackets, the thirty remaining hexagram pairs are grouped
into five sets, the first of which (3/4 through 15/16) centers on Hexagrams
9 and 10. This pair make as theme that our human life-- this venturing and
risking on earth under the heavens-- endemically becomes involved in troubles, in troubled situations. A subsequent group (17/18 through 41/42) centers on Hexagrams 29 and 30. This pair concerns divine powers manifest in
the earth's higher and lower places, and the various pairs which belong to this
group all develop themes which relate to earthly life under Heaven, particularly in its social aspects and in the general features of its being a temporal (mortal) affair.

The next set of hexagram pairs (43/44 through 49/50) has no central or
organizing pair; its coherence is found in the common reference of all four
pairs back to conditions of a being whose life is an active affair involving
risk. In the venturing involved, such a being's efforts are caught up in various polar conditions.

Hexagrams 45 (Weighed down in distress) and 46 (Rising up in ascent)
are linked in contrasting focus on the up and down character of our existence. The first hexagram has a being weighed down as its theme, while the
second makes a rising up in ascent be thematic.

The present hexagram does not tell a story but starting from a setting (that
of the king approaching and entering his own temple) the lines provide a

grouped (two-one-two-one) and correlated (Lines 1-2 and 4-5 correspond, as do Lines 3 and 6) set of images which speak to the condition of distress as something shared first, by captives, and second, by men of rank.

The Hexagram Text sets the scene: it is a situation that calls for the King to undertake sacrifice. From the lines which follow, it would seem to be more precisely a situation in which human sacrifice is to be undertaken, apparently after a battle and using prisoners made captive in that battle. Taken overall, the lines point, on the one hand, to the contrasting status of captive and captor, and on the other hand, to a commonality nonetheless.

The images start (Line 1) with the distress of the captives who are being offered for sacrifice. If that offering is unending, then the consequences will be disorder; so an end is made, and the captives that remain turn from crying and cajoling to smiling and laughing. The distress here at the prospect of death is relieved.

Since the image is missing from Line 2, how this beginning with the distress-then-relief of captives being saved from sacrifice was followed up can not be ascertained. But presumably it also concerned the distress of captives who are unwilling participants in what is taking place.

However, in the next line which has an image (Line 3) we find simply a condition attributed to no one in particular: the appearance and likeness of someone who is sighing and weighed down in distress. Since this anonymous imagery is echoed in the comparable culminating line of the upper three (in Line 6), the parallel suggests that these two lines are meant to point into a common human condition in the two otherwise quite differently placed parties.

In the upper half of the figure, the line-images proceed in parallel fashion.

Line 4 speaks to the men of ranks, and to a correlative distress weighing down the upper classes, and probably more particularly, those members who hold positions at court. Presumably the carrying out of the ritual involved them. Presumably also such distress is auspicious because the sacrifice will involve captives who have brought this distress upon those upper class figures, in battle (say) before the captives were taken.

Line 5 speaks of another sort of distress, that arising from an absence of captives and thus a lack of human sacrificial offerings for the ritual. Without such offerings, the distress pointed to in the preceding line could not be alleviated.

Line 6 ends the set with an echo of Line 3, an image of a sighing and sobbing, weeping and sniffling, which are attributed to no one in particular. The anonymity is significant in both cases: both of the differentiated parties stand subject to the same feelings.

What the set of six lines and images together does, then, is point into distress as a common element in the human condition, grounded in the mortality and the vulnerability to suffering and injury which we share, along with the capacity to inflict suffering and injury on each other.

****

◆ TEXTUAL NOTES ◆

a. The title-name seems best understood as a loan-word. The Mawangdui text provides the original simple graph, and the question really is what classifier is the proper one. The meaning of the lines seems to point to Radical 104 (疒) as the appropriate one. Li (*ZTong*, 89) points to this one as well as Radical 61 (忄), while Gao points to this one as well as Radical 181 (頁). Karlgren (*Grammata Serica Recensa*, 134, under entry 490)(later cited as *GSR*) links the three, and of his references the oldest is to the *Book of Poetry* on Radical 104, with meanings "suffering, fatigue, distress". Radical 104 seems the best alternative. I have used it here and throughout the lines of this hexagram.

b. In its traditional form the Hexagram Text seems to contain two sets of text, as if we have another case here of alternatives which have been both preserved, or of a line displaced from the Hexagram Text of another hexagram. I have taken the former alternative as most plausible, and have also collapsed the two to form one Text.

c. I read yi^1-wo^4 (嗌 喔) for yi^1-wo^4 (一 握), as Kunst does.

d. In the traditional and Mawangdui versions this line has no line-image, whereas Line 5 has a dual image. The pattern of the writing, and of the set of six lines, together suggest that a copy error has produced a mistaken line division between Lines 4 and 5. I have restored the first image in Line 5 to this line.

e. The pattern $yuan^2$ $yong^3$ $zhen^1$ (元 永 貞) occurs also in the Hexagram Text of Hexagram 8; but in its context there the $yuan^2$ does not modify the $yong^3$ and the three characters do not form a single phrase. Throughout the whole text of the *Zhouyi yuan²* appears in only two contexts except for a single occurrence of "primary man" and these two instances where it might be taken with a following $yong^3$. One is in the regular Hexagram Judgment phrase $yuan^2$ $heng^1$ (元 亨); the other is in a phrase which regularly occurs in the lines, *yuan² ji²* (元吉). Gao, Kunst, and Shaughnessy all emend here by adding *ji²*; but that creates a scarcely credible prognostication for Line 5. So I have preferred to treat the *yuan²* as here, alone in its occurrences in the text, modifying *yong³*, and have translated accordingly.

HEXAGRAM 46

ASCENT

HEXAGRAM TEXT:
(The occasion calls for a) **grand sacrifice.** [H-O]
Beneficial[a] to see the big man. Do not worry! [H-A]
Auspicious for a southern campaign. [H-SP]

LINES:
6 at the beginning:
Allowable to ascend.[12] [L-I]
Greatly auspicious. [L-P]

9 at LINE 2:
**If one has captives, then it is beneficial to employ the *yue*-
sacrifice.[13]** [L-A]
Without harmful mishap. [L-P]

9 at LINE 3:
Ascend to the hill town. [L-I]

6 at LINE 4:
The King acts to sacrifice[c] on-and-to Mt. Qi. [L-I]
Auspicious, without harmful mishap. [L-P]

6 at LINE 5:
Ascend the stairs. [L-I]
As a divination, auspicious. [L-P]

6 on top:
Ascent into the world of darkness.[14] [L-I]
A divination beneficial for not resting. [L-SP]

****

COMMENTARY

For the place of Hexagram 46 in the overall structure of the *Zhouyi*, and for the meaning of its pairing with Hexagram 45, see the first three paragraphs of the Commentary on Hexagram 45.

The present hexagram seems to address a religious affair, this time in a story which is not easy to decipher because of the brevity of the images and the absence of any image in one line. But it seems to relate to a royal sacrifice at-and-to Mt. Qi and to the ascents involved in this.

The start of the story (Line 1) is a pointer to such a royal sacrifice as involving an ascent which is sanctioned, as one connected with a ceremony--in contrast to (say) any ordinary climb of a mountain or climb into high places.

The next image (in Line 2) is missing, but it seems that whatever facet of ascent is being recalled, the journey to Mt. Qi is for a ceremonial purpose which would be best conducted if it involved using captives in a sacrificial ritual.

The upward journey that will take the royal party into the mountains involves climbing to a town on a hill or in the hills (Line 3), presumably one in the vicinity of Mt. Qi.

From there, the King can carry out the purpose of the upward journeying, in a sacrificial ritual at a place in the mountains (Line 4).

The ritual itself involves an ascent of stairs (Line 5). Is it that the captives are to be sacrificed at the top of an altar?

Finally, the ritual involves a further element of ascent, whose character is not unambiguously conveyed by the phrasing of the line image (Line 6). It could refer to an ascent in the darkness (the ritual is carried out at night), or to the ascent of the sacrificial victims into the dark-world. If it is the latter, and if the dark-world is (despite the paradox) conceived as lying in a downward direction, this 'ascent' would involve a culmination to the story whose directional element brings this hexagram back to the 'down' of its pair (Hexagram 45). Thus the line would both culminate Hexagram 46 and lead back into Hexagram 45 and its thematic of distress that weighs one down.

****

◆ TEXTUAL NOTES ◆

a. I follow the Mawangdui text, reading *li⁴* (利) instead of *yong⁴* (用) here, in keeping with the pattern throughout the *Zhouyi* except in this one case.

b. Reading *yun³* (𣉜) instead of *yun³* (允).

c. I read *xiang³* (享) for *heng¹* (亨), since this appears in a Line Statement rather than in the Hexagram Texts.

HEXAGRAM 47

HEDGED IN AND DISTRESSED[15]

HEXAGRAM TEXT:
(The occasion calls for a) **sacrifice.** [H-O]
Things are said, but do not believe them. [H-A]
As a divination for a big man, auspicious, without harmful mishap.
[H-SP]

LINES:
6 at the beginning:
**Buttocks hedged-in-and-distressed by a wooden staff. Entering into
'hidden valley', for three years he is not seen face-to-face.** [L-I]
Ominous.[a] [L-P]

9 at LINE 2:
**Hedged-in-and-distressed[16] by food and drink: the vermillion-knee-
cover border-state (people)[17] have come.** [L-I]
Beneficial to act to make a sacrificial offering. [L-A]
Without harmful mishap. Ominous for campaigning. [L-P, and
L-SP]

6 at LINE 3:
**Hedged-in-and-distressed by the rocks, grasping onto the spiny
caltrop: he enters his own palace, does not see his wife.** [L-I]
Ominous. [L-P]

9 at LINE 4:
They come slowly, hedged-in-and-distressed by bronze-metal carts.
[L-I]
Difficulties have an end. [L-P]

9 at LINE 5:
With nose and feet cut off, he slowly has gained release[b] **after being
hedged-in-and-distressed by red-knee-cap (people).[18]** [L-I]

Beneficial to act to make a sacrificial offering. [L-A]

6 on top:
Hedged-in-and-distressed by vines and by stumps, to the point that moving is trouble piled on trouble. [L-I]
Auspicious for campaigning. [L-SP]

****

COMMENTARY

In its overall structure the *Zhouyi* begins (Hexagrams 1 and 2) with the seasonal rhythm and life in an agriculture-dependent mode fitting itself into that rhythm, and ends (Hexagrams 63 and 64) with life placed within the matrix of the collective political/historical venturing which the Mandate of Heaven and the Shang and Zhou leadership of human life on earth provides.

Within these brackets, the thirty remaining hexagram pairs are grouped into five sets, the first of which (3/4 through 15/16) centers on Hexagrams 9 and 10. This pair make as theme that our human life-- this venturing and risking on earth under the heavens-- endemically becomes involved in troubles, in troubled situations. A subsequent group (17/18 through 41/42) centers on Hexagrams 29 and 30. This pair concerns divine powers manifest in the earth's higher and lower places, and the various pairs which belong to this group all develop themes which relate to earthly life under Heaven, particularly in its social aspects and in the general features of its being a temporal (mortal) affair.

The next set of hexagram pairs (43/44 through 49/50) has no central or organizing pair; its coherence is found in the common reference of all four pairs back to conditions of a being whose life is an active affair involving risk. In the venturing involved, such a being's efforts are caught up in various polar conditions.

Hexagrams 47 (Hedged in and distressed) and 48 (Well) are linked in focus on the thematic contrast of what is hedged in and inhibited, beset and frustrated vs. what flows freely.

The present hexagram unfolds as a series of variations on a phrase. There does not seem to be a story being told, and while there are contrasts and connections of the line-images which link Lines 1 and 4, 2 and 5, 3 and 6, the ordering of the series remains loose.

The theme of being hedged in and distressed is first (in Line 1) pointed to in the image of someone being beaten on the backside with a wooden staff, then imprisoned and disappearing from view for three years. Here the theme is realized in an obvious and physical reference, and by the instrumentality of other persons.

The next pointer (Line 2) realizes the theme in quite different circumstances: visitors from a border-state have come and are being entertained, and everyone is oppressed by food and drink (suffering from too much?). Here the realization is more subtle, but the oppressing circumstance is still a physical one.

The third pointer (Line 3) envisions a more inward realization of the theme. Here, the character of someone's distraction is being imaged-- it is as if, feeling hedged in by rocks, he inattentively grasped a spiny shrub/ tree to help him climb out; and distracted in this oppressed and self-inflicted pained fashion, that person enters his own house and does not see his wife, not because she is not there but because his mind is elsewhere.

The fourth pointer (Line 4) recalls the first in realizing the theme in an obvious and physical form, and in a way that involves the instrumentality of other persons. Someone seeking to go somewhere is only able to move ahead slowly because of harrassment by persons in bronze chariots.

The fifth pointer (Line 5) recalls the second to the extent of its reference to people at a distance by their dress; but the realization of the theme is more obvious, being found in the sense of being hedged in on the part of someone who has received punishment at the hands of that distant people (having his nose and feet cut off) and who slowly, only after a time, gains his release.

The final pointer (Line 6) recalls the third to the extent of its reference to vegetative obstacles, in this case, vines, stumps; but the realization is outward, the vines and stumps hedging in someone to the extent that the person finds it quite troublesome simply to move.

****

♦ TEXTUAL NOTES ♦

a. I follow the Mawangdui version here.

b. I read *tuo¹* (脫) instead of *shuo¹* (說); an alternative reading would be *tuo¹* (挩).

HEXAGRAM 48

WELL

HEXAGRAM TEXT:
> Changing the town but not changing the well is without loss or gain. But coming and going constantly-and-regularly, the well reaching the point of exhaustion and still not being dug out, the earthen jar becoming damaged: (that is something) ominous. [H-SSI]

LINES:

6 at the beginning:
> The well is muddy, not drinkable; the old pitfall is without game. [L-I]

9 at LINE 2:
> In the depths of the well, shoot silver carp; the earthen jar is ruined and leaks. [L-I]

9 at LINE 3:[a]
> The well suffers seepage, is not drinkable; it makes our hearts sorrowful. [L-I]

6 at LINE 4:[a]
> The well is tiled, it is fit for use in drawing water (to drink). [L-I]
>> Without harmful mishap. [L-P]

9 at LINE 5:
> The well is clear, a cold spring for drinking. [L-I]

6 on top:
> The well is brought to an end of its use. [L-I]
>> Do not cover! (Using it) make captures! [L-A]
>> Greatly auspicious. [L-P]

****

COMMENTARY

For the place of Hexagram 48 in the overall structure of the *Zhouyi*, and for the meaning of its pairing with Hexagram 47, see the first three paragraphs of the Commentary on Hexagram 47.

The Hexagram Text in the present case holds an image which sets the context for the lines and the story they tell. It is a time when the town has been moved, a move which by itself is neither a loss nor a gain; the old well has been kept, however, but there are problems. For after all the previous use of the well, it has reached a point of seeming exhaustion and has not been dug deeper, and the earthen jar used to draw water from it has been damaged. None of this bodes well for its continued use.[19]

The story, such as it is, proceeds by pairs of lines.

The first two lines adumbrate further the state of things expressed in the Hexagram Text image. Line 1 points to the uselessness of the well in its current state: the well-water is muddy and undrinkable, and even if one were to turn it into a pitfall it would be able to catch no game. Line 2 points to other sides of the present situation: even if the well-water were drinkable, the jar for drawing drinking water is ruined; the best that can be said is that the well has become a fish-pond which holds some fish.

The third and fourth lines bring action. First is the motivating sadness at the pollution of the well-water: community members apparently do not want to abandon the well (Line 3). This "sorrowful heart" provides the impetus toward corrective action. With successful repair action in the form of a tiling of the well (presumably after it has been cleared out and dug deeper), it is now fit for use in drawing water to drink (Line 4).

Finally come two lines pointing to the conditions which are the outcome of this action: the well clears up and becomes again a cold spring of drinkable water (Line 5); and when its use as a source of drinking water is over, it can be used as a pit and pitfall for hunting game (Line 6).

****

◆ TEXTUAL NOTES ◆

a. Lines 3 and 4 as they appear in the traditional and Mawangdui versions have been wrongly divided. I treat the last 9 characters of Line 3 (*ke³ yong⁴ ji¹, wang² ming² bing⁴ shou⁴ qi² fu²*: 可用汲王明並受其福) as in fact belonging in Line 4. The first three of these characters form part of the line-image, while the last six ("The royal covenant: together receive this blessing": I read *ming²* [明] here as *meng²* [盟]) form an intrusive editorial/commentary note which addresses the matter in Line 4. The note treats of the well as to be maintained and to function as a common source of water (this is the 'blessing').

HEXAGRAM 49

HIDE TANNED AND CHANGED[1]

HEXAGRAM TEXT:[a]
(The occasion calls for a) **grand sacrifice.**
It is a beneficial divination. [H-O]
　　It is a sacrifice[b] day, so they take captives. [H-SSI]

LINES:
9 at the beginning:
Bind using the tanned-hide of a yellow ox. [L-I]
　　Troubles vanish.[a] [L-P]

6 at LINE 2:
When the sacrifice[b] day came, they changed it. [L-I]
　　Without harmful mishap; auspicious for campaigning. [L-P, and
　　L-SP]

9 at LINE 3:
Change words (= commands), three accomodations to circumstance.[c]
[L-I]
　　As a divination, danger. For campaigning, ominous. [L-P, and L-
　　SP]

9 at LINE 4:
They hold the captives while changing the commands. [L-I]
　　Troubles vanish. [L-P]

9 at LINE 5:
**The big men underwent a tiger-transformation, even before (the
diviner) divined this 'holding the captives'.** [L-I]
　　Auspicious.[d] [L-P]

6 on top:

The nobleman underwent a leopard-transformation, and the little men had faces of tanned-hide.[2] [L-I]

Ominous for campaigning; auspicious as a dwelling-divination. [L-SP]

****

COMMENTARY

In its overall structure the *Zhouyi* begins (Hexagrams 1 and 2) with the seasonal rhythm and life in an agriculture-dependent mode fitting itself into that rhythm, and ends (Hexagrams 63 and 64) with life placed within the matrix of the collective political/historical venturing which the Mandate of Heaven and the Shang and Zhou leadership of human life on earth provides.

Within these brackets, the thirty remaining hexagram pairs are grouped into five sets, the first of which (3/4 through 15/16) centers on Hexagrams 9 and 10. This pair make as theme that our human life-- this venturing and risking on earth under the heavens-- endemically becomes involved in troubles, in troubled situations. A subsequent group (17/18 through 41/42) centers on Hexagrams 29 and 30. This pair concerns divine powers manifest in the earth's higher and lower places, and the various pairs which belong to this group all develop themes which relate to earthly life under Heaven, particularly in its social aspects and in the general features of its being a temporal (mortal) affair.

The next set of hexagram pairs (43/44 through 49/50) has no central or organizing pair; its coherence is found in the common reference of all four pairs back to conditions of a being whose life is an active affair involving risk. In the venturing involved, such a being's efforts are caught up in various polar conditions.

Hexagrams 49 (Hide tanned and changed) and 50 (Cauldron) are linked in focus around the theme of change and metamorphosis vs. stability and domesticity.

The present hexagram takes shape in its lines as telling a kind of story, but in a telling which makes use of different meanings of the title-name. For *ge*[4] (革) can signify a tanned-hide (as in Line 1); but it can also signify change, particularly one which involves removing, getting rid of, eliminating, and making into something new (as in Lines 2 and 3). And it is this-- various kinds of (transformative) change, signified not only by 革 but also by 改 and

變-- that lies at the heart of the story.

The scene is set by the image in the Hexagram Text: the story is to take place in a situation in which, given that a sacrifice day is approaching, there is need to secure captives for the sacrifice.

The story starts with the captives having been taken and then bound using strips of a yellow-ox tanned-hide (Line 1).

When the appointed day arrives, the sacrifice day is changed even though the captives have been taken and bound who were to be part of the sacrificial ritual (Line 2). The reason for the posponement is not mentioned, but presumably it has something to do with the day originally chosen turning out later not to be auspicious for such a sacrifice.

Three attempts to find a good day are made before an auspicious day was found (Line 3).

All while these changes in the commands were occurring the captives have been held (Line 4).

The delay had an impact upon some of the people involved: even before the divination took place concerning whether it was auspicious to keep holding the captives, the 'big men' supported holding the captives and became 'tiger-like' (thus aggressive, ready to go ahead) (Line 5).

The response of others was different: the nobleman, becoming leopard-like himself, restrained any action until the divination showed it to be auspicious. The 'little men', however, were basically bystanders who had faces of tanned-hide: that is, their faces changed as the nobleman asserted himself,[3] and they followed him (Line 6).

****

◆ TEXTUAL NOTES ◆

a. In the traditional and Mawangdui versions, there is a phrase (*hui³ wang²*: 悔亡) which (due to a faulty line-division) has been placed in the Hexagram Text whereas it belongs with Line 1, which otherwise is without prognostication words. I have restored it to its proper place.

b. I read *si⁴* (祀) for *si⁴* (巳).

c. That is, the date was three times adapted to the circumstance of a divination which indicated that the proposed date was inauspicious. I have omitted here a *you³ fu²* (有俘: 'take and hold captives', 'offer captives as sacrificial animals') as a misplaced repetition of that phrase in Lines 4 and 5.

Its appearance here would make Line 4 a mere repetition of the idea already in Line 3. An alternative treatment of the 2-character phrase would be to understand it as *yu² fu²* (于俘), thus meaning "three accommodations (in dates) relating to the captives".

d. Due to a faulty line-division, this prognostication word appears at the end of Line 4 in the traditional and Mawangdui versions, separate from the other such phrase in that line.

HEXAGRAM 50

CAULDRON[4]

HEXAGRAM TEXT:
(The occasion calls for a) **sacrifice.**
A beneficial divination.[a] [H-O]

LINES:
6 at the beginning:[b]
 The cauldron is overturned, its feet turned up. [L-I]
  **Beneficial to expel evil, acquire female-bondsmaid(s) along with
  her/their offspring.** [L-A]
  Without harmful mishap. [L-P]

9 at LINE 2:
 **The cauldron holds contents; 'my mate is ill, the illness is not able to
 reach me'.** [L-I]
  Auspicious. [L-P]

9 at LINE 3:
 **The cauldron's ear is removed, its going is blocked, the fat meat of
 the pheasant is not eaten. It is just about to rain; there will be
 damage.** [L-I]
  Troubles, in the end auspicious. [L-P]

9 at LINE 4:
 The cauldron breaks off its feet, overturning the Duke's stew; his (=
 the person responsible) **punishment**[c] **is being put to death.** [L-I]
  Ominous. [L-P]

6 at LINE 5:
 A cauldron with yellow ears and a metal carrying-bar. [L-I]
  Greatly auspicious.[a] [L-P]

9 on top:
  A cauldron with jade carrying-bar. [L-I]
  Greatly auspicious, nothing not beneficial. [L-P]

****

COMMENTARY

For the place of Hexagram 50 in the overall structure of the *Zhouyi*, and for the meaning of its pairing with Hexagram 49, see the first four paragraphs of the Commentary on Hexagram 49.

The present hexagram takes shape as a set of variant images of a cauldron. They are ordered in contrasting line-pairs, and while not apparently telling any story nor setting forth any type-analysis, the pairs focus attention sometimes on the functioning of the cauldron, sometimes on one or another part of it or separate part needed for its functioning.

In Line 1, the cauldron is overturned, its feet are sticking up: it has been emptied, apparently, or at least, it is presently empty. This is the cauldron when it is not functioning as such. In contrast, in Line 2 the cauldron is right side up and full. And yet while it is now functioning, the lord's mate is ill and can not join him in eating; on the brighter side, the illness is thereby not able to reach the husband.

In Line 3, the cauldron's ears have become stripped off, and and its consequent non-functionality introduces troubles. For since the cauldron now can not be carried and the food served, the food will not be eaten. What is worse, rain is imminent and with it damage to the food. Thus we have an image of things gone wrong and about to get worse. In Line 4, it is the cauldron's feet which are broken off: it was full, and the stew was thus spilled, so as a result someone was punished (death: after all, it was the *Duke's* stew!).

In the final two lines, it is not the functioning of the cauldron which is pointed to, but only certain of its functional elements. In Line 5, the cauldron has yellow ears and a metal carrying-bar, while in contrast, in Line 6 the cauldron has a jade carrying-bar.

****

◆ TEXTUAL NOTES ◆

a. For some reason, the prognostication words in the Hexagram Text and in

Line 5 seem to have been exchanged, so that the Hexagram Text contains a phrase that is found only in the Lines and the Line contains a phrase found unqualified only in the Hexagram Texts. I have restored the phrases to their proper places.

b. Kunst (*OY*, 421-38) offers extended glosses of each of the six lines; Shaughnessy (*CZ*, 177-82) provides a briefer discussion of the Line Statements also. Both warrant consultation.

c. Reading *xing² wu¹* (刑劓) for *xing² wo⁴* (形渥).

HEXAGRAM 51

THUNDER⁵

HEXAGRAM TEXT:ᵃ
(The occasion calls for a) **sacrifice.** [H-O]
> **Thunder startles and arouses the hundred villages, but he** (the leader of the ritual) **does not lose the sacrificial ladle and the fragrant wine.** [H-SSI]

LINES:
9 at the beginning:ᵃ
> **Thunder is coming, crack-crack** (sound of thunder) **and then afterwards, laughter and talk, ha-ha** (sound of laughter). [L-I]
> > **Auspicious.** [L-P]

6 at LINE 2:
> **Thunder is coming, a threat; perhaps we will lose 'cowries'.** [L-I]
> > **They** (= horses?) **climb in the Nine Hills; do not pursue, you will get them after seven days.** [L-A]

6 at LINE 3:
> **Thunder rumble-rumble** (sound of rolling thunder), **thunder is traveling.** [L-I]
> > **Without calamity.** [L-P]

9 at LINE 4:
> **Thunder, then mud.** [L-I]

6 at LINE 5:
> **The thunder in its coming and going was forceful:** 'ah (sighing-sound, with a sense of relief), **it was without loss in my own affairs'**ᵇ. [L-I]

6 on top:[c]
  Thunder does not concern themselves, it concerns their neighbors.
  [L-I]
    **Without harmful mishap. As to a marriage match, there will be
    talk.** [L-P, and L-SP]

****

COMMENTARY

In its overall structure the *Zhouyi* begins (Hexagrams 1 and 2) with the
seasonal rhythm and life in an agriculture-dependent mode fitting itself into
that rhythm, and ends (Hexagrams 63 and 64) with life placed within the
matrix of the collective political/historical venturing which the Mandate of
Heaven and the Shang and Zhou leadership of human life on earth provides.

Within these brackets, the thirty remaining hexagram pairs are grouped
into five sets, the first of which (3/4 through 15/16) centers on Hexagrams
9 and 10. This pair make as theme that our human life-- this venturing and
risking on earth under the heavens-- endemically becomes involved in troubles, in troubled situations. A subsequent group (17/18 through 41/42) centers on Hexagrams 29 and 30. This pair concerns divine powers manifest in
the earth's higher and lower places, and the various pairs which belong to this
group all develop themes which relate to earthly life under Heaven, particularly in its social aspects and in the general features of its being a temporal (mortal) affair. The next group of hexagram pairs (43/44 through 49/
50) has no central or organizing pair; its coherence is found in the common
reference of all four pairs back to conditions of a being whose life is an active affair involving risk. In the venturing involved, such a being's efforts are
caught up in various polar conditions.

The next to last group of hexagram pairs (51/52 through 55/56) is structured as a lead pair followed by two complementary pairs. The unifying
theme for the group is sexuality between male and female, man and wife: the
most intimate connection of human beings with each other out of their inwardness.

Hexagrams 51 (Thunder) and 52 (Glaring) form the head pair of this
group. They are linked in focus upon the contrast of sexual intimacy and
hostile distance.

The present hexagram sets forth, in an ordered group of variations on a
phrase, a 'story' which exhibits the phases in an event involving thunder.

The scene is set in the image of the Hexagram Text: the context of the lines is a springtime festival ceremony which celebrates survival through the winter and which ritually ensures the fertility of the soil for the coming growing season. It is a rite of spring, and with that, a rousing to life which includes importantly, both symbolically and actually, sexual attraction and an erotic undertone investing interaction between the sexes.

The start of the story of the coming and passing of thunder on such an occasion is with the distant sounding of thunder, an initiating force in the spring fertility festivals, and with laughing and talking among participants in the ritual celebration.

In Line 2, while still at a distance the thunder is nonetheless coming closer and it is becoming noticed now as a threat: a possible loss of valuables, presumably from flood occasioned by the rain, but perhaps from other causes associated with thunderstorms (for example, the scattering to and in the hills of horses frightened by the sound).

In Line 3, the approach of the thunder is manifest now in its rolling sound; it is almost upon the people.

In Line 4, the thunderstorm has has arrived, bringing rain and thus mud.

In Line 5, the thunderstorm has now passed; its coming had been forceful but apparently-- to their relief-- had brought no loss to the affairs of the celebrants.

And finally, in Line 6, with the thunder in the distance again, the image is of this contrast: it does not concern one's own person now, but concerns one's neighbors.

****

◆ TEXTUAL NOTES ◆

a. The Hexagram Text in the traditional and Mawangdui versions contains a phrase ("Thunder coming, crack-crack [sound of thunder], laughter and talk, ha-ha [sound of laughter]") which forms an alternative version of Line 1. In this case the Text is functioning as a convenient place to 'store' this variant line (it differs from the traditional Line 1 only by one character). I remove it from the Text, and retain Line 1 as it is in those versions. See also Shaughnessy (*CZ*, 215-16) for a treatment of the Hexagram Text phrase as a reduplication of Line 1.

b. For the grammar of the *you³ shi⁴* (有事), see Kunst (*OY*, 108 and 197).

c. In the traditional and Mawangdui versions, Line 6 holds an alternative line 'stored' there for retention, namely: "Thunder going boom-boom (sound of thunder), looking around here-and-there.[6] Ominous for campaigning." This 'extra' and variant Line may not have been meant to be alternative to the present Line 6, but perhaps to Line 3.

HEXAGRAM 52

GLARING[a]

HEXAGRAM TEXT:

[Whatever may have been a part of this Text is lost now.][b]

LINES:
6 at the beginning:
Glare at his/their feet. [L-I]
Without harmful mishap. A beneficial long-term divination. [L-P, and L-SP]

6 at LINE 2:
Glare at his/their lower-leg, do not help his/their followers, his/their heart is not happy.[c] [L-I]

9 at LINE 3:
Glare at his/their mid-section, pierce (with one's eyes) the small of his/their back(s): a threatening and aflame/fuming/beclouded heart. [L-I]

6 at LINE 4:[b]
Glare at his back, but not catch his whole torso; walk in his courtyard, but not see the others. [L-I]
Without harmful mishap. [L-P]

6 at LINE 5:[b]
Glare at the whole torso.[7] [L-I]
Without harmful mishap. [L-P]

9 on top:[b]
Glare at his/their[c] **cheeks-and-jaws; speak words that have order.** [L-I]
Auspicious; troubles vanish. [L-P]

****

COMMENTARY

For the place of Hexagram 62 in the overall structure of the *Zhouyi*, and for the meaning of its pairing with Hexagram 51, see the first four paragraphs of the Commentary on Hexagram 51.

In an ordered series of variations but this time without story, the present hexagram sets forth a series of 'staring at' examples. These express human relations that embody varying degrees of distance and hostility. The order includes an ascending focus on different bodily parts.

The beginning (Line 1) is with a glaring at the lowest part of the body of another person, the feet.

The next step moves the glaring up a bit, to the calf area of the leg (Line 2), and takes note of something that goes into the glaring: an unhappy heart that is not willing to help his/their followers.

The next step is similar: the glaring shifts to the waist or mid-section (Line 3), and this time, the heart is even more hostile: a fuming heart, beclouded with anger, and threatening. The glance of such a person pierces through to the small of the back of the person upon whom it is directed.

Again the glare moves upward, this time to someone's back (Line 4); it is a glaring whose limited focus (it does not catch even the whole torso) is underlined in a counterpart image of someone moving about his courtyard oblivious to anyone else that is there.

In Line 5 the glaring expands to the whole torso.

The series ends in Line 6, with a glaring at someone's cheeks-and-jaw. Such glaring continues the expansion of attention and awareness started in Line 5, for in reaching to the high point of the body (the face), it reaches also to the part which involves speech. And with that, glaring seems itself to become modified and to be able to issue in orderly speech.

****

◆ TEXTUAL NOTES ◆

a. Shaughnessy (*CZ*, 187) provides good reasons for understanding the title-name to mean "glaring at". See also Gao's analysis (*ZGJ*, 179-80).

b. In the traditional and Mawangdui versions there are two significant textual emendations to be made. Line 6, which falls outside the pattern in its line-image, in fact seems more like an editorial/commentary note that has mistakenly been entered into the text. The note ("Intensely stare at") comments on the meaning of the title-name to the Hexagram, emphasizing the intensity of the looking or staring that is involved: it is an "intense staring", that is, it is a glaring with an inner intensity to the looking that manifests itself in the act itself. I have excised the phrase from the text. There is also a line with two images present in the traditional and Mawangdui versions of the Hexagram Text. This line has the character of a Line Statement, and in terms of its image-content, it should be a displaced Line 4. I have restored it to its proper place, and shifted what in the traditional and Mawangdui versions are Lines 4 and 5 to be Lines 5 and 6 respectively. [In the latter case, I have retained the *ji²* (吉) of Line 6 in the traditional and Mawangdui versions, and joined it to what before was Line 5.]. When all this is done, there is nothing left in the Hexagram Text. Shaughnessy (*CZ*, 187-88), taking his cue from the anatomical organization of the topics, also argues that the Hexagram Text phrase in question is a displaced line statement; but he would place it as Line 5, whereas I think the order is better served by making it Line 4. That is particularly so if one adopted the suggestive reading of 身 which Li points to in considering the 身 in the traditional Line 4 (what I place as Line 5). There he claims that the ancient writing of this character resembled the form of a protuding chest and belly, and that a pregnant woman was said to 有身 (we might translate, "have a belly"); thus he urges understanding the term to signify our front section (breast and belly). That makes good sense in the line-phrase in which it is explicitly contrasted with the back (the one I place as Line 4), and not as good for the line-phrase in which it appears alone (what I place as Line 5). I would reserve the meaning of "whole torso" for the term in Line 5, which forms a fitting transition to the reference in Line 6 to a part of the head (cheeks-and-jaws).

c. The Chinese here (*qi²*: 其) is indeterminate, and since there is no context to give us a clue, it could mean either "his" or "their".

HEXAGRAM 53

ADVANCE

HEXAGRAM TEXT:
It is a beneficial divination. [H-O]
    Auspicious for a female to be given in marriage. [H-SP]

LINES:
6 at the beginning:
    Wild geese advance to the mountain stream[a]. Small ones are in danger, there are scolding words[b]. [L-I]
    Without harmful mishap. [L-P]

6 at LINE 2:
    The wild geese advance to the large boulders, and drink and eat happily ('honk-honk'). [L-I]
    Auspicious. [L-P]

9 at LINE 3:
    The wild geese advance to higher ground; a husband on campaign and not yet returned, a wife pregnant and not yet having given birth. [L-I]
    Beneficial for warding off bandits. [L-A]
    Ominous. [L-P]

6 at LINE 4:
    The wild geese advance to the trees, and now[c] gain their perch [= a horizontal branch on which to perch]. [L-I]
    Without harmful mishap. [L-P]

9 at LINE 5:
    The wild geese advance to high mounds which form hillocks; the wife has not been pregnant for three years, but in the end nothing overcomes her. [L-I]
    Auspicious. [L-P]

9 on top:
The wild geese advance to the high ground of hilltops[d]; their feathers are suitable for using to make ceremonial dance paraphenalia. [L-I]
Auspicious. [L-P]

****

COMMENTARY

In its overall structure the *Zhouyi* begins (Hexagrams 1 and 2) with the seasonal rhythm and life in an agriculture-dependent mode fitting itself into that rhythm, and ends (Hexagrams 63 and 64) with life placed within the matrix of the collective political/historical venturing which the Mandate of Heaven and the Shang and Zhou leadership of human life on earth provides.

Within these brackets, the thirty remaining hexagram pairs are grouped into five sets, the first of which (3/4 through 15/16) centers on Hexagrams 9 and 10. This pair make as theme that our human life-- this venturing and risking on earth under the heavens-- endemically becomes involved in troubles, in troubled situations. A subsequent group (17/18 through 41/42) centers on Hexagrams 29 and 30. This pair concerns divine powers manifest in the earth's higher and lower places, and the various pairs which belong to this group all develop themes which relate to earthly life under Heaven, particularly in its social aspects and in the general features of its being a temporal (mortal) affair. The next group of hexagram pairs (43/44 through 49/50) has no central or organizing pair; its coherence is found in the common reference of all four pairs back to conditions of a being whose life is an active affair involving risk. In the venturing involved, such a being's efforts are caught up in various polar conditions.

The next to last group of hexagram pairs (51/52 through 55/56) is structured as a lead pair followed by two complementary pairs. The unifying theme for the group is sexuality between male and female, man and wife: the most intimate connection of human beings with each other out of their inwardness.

Hexagrams 53 (Advance) and 54 (Marrying Maiden) are linked in focus upon the contrast of the state of the connection formed between man and woman, husband and wife: a distance between them being closed vs. a distance opening up between them.

The present hexagram develops as a set of variations, which also tells the story of the return of wild geese to their upland home-country. The core to the story is the advance of the geese to a mountain stream (Line 1), to large rocks/boulders (Line 2), to higher ground (Line 3), to trees (Line 4), to hillocks or high mounds (Line 5), and finally (Line 6) to high hilltops and ground. Yet the lines which convey this also amplify the imagery.

Lines 1 and 2 do so by reference to the geese alone: at the first stop, the parents scold their small offspring who are oblivious to the dangers they are getting themselves into, and at the second, the geese happily eat, drink, and socialize.

Lines 3 and 5, however, introduce an explicit counterpoint with human beings and affairs in human life. Thus in Line 3, it is a husband on campaign and not yet returned, and a wife pregnant and not yet having given birth; the conjunction of the two images (bird and human) would seem to intensify the sense related to the wild geese, that 'we are getting close to being home', with the sense of almost-home strengthening the feeling of still being at a distance, still not yet there. In Line 5, it is a wife for three years not pregnant, but in the end nothing overcomes her; again, the conjunction of the two images (bird and human) would seem to intensify the sense related to the wild geese, that an invincible steadfastness over a long journey has brought them almost home.

Finally, in Line 6, the human and avian are brought together in a different way: the moulted feathers of the birds who have returned home are suitable for use in making ceremonial-dance paraphenalia.[8]

The return of the geese to their home evokes, along the way, the separation that is being overcome, and in the human counterpart images in Lines 3 and 5 at least, particularly marital separation. This theme of overcoming marital separation is confirmed and strengthened by the Hexagram's being paired with Hexagram 54 (Marrying Maiden).[9] And when this is amplified by the wife's faithfulness, then the imagery enhances the pairing of the two hexagrams.

****

◆ TEXTUAL NOTES ◆

a. Shaughnessy (*CZ*, 190-92) points to two meanings of *gan¹* (干: bank of a stream, or mountain stream), and to linkages of words in a *Shijing* poem which suggest that "mountain stream" is the better translation here. Li (*ZTong*, 105) also takes "mountain stream" for the meaning, as do I. But Kunst (*OY*, 344-5) and Gao (*ZGJ*, 183) interpret it as "river-bank".

b. Li (*ZTong*, 105) reads *yan²* (言) as a loan for *e¹* (詻) (scolding and opposing words); but even without that, the *you³ yan²* (有言) could mean something like that.

c. Reading *huo⁴* (或) as "and now" with Shaughnessy (*CZ*, 189); but this could also be taken to mean "some", as Kunst (*OY*, 344) and Li (*ZTong*, 106) do.

d. I read *e⁴* (阿: hilltop) instead of *lu⁴* (陸: land), the latter being a mistaken repetition of Line 3 and lacking the sound to carry the rhyme here. See Shaughnessy (*CZ*, 192-3) for a discussion; Li reads *e⁴* also.

HEXAGRAM 54

MARRYING MAIDEN

HEXAGRAM TEXT:
Ominous for campaigning, without anything beneficial. [H-SP]

LINES:
9 at the beginning:
Sending the maiden in marriage accompanied by her younger sister(s):[10] the lame are able to walk. [L-I]
Auspicious for campaigning. [L-SP]

9 at LINE 2:
The feeble-sighted are able to see. [L-I]
A beneficial prisoner-divination. [L-SP]

6 at LINE 3:
Sending the maiden in marriage accompanied by her elder sister(s)[a]; they return home accompanied by her younger sister(s). [L-I]

9 at LINE 4:
The marrying maiden exceeded her time-period;[11] but sent late in marriage there (still) was time. [L-I]

6 at LINE 5:
Emperor Yi[12] sent his daughter in marriage, the primary bride's sleeves were not as beautiful as those of the secondary wife. [L-I]
Auspicious when the moon is almost full. [L-SP]

6 on top:
The women held in outstretched hands baskets without fruit, the men stabbed sheep but there was no blood.[13] [L-I]
Without anything beneficial. [L-P]

****

COMMENTARY

For the place of Hexagram 54 in the overall structure of the *Zhouyi*, and for the meaning of its pairing with Hexagram 53, see the first four paragraphs of the Commentary on Hexagram 53.

The present hexagram unfolds as telling the story of the unsuccessful marriage of the Yin-Shang ruler Di Yi's daughter to King Wen of the Zhou.[14]

It begins (Lines 1 and 2) with the daughter being sent in marriage accompanied by her younger sisters, and with a hint that something was amiss. For an accompanying image in Line 1 points implicitly to what is to be discovered in time: although she is able to be married (can "walk"), she is not able to produce as wife (is "lame"). And this hint is continued in another accompanying image in Line 2 (the main line image is missing there); this time, it concerns her "sight" being "feeble".

Even though the new family situation is apparently not all that it could and should be, Di Yi's daughter remains in it while her sisters older and younger return to their original family and family situation (Line 3).

In Line 4, we get closer to a disclosure of what was hinted at in the first two lines; for she is pointed to as having been older than the norm when married, and yet still having time, presumably for bearing male offspring.

In Line 5, her deficiency in comparison with another woman, the secondary wife of King Wen's who was eventually to be the mother of King Wu, is pointed out.

And finally the unsuccessful character of the marriage comes out into the open, in images of the fruit-less and blood-less (Line 6).

The story-movement that is achieved through the lines-- a beginning in closeness, the emergence of a distance, and finally failure-- provides a thematic contrast with the success-story of Hexagram 53, with its beginning in distance, then the distance gradually being closed, and its end in the successful arrival at the nesting ground.

****

◆ TEXTUAL NOTES ◆

a. I read *xu¹* (鬚) for *xu¹* (須). The term translated "elder sisters" here is also used as a familiar name for bondmaids, so it need not necessarily mean the marrying maiden had older sisters who accompanied her-- especially if she was already a woman older than normal for marriage.

HEXAGRAM 55

FULLNESS[15]

HEXAGRAM TEXT:
(The occasion calls for a) **sacrifice.** [H-O]
> The King proceeded to and entered it,[16] do not worry, it is fitting (for him to do this) at mid-day. [H-SSI]

LINES:
9 at the beginning:
> He[17] meets the chief concubine[a]. [L-I]
>> As for going, it has its rewards[b]; as for there being man-woman combining[c], that would be without harmful mishap. [L-SP]

6 at LINE 2:
> Grand-and-full is the darkness, at midday see the Dipper. [L-I]
>> As for going, obtain mistrust and hate; auspicious for offering in sacrifice captives bristling with anger. [L-SP]

9 at LINE 3:
> Full-and-grand the screening, at midday see darkness[d]; break one's right forearm. [L-I]
>> Without harmful mishap. [L-P]

9 at LINE 4:[e]
> He meets the barbarian chief: coming splendor-and-brilliance, will have rejoicing and praise. [L-I]
>> Auspicious. [L-P]

6 at LINE 5:[e]
> Grand-and-full the darkness, at midday see the Dipper. [L-I]

6 on top:
  **Grand-and-full the roof[, dark the home; peek in the door, desolate
  its being without anyone there; three years, not see face to face. [L-I]
  Ominous.** [L-P]

****

COMMENTARY

In its overall structure the *Zhouyi* begins (Hexagrams 1 and 2) with the
seasonal rhythm and life in an agriculture-dependent mode fitting itself into
that rhythm, and ends (Hexagrams 63 and 64) with life placed within the
matrix of the collective political/historical venturing which the Mandate of
Heaven and the Shang and Zhou leadership of human life on earth provides.

Within these brackets, the thirty remaining hexagram pairs are grouped
into five sets, the first of which (3/4 through 15/16) centers on Hexagrams
9 and 10. This pair make as theme that our human life-- this venturing and
risking on earth under the heavens-- endemically becomes involved in troubles, in troubled situations. A subsequent group (17/18 through 41/42) centers on Hexagrams 29 and 30. This pair concerns divine powers manifest in
the earth's higher and lower places, and the various pairs which belong to this
group all develop themes which relate to earthly life under Heaven, particularly in its social aspects and in the general features of its being a temporal (mortal) affair. The next group of hexagram pairs (43/44 through 49/
50) has no central or organizing pair; its coherence is found in the common
reference of all four pairs back to conditions of a being whose life is an active affair involving risk. In the venturing involved, such a being's efforts are
caught up in various polar conditions.

The next to last group of hexagram pairs (51/52 through 55/56) is structured as a lead pair followed by two complementary pairs. The unifying
theme for the group is sexuality between male and female, man and wife: the
most intimate connection of human beings with each other out of their inwardness.

Hexagrams 55 (Fulness) and 56 (Traveller) are linked to form the continuing story of Prince Hai, a member of the royal family in early Shang
dynasty times.[18] The two phases of the story concern his exploits when taking over and inheriting a large estate and then when he has rejected that and
gone on the move.

Included in the Text of the present hexagram is a scene setting image which places the story to be told in the context of an unusual (and therefore worrisome) action of the Prince, which is nonetheless something fitting for him to carry out at the mid-day time he does it.

The succession of lines that follows sets forth sufficient of his exploits as a youth for us to get his character. It begins (Line 1) with Prince Hai meeting with the chief concubine or consort at court, with the implication (in the prognostication) of 'combining' (sexually) and of the initially rewarding and harmless character of the going.

But soon, the liaison changes character. The image in this line (Line 2), in its literal sense altogether unconnected with that in Line 1, is of an extreme darkness that has come at midday (presumably through an eclipse) and has made the Dipper visible then. The prognostication, speaking again of 'going' and presumably (as in Line 1) meaning going to meet a woman, suggests that the affair has turned sour. Mistrust and hate have arisen.

Apparently the affair ends in frustration (Line 3). For the image in this line, in its literal sense again unconnected with that in Line 1, is of a full screening out of the light, such that at midday one can only see darkness (as in a thicket, the dense vegetation turns day into night; as in heavy cloud cover also). This leads to a "breaking of one's right forearm": an expression which means "to fail in accomplishing one's purposes". Such imagery is symbolic of being plunged inwardly into darkness, this time into such deep darkness that all light is obscured; and this is the matrix of the acknowledgement of failure (here, presumably, in the affair).

With Line 4, a second venture is initiated, this time a meeting with a barbarian chief; with this meeting comes what seems to be imminent glory and splendor, what promises joy and praise. The 'darkness' vanishes for a moment, and Prince Hai seems on the rise.

But as in the sexual affair, so again here (Line 5): the same darkness descends at midday, an eclipse such that the Dipper is visible at noon. Presumably this is again symbolic: the promise has fallen through.

Prince Hai's response is intimated in the final line, which presents a picture of desolation-- a deserted homestead, no sign of the owner for three years (Line 6).

****

◆ TEXTUAL NOTES ◆

a. I read *fei¹* (妃) for *pei⁴* (配), treating the latter as loan for the former. Kunst (*OY*, 349) translates: "He meets his mistress." Li (*ZTong*, 109-10) takes the woman to be a hostess whom a traveller meets and ends up marrying; Gao (*ZGJ*, 191) interprets similarly.

b. I read *shang³* (賞) for *shang⁴* (尚).

c. In this two-character phrase, I read *sui²* (雖) as *wei²* (唯); and I read *xun²* (旬) as the primitive graph for *jun¹* (昀).

d. I read *mei⁴* (昧) for *mei⁴* (沬).

e. There is a faulty line-division between Lines 4 and 5; I have moved the first part of Line 4 in the traditional and the Mawangdui texts to Line 5, and what was Line 5 to Line 4, to restore the text to order.

f. Or, "canopy" (see Kunst, *OY*, 349).

HEXAGRAM 56

TRAVELER

HEXAGRAM TEXT:
   (The occasion calls for a) **minor sacrifice.** [H-O]
      Auspicious as a traveler-divination. [H-SP]

LINES:
6 at the beginning:
   The traveling-visitor, chopping up his place bit by bit,[19] fetched
   disaster. [L-I]

6 at LINE 2:
   The traveling-visitor arrives at a hostel, carrying wealth in his
   bosom, and acquires young slaves. [L-I]
      As a divination, auspicious.[a] [L-P]

9 at LINE 3:
   The traveling-visitor burns the hostel, and loses his young slave-boys.
   [L-I]
      As a divination, danger. [L-P]

9 at LINE 4:
   The traveling-visitor, on his sojourn, acquires wealth, but ...'My
   heart is unhappy'. [L-I]

6 at LINE 5:
   He shot a pheasant with one arrow; it disappeared, (but) in the end
   by this means (he gained) praise and a mandate-and-command. [L-I]

9 on top:
   A bird burning its own nest: the traveling-visitor at first laughed, but
   later wept and wailed; he lost his cows at Yi. [L-I]
      Ominous. [L-P]

****

COMMENTARY

For the place of Hexagram 56 in the overall structure of the *Zhouyi*, and for the meaning of its pairing with Hexagram 55, see the first three paragraphs of the Commentary on Hexagram 55.

The present hexagram takes up where the story left off in 55: the owner (Prince Hai) has returned, but only in order to destroy the place, and to that extent he brings disaster on himself (Line 1).

Setting out as a traveler, he carries wealth with him and acquires slaves at a hostel where he stays (Line 2).

But once again, in a self-destructive action that recalls that of Line 1, he destroys his 'home' (setting fire to the hostel) and in the bargain loses his newly-purchased slaves (Line 3).

Setting off again, he acquires wealth on his sojourn, but still feels unhappy (Line 4).

Yet having established himself enough and built up holdings enough to take part in the noble pastime of hunting, by a strange turn (a pheasant he shot disappeared, and yet somehow that was the means for ...), he gains praise and a mandate-and-command (Line 5).

But finally, in a repeat of the pattern, he undermines himself: like the bird burning its own nest, he first indulges himself enjoyably (presumably, adultery) and then later weeps and wails (as the offended lord conspires against him). The upshot is 'he lost his cattle at Yi' (his herds were confiscated and he was killed) (Line 6).

****

◆ TEXTUAL NOTES ◆

a. The *jt²* (吉: 'auspicious') has been inadvertently omitted from the traditional and the Mawangdui texts; I restore it here.

HEXAGRAM 57

LAYING OUT FOOD OFFERINGS[a]

HEXAGRAM TEXT:
(The occasion calls for a) **minor sacrifice.** [H-O]
Beneficial to have a place to go. Beneficial to see the big man. [H-A]

LINES:
6 at the beginning:
Advance and withdraw. [L-I]
Beneficial military-man divination. [L-SP]

9 at LINE 2:
Lay out food offerings under the platform, use diviners and shamans in good numbers. [L-I]
Auspicious, without harmful mishap. [L-P]

9 at LINE 3:
Repeatedly lay out food offerings. [L-I]
Difficulty. [L-P]

6 at LINE 4:
Hunting, catch three kinds (of game). [L-I]
Troubles vanish. [L-P]

9 at LINE 5:
As a divination, auspicious, troubles vanish, nothing not beneficial.
As for having an end without a beginning: auspicious for three days before a *geng*-stem day[1] and three days after such a day. [L-P, and L-SP]

9 on top:
Lay out food offerings below the platform, lose the money-axes.[2] [L-I]
    As a divination, ominous. [L-P]

****

COMMENTARY

In its overall structure the *Zhouyi* begins (Hexagrams 1 and 2) with the seasonal rhythm and life in an agriculture-dependent mode fitting itself into that rhythm, and ends (Hexagrams 63 and 64) with life placed within the matrix of the collective political/historical venturing which the Mandate of Heaven and the Shang and Zhou leadership of human life on earth provides.

Within these brackets, the thirty remaining hexagram pairs are grouped into five sets, the first of which (3/4 through 15/16) centers on Hexagrams 9 and 10. This pair make as theme that our human life-- this venturing and risking on earth under the heavens-- endemically becomes involved in troubles, in troubled situations. A subsequent group (17/18 through 41/42) centers on Hexagrams 29 and 30. This pair concerns divine powers manifest in the earth's higher and lower places, and the various pairs which belong to this group all develop themes which relate to earthly life under Heaven, particularly in its social aspects and in general features of its being a temporal (mortal) affair. The next group of hexagram pairs (43/44 through 49/50) has no central or organizing pair; its coherence is found in the common reference of all four pairs back to conditions of a being whose life is an active affair involving risk. In the venturing involved, such a being's efforts are caught up in various polar conditions. The next to last group of hexagram pairs (51/52 through 55/56) is structured as a lead pair followed by two complementary pairs. The unifying theme for the group is sexuality between male and female, man and wife: the most intimate connection of human beings with each other out of their inwardness.

The final group of hexagram pairs (57/58 through 61/62) has the same structure as the preceding group: a lead pair followed by two complementary pairs. The unifying theme for the group is an even more intimate connection than the sexuality that was theme for the preceding group: it is the connection of human beings with the divine and not simply with each other.

Hexagrams 57 (Laying out food offerings) and 58 (Pleasure) are linked in focus on contrasting attitudes: a reverence (submissiveness, yieldingness) that would make offerings to the gods and spirits vs. the joy which, while it would begin and end in harmony (among human beings), is achieved also in war and negotiation as well as in the willingness to continue fighting-- which would also ask the gods to help but ... would not stop acting. The contrasts are also connected by the faint traces of a 'story' which, beginning with delineating the pervasive relevance of reverence throughout victory, defeat, and indecisiveness, ends with delineating how pleasure may also pervade life's different conditions.

The underlying issue in this pair is the King as religious and political figure, with a mandate for exercise of authority in the name of a reaching for civilized existence. The task his exercise of authority is implicated in is a cooperative one that is demanding and unending, marked by ups and downs along the way, but to be enjoyed in its challenge.

The 'story' adumbrated through the lines of the present hexagram starts with a time and condition of indecisive conflict, of an advancing and retreating (Line 1).[3]

This indecisiveness calls forth a sacrificial ritual on a grand scale, including the laying out of food offerings and the use of diviners and shamans (Line 2).

Indeed, it calls for repeated sacrificial ritual and offering of food-offerings before the conflict (in Line 1) is settled (Line 3).

If some peace has followed on this, it has given time for hunting, and the hunt is successful (Line 4). Thus although there is no image to explain it,[4] it is a time when troubles have vanished (Line 5).

But the 'story' ends on a different note: another laying out of offerings, this time in a time of difficulty in which one's wealth is being lost. There is an ominous foreboding here (Line 6).

Together, the lines convey a sense of the religious address to life and things, that it is a steadying force relevant to times of all sort-- of indecisive conflict, of victory and secure peace, and of loss-- but that it by no means always succeeds in bringing fortunate eventualities.

****

◆ TEXTUAL NOTES ◆

a. The title-name in the traditional texts is the primary graph *sun¹* (巽), but that graph is used in the sense of *zhuan¹*, the primary graph given the food-radical (饌). The primary graph is, etymologically, a picture of two men kneeling on a small table; its meaning lies in the idea of being compliant and submissive. In the title-name the element of food is added, and the combined character indicates what the act of laying out food offerings is supposed to express, namely, a submissive and humble reverence that would make offerings to the gods/spirits. And yet... as the pair-hexagram would suggest, this means an attitude which is in concert with the sense of willingness and ability to assume responsibility which the notion of the Mandate of Heaven (with its call upon initiative and venturing, upon one's own effort) conveys. The above suggested reading of the graph, which agrees with that of Kunst (*OY*, 352-3), is found throughout this hexagram.

HEXAGRAM 58

PLEASURE[a]

HEXAGRAM TEXT:
(The occasion calls for a) **sacrifice.**
It is a beneficial divination. [H-O]

LINES:
9 at the beginning:
 Pleasure in harmony. [L-I]
  Auspicious. [L-P]

9 at LINE 2:
 Pleasure in capturing. [L-I]
  Auspicious, troubles vanish. [L-P]

6 at LINE 3:
 Pleasure in making come (in submission). [L-I]
  Ominous. [L-P]

9 at LINE 4:
 Taking pleasure in discussion, not yet pacified. [L-I]
  Great illness has a cure. [L-SP]

9 at LINE 5:
 Captives at a flaying[b]. [L-I]
  Have danger. [L-P]

6 on top:
 Pleasure in leading-and-guiding. [L-I]

****

COMMENTARY

For the place of Hexagram 58 in the overall structure of the *Zhouyi*, and for the meaning of its pairing with Hexagram 57, see the first five paragraphs of the Commentary on Hexagram 57.

The present hexagram starts with pleasure taken in the harmonious coming together of all, thus a pleasure that can be shared with all. Such coming together forms a condition of peaceful integration of human beings with each other, in particular, of integration within a civilized existence (Line 1).

But such existence does not come without effort, and effort of various sorts. The King needs to be able to take pleasure occasionally in taking others captive, in the control over others through the exercise of force, in the having superior power which is made manifest in this act (Line 2).

He also needs to be able to take pleasure in making others come to his own place (the court) and submit, in intimidating others with a show of force (Line 3). This is a second form of aggressive action mentioned in the lines.

However, the enjoyment of this form of aggression does not necessarily bode well. In situations of conflict, he needs also to be able to enter upon negotiation, discussion, and to take pleasure in this (Line 4). And even if this does not settle everything so that all are pacified, there is the prospect that the 'great illness' will have a cure eventually.

He needs also to be able to acknowledge Heaven in a sacrificial act that brings human beings together in a reference to Heaven whereby Heaven's purpose-- and the King's work in service to that purpose-- is being acknowledged as binding even at the cost of human life (Line 5).

But there is, finally and in sum, the need for the King to take pleasure in leadership, in guidance, such as brings on the harmonious condition pointed to in Line 1.[5]

****

◆ TEXTUAL NOTES ◆

a. The title-name *dui*[4] (兌) is the protograph for *yue*[4] (悅), "pleasure, joy".

b. The *bo*[1] (剝) here could be taken as Li does (*ZTong*, 116), as a place name (the name of a country, in Li's case). This would mean that the line lacks a religious reference, but it links well with Line 4's sense of a still not completely pacified state of things. It also has the pattern of Hexagram 17/Line 5, where I choose the place-name alternative over the religious one.

HEXAGRAM 59

SPURTING AND SPATTERING

HEXAGRAM TEXT:
(The occasion calls for a) **sacrifice.**
A beneficial divination. [H-O]
  Beneficial to cross the big river. [H-A]
    The King proceeds to his own temple. [H-SSI]

LINES:
6 at the beginning:[a]
Spurting-and-spattering and running over the small table. [L-I]
  Use for gelding a horse, making it healthy. [L-A]
  Auspicious. [L-P]

9 at LINE 2:[a]
Spurting-and-spattering his body. [L-I]
  Troubles vanish. [L-P]

6 at LINE 3:[a b]
Spurting-and-spattering his own mound. [L-I]
  Without troubles. [L-P]

6 at LINE 4:[a]
Spurting-and-spattering the crowd. [L-I]
  Greatly auspicious. [L-P]

9 at LINE 5:[a]
Spurting-and-spattering the royal dwelling. [L-I]
  Without harmful mishap. [L-P]

9 on top:[a]
Spurting-and-spattering guards[c] **the great commands.** [L-I]
  Without harmful mishap. [L-P]

****

COMMENTARY

In its overall structure the *Zhouyi* begins (Hexagrams 1 and 2) with the seasonal rhythm and life in an agriculture-dependent mode fitting itself into that rhythm, and ends (Hexagrams 63 and 64) with life placed within the matrix of the collective political/historical venturing which the Mandate of Heaven and the Shang and Zhou leadership of human life on earth provides.

Within these brackets, the thirty remaining hexagram pairs are grouped into five sets, the first of which (3/4 through 15/16) centers on Hexagrams 9 and 10. This pair make as theme that our human life-- this venturing and risking on earth under the heavens-- endemically becomes involved in troubles, in troubled situations. A subsequent group (17/18 through 41/42) centers on Hexagrams 29 and 30. This pair concerns divine powers manifest in the earth's higher and lower places, and the various pairs which belong to this group all develop themes which relate to earthly life under Heaven, particularly in its social aspects and in general features of its being a temporal (mortal) affair. The next group of hexagram pairs (43/44 through 49/50) has no central or organizing pair; its coherence is found in the common reference of all four pairs back to conditions of a being whose life is an active affair involving risk. In the venturing involved, such a being's efforts are caught up in various polar conditions. The next to last group of hexagram pairs (51/52 through 55/56) is structured as a lead pair followed by two complementary pairs. The unifying theme for the group is sexuality between male and female, man and wife: the most intimate connection of human beings with each other out of their inwardness.

The final group of hexagram pairs (57/58 through 61/62) has the same structure as the preceding group: a lead pair followed by two complementary pairs. The unifying theme for the group is an even more intimate connection than the sexuality that was theme for the preceding group: it is the connection of human beings with the divine and not simply with each other.

Hexagrams 59 (Spurting-and-spattering) and 60 (Restraint) are linked in their focus on the contrast of the spurting blood of a sacrificial victim, a releasing from confinement of the life-blood of such a living creature which is of the essence in the sacrificial ritual, with the holding back, holding within bounds and limits, which is of the essence in the moral life. Together they echo the pairing of Hexagrams 57 (Laying out food offerings) and 58 (Pleasure), with their emphasis on religious reaching and political uniting. In virtue of this echoing, the reaching is seen as carrying with it an act of killing which is to function in a giving addressed to the divine powers and ancestral spirits; and the political uniting has to be founded in a restraint which would find for all a place in a harmonious existence.

The image found in the Hexagram Text of the present hexagram sets the context for the lines to follow, which evolve as an ordered set of variations on a sacrificial theme in which the King is the one making the sacrificial act.

The beginning is with the blood of the sacrificial victim being released, spurting-and-spattering, to run over a small table (one used in the act of sacrifice, presumably) (Line 1).

This is followed by the blood of the sacrificial victim spurting a bit farther, spattering the body of the person who is performing the ritual act (Line 2).

Next comes a spurting of the blood of the sacrificial victim ever farther, reaching the royal burial-mound in the sacrifice area (Line 3).

This is followed by the spurting blood of the sacrificial victim going even farther, this time reaching to the crowd attending the ritual (Line 4).

Next comes a spurting of the blood of the sacrificial victim which reaches to the King's dwelling nearby the place where the sacrifice is taking place (Line 5).

The final line, rather than introducing a further step in the expansion of the range of the spurting-and-spattering of the sacrificial victim's blood, addresses the function of the sacrificial ritual itself. It is meant to support and protect the commands which the King gives by showing the regard for the ancestral and divine powers that assures that they will function supportively and protectively (Line 6).

****

◆ TEXTUAL NOTES ◆

a. The very regular and orderly pattern of these lines is concealed by two dislocations with wide-ranging ramifications involved in the traditional and Mawangdui versions, by some accompanying faulty line-divisions in each case, and by two intrusions into the text from commentaries. (1) Line 4 holds two line-images, whereas Line 1 has none; this seems likely to have been the result of a very simple copy error to start with. I have restored a line-image to each line simply by relocating the line-divisions. Thus the line-image of Line 2 is moved to Line 1, to be rejoined with the action and prognostication elements already present there. The line-image of Line 3 is moved to Line 2, to join the prognostication phrase already present there. And in keeping with the order of images according to the expanding range of the spurting and spattering, I have moved the second line-image of Line 4 to Line 3, to join the prognostication phrase already present there. [For an omitted commentary intrusion, see Note b. below.] (2) Line 5 also has two line images, one of which belongs there and one of which belongs as the image of Line 6. What serves as Line 6 in the traditional and Mawangdui versions ("Spurt-and-spatter: the blood goes far forth") is not a line image but a definition/explanation of the title-name which has intruded from some commentary and become taken as text. In keeping with the order of images according to the expanding range of the spurting and spattering, I have retained the second line image of Line 5 as its proper one, and moved the first to Line 6, to join the prognostication phrase already present there. [The definitional phrase is similar to a phrase which is part of the text in Hexagram 9/Line 4.]

b. In the traditional and Mawangdui versions, the last four characters of Line 4 ("It is not what one would ordinarily think of") are an editorial/ commentary intrusion, not part of the original text. While the phrase is traditionally a part of Line 4, it seems to belong with the line-image I have transferred from there to Line 3, and originally then to have related to that line.

c. I read *gan¹* (扞) for *han¹* (汗) here, the latter being a loan substituted for the original character under a misreading which would make the pattern of this line fit that of the preceding four. For that, one needs a kind of 'flow'-word, and the 'water'-classifier provides that.

HEXAGRAM 60

RESTRAINT

HEXAGRAM TEXT:[a]
(The occasion calls for a) **sacrifice.** [H-O]

LINES:
9 at the beginning:
  Not go out the courtyard door. [L-I]
    Without harmful mishap. [L-P]

9 at LINE 2:
  Not go out the courtyard gate. [L-I]
    Ominous. [L-P]

6 at LINE 3:
  Not restraint-wise, then 'alas'-wise. [L-I]
    Without harmful mishap. [L-P]

6 at LINE 4:
  Contented restraint. [L-I]
    Auspicious[b]. [L-P]

9 at LINE 5:
  Pleasurable restraint. [L-I]
    Auspicious; going has a reward.[c] [L-P, and L-SP]

6 on top:[d]
  Bitter restraint. [L-I]
    As a divination, ominous. [L-P]

****

COMMENTARY

For the place of Hexagram 60 in the overall structure of the *Zhouyi*, and for the meaning of its pairing with Hexagram 59, see the first four paragraphs of the Commentary on Hexagram 59.

The present hexagram develops as an ordered set of variations whose focus shifts from outward to inward in the course of the series of lines. It begins with restraint in an outward sense, of holding back and keeping within the courtyard door (Line 1) and then the courtyard gate (Line 2). It moves to the consequences of unrestraint (grief) (Line 3), and culminates in three inward conditions in an agent who has restraint: a condition in which the restraint being exercised leaves the person contented (Line 4), a condition in which the person takes pleasure in the restraint being exercised (Line 5), and a condition in which the restraint being exercised is not felt to be enjoyable but rather to be something bitter, something constraining or oppressing (Line 6).

****

◆ TEXTUAL NOTES ◆

a. In the traditional and Mawangdui versions, the Text holds a phrase ("Bitter restraint; as a divination, not acceptable") which is an alternative form of Line 6. It is 'stored' here, but is not part of the Text itself.

b. I read *heng¹* (亨) here as a copy error for *ji²* (吉); there is no change in sense.

c. I read *shang⁴* (尚) here as shang³ (賞).

d. In the traditional Mawangdui versions, there is a prognostication phrase (*hui³ wang²* [悔亡]: "Troubles vanish") which seems an intrusion-- but from where, I can not say. In any case, it does not belong here.

HEXAGRAM 61

BULL'S-EYEING THE CAPTIVES

HEXAGRAM TEXT:
 A beneficial divination. [H-O]
  Beneficial to cross the big river. [H-A]

LINES:
9 at the beginning:
 Pigs and fish[b]: a *yu*-burial-sacrifice.[6] [L-I]
  Auspicious, but have unanticipated obstacle and no repose. [L-P]

9 at LINE 2:
 A crane calling in the shade, its offspring answer it; "I have a fine *jue*-beaker, let's you and I join in emptying it." [L-I]

6 at LINE 3:
 When we caught the enemy, some drummed, some rested, some wept, some sang. [L-I]

6 at LINE 4:
 The moon is almost full, the horse's mate vanishes. [L-I]
  Without harmful mishap. [L-P]

9 at LINE 5:
 Offer captives in sacrifice, trussed up together. [L-I]
  Without harmful mishap. [L-P]

9 on top:
 The sound of wings rises to the heavens. [L-I]
  As a divination, ominous. [L-P]

****

COMMENTARY

In its overall structure the *Zhouyi* begins (Hexagrams 1 and 2) with the seasonal rhythm and life in an agriculture-dependent mode fitting itself into that rhythm, and ends (Hexagrams 63 and 64) with life placed within the matrix of the collective political/historical venturing which the Mandate of Heaven and the Shang and Zhou leadership of human life on earth provides.

Within these brackets, the thirty remaining hexagram pairs are grouped into five sets, the first of which (3/4 through 15/16) centers on Hexagrams 9 and 10. This pair make as theme that our human life-- this venturing and risking on earth under the heavens-- endemically becomes involved in troubles, in troubled situations. A subsequent group (17/18 through 41/42) centers on Hexagrams 29 and 30. This pair concerns divine powers manifest in the earth's higher and lower places, and the various pairs which belong to this group all develop themes which relate to earthly life under Heaven, particularly in its social aspects and in general features of its being a temporal (mortal) affair. The next group of hexagram pairs (43/44 through 49/50) has no central or organizing pair; its coherence is found in the common reference of all four pairs back to conditions of a being whose life is an active affair involving risk. In the venturing involved, such a being's efforts are caught up in various polar conditions. The next to last group of hexagram pairs (51/52 through 55/56) is structured as a lead pair followed by two complementary pairs. The unifying theme for the group is sexuality between male and female, man and wife: the most intimate connection of human beings with each other out of their inwardness.

The final group of hexagram pairs (57/58 through 61/62) has the same structure as the preceding group: a lead pair followed by two complementary pairs. The unifying theme for the group is an even more intimate connection than the sexuality that was theme for the preceding group: it is the connection of human beings with the divine and not simply with each other.

Hexagrams 61 (Bull's-eyeing the captives) and 62 (Passing-by by a little) are linked in their focus on the intertwining of death with life as an affair of connecting, of encountering or missing each other, and of making something of those connective encounters.

The present hexagram unfolds in a pointing to our common human condition, friend and enemy alike-- a pointing to our mortality and the vulnerability of ourselves in our connectedness with each other.

Lines 1 and 2 address the death of someone close: the burial rite, with its element of an animal sacrifice (pigs and fish) to appease the spirits (Line 1), and the poignant memory of a connection and companionship such as might come back to mind at the death of someone dear, celebrated in shared drinking (Line 2).

Lines 3, 4, and 5 address death to captive enemies. Line 3 speaks of their capture, and of the different response of the captives to their being held captive. Line 4 uses the animal to voice the human in its alien (here, enemy) guise, and by alluding to a horse's loss of its mate, speaks to the sense of separation the captives feel from their mates. Is that what lies in store for the enemy who was captured? for the wives of the enemy troops captured? And Line 5 speaks to the finalization of that separation in the death of the prisoners (as sacrificial victims trussed up together and sharing their common fate bound to each other).

In Line 6 the common sense or meaning of death-- for friend and foe alike in the context, for all mortal human beings-- is evoked in an image of birds: their wing-sounds rise to the heavens/Heaven, signifying not only a departing and passing on (as migrating flocks rising off a lake and proceeding onward with their migration) but also the sense of the whole in which human beings find themselves as a religious one (*tian* as not simply the heavens but also Heaven).[7]

****

◆ TEXTUAL NOTES ◆

a. The title-name *zhong¹ fu²* (中孚) does not appear in the lines and is not obvious in its connection with the lines. But given the thematic focus of those lines, it seems most obviously to be pointing to Lines 3-5 and underlining the theme as it appears there. Narrowly speaking, that regards the capacity to see enemy captives as human beings with family and intimate ties, yet nonetheless to offer them in sacrifice in a religious ritual addressing the highest divine powers. More broadly, the theme is human beings as mortal, as captives to time, as targeted for eventual death. I understand the title-name, then, to stand for that most forceful act for bringing these matters to the fore, namely, the making captives be targets, making them stand in the bull's-eye; or putting the focus on the captives, I understand it to mean "bull's-eyed captives".

b. The phrase "pigs and fish: auspicious" has been displaced to the Hexagram Text; I restore it here, and join it with what was left in Line 1. The "auspicious" occurring in both places, I collapse into one occurrence.

HEXAGRAM 62

PASSING-BY BY A LITTLE

HEXAGRAM TEXT:[a]
(The occasion calls for a) **sacrifice.**
It is a beneficial divination. [H-O]
> **Acceptable in regard to minor affairs, not acceptable in regard to major affairs.** [H-SP]

LINES:
6 at the beginning:[a]
As to the sound which flying birds leave behind: it is not suitable for it to rise but rather to descend.[8] [L-I]
> **Greatly auspicious.** [L-P]

6 at LINE 2:
Pass by his grandfather, meet[9] his grandmother; not reach to his lord, meet his servant. [L-I]
> **Without harmful mishap.** [L-P]

9 at LINE 3:
He does not pass them by, they prevent him doing that; while following behind them, someone injures him.[10] [L-I]
> **Ominous.** [L-P]

9 at LINE 4:
He does not pass them by but encounters-and-meets them. [L-I]
> **Do not act!** [L-A]
> > **As a long-term divination, without harmful mishap. As for going, there is danger, one must be cautious.** [L-SP]

6 at LINE 5:[b]
He does not encounter-and-meet them but passes them by.
> [L-I]

6 on top:[b]
   **The Duke shoots with a string-attached arrow, he fetches that (bird
   he shot) in the cave; the** (still) **flying bird, he nets it.** [L-I]
   Ominous. [L-P]

****

COMMENTARY

For the place of Hexagram 62 in the overall structure of the *Zhouyi,* and
for the meaning of its pairing with Hexagram 61, see the first four paragraphs of the Commentary on Hexagram 61.

The present hexagram develops in contrasting ways the encounter of
human beings with each other in the interim between birth and death. The
images begin and end with bird-imagery that bodies forth the two-sided end
of life (its culmination, and its termination) and links the paired hexagrams
closely.[11]

Line 1 images the sounds which birds in flight leave behind; it is fitting
for such sounds to descend to earth. This image points to one side of the
matter of human life on earth, that its openness to the heavenly (we are
'birds') fits it to transform the earthly. Such an image might well call to mind
the King as committed to the Mandate of Heaven, thus to work on earth
which resonates of Heaven and which gives meaning to a life which is
nonetheless finite, transient, mortal.

Line 6 images a bird, shot and downed by the Duke using an attached
arrow, sought out by him in a cave and finally enmeshed in a net. This
image points to another side of the matter of human life on earth, that it is
unavoidably mortal, and apt to a death after having become caught and entangled in the ties which brings us down to the ground. We are all targeted
by death, as the pair hexagram reminds us.

Given this bracketing by bird-images of the life that is suited to resonate
of the heavenly but at the same time ends in death, the lines in between develop the sense of that earthly life, that it is lived in one form or another of
an encountering or passing-by (not-encountering) one another in its course.
Four variations on this theme are set forth, pointing to different facets of
ongoing life.

In Line 2 there is encounter, but it results in meeting not the primary person one was to meet but instead a secondary (yet related, connected) person.
That is, the being one encounters is slightly different from the being one

might have-- even perhaps was meant to have-- encountered.

In Line 3 there is an attempt of one traveler to pass by another, but a resistance on the part of the other to being overtaken. The latter, indeed, prevents that passing by, and what ensues is an injury to the person who is being forced to follow.

Lines 4 and 5 link closely with each other. Line 4 points to an encountering which takes place instead of a passing by, while Line 5 points to the reverse: one passes someone by and does not meet him.

In life, then, we meet and connect, or we do not; and when we connect, it may be in a competitive vein, or it may be in discovery of others who do not measure up to what would most draw out and support the life within us.

****

◆ TEXTUAL NOTES ◆

a. In the traditional and the Mawangdui texts, what originally was Line 1 has been displaced to the Hexagram Text, and replaced by what is best understood as a copyist's note. It reads: "'Flying birds' on to 'ominous'." That is, it refers to the beginning and ending of the set of hexagram lines in their original form. Line 1 begins with "flying birds", and Line 6 ends with "ominous". The *shi⁴ wei⁴* phrase which is currently found after the "ominous" in Line 6 (是謂災眚: "This means 'a disaster'") is a much later addition, an intrusion from an editorial/commentary note (as its very form suggests). It seems to be explaining the term "ominous".

b. The last two lines of the traditional and Mawangdui versions exhibit some textual dislocation. The first part of traditional Line 5 ("Extremely cloudy, but no rain comes from our western outskirts.") is an intrusion repeating (for some unknown reason) the phrase which functions as scene setting image in Hexagram 9. The second half of traditional Line 5 belongs with the second half of traditional Line 6, to form original Line 6; while the first half of traditional Line 6 is properly Line 5. The general structure of the hexagram line-images strongly suggests this ordering. I have restored the text accordingly. For a phrase ("This means 'a disaster'") at the end of Line 6 in the traditional and Mawangdui versions, see Textual Note a. above; I have omitted it.

HEXAGRAM 63

ALREADY HAVING FORDED ACROSS

HEXAGRAM TEXT:
(The occasion calls for a) **minor sacrifice.**[a]
A beneficial divination. [H-O]
   At first auspicious, but there is disorder in the end. [H-SP]

LINES:
9 at the beginning:
Dragging its wheels, wetting its tail. [L-I]
   Without harmful mishap. [L-P]

6 at LINE 2:
The matron loses her head-ornament. [L-I]
   Do not pursue, in seven days you will get it (back). [L-A]

9 at LINE 3:
Our High Ancestor[12] attacked the border-state of Gui, and in three years overcame it. [L-I]
   Little men, do not act! [L-A]

6 at LINE 4:
He wets[b] his own clothes and rags, throughout the day he is on-guard-and-cautious. [L-I]

9 at LINE 5:
As regards really receiving blessings, the eastern neighbor's slaying oxen for sacrifice[c] is not as good as the western neighbor's *yue*[-]sacrifice. [L-I]
   Auspicious.[d] [L-P]

6 on top:
He wets his head. [L-I]
   Danger. [L-P]

****

COMMENTARY

In the overall structure of the *Zhouyi* Hexagrams 1 and 2 are paired with each other, as are Hexagrams 63 and 64. These two sets of pairs form a bracket around the whole work, and utilize images which recall the embracing temporal and historical frame of human life. Hexagrams 1 and 2 are concerned with the seasonal rhythm and life in an agriculture-dependent mode fitting itself into that rhythm. Hexagrams 63 and 64 are concerned with life placed within the matrix of the collective political/historical venturing which the Mandate of Heaven and the Shang and Zhou leadership of human life on earth provides. Such, at least, is the matrix claimed here and in the traditional Zhou view of life in the world known to the author of the *Zhouyi*

Neither Hexagram 63 nor Hexagram 64 speaks solely of the political, or uses throughout images from the political sphere. But by the placement of this pair as the counterpart to the opening pair and the last in the set of pairs which make up this whole work, the author places weight on venturing, hazarding, as endemic to human life on earth, individual and collective ... and on political venturing as the broadest human horizon for our lives.[13]

The present hexagram does not give focus to its adumbration of the theme of hazardous-venturing by means of repetition of the title-name or any other verbal continuity. Nor is there a story of the Shang dynasty being told in any straightforward sense. Indeed, only two lines explicitly address the Shang: Line 3, which points to an event attesting the political supremacy of the Shang[14], and Line 5, which points beyond the Shang (they are "already finished") by intimating the religious superiority of the Zhou to the Shang.

Instead, the hexagram lines exhibit a thematic alternation.

Lines 1 and 2 point to a difficult river-passage in a literal way and in reference to individuals. In Line 1, the crossing is difficult enough that the cart, having to be aided through a deep spot, gets stuck, has to be dragged or pulled, and wets its own tail. In Line 2 the river crossing is difficult enough that the passenger, in the flurry and excitement, loses her head ornament.

Line 3 introduces the embracing historical and political dimension explicitly. The image refers to the Shang King, Wuding, whose reign marked the high-water mark of the Shang dynasty. Under his leadership the Shang expanded their territory; the border-state of Gui seems to have been a western tribe, possibly affiliated with the Huns, or the Tibetans. "Three years" means that the campaign was long and arduous.

Line 4 returns to the literal passage, as before in an individual vein. This time the image points to the person carried on the cart across the river as having gotten wet, and as maintaining a sense of caution throughout the day, as if threatened or at least desiring to be careful just in case. For pausing to dry out the clothing and thus not being in a position to advance, could make him vulnerable to attackers (bandits, say).

Line 5 brings back the embracing historical and political context. The image contrasts two sacrifices. The nature of the contrast is not transparent, since precisely what was involved in the Zhou (= western neighbor) *yue^4*-sacrifice is not known.[15] Was it an agricultural offering, thus one less rich than the oxen-offering of the Shang (= eastern neighbor), but one more than compensated for because of the superior virtue of the Zhou? Or was it a ritual involving human sacrifice, and thus more successful because it also made use of a more valuable offering, a human life? In either case, the line points historically to a time when the Shang had become religiously inadequate, if still supreme in terms of political force. Thus the Shang were in principle 'already finished' as the world's political leaders; and time would eventually show this fully and bring even their political supremacy to an end.

Line 6 ends with a suggestion relating both to the literal passage and to the historical-political venture: both river-forders and civilization-leaders have gotten in over their heads and are threatened. In this second reference, with the Zhou religious superiority the shift in Mandate was accomplished in principle, and the Shang were about to be drowned, their leadership in the venture toward civilization being over with.

****

◆ TEXTUAL NOTES ◆

a. I read *xiao³ heng¹ li⁴ zhen¹* (小亨利貞), reversing *xiao³* and *heng¹* from their order in the traditional and Mawangdui versions. See Hexagram 33 for the same emendation. These are the only two cases where the *li⁴ zhen¹* phrase is modified in the traditional version of the Hexagram Texts, whereas *heng¹* is commonly modified (12 times by *yuan²* [元], 2 by *xiao³* in addition to the two in question here). In the Mawangdui version of Hexagram 58 we also find *heng¹ xiao³ li⁴ zhen¹*, although the traditional text has no *xiao³* at all. [This reversal might also be called for in Hexagram 22, which reads *heng¹ xiao³ li⁴ you³ you¹ wang³* (亨小利有攸往). Reversal here would make both phrases fit normal patterns.]

b. I read ru^3 (濡) for xu^1 (繻).

c. I follow the Mawangdui version in entering this phrase (以祭: $yi^3 ji^4$, "for sacrifice") into the line at this point.

d. I enter this prognostication word (吉: ji^2) into this line, following the Mawangdui version.

HEXAGRAM 64

NOT YET HAVING COMPLETED THE FORD

HEXAGRAM TEXT:[a]
(The occasion calls for a) **sacrifice.** [H-O]
   Beneficial to cross the big river. [H-A]
   Ominous for campaigning. [H-SP]

LINES:
6 at the beginning:[a]
   The small fox, on the point of completing a ford across the river, wets his tail. [L-I]
      Difficulty, without anything beneficial. [L-P]

9 at LINE 2:
   They drag-and-pull its wheels. [L-I]
      As a divination, auspicious. [L-P]

6 at LINE 3:[a] [b]
   Zhen[16] **acted to attack the Gui border-state; after three years he had his reward from the 'big country'.**[17] [L-I]
      As a divination, auspicious, troubles vanish. [L-P]

9 at LINE 4:[b]
   The noblemen arrive at splendid-glory, they offer captives as sacrificial victims. [L-I]
      As a divination, auspicious, without troubles. [L-P]

6 at LINE 5:[b]
   Offering captives as sacrificial victims, they go on drinking wine. [L-I]
      Auspicious. [L-P]

9 on top:[b]
   They wet their heads, and offering captives in sacrifice they lose the spoon[c]. [L-I]
      Without harmful mishap. [L-P]

****

COMMENTARY

In the overall structure of the *Zhouyi* Hexagrams 1 and 2 are paired with each other, as are Hexagrams 63 and 64. These two sets of pairs form a bracket around the whole work, and utilize images which recall the embracing temporal and historical frame of human life. Hexagrams 1 and 2 are concerned with the seasonal rhythm and life in an agriculture-dependent mode fitting itself into that rhythm. Hexagrams 63 and 64 are concerned with life placed within the matrix of the collective political/historical venturing which the Mandate of Heaven and the Shang and Zhou leadership of human life on earth provides. Such, at least, is the matrix claimed here and in the traditional Zhou view of life in the world known to the author of the *Zhouyi.*

Neither Hexagram 63 nor Hexagram 64 speaks solely of the political, or uses throughout images from the political sphere. But by the placement of this pair as the counterpart to the opening pair and the last in the set of pairs which make up this whole work, the author places weight on venturing, hazarding, as endemic to human life on earth, individual and collective ... and on political venturing as the broadest human horizon for our lives.[18]

The present hexagram does not give focus to its adumbration of the theme of hazardous-venturing by means of repetition of the title-name or any other verbal continuity. Nor is there a story of the Zhou dynasty being told in any straightforward and explicit sense. In fact, there is just one line which expressly addresses the Zhou: Line 3 points to the rise of the Zhou militarily while the Shang still held the dynastic authority. But Lines 4, 5, and 6 implicitly relate to the Zhou as well.

Line 1 takes up not yet completed venturing in the image of a fox. If this has meaning in relation to the Zhou, it would seem to symbolize the early venturing of the Zhou people westward across the Yellow River and into what was to become the area of their homeland; thus it would point to a memory of their early sojourn as a people before they became the people of the Zhou plain, their start on the journey that led (as with the Shang earlier) to the assumption of the Mandate of Heaven.

Line 2 moves from the tail-wetting beginning to a difficult fording imaged through the same image as in Hexagram 63: a cart aided through a difficult place by being dragged and pulled.

Line 3 introduces explicit reference to the historical-political venturing, pointing to the Zhou at a time before they had reached the place where they would challenge the Shang. This is the time of Ji Li, when the Zhou first appear as a major military and political force, and are first recognized by the Shang as having an important standing. The allusion is to the beginning of the rise of the Zhou.

Line 4, while not expressly identifying the Zhou, speaks nonetheless of the noble Zhou leaders and their arrival at brightness, at splendor and glory, as rulers in a new dynasty. That occurred through force (a 'taking of prisoners'), although it was grounded in virtue. The image then points to the Zhou nobility, through the work of Kings Wen and Wu, arriving at the height of power.

Line 5 alludes to the development of the Zhou dynasty and to the seeds of the 'future' which includes the time when the author of this work is writing. The time since the early glory days has been marked by two things: by continued involvement in war and a reliance on force, and by the 'wine drinking' that symbolizes the degeneration that marked the later Zhou dynasty. In the early Zhou it was the spirit, not force, that was the deepest power; and at the same time wine-drinking was thought of as undermining the commitment and values central to the leadership role the Zhou were assuming, and was something strongly warned against. By the time near the end of the Western Zhou when the author is writing, these two things (or what they symbolize) have brought the dynasty to a low ebb.

Line 6 both hearkens to the literal river-fording (presumably as in Hexagram 63, on the individual level) and completes the historical-political focus started in Line 3. In effect, it culminates the lines of this Hexagram and ends the whole divination work by posing a question in its anticipation of the future: have the Zhou now gotten into the stream over their heads, so that while taking prisoners and focusing thus on military might, they have lost the spoon, that is, lost touch with the spirit which ritual celebrated and confirmed, the spirit called for in the Mandate which is Heaven's to withhold *if* the present claimants do not live up to the moral conditions and the task of effective leadership toward a more civilized human existence on earth?

****

◆ TEXTUAL NOTES ◆

a. In the traditional and Mawangdui versions there are two displacements that affect the Hexagram Text and Lines 1 and 3. One, is the displacement of the two phrases I treat as H-A and H-P, along with the title-name, into Line 3. I have restored them to the Hexagram Text, to go with the *heng¹* (亨) that is already there. Two, is original Line 1, which has been displaced into the Hexagram Text and been replaced by an alternate and truncated version of itself. I have restored Line 1 by bringing the full and truncated versions together into one.

b. When the title-name and Hexagram Text material was displaced to Line 3, original Lines 3, 4, and 5 were copied as Lines 4, 5, and 6, and original Line 6 was retained as a second image in that line. With the restoration of the displaced Hexagram Text material, these consequences of the displacement can be undone. In this reshuffling, I have retained the final *ji²* (吉) of Line 5, and added to it the first image of traditional and Mawangdui Line 6. The amount of displacement involved in the last hexagram of the whole work-- involving all but Line 2-- is considerable, but intelligible as the consequence of three simple displacements in the copying.

c. I read *shi⁴* (是) as protograph/loan for *chi²* (匙) .

APPENDIX
The earliest records of divination
using the *Zhouyi*

The *Zhouyi* is a work of the late 9th century BC. Early in the 8th century, less than fifty years after its composition, Western Zhou rule ended. Through actions of some of the feudal lords, the capital was moved, King Ping was placed on the throne, and a nominal continuation of the Zhou leadership of the civilized world was arranged. But it was merely nominal, since belief in the Zhou as effective leaders holding a Mandate from Heaven had withered away. In the arrangement that was settled upon, the Zhou King was mainly a religious focal point without an effective political role. In the Eastern Zhou times which followed, much that had been definitive for the early Western Zhou and its revival in the time of King Xuan was modified or left behind as a living reality. Politically and religiously, life within the civilized world was now marked by greater assertiveness on the part of the feudal lords, increasing autonomy for the major states, shifting arrangements for some feudal lord instead of the Zhou ruler to look out for the civilized world against the barbarians, and increasing focus on alliances and force as the means for each of the states to remain independent.

One consequence of the effective political decentralization was the appropriation by other rulers of the rights and trappings of power which had belonged to the Zhou King, and eventually, in some aspects, appropriation of these by the aristocracy generally. The aspect of this which concerns us most here is a spread in the use of the *Zhouyi*, thus its adaptation for use by other than the Zhou King in circumstances and for purposes other than the original ones for which it was created and suited.[1]

We have no contemporary (9th century BC) evidence on the use of the original *Zhouyi*-- on the method of stalk-divination to select the sign, on the nature of the sign itself, or on the manner in which the sign was interpreted. But in Part I and then again in the commentary on the text, I have indicated how, from the work itself and from the historical background and context of its composition, we might most plausibly understand the distinctive character, features, and use, of the original work, and in particular, the way its imagery functioned, and the sense in which it anticipated the future. When in historical accounts we first catch sight of the *Zhouyi* in use, it is being employed in ways that already reflect its adaptation for functioning in the different conditions of Eastern Zhou times. The records giving us a glimpse of this adapted functioning are to be found in the *Zuozhuan* and the *Guoyu*.

In initial appearance the *Zuozhuan* is a commentary on the *Chunqiu* (Springs-and-Autumns[2]), which was composed by Zuo Qiu-ming, a contemporary of Confucius[3]. But closer study has brought both appearances into question, and left us able to say at best that it is a work which may have been composed somewhere between 468 and 300 BC[4], and probably closer to the end of that time (the late 4th century) than to the beginning. Somewhat similarly, the *Guoyu*, whose material concerns events taking place within 956 to 476 BC, was a compilation whose elements seem to have been composed sometime between 431 and 314 BC.[5] In both cases, then, we are dealing with-- at the earliest-- 5th century records which, although they may incorporate material from earlier times, were themselves composed roughly 400 years after the composition of the *Zhouyi*.

Two things need to be noted then at this point.

One is that the mentions of the *Zhouyi* begin in records which concern the second quarter of the 7th century BC, a century and a half later than the composition of the work. That is time for considerable evolution in the use of the method, particularly if life in many fundamental respects was changing and if the distinctive character of *Zhouyi* divination had not had time to establish itself in a tradition before the dislocating events of the early eighth century.

The other is that the composition of these records, itself dating to a time more than two centuries after the events being recorded, may perhaps have been framed in language that was appropriate to the later times of the composition, more so than to the times of the events themselves.[6]

In the following discussion, I begin by addressing the records that give us our earliest view of the use of the *Zhouyi*; in this, I seek mainly to note what the records have to tell us as we go through them one by one. Once this address to the separate cases is completed, I end by placing the practices noted into historical context, and on the background of the general historical conditions I seek to understand what the records tell us was happening in the early Eastern Zhou time of adaptation of the work for use in the different conditions. Because of the paucity of the records and the length of time involved, I do not presume to give a comprehensive or detailed history of the divinatory practice and the text involved during this period, only to point to different facets of a development in use to which the records give us access and to illuminate the meaning of what we see.

In this discussion I suppose generally that the language of the records is appropriately framed for the time which is being recorded, but I do not assume that all the records are genuine, that there is nothing in the way of later forgery to be found in them.[7] I also do not assume that all the cases of stalk-divination referred to involved use of the *Zhouyi* or that, even in those cases where the *Zhouyi* is clearly involved, there was only one method used in every case to bring the divinatory elements into play.

Let us take for our consideration the entries in these two works which introduce stalk-divination at sufficient length and in sufficient detail that we can have some idea of the method of divination being practised in the reference. And let us focus mostly on the *Zuozhuan* both for its greater trust-worthiness as a historical record and for its more extensive record of Eastern Zhou use of stalk-divination.[8] Overall, when we approach the early records in this fashion, we see the following.

First, only in some cases are stalk-divination inquiries expressly claimed to have involved the *Zhouyi*. There are others which, given the language used, probably involved such use, even though the record contains no explicit mention of the *Zhouyi* as being employed. But there are some cases in which line-figures were involved in some stalk-divination method but were apparently associated with verbal elements other than those in the version of the *Zhouyi* which we know; they might therefore reflect use of another text than the *Zhouyi*.[9]

Second, in no case do we have clear indication of what the procedure was in the manipulation of the stalks. Nonetheless, we do have various ways of recording the results of the selection process (which may in fact reflect different ways of manipulating the stalks), and various ways of interpreting those results and relating them to the matters being inquired into.

Third, this variety represents one or both of two things. On the one hand, some of the differences in question reflect that divination is an art and practice which depends on individual creativity and which involves individual variation in the conduct of the act. Even when the *Zhouyi* is employed by contemporary diviners in 'the same way', reading the signs is an art, a creative act, and different practitioners will exhibit significant differences in their taking up with the medium and the work. On the other hand, some of the differences reflect the uprooting of the *Zhouyi* as a divinatory work from its original setting and use, and express the evolution over time of new ways of using the stalks and line-figures, new ways of giving the latter meaning as signs, indeed new ways of taking up with the work itself and employing it in a non-divinatory reference.

In short: what the earliest records indicate is that the tradition of stalk-divination generally and of use of the *Zhouyi* in particular were not monolithic at any one time, let alone over time. The employment of the *Zhouyi* shows variety, and in particular, both types of difference mentioned above. And this makes good sense for the time after 771, which was marked by the loss of Zhou centrality and by the appropriation of the *Zhouyi* by persons outside the Zhou court who would have had no first-hand experience in the original method of use of this particular text for the purposes of divination.[10]

1. *Zuozhuan* examples: mention of *Zhouyi*

In the *Zuozhuan* there are fourteen cases of stalk-divination which have sufficient content to their exposition to make some assessment of how the signs are being treated in the interpretation. Of these, the account of the divination expressly mentions the *Zhouyi* in only five cases. These appear in the events of the years 672, 565, 537, 535 and 484. Let us start with these.

a. First case: 672 BC

The first case is reported as occurring almost a century and a half after the composition of the *Zhouyi*.[11] In it, a Zhou royal scribe[12] is described as having come to see the Marquis of Chen. Bringing the *Zhouyi* with him, he stalk-divined at the request of the Marquis. The inquiry concerned his young son Wan, and in particular, whether Wan would succeed him in ruling Chen. Thus while we have here as diviner the Zhou court official who would serve the Zhou King in that capacity in inquiries relating to royal affairs, we also see stalk-divination using the *Zhouyi* as it is being carried out in a new context and reference-- at the behest of the ruler of the state of Chen, on a matter that does not concern the Zhou King and affairs of royal government.[13]

What is the character of the divination method here, and how does it compare with what we proposed was involved in the original use of the *Zhouyi*?

When the Zhou scribe manipulated the stalks, he encountered Line 4 of Hexagram 20 (entitled "Contemplation").[14] It is the line image of that line which, in the original *Zhouyi* method, would have formed the basic sign to be regarded as the response from the spirits. It is taken here also as the first and most significant element of the sign, and is set forth with the rest of the line statement: "Contemplate the country's bright light; beneficial to act to be the guest of the King".

After the announcement of the complete line statement, comes a question, which presumably[15] represents the matter at issue as it was posed at the start of this consultation: "Will he[16] hold the country in succession [upon the Marquis] in Chen?" The interpretation of the sign is formed as an answer to that question.

The general answer is stated first: "No, he will not hold the country in succession (upon you) in Chen, but will (hold the country) in a different country, and he will do so not in his own person but in his descendants." The sign, as the Zhou scribe interprets it, points to this as the future to come, instead of that hoped for by the Marquis and anticipated in his question.

How is this answer grounded in the sign? In this new context of the use of the *Zhouyi*, we find a significant change having taken place in what the sign is which the diviner takes for interpretation and which he regards as conveying the response of the spirits to the question posed.

a1. First step: line image

The first step in explaining the sign is an interpretation of the line image: "The bright light is far away, yet from that (distant place) there is a radiant-shining." In this reading, the line image "contemplate the country's bright light" is being interpreted as follows: the country's bright light (symbolizing its illustrious ruler) whom you are looking for in the person of your own son will be found only at some distance from Chen, but from that bright light there will be even at that distance an observable radiance-- observable, presumably, from Chen. The "distant-yet-visible" is an idea introduced as part of the meaning of contemplation, that it is an observing of something at a distance. A further side to the meaning of the image is brought out in a moment, when the distance is understood symbolically both as socio-political, as pointing to another country in which the light is shining, and as generational, as referent to the posterity of the Marquis's son.

Before that follow-up reading of the line image is made, the exposition indicates that the interpreter brought in the line figures as themselves bearers of meaning and thus as functioning elements of the total sign. If the first step, and some of the follow-up which completes it, is one generally in keeping with the original *Zhouyi* method, this step is not, and represents something which is unlikely to have been part of the original *Zhouyi* method.

a2. Second step: trigrams

In the pre-*Zhouyi* records of stalk-divination, we saw sets of numbers which can plausibly be understood as precursors to line figures. Commonly those were sets of six, but sometimes sets of different size, especially of three. Even if we accept those number-sets as precursors for line figures, we have no reason in our evidence for thinking that those number-sets were anything but more or less complex formulations of the auspicious and in-auspicious, let alone that such sets had any specific meanings associated with them. But it does make some sense to see associated meanings as something which might be introduced *after* the *Zhouyi* system of verbal elements accessed through numbers and line figures has been created and *after* the idea of such divination as addressing through verbal images more than the auspicious/inauspicious and yes/no has taken hold. Once those things have happened, one might then be led to ask: if the verbally formulated line images are symbols, what about the line figures which are the vehicles for selecting those line images?

We have already suggested that in the original *Zhouyi* approach, those figures did have a minimal symbolic function: they symbolized the limited many-in-one which is the complex situation whose outworking in future would hold the matter at issue in the divination inquiry. We have also already noted that any single line, selected out in the process as moving, symbolizes matters of further change within the initial complex situation, matters which the line image associated with the moving line points one to symbolically. Even if we do not commit ourselves to any reading of the pre-*Zhouyi* number-sets that sees them as more than complex formulations of the auspicious and inauspicious, we may still see their presence in the back-ground as providing a context in which, when line figures become generated and represent sets of numbers, aspects of the line figures not already drawn explicitly into play in the *Zhouyi* might subsequently be so drawn. For if the set of six, and the single lines which move, have some symbolizing function in the original *Zhouyi* system, why not also the three-line figures which are readily discernible units contained within the six-line figures?

This is what we find having developed by early 7th C and being attested in this first example: an interpreting of the line figures as themselves bearing symbolic meaning in virtue of the meanings attached to the three-line figures (trigrams) which are taken to be components of the whole six-line figure. In this divination record trigrams are appealed to under the same "names" that later times know them under. Each also has a dominant association with a part or power in "nature", and secondary associations with other parts or powers, just as in later tradition. There is, however, no reason for thinking that the complex set of associations found in some parts of later tradition are already fully present here.[17]

A brief consideration of the general question of these names and associations seems to confirm that this way of reading the sign is a later modification of the original *Zhouyi* method with its focus on the verbal images.[18]

In the cases of *Qian²*, *Kun¹*, *Kan³*, and *Zhen⁴*, the same character serves as name of the trigram and as title-name of the hexagram whose form harbors the trigram in question doubled, with one example of the trigram placed on top of the other. Moreover, that same character is to be understood in both cases in its own intrinsic sense; it is not functioning as a loan word. Finally, the meaning of the hexagram title-name, as this is visible in reflection of the themes of the hexagrams in question, is closely connected with the main association being assigned to the corresponding trigram. Thus the hexagram *Qian²* thematizes the celestial dragon and seasonal changes reflected in its different appearances in the night sky; as trigram, the figure is assigned the meaning of the "heavens". The hexagram *Kun¹* thematizes the seasonal changes affecting the crucial months in agricultural life and the growth of grain and foodstuffs on earth; as trigram, the figure is assigned the meaning of the "earth". The hexagram *Kan³* thematizes pits which serve as water wells (although they can also serve as game traps); as trigram, the figure is assigned the meaning of the "waters". The hexagram *Zhen⁴* thematizes (spring) thunder; as trigram, the figure is assigned the meaning of "thunder".

In these first four cases, then, we can be fairly well assured that the sameness in character signifies the same meaning being intended through the character in both title usages. But in the other four cases there are significant differences involved. *Li²*, *Sun⁴*, *Dui⁴* and *Gen¹* as names of trigrams are represented by characters which, in their function and meaning as the original title-names of the hexagrams which are the double trigram forms of each corresponding trigram, are quite different from those same characters in their function and meaning as trigram names.

In the cases of *Sun⁴* and *Dui⁴*, the hexagram title-name characters are protographs for other characters, namely, *zhuan⁴* (饌) and *yue⁴* (悅). Moreover, the thematic foci of the hexagrams which confirm this reading of the title-name as the one intended (the laying out of food offerings, and a joy in leadership achievement even in situations involving conflict) do not refer in any direct way to the powers of nature which form the primary associations of the trigrams (marshes, and still waters as in lakes).

In the case of *Li²*, the hexagram title-name is a loan word for its simpler

form; and the thematic focus of the hexagram exhibited in the six line statements confirms that the meaning is that conveyed by that simpler form,
namely, a "mountain spirit". *Li²* as it is used as name of the trigram is presumably a loan-word for something which would ground the association
which is assigned to the trigram, namely, fire, although what that something
is, I do not know. In any case, it would not be the same as the title-name of
the hexagram.

In the case of *Gen¹*, the hexagram title-name is used in its intrinsic sense,
"glaring", and that is the theme of the six line statements of the hexagram.
But the trigram name is the protograph for another form, one whose meaning
(when written with a suitable radical, say 限) would be appropriate for the
association assigned to the trigram, namely, "mountains".

In short: the sameness of character being used in these last four cases both
for the traditional hexagram title-name and for the name of the trigram obscures significantly different meanings as being intended in the two different
uses. And when the appropriate meanings are discerned and the differences
are analyzed, the kind of linguistic situation we find suggests the likelihood
that while all the trigram names were borrowed from the hexagram title-
names as then written, this borrowing took place at a late enough time that
the differences in meaning of the same character in these two different roles
were either unrecognized or were deliberately ignored in view of the purpose
at hand. The meanings which I have suggested to belong to the title-names
of the hexagrams are confirmed as original through the discernment of the
theme intended through those names and embodied in the line statements of
the hexagram. Not only does the difference in relation of the two sets of four
title-names seem a clear indication that there was a later act of borrowing
involved; it seems to indicate as well that the hexagrams were not formed out
of the trigrams as intrinsically having such associated basic meanings, and
the imagery of the original hexagram title-names and line statements was not
formed on the basis of any such associations of the internal trigrams of the
hexagrams.[19]

What we are finding in this oldest case of *Zhouyi* divination in the *Zuozhuan*, then, is a use of trigrams with associated meanings in the interpretation of the divinatory sign, which use seems clearly to be a later development than the original *Zhouyi*. It could be that the emergence of the non-
traditional way of thinking manifest in the basic trigram associations[20] took
place simply within the divination tradition. But it might also be that the
thinking involved in this evolution of the *Zhouyi* divination method reflects
developments arising outside the divinatory context altogether,[21] and devel-

opments which, because we have no clue to their starting-time, may even have begun in some form before the Late Western Zhou time of the composition of the *Zhouyi*. It might even be that this appropriation of the *Zhouyi* divination into broader streams in the development of thought in Eastern Zhou times involved its appropriation into that way of thinking which A. C. Graham calls "correlative thinking". If so, that would have taken place well before such thinking with its cosmological bent emerged in the third century in that influential form associated with the name Zou Yan.[22] It would also have taken place well before the most extensive and decisive connection of this way of thinking with the *Zhouyi* in the various appendices which by Han dynasty times had become attached to the divination work and which transformed it into what came to be called the *Yijing*.[23] But regardless of what part of the broader stream of thought was involved, or of whether this was a development that began with reflection on the *Zhouyi* line figures and their possible symbolic meaning, the point immediately relevant here is twofold: first, that the evidence which we have indicates that this introduction of associated meanings into the trigrams and this use of the line figures as symbols enriched by such associated meanings took place some time after the original composition of the *Zhouyi*, and second, that this was one early part of changes in the divinatory use of the *Zhouyi* which altered it from its original nature.

Returning now to the case at hand: when the interpreter takes the two hexagrams in question here as each composed of two (upper and lower) trigrams, he recognizes that among the four trigrams involved there are three different ones included in the two line figures. The major powers associated with the three are the heavens, the earth, and the wind. But analyzed more closely, one can find other trigrams, represented by lines 2-3-4 and 3-4-5 of any hexagram. Considering the hexagrams in question in this way, one further different trigram can be seen as present; associated with it is the mountains.[24] It is these four constituent trigrams, which together enter into the composition of *both* hexagram figures, that are appealed to, under those meanings, as another basis for talking of the country's bright light.

Such a reading is ventured on the basis of the trigram-associations and the way in which the different trigrams are present in the two hexagrams. Thus:

1. In each hexagram, the lower trigram is the one being associated with the earth, the upper trigram of the first is the one being associated with the wind and that of the second with the heavens;
2. Because the first top trigram is seen as becoming the top trigram in the second (thus, the wind becoming the heavens):

a. The mountain trigram is generated, in the form of the 2-3-4 trigram of the second hexagram;

b. The woods trigram also appears (as 3-4-5 trigram of the second hexagram), and appears in relation to the mountain trigram 2-3-4 as rising higher than the latter (its top line is higher within the hexagram figure than that of the mountain trigram);

c. In turn, the upper trigram of the second hexagram (involving lines 4-5-6) is the heavens trigram, which rises higher than the woods trigram and thus (taking the heavens as "shining" either through itself or through the sun which appears in it) "shines down on" those below it.

Understood in this way, the trigram-interpretation ventured includes not only the associations of the upper and lower trigrams of the two hexagrams, but also those of the three trigrams which contain the line in the second hexagram which is different from its counterpart in the first.

This initial trigram-reading concludes: "Thereupon, the bright light dwells above the earth. Therefore (the line statement) says: 'Contemplate the country's bright light.'"

The connection of the trigram reading (introduced by "thereupon") with the line image is indicated by a "therefore". In fact, this is stretching the point. For while the trigram symbols so far place the bright light (the heavens) on top of the earth[25], it is only later when other associations of the trigrams are introduced that the "distance" idea contained also in the line image (or more precisely, in the interpretation of that image) is accounted for.

So far, the trigram symbolism is used to provide a figure-based imagery that basically grounds or confirms the line image symbolism and in addition enables refinement of it. Taking the trigrams as themselves figuring forth in symbolic fashion[26] certain forces and factors in the natural world, the interpreter has made the relations of those trigrams within the hexagrams a vehicle for laying out certain relations among the associated (natural) factors. And in turn-- this is the important point-- this set of forces and their relations are taken as representations of realities in the present-unfolding-into-the-future that holds the matter being asked about. Those representations, when taken as symbols and connected with the line image symbols, are understood to say: the forces in the present portend an unfolding in which there is a shining light (i.e. illustrious ruler) atop the earth (and in virtue of a follow up exposition, the interpretation will add: at some distance from Chen but still observable from there).

Connected back with the question and the matter at issue in it, the interpreter is so far saying: the future does indeed hold some illustrious successor such as the Marquis is hoping his son will be to him in Chen.

a3. Third step: action indicator

After the first trigram analysis has reaffirmed the reading of the line image (more precisely, of one part of it), the exposition turns to the second part of the line statement, what I have called an action-indicator in the way I have been understanding the *Zhouyi* in its original character. However, this phrase-- "beneficial to act to be guest to the King"-- is now taken in a different vein, as if it were part of the image that functions as disclosive symbol and were to be reaffirmed in its meaning by a further trigram analysis. This analysis proceeds by drawing on the previous associations of the lower trigram of both hexagrams (earth) and of the upper trigram of the second hexagram (heavens). But this time, other associations also come into play: of an inner trigram (meaning "gates and halls"), and of the upper and lower trigrams (meaning "metal and jade", then "cloth and silk", respectively)-- all of the second hexagram. Together the associations point to the fair things-- produce of heaven and earth-- present and offered within the audience-hall by the King to those who come to have audience with the him. "Therefore" the line statement says ...: that is, that set of trigram-associations is the ground for, or a confirmation of, the phrase "Beneficial to act to be guest to the King". The implication here-- and it is not drawn out explicitly-- seems to be: that illustrious ruler will indeed be highly honored within the Zhou King's court.

a4. Further steps

The interpretation continues by completing the line image reading: "'still, there is [the word] 'contemplation' in it'"-- that is, the shining light is not too distant to observe-- "therefore I said, 'it is found in his descendants'". This takes no account of the trigram analysis, but only addresses the contemplation in the line image. If this introduces distance, it also maintains connection and does not place what is seen at such a distance that it cannot be seen. As symbol here, this 'distance yet contemplatability' is understood in generational terms, as meaning that such a future ruler reaching such heights will be found among his descendants, within a limited number of generations.

The next-to-last step in the sign reading has recourse back to the trigrams. "The wind travels and (the heavens, or the sun) shines-brightly on the earth".

This refers to the two upper trigrams and the change ("travels") of the first (wind) into the second (heavens). Presumably it is in relation to the imagery of travel and distance (the wind traveling to another place on the earth, where the heavens are shining brightly down on earth) that the symbolism here is interpreted to mean: "it will be in a different country."

As the final interpretative step which the exposition records, the interpreter draws out the meaning of the signs as he understands it in more concrete reference, and seeks specific reference points in the imagery for what he is concluding as being pointed to through the sign. The point is to bring the symbolic pointers to bear on the known world and context of this matter of succession to rule, and to set forth the matter a bit more concretely. Drawing on the symbolism of the relation of the heavens trigram (4-5-6 in the second hexagram) to the mountain trigram (2-3-4 in the second hexagram)-- both are elevated, but one is grander than the other-- the interpreter concludes: "If it is in another country, it is bound to be a Jiang-clan country; the Jiang are descendants of the Great Peak: since mountains are high-peaked (= majestic), they are then a match for the heavens. But among things, there cannot be two that are greatest; will not Chen decline and this (Jiang-clan country) flourish?"

a5. The method, seen overall

In this example as it has been recorded in the *Zuozhuan* the interpreter takes a complex symbol, composed of the two line statement elements and the line figures (the trigrams composing both hexagrams, as having associated meanings), and interprets the joint disclosure of all these factors for the matter at issue.

He understands through the signs that the forces of the present harbor a future in which the succession by an illustrious son in Chen which the Marquis was anticipating in the question is not being confirmed in that form. But some sort of succession is seen as harbored there, one which is to take place in a distant future and a different place which is yet not so far away as not to be visible back in Chen. It involves the posterity of the Marquis's son eventually rising in some Jiang-clan country and becoming the illustrious ruler that the Marquis was hoping his own son would be as his (anticipated and hoped for) successor in Chen.

How does the interpreter ground that vision of the future in the complex symbol he starts from?

In the interpretation, he makes no use of the title-name of either hexagram, but focuses initially on the line statement, and in supplementation and amplification of that, on certain associations of the trigram constituents of the two hexagrams. These are all interpreted in a way that relates to elements in the situation of the question being posed, and their symbolism is utilized to anticipate the course of the future. The complex sign has thus been read as symbol pointing to one future coming actually to pass from out of the present rather than another.

Two things of considerable significance need to be noted in regard to the character of this interpretation.

First: in this reading, the complex of symbols provided as starting-point for interpretation in the divinatory act has a richness in meanings that is far from exhausted by the interpreter; his interpretation involves a selection from this richness and a use of only those selected aspects in his reading. Furthermore, in order to apply those selected symbols and meanings concretely, the interpreter uses his assessment of the present and his judgment as to what it bodes for the future. In keeping with his knowledge and judgment, and with whatever amplification of these is born in the interplay of the symbolism with his own capacities for seeing and understanding, he applies the chosen symbolic meanings concretely, in the specific fashion that takes place. Thus much of what composes the interpretation in each case is dependent on who the interpreter is, and often on capacities, experience, and insight that are peculiar to the interpreter.

Second: next to nothing is done[27] to use the symbolism as a guide to attend to the present, and so to understand concretely how it is that whatever future is being anticipated is grounded in the forces of the present. If the interpretation is not focused simply on the auspicious and the inauspicious, it also does not reflect the same sort of focus on the present and its futural implications as is to be found in the original *Zhouyi*. Its interest is more in predicting or deriving a predictive side of the sign and telling what will happen, than in using the sign to pay attention closely to *how* things are currently constituted and what that means for the future. Thus factors whose futural implications are being pointed out are being ignored in favor of the future being envisioned.

Even so, at the end the sign-reading is placed back into the context of an understanding of the situation at the time, so that one knows its anticipation emerges also out of a grasp of current conditions and of trends and possibilities as these are rooted in those conditions, in the human beings involved and the states and families, the horizon of history, and the like. One definite manifestation of this: that it would be in a Jiang-clan country that the successor illustrious light would appear (reflecting the clan circumscription of the general possibilities for advancement in countries not one's own by

birth). Implicitly, there is much in the ken of the interpreter, in his knowledge and assessment of conditions at the time, that must have been called
upon, organized, and focused in his interpretation of the sign, even if most
of that was not conveyed in the exposition and perhaps was not even explicitly made part of his verbalization of his insight into the signs.

a6. Comparison with the original *Zhouyi* method

In the above case, what we have in the interpretation of the sign selected
in the use of the *Zhouyi* system keeps something like a reading of the line
image as symbol that we saw in discussing the original system, and it keeps
it still as primary, or at least, as to be addressed first. But it introduces two
further elements as if they were part of the sign, and in both cases makes the
divination vehicle somewhat different from what I urged was found in the
original *Zhouyi*.

One is the treatment of the action-indicator in the line statement as if it
were part of the disclosive sign. In contrast, I took it as an additional and
imperative element for the inquirer to attend to, but one not necessarily connected with the issue which the line image addresses. If it is connected with
that issue, it is as promising a good for the inquirer as agent, whereas the
interpreter here makes it into a symbol of a certain future condition.

The other is the introduction of trigrams as part of the sign, or more
precisely, as holding associations with meanings in virtue of which those line
figures become symbols. The use of the constituent trigrams of (in this case)
both hexagram elements selected in the divination reflects the emergence of
an analytic focus on the line figures themselves and their possibilities of
functioning as symbols. Here that line figure symbol analysis provides a
complement and grounding of the verbal components and the symbolism
they involve. Thus in this case the word-conveyed signs seem to retain primacy, and the trigram symbols are drawn out to support and in some measure to fill out the meaning of those signs. As time passes this supportive
function of the trigram symbols gives way to the elevation to primacy of the
line figure associations that are attributed to the various component trigrams
of the hexagrams. With this, attention to the line images themselves as divinatory factors virtually disappears.

a7. Final comments on this first example

I have said that the line image is used in something like the *Zhouyi* manner as I have sketched it out in Part I. But this needs to be made a bit more

precise. The imagery is used as symbolism, but the concern with symbolism is different. It lies simply in the power of the symbolism to point out in advance what will be, to predict the future. In contrast, in the *Zhouyi* originally, symbols were used to focus attention on the futural implications of the current present, and that means: to guide an attention to the present through which the inquirer can become more knowledgeable about what he/she is involved in, and in particular can descry a future which is harbored in that present and whose working out concretely over time is to involve the inquirer and his/her more informed involvement in that outworking. In this latter case, the complicity of the inquirer agent in the coming to pass of the future in question is maintained, and the projection of the future is adapted to that-- it is prophetic in character. But in the former case, it is as if the matter which is of concern (perhaps in the case at hand because of the distant future being held out as the relevant one) *will* happen *apart from* the manner of complicity of the inquirer agent, so that it is being predicted in some absolute sense, and the divination is no longer functionally prophetic.

The *Zuozhuan* exposition of this first example is followed by a comment by the author of the passage (Zuo, in the traditional understanding), to the effect that in fact, Chen did decline and an eighth generation descendant of the Marquis of Chen's son Wan did gain governance in Qi. This concern to indicate the accuracy of the sign-reading by the Zhou court scribe attests that the author of this comment also looked at the divination only as predictive in force. When the examples of divination which the *Zuozhuan* recalls are looked at in this predictive vein, the accuracy of those 'predictions' is one of their common features. It is this feature, however, which has also aroused suspicion and has led later commentators to regard these cases as composed after the fact and introduced much later into the text, and as formulated then in such way as to assure their accuracy since one knew what had come of the matters.[28]

Even if the the author/editor of this whole passage made it up with only a minimum of basis in the actual historical record so that the record in its details reflects a way of thought of the 5th century or later author/ editor, there are general features of the kind of interpretation being exhibited as having been ventured in 672 BC that seem historically plausible. In particular, I have in mind the presence of only the vestiges of the sort of line image use that was part of the original *Zhouyi* (even as those vestiges have a primacy still for the interpretation), and the fairly strong function of the line figures (under a trigram analysis and set of trigram associations) as part of the basic sign through which the ancestral spirits are communicating. What we find as time goes on is a continuation of both of these trends: eventually the almost total disappearance of consideration of the line image, and the increasing preoccupation with trigram-associations as providing the heart of the symbolism to be interpreted in order to understand the response of the spirits to the inquiry being made.

b. Three subsequent cases: 565, 537, 535 BC

Our next examples of cases in the *Zuozhuan* in which the *Zhouyi* is expressly said to have been used in a divinatory vein, come about another century later, in the mid-sixth century. In the latter two of these, we find ourselves in times soon after the birth of Confucius. None of the cases involve a Zhou royal scribe or official. Each introduces us to significant aspects of the modifications being made over time in the approach to the *Zhouyi* as a divination work.

b1. 565

The first example is found in the story of the impending death of Mu Jiang, the mother of Duke Cheng of Lu.[29] When she had been placed under house arrest in the Eastern Palace for her part in an attempt to subvert the government of her son, she had stalk-divined about her future. Although the divination method she used involved hexagrams with title-names found in the *Zhouyi*, the manner of recounting the sign set forth and the brief interpretation offered are difficult to comprehend.[30] It might be that the stalk-divining in this case did not in fact draw on the *Zhouyi* but on some other system; indeed, when Mu Jiang heard what the scribe offered as interpretation of the answer to her inquiry, she disputed his interpretation, and did this by appealing expressly to the *Zhouyi*. This could be read as indicating that the *Zhouyi* was not what was used in the first case but that she is appealing to it now because it offers the better way to read the sign. Yet it is more likely that it only signifies that while the *Zhouyi* was being used, the relevant part of the sign was not being selected for interpretation in the first case.[31] In that case, she would be correcting the scribe's use of the *Zhouyi*; perhaps he was letting his wishful thinking guide his interpretation of the significant element of the sign and of what it meant.

When the Duke's mother goes on to cite not simply the title-name[32] but also some words from the hexagram text to explain why she disputes the scribe, she cites the words which we find in the *Zhouyi* text as we have it today. Yet her way of reading the meaning of the terms reflects the sort of moralization of divinatory language which our records indicate becomes common starting in the 6th century. After setting forth the title-name and the hexagram statement ("*Sui²: yuan² heng¹ li⁴ zhen¹, wu² jiu⁴*"), she gives meaning to the four occasion-response characters as representing four separate virtues. But she does more: pointing to part of the the sign (the "come forth" of the title-name) as being accompanied by "without blame" (a moral interpretation of the meaning of a prognostication phrase in the hexagram text), and noting that she is lacking in those virtues (indeed, is evil) and thus is not blameless, she disclaims the applicability of the "come forth" to herself, and claims instead that she is bound to die, not to get out alive from the imprisonment which she suffers.[33]

It is not clear whether this moralized reading of the meaning of occasion response and prognostication words was grounded in an attempt to give meaning to terms which had become unintelligible in their original sense, or whether it was part of an attempt consciously to modify and adapt the divination method to 'modern' ideas and the 'modern' spirit. However that may be, we find here one expression of a second radical shift in address to the *Zhouyi*, one much broader than this one case and one whose further evolution is companion to the transformation of the divination work into a wisdom work.

In contrast to the first shift constituted by the amplification of and focus on the line figures themselves as significant functional parts of the divinatory symbol, this shift expresses an attempt to reconceive the nature and grounds of the divinatory process itself and not simply to focus on the symbols that intimate a future. As I mentioned before, the original employment of the *Zhouyi* was as part of a moral effort being undertaken by the royal inquirer. Yet while the Mandate called for his moral address to his responsibilities as ruler, his divinatory use of the *Zhouyi* was not a vehicle for addressing the moral dimension of the situation. It was rather fitted for helping him (the inquirer) concentrate his attention and inquiry upon the realities of that situation.

Because the text set forth elements in the divinatory act which had such a function, it did not make explicit in its terms this moral dimension that was to invest the very act which brought those terms into appropriate use. Thus when in Eastern Zhou times the employment of the text was detached from the concrete situation of the Zhou King responding to the Mandate, the text itself carried no directives concerning its own employment, not even that it was presumed to be the act of a King assuming his responsibilities in an effort to live up to the Mandate concretely. When in this new context of use the absence of the moral nerve in the employment of the *Zhouyi* became felt as problematic and an attempt was eventually made to redress this, that attempt at moralization took more than one form.

In the particular example of use which we are considering, the moralization of *Zhouyi* divination seems to operate on the background of a moralistic view of the world and of what happens to human beings in it. It also exhibits the shift from reading the sign as a disclosive pointer to the concrete present and its futural import, to reading it as predictive in its significance. Given such a moral world-view and such a predictive reading of the title-name image, the example introduces the moral into the act of divination by interpreting certain terms of the *Zhouyi* vehicle itself in a moral vein, and by taking the presence of those terms in the selected text as signifying the moral precondition for the predictive force of its symbols.

b2. 537

The second example is a divination by a Lu noble concerning his newborn son.[34] Encountering the change of Hexagram 36 ("Injured brightness") into Hexagram 15 ("Modesty")[35], thus encountering Line 1 of Hexagram 36 as the sign selected, he took this result and showed it to a diviner. The line statement of Line 1 reads: "Injured brightness in flight, drooping its wings; a nobleman goes on a travel trip, three days he does not eat. He has a place to go, the hosts have words."[36]

The diviner's interpretation makes the complex sign from the spirits point to a particular future course of events. That course: "He will travel, but return to make the son's sacrifice; (yet on his return) he will bring with him a slanderous man, by name Niu, and he himself will eventually die by starvation."

The rest of the narrative is the exhibition of the basis of this reading in the aspects of the sign. The analysis of the sign in its relevant elements is complex, elliptical, and incomplete, and the text seems jumbled at places. But so far as I can make sense of it, the analysis achieves its end (the displaying of the meaning of the complex sign) by the following means. First, in the consideration of the imagery of the traditional line statement, that imagery itself is analyzed, amplified and interpreted, so that a more complex set of images is claimed to be involved; in the course of this analysis, some of the imagery is grounded in trigram-associations. Second, this amplified imagery is made the basis for pointing to the series of events representing the future of the new-born child. In the achieving of both of these, we have elements to the interpretative effort which we have not seen before.

The first phase of the interpretation focuses on two things: the title-name of the first hexagram[37], and the hexagram change. The title-name, *ming² yi²*, is understood as "injured brightness", and the phrase is taken as an allusion to the sun. Certain associations of the sun with the 10 time-periods (three of them in particular) are then set forth, as well as its association with the 10 ranks (two of these in particular). Then the change from the hexagram with that name, to the second hexagram is considered and its meaning is brought out: the change signifies a brightness which (because of its change into 'modesty') is not overpowering (glaring), and the time of day at which the sun is of this character is dawn. That is also the time of day for a certain sacrifice (that made by a son and addressed to his father). So the first element of the diviner's reading of the future implied in the sign is this: that the son will be making the son-sacrifice.

The second phase of the interpretation focuses on the line image in the line statement, and provides for each of the four phrase-parts of that image an explanation of the imagery-- but no application of it to the future in hand. According to that explanation: in this line, the change of the sun so that it is 'modest' is symbolized in the line image by taking the sun as a bird. Given this way of alluding to the sun, then: (1) it is the change of the sun-hexagram into the modesty-hexagram that is expressed in the first phrase of the line image ("injured brightness in flight"); (2) it is the sun's muted brightness that is expressed in the second phrase ("its wings drooping"); (3) it is the sun's movement that is expressed in the third phrase ("a nobleman on a travel-trip"); and (4) it is the sun in its muted glowing at dawn (with dawn being associated with the number 3) that is expressed in the fourth phrase ("three days, not eat"). In all four cases, the interpreter is simply analyzing, ampli-fying and explaining the given imagery and introducing further imagery; what the meaning of all this is for the question being asked about the future of the new-born son is not yet developed.

The third phase of the interpretation starts from the trigrams that are har-bored in the two hexagrams, and in particular, from the lower trigrams which hold the changing line and are different from each other in virtue of it. Those lower trigrams stand, respectively, for fire and for mountains, and the change whereby the first becomes the second is read as signifying the burning and destroying of the mountains by the fire. The destroying-element of this imagery is then related to something in the sphere not of nature but of human beings, namely, that of language; in particular, 'destroying words' are slanderous words. At this point in the exposition, the text seems corrupt; rather than using this analysis to ground the final phrase in the line statement ("Hosts have words": a phrase which would make much more sense as being grounded in these trigram-based associations than anything having to do with "going"), the "therefore" makes it be claimed as grounding the next-to-last phrase, "Have a place to go." It seems likely that the original record contained two parallel constructions: explanatory phrase ➔ "Hosts have words"; explanatory phrase ➔ "Have a place to go"; the first phrase to be explained, and the explanatory phrase for the second, have accidentally dropped out of the text, making the first explanatory phrase be followed by the second phrase to be explained and leaving the impression this explanatory phrase was meant to explain this phrase.

However that may be, phases two and three of the exposition of the interpretation work with imagery to explain or ground elements of the line statement, without bringing any of this to bear on the matter of the new-born son and the future presumably being pointed to by the line statement (at least, by the line image). These phases are followed by a fourth phase; it is incomplete, but it does seek to do what the first phase sought to do, namely, point to how the reading of the diviner whereby he applies the imagery to the future in question is based in the imagery. And in making this attempt, it draws on the analysis of imagery presented in phases two and three.

Phase four has two steps[38], each of which expressly grounds an element in the diviner's reading of the future. First: the lower trigram of the first hexagram is associated not only with fire, but also with oxen (*niu²*); now in a disorderly world slander is victorious, and the trigram *li²* (as is displayed in its overpowering the mountains[39]) is suitable as a victor, thus "his name is Niu".[40] Second: a series of four images ("modesty meaning not sufficient, flying meaning not soaring, drooping meaning not flying high, wings not being broad") all point to some sort of insufficiency, in particular, to some sort of not being able to fly high and far away; and it is this, it seems, which is expressed in "this makes his son return". This is presumably the second part of the diviner's reading of the future, and linked with the third which has already been explained: "(the son) will return home to make the son's offering sacrifice".

So far, the middle portions of the reading of the future by the diviner have been grounded in phases one and four: "He will return to make the son's sacrifice; (yet on his return) he will bring with him a slanderous man, by name Niu." What is as yet unaccounted for is the start ("he will travel") and the end ("he himself eventually died by starvation"). Perhaps these are too obvious in their grounding to need separate and explicit explanation: the first hearkens back to the "nobleman goes on a travel trip", the last to "three days, not eat".

In this example taken as a whole, the ultimate concern is to formulate the meaning of the sign for the future involved in the question. This is done by taking the complex sign-elements as, in one way or another, marking out certain aspects of the future, certain events and eventualities. But the determination of which aspects are marked out is grounded directly[41] in various aspects of the sign: the title-name, the line statement, and the lower hexagrams and their associations. The interpretation does not focus the inquirer's attention back on the present in its futural aspects, but instead proceeds in a predictive vein from the signs alone.

In the context of the known examples, what is new and notable about this example are two things.

One is the extraordinary attention paid to extending and refining the imagery itself. In this the trigram figures and their associations, the line statement and the associations of its components, and the title-name images and their associations are all drawn upon. But perhaps because of the incompleteness of the expository record of this case, much of that work bears no direct and indispensable relation to the interpretation of the sign in regard to the matter at issue; nonetheless, it discloses the way in which the range of imagery which can be drawn out of any example can be expanded, giving the interpreter much more to work with than otherwise.

The second thing is the way in which the imagery functions in regard to the matter at issue. When it is applied, the "he will travel" becomes drawn on in literal vein from the line statement, and the "will die a starvation death" seems to come in literal vein from "three days, not eat", but by an extension of what is directly said (even if one takes the "three" to be metaphor for a good period of time) to a possible consequence of not eating for a lengthy period of time. Where the imagery becomes used in some other vein than literal picture-like application, the roots of the meaning are very complex, involving going back to the first hexagram title-name and taking it to allude to the sun, and the sun to be represented in the line statement as a bird. Taking the associations of these, some sort of grounding of most of the interpretation is provided with the help of associative chains and analogical leaps; but this grounding is not fully worked out[42] and the state of the text obscures much[43]. What is new here is the mixture of a complex symbolic reading with a measure of literalism which, if we can regard it as addressing symbols as symbols at all, does so at most in a minimalist fashion. It is as if the classificatory mind is invading and taking over the realm of symbol and inhibiting the imaginative address to symbols as symbolic.[44]

b3. 535

The third example in this cluster of records involves two divinations on the same matter (succession of the Duke in Wei). Each was focused on a different son of his by the same consort: the first was named Meng-zhi, the second was named Yuan (a name which means 'first').[45] In the divinatory inquiries undertaken on behalf of the Duke, one was phrased: "Would that Yuan enjoy Wei, being the master of its god of the crops!", while the other was phrased: "Would that I establish Zhi, would that I be able to commend him!" In the first case, the stalk-divining elicited Hexagram 3, in the second, Hexagram 3 changing to be Hexagram 8 (this making Line 1 be the moving line).

When these divinations were interpreted by a scribe, the latter made no appeal to the imagery in the title-name when the first one was considered, but looked only to what I have called the occasion responses, interpreted by him in very different vein. He reads the *yuan² heng¹* as "Yuan will be successful"-- reading the *yuan²* as singling out the son by that name. "What further doubt is there of it?"

When it was pointed out to him that "*yuan²*" means "oldest", his response was that the "oldest" son (Meng-zhi) was a non-person (he was crippled in the feet); since it would not be proper for him to be in charge in the ancestral temple, one could not possibly call him "oldest".

Besides, the appended words-- both in the hexagram text and in the particular line statement selected (Hexagram 3, Line 1)-- have the phrase, "Beneficial to establish feudal lords". Now if succession simply went to the oldest in age, there would be nothing to "establish"; but since there apparently is, then ... this too confirms that the youngest, named Yuan, should enjoy Wei.

In this example, we have moved away altogether from the use of imagery as symbol. Indeed, even the trigram associations are ignored here. Only the chance identity of the name of one of the sons with a character in a two-character phrase, and the reading of that phrase to make it a sentence using the name as subject, gives one response; the other comes by the chance appearance of a phrase harboring a word whose literal sense and application could be twisted to imply something other than natural succession. The crucial words in both cases belong to the added verbal elements in the hexagrams, not to the words which convey the images. From this, we can recognize that we have moved quite far from the 9th century spirit and method of divination originally expressed in the *Zhouyi*. Not only is divination not something being undertaken by a member of the royal court, by the ruler or his diviner, but the scribe's reading shows no feeling for the matter of divination as the *Zhouyi* conceived and carried it out.[46]

c. Final case: 484 BC

Our final example from cases in the *Zuozhuan* in which the *Zhouyi* is expressly said to have been used in a divinatory vein, comes from a half century after the three preceding cases, well into the fifth century and toward the end of the lifetime of Confucius.

In this case[47] we find that after three different diviners used turtle divination and obtained three different answers on a certain matter, a personage of the state of Jin took the *Zhouyi* and stalk-divined the matter. What was at issue was whether Jin should enter into battle with Song, to save Zheng. The diviner encountered Hexagram 11 changing to Hexagram 5 (thus Line 5 of Hexagram 11). Although this line is not set forth straightforwardly in the exposition, as the discussion proceeds parts of it emerge, and it appears to have been the same as in the *Zhouyi* text: "Emperor Yi giving his daughter in marriage, thereby happiness, extremely auspicious".

The interpretation ventured makes use only of the line image, and takes it up in two regards. The first concerns Emperor Yi: reference to him recalls the intimate connection of Song and its founding with the Shang (and in particular, with the oldest son of Emperor Yi), and given the relation of Song and Zheng as a sort of uncle-nephew one, it is not acceptable for Jin to inter-ject itself into this family quarrel. The second continues that thought: if (as in the line image) happiness (prosperity) belongs to Emperor Yi's giving his daughter (thus his oldest son's sister) in marriage, what that is auspicious could come from going into battle against Song on behalf of Zheng?

In this interpretation, the title-name image is ignored, and no trigram associations are introduced; yet even though the focus here is on the line image, just as in the 9th century *Zhouyi*, it is not on that image as symbol pointing attention to the present and to the forces at work in it that would bear upon the matter of of Jin intervention. It is rather on that image as, in its literal sense, recalling historical relations and connections. Because the image, when used in its literal meaning, highlights certain aspects of the current situation about which the question is being posed, and because those aspects (e.g. prosperity as a heritage for Song) suggest that Jin intervention might not be an auspicious thing for Jin, the interpretation concludes to the absence of good reason to try coming to the rescue of Zheng.

2. A *Guoyu* example, mentioning *Zhouyi*

Before passing on to a consideration of examples in the *Zuozhuan* of stalk-divination which might be compared with those cases we have been reviewing, let us take up with the one example from the *Guoyu* in which the *Zhouyi* is mentioned as being involved in the consultation.

This example belongs to events of 637 BC, and thus belongs 35 years after the first of the *Zuozhuan* examples we discussed above. The initiator of the divination is the Duke of Jin, so we have here an employment of the *Zhouyi* outside the royal court. The divination tests a desire of the Duke: "I would like to have-and-hold the country of Jin." That is, the 'charge' (*ming⁴*) to the stalks is to convey to the spirits this wish of the Duke, to mediate their response, and thereby to indicate whether that wish is consonant with the forces which are at work in the present (including those spirits) and whose working bears on how the future will be defined in regard to that matter.

The exposition continues: "He obtained as *zhen¹*, Hexagram 3 (*Zhun¹*), as *hui³*, Hexagram 16 (*Yu⁴*). Both were 8's." This way of phrasing the stalk-divination result is different from anything we have encountered up to here. In other and later reports, the terms *zhen¹* and *hui³*, used as a linked pair, seem to signify trigrams (the lower and upper trigrams of a hexagram); here they seem to stand for hexagrams, presumably the first and second hexagrams obtained in the divining process. Apparently these have no moving lines[48] and thus no connections with each other through such lines. They are simply two responses, to be interpreted together in order to grasp what the spirits are saying in response to the desire communicated to them in the charging of the stalks.

The initial interpretation, by milfoil scribes, is reported as having been in every case "not auspicious", with an added comment to the effect: "closed and not communicating-or-exchanging, lines are without action". Presumably the comment indicates that neither involves a moving line: the lines are all inert, unmoving, neither hexagram opens out beyond itself and through one or more moving line becomes the other. But the "not auspicious" is a puzzle: in the *Zhouyi* the hexagram texts in both cases contain nothing of that sort. Now it may be that this is a use of the line figures in a different system, fitted simply to disclose the auspicious and the inauspicious. For immediately the Minister of Public Works gives a different reading-- "auspicious"-- and says: "In the *Zhouyi* these are both 'beneficial to establish feudal lords'." That could be read as distinguishing the first readings from this one, they not belonging to the *Zhouyi* whereas the last reading does. Or it could mean that, when we look to the hexagram texts and not simply to the character of the lines,[49] we find in both cases the same phrase. And that phrase is relevant to the matter at issue; indeed, it is the key to the response which the spirits are making.

The phrase in question is one I have called an action indicator. Here its import is taken to be this: you have expressed your wish in the charge, the response has selected out the words in question; and "in regard to the matter of acquiring a country: what could be more auspicious than that? If you do not hold the country of Jin so as to aid the royal house, how could you 'establish feudal lords'?" That is, the sign-- taken to be a phrase common to both of the hexagram texts-- indirectly indicates that you will have-and-hold Jin, for that would be the precondition which alone would give appropriate sense to the action indicated as beneficial.

In the reading so far, no use has been made of the title-names and the matters which those names stand for; nor has the whole of the either hexagram text been invoked.[50]

The interpretation proceeds, this time in another vein. It introduces trigram associations and hexagram title-name meanings, and uses them to justify the language elements selected from the hexagram texts, to show those words as grounded in these associations. There is no attempt, however, to employ them in the fathoming of the future in any other sense than that they explain the auspiciousness noted.

The start is simple: three trigram associations ("Thunder is cart, pit is water, the receptive is earth") relating to the three different trigram components of the two hexagrams are set out; then the two hexagram title-names are interpreted ("*zhun¹* is generosity, *yu⁴* is pleasure").

Next, each of these first trigram-associations is related to its hexagram whole. The first step: through the association of lower trigram of the first Hexagram with "carts", and the presence in Lines 2, 4, and 6, of the same Hexagram of a recurrent phrase whose image involves carts ("teams of horses circling round"), the interpreter notes: "'Carts are circling round': the outer and inner[51] are in accord, use this for interpretation." The second step: through the association of the upper trigram of the first Hexagram with "water", the interpreter notes: "A spring: a (water) source, whereby one provides aid-and-assistance" (i.e. is generous). The third step: through the association of the lower trigram of the second Hexagram with "earth", the interpreter notes: "The earth: it is generous, and one may take pleasure in its fruits."[52]

Finally, the interpretation focuses on the two hexagram wholes, and provides a trigram analysis which grounds the title-name and the hexagram text ("appended words": *zhou⁴*) of each. This step takes place as follows.

1. Hexagram 3, its title-name (*Zhun¹*): the analysis proceeds
   a. By extending the associations of the component trigrams ("Thunder is lightning, cart; pit is labor, water, the masses");
   b. By introducing associations based on the place of the trigrams, "thunder" being below and "pit" above ("Lightning and cart are master⁵³, water and masses are elevated");
   c. By introducing further associations, this time with the two sides of public life (the military and the civil⁵⁴): "Carts which have 'thunder' (i.e. majesty: they are awe-inspiring) are military; the masses are compliant with the civil-and-cultured; the military and the civil both are the extreme of generosity. Therefore the (title-name) is *Zhun¹*" (which in the initial exposition was interpreted as meaning "generosity").
2. Hexagram 3, its hexagram text:
   a. *Yuan²* (understood as 'first') is explained by "being master is being the superior of thunder and lightning"; *heng¹* (understood as 'successful (?)) is explained by "the masses and their compliance with the good"; *li⁴ zhen¹* (understood as ...(?)) is explained by "holding lightning and thunder inward to itself" (presumably, having such a trigram interior to the hexagram).
   b. *Wu⁴ yong⁴ you³ you¹ wang³* (presumably understood as 'do not act to have a place to go') is explained by the following associations: "With the cart below and water above⁵⁵, matters are bound to be distressing⁵⁶; minor affairs are unsuccessful, obstructed".
   c. *Li⁴ jian⁴ hou²* (presumably understood as 'beneficial to establish feudal lords') is explained by the following associations: "When the single man acts, the masses are compliant and hold the military in awe."
3. Hexagram 16, its title-name:
   a. This title-name (*Yu⁴*: earlier said to mean "pleasure") is explained by certain associations of the component trigrams: "*kun¹* is mother, *zhen⁴* is elder male; mother and oldest son are strong".
4. Hexagram 16, its hexagram text:
   a. *Li⁴ jian⁴ hou², xing² shi¹* (presumably meaning 'beneficial to establish feudal lords and to mobilize armies') is explained: "This has the meaning of dwelling in joy and putting forth majesty-and-awe." Presumably that refers to the trigram associations: the earth below with joy, the thunder above with what inspires awe; the first half would be the basis for the establishing of the feudal lords, the latter half for the mobilizing of the armies.

It is on the basis of such an analysis, that the interpreter then concludes: "These two (hexagrams) are gaining-a-country line figures." Apparently this association-analysis through the line figures is meant simply to display how it is that the two hexagram response can be understood as favorable in this matter of the Duke's gaining Jin as the country for him to rule.

What this interpretation shows, overall, is a distinctive method (using two separate hexagrams as independent signs), a focus on a common phrase in the hexagram texts which is basis for the judgment that the sign is auspicious in regard to what the Duke wants, and a complex analysis of the trigram-associations and the title-name meanings to show how such a meaning to the words is substantiated in the line figures themselves, in the meanings assigned to these. This latter contributes nothing independently to the response which the spirits are grasped as having made in the word-elements; but its complexity indicates a developed system of assigned meanings and associations is already present when this divination took place.[57] The subordination of all sign analysis to the mere matter of the auspicious or inauspicious is a feature rather different from the distinctive *Zhouyi* use of images and symbols.

3. *Zuozhuan* examples: probably *Zhouyi* but no mention

Of the fourteen examples of stalk-divination in the *Zuozhuan* which are presented with sufficient detail and content that we can make some assessment of how the signs are being treated in the interpretation, we have considered the five in which the *Zhouyi* is expressly mentioned. There are five further cases in which, although the *Zhouyi* is not mentioned by name, the divinatory elements and method so far as we can see these seem to reflect use of the *Zhouyi* as we know the text. These appear in the records of events of the years 661, 645, 635, 546, and 528. Let us briefly consider these cases for any further light they might throw on the use of the *Zhouyi*, assuming that in fact it was being used in them.

a. Three cases from the middle third of the 7th century

a1. 661

In the first case, in 661[58], we find a certain Bi Wan, at a time long before he became a *dai¹-fu¹* in Jin with Wei as a fief, stalk-divining concerning his employment as an official in the state of Jin. He encountered Hexagram 3 changing into Hexagram 8, making Hexagram 3, Line 1, be the sign he received. A Jin *dai⁴-fu¹*, Xin Liao, interpreted this for him, in the following fashion.

The first step was to affirm: this was an auspicious divination. No basis for this is given: the line itself is not set forth or even alluded to in its content in the course of the discussion.[59] And if indeed the *Zhouyi* is being used, this line as we know it holds no explicit prognostication element relating to the line image in it, although it has two accompanying but independent action indicators both of which are "beneficial".

The second step is to set forth the meaning of each title-name: the first (Hexagram 3, *Zhun¹*) is "firm", while the second (Hexagram 8, *Bi³*) is "intimate". "What is more auspicious than that? You will be bound to flourish." Again, the exposition provides nothing to explain this interpretation and judgment. Are the two characterizations meant to be translations of the title-names, or additional associations? Is it simply that the firm-and-resolute changes into the intimate, and that the latter indicates some success in reaching into the inner circles of the Jin court? In any case, the images which the title-names convey are not explored directly or used to fathom the present in its futural bearing. The focus is simply on the auspicious or inauspicious.

The third step is to put forth a set of trigram associations and relations, to be used for two things: a) grounding this judgment of "auspicious" in the meanings assigned to the trigrams, and b) developing out of the latter further facets of the situation than those apparent simply through the title-name associations. The exposition of trigram meanings and relations begins with three versions of the change of the lower trigram of the first hexagram into the lower trigram of the second:

1. "Thunder becomes earth": the first is "thunder", the second "earth", and through the changing line the first changes into the second.
2. "The cart follows the horses": the first is "horses", the second "cart";
3. "The feet occupy it (i.e. the ground)": the first is "feet", the second is "earth".

The exposition continues with three further associations, this time with each of these lower hexagrams separately:

4. "The older brother has precedence": this refers to an element in the meaning of "older brother", which in turn is associated with the 'thunder' trigram;
5. "The mother covers-and-protects him": this refers to an element in the meaning of "mother", which in turn is associated with the 'earth'

trigram;

6. "The masses return-in-allegiance to him": this refers to an element
in the meaning of "masses", which in turn is associated with the
'earth' trigram.

The exposition of these trigram meanings and associations ends with the
puzzling comment: "These six parts will not change." The exposition records nothing being done with this set of associations beyond this simple
enumeration. As a result it is difficult to know how they were supposed to
figure in the divination. Were they the vehicle for defining in concrete reference that course into the future which the overall change of the hexagrams
intimates (the movement from firmness to intimacy)? Or were they meant
to amplify the meanings of "firm" and "intimate"? Or ... ? The record which
we have gives us no help in answering such questions.

The fourth step is to conclude, in a fashion that draws on what has been
already set forth but brings it back to the question being asked: "to join
together and yet be able to be firm, to maintain security-and-peace and yet
be able to slay[60]: (these qualities and capacities make clear that the) line figures (pertain to) Dukes and Lords. The descendants of Dukes and Lords are
bound to return to the beginning." That is, in such Hexagrams and their uniting of such contrasting things, we have line figures which manifest qualities
and capacities which are to belong to Dukes and Lords. That being so, as responses to the question posed in the divination, they signify that Bi Wan is
bound to regain the position of his forefathers (in particular, Duke Gao of
Bi).

The concluding step would seem to reassert that the primordial horizon
of the divination is the question of the auspicious and the inauspicious. Is Bi
Wan's desire to become an official at the Jin court aligned with the forces at
work (the spirits, for example), or is it not? The absence of any reference to
the line image in the moving line would seem to provide some further confirmation that the auspicious/inauspicious is the limiting horizon of the interpretation.

a2. 645

In the second case, in 645[61], we have a series of events in the course of
which two different stalk-divination actions are taken. From the language
used, it seems likely that the *Zhouyi* was used in the one case-- which I will
take up here-- but another method may have been involved in the other case.

The case in point here concerns Duke Xian of Jin and his consultation
concerning his giving his oldest daughter in marriage to the ruler in Qin. In

the stalk-divination, he encountered Hexagram 54 changing into Hexagram 38, making Line 6 of Hexagram 54 be the sign involved.

The first step by the diviner who offers the interpretation is to note that it is "not auspicious". He then announces the line statement (more precisely, the "appended words" [*zhou*[t]]), and it is the same as is found in the *Zhouyi* for that line with two exceptions: it lacks the prognosticatory element at the end of the *Zhouyi* line statement[62], and it has the two components of the line image in an order reversed from that in the *Zhouyi* as we have it. As he announces it, it reads: "The man stabs the sheep, there is no blood; the woman holds out a basket, there are no gifts."

What immediately follows in the exposition is an application of the prognosticatory "inauspicious" to the situation involved in the question. "Our western neighbor's chiding words are not able to be undone by compensation. The sign (Hexagram 54 changing into Hexagram 38) is tantamount to being without help." That is: if you are seeking to appease Qin by this marriage, you will not succeed. Qin's criticism of Jin is not to be assuaged in that fashion. The act of daughter-marriage will not provide any help. Such is the meaning of this sign, according to the diviner.

This application of the prognostication to the situation in question is followed immediately by further interpretation which draws upon and applies, first some trigram associations, then some of the imagery in the line in the second Hexagram (38/6) corresponding to the moving line (54/6).

The first step: alluding to the upper trigrams in each hexagram, the interpreter reads not simply the one becoming the other but the reverse movement, and (in virtue of the associations of the one with thunder[63], the other with fire) applies the sign: "this is the Ying clan defeating the Ji clan."[64] This would seem to be an attempt to apply imagery involved in the sign, to relate it to the future that is to come out of the present: this situation of a possible daughter-marriage is, in broader terms, one of a conflict of Qin and Jin, the ultimate issue of which seems to be being anticipated here.

The second step: "The cart loses its axle-bindings[65], fire burns the banners: it is not beneficial to march armies, defeat at the ancestral mound." Although "cart" might be derived from the imagery of 38/6, it is more likely to fit with "fire" and be based, like the latter, on trigram associations: "cart" is associated with the thunder trigram (the upper one of the first hexagram), "fire" with the upper trigram of the second hexagram. But the use of the two elements here is puzzling. It could be that, using the two trigram associations, the interpreter is applying them to the situation in a specific reference-- to the military struggle between Qin and Jin-- and then framing the inauspicious sense in a way suited to that situation. But actually, the whole set of phrases here sounds more like a set of four four-character phrases which, while it may have a comparable sense to the moving line's line statement (a double image of inauspicious matters), was being drawn from elsewhere than the *Zhouyi* as we have it and being used here, perhaps on the basis of the trigram associations I just mentioned. In any case, as with the first interpretative step just discussed there seems to be here also an effort to interpret imagery in a relation to the future in question, and to address the military context of the daughter-marriage question.

The third step[66]: here interpretation seems to draw not on the moving line's imagery, but on imagery present in the corresponding line in the second hexagram.[67] Thus: "The marrying maiden observes the fox, the bandits stretch out their bows." This takes three elements of the complex imagery of 38/6 ("observes the fox", "outstretched bows", and "bandits"), and brings them to bear on the situation which the Jin ruler's daughter would be in if in fact the marriage went through: she would be in position to observe the Qin leader (the "fox") and his army ready for battle (the "bandits" with their "bows outstretched"). As in the two previous steps, if this is so then there is another attempt being made here to use the imagery to elicit the character of the future involved in the situation and matter at issue in the question relating to that situation.

a3. 635

In the third case, in 635[68], the Qin army was encamped on its side of the Yellow River, on its way across Jin to see to the safe return of the Zhou King to his capital after a Zhou defeat by some Rong forces. The Jin ruler was urged himself to undertake this service to the Zhou King: 'there's nothing like diligent service of that sort to serve you in gaining the allegiance of the other feudal lords, and besides, it's the just thing to do. Is it not the acceptable thing for you at present, to continue earlier Jin service in the affairs of the King and to build trust among the other feudal lords?' The Jin ruler asked that the matter be put to the tortoise shell, and the report was "auspicious"[69] But the Jin Duke claimed he was not up to that, and when told that the Zhou ritual was unchanged (the present King is the Emperor of old, thus it was his obligation in this regard that was in question), he asked that this be put to stalk-divination.

The divining encountered Hexagram 14 changing into Hexagram 38, making Line 3 of Hexagram 14 the sign selected.

The first step in the interpretation was to note: "entirely auspicious".

The next step was to set forth the line statement encountered: "The Duke acted to make sacrifice to the Son of Heaven."[70]

The third step was to interpret the sign in what it disclosed of the situation harboring the matter at issue in the consultation. The interpreter did this by interpreting the act of sacrifice mentioned in the line image as one celebrating a successful battle, and then by applying that in straightfoward literal fashion to the situation: 'the fighting will be successful and the King will enjoy a feast, what could be more auspicious than that?'

The fourth step ("moreover") was to draw upon trigram associations to fill out the interpretation being ventured. The sun (that is, the upper trigram in both hexagrams) is found above the changing lower trigrams, which represent heaven becoming a watery marsh; the interpreter notes: "In this line figure, heaven becomes a watery marsh, so as to be a match for the sun." This is then interpreted in relation to the situation holding the matter at issue: "The Son of Heaven will lower his heart to you, is that not acceptable?" The reference is to royal action to honor the Duke for his service.[71]

b. Two cases in the third quarter of the 6th century

There are two examples from the 6th century which might also involve use of the *Zhouyi*, although no mention of the divination work by name is found in either record.

b1. 546

In the first case, in 546[72], the stalk-divination arises in a setting in which marriage is the matter at issue. The sister of the Cui ruler's minister was widowed by the death of her husband, a Qi Duke, and the Cui ruler, attracted to her, sent her brother to fetch her so that he could marry her. The brother resisted (the kinship relations were wrong, marriage would create incest), and the Cui ruler stalk-divined the matter. He encountered Hexagram 47 changing into Hexagram 28, thus Line 3 of Hexagram 47 was the sign-- supposing that it is the *Zhouyi* that is involved here. The scribes all interpreted this as "auspicious"[73], but when the Cui ruler made known all this to Wen-zi of Chen, the latter interpreted it differently.[74]

His interpretation begins with associations pertaining to the trigrams of both hexagrams. The lower trigram of the first is associated with "man", and the upper and lower trigrams of the second with "woman" and "wind" respectively.[75] Then the change in lower trigrams is taken to mean "a man follows the wind", while the relation of the two trigrams of the second hexagram is taken to mean "wind topples a woman". From this the is conclusion drawn : "not acceptable to marry".

His interpretation continues ("moreover"), this time by reference to the line statement (*zhou⁴*), which is set forth here and, apart from a loan-word difference, is exactly as in the *Zhouyi* for 47/3. Separating out its three images for individual reading, he gives a brief interpretation of each, and in each case gives the imagery a sense that points up the injurious or defective character of the proposed marriage as he sees it. Thus:

1. "'Distressed by stones', he proceeds but does not get across": presumably, stones hamper travel sufficiently to prevent a successful ford;
2. "'Relying on the spiny caltrop', what one relies on injures one"; presumably, the attachment is injurious;
3. "'Entering into his palace, not seeing his wife: ominous', nothing to go home to."

The images seem to be taken simply in their negative force, as underlining the inauspiciousness of the proposed marriage. They do not seem to be interpreted in terms of their content, as pointing symbolically into the unfolding of the future out of the present and focusing attention on problematic aspects of the proposed marriage, on specific defects or inauspicious conditions or events which loom ahead if the marriage takes place and which together make the proposal something unacceptable.[76]

b2. 528

In the second case, in 528[77] (well into the lifetime of Confucius), we have a situation in which the current ruler of Lu has shown disrespect to Nan Kuai, one of his ministers, and provoked him to consider rebellion and restoration of the Lord of Lu to his throne. Nan Kuai stalk-divines on this matter of rebellion and encounters Hexagram 2 changing to Hexagram 8. The selected sign-- Line 5 of Hexagram 2-- says: "Yellow skirts, extremely auspicious" (exactly as in the *Zhouyi*). He shows the result to a friend, Zifu Huibo, and asks, if he wanted to undertake the affair, what would that friend say.

Zifu Huibo's considered opinion is to the effect that if the rebel leader's undertaking is an affair of loyalty and good faith, it is acceptable, but if not, then it is bound to fail. Then after he explains what he means by the two terms he has just used ("loyalty" is "outer strength, inner warmth", "good faith" is "harmony along with frank honesty"), he turns to the line image which is the divination sign, to develop his thoughts out of it.

His is a moralizing type of analysis, which does not address so much the meaning of the sign as something pointing into the future, as the conditions under which it is appropriate to act upon a divinatory sign, even an auspicious one. More precisely, it interprets the first three characters of the auspicious sign as intimating the moral conditions that are requisite if the inquirer receiving this response of 'auspicious' is to act upon it and that acting is to be acceptable.

First step: after characterizing what each of the first three characters in the line statement means[78], he says: a middle which is not loyal would not gain (the name of) this color, a lower (part) which does not work together[79] would not gain (the name of) this adornment, affairs which are not good would not gain (the name of) this utmost high-point[80].

Second step: he characterizes what each of the terms he had just used means, loyalty (the outer and inner entirely united), working together[81] (to lead affairs using good faith), and goodness (to offer nourishment to the three virtues), and he concludes: if these three are not present, it does not fit.[82]

Final step: "Inward beauty enables 'yellow'; upper beauty makes for 'extreme'; if there is beauty below, then there is 'skirt'. If one's share in these three is perfected, then it is acceptable to stalk-divine; if one still has a deficiency, then even though the stalk-divination is 'auspicious', it is not."

In effect, the interpreter says: it is not acceptable to act upon even an auspicious divination, unless in that acting one is acting out of certain virtues, certain inner conditions. That is, if one does not measure up to a certain inward completeness in virtue, then one should not be acting even upon an auspicious divination.

In this case of use of the *Zhouyi* we have a second example[83] reflecting in another form the moralizing reading which is part of some users attempt to bring *Zhouyi* divination into what they felt was the moral nerve of human life. In this case as in the first, the moralization involves giving a moral reading to certain terms within the *Zhouyi* vehicle itself, and from that starting point working back in the act of interpretation to claim a moral precondition for the predictive force of its symbols. In this case, the starting point is not a hexagram text but a line statement, in which the two characters which form the line image and one character which is part of the prognostication are separated off from the second prognostication character and treated as standing for three virtues. It is the presence of these virtues in the agent who is making a divination inquiry concerning a proposed action of his/hers which, according to this reading, is being pointed to by the sign as necessary condition for any appropriate use of *Zhouyi* divination.

4. *Zuozhuan* examples: other cases

Of the fourteen examples of stalk-divination we set out to consider, four remain to be looked at. Three of these-- appearing in the record of the years 660, 645, and 576-- might involve the *Zhouyi* although this would require special explanations to make the examples plausible. The fourth and final example, in 656, might also involve a use of the *Zhouyi* although nothing in the record indicates that it is that type of stalk-divination.

a. Perhaps *Zhouyi* but no mention

The first two cases here belong in the middle third of the 7th century.

a1. 660

In the first example, in 660[84], the divination concerns the future of the new-born son of Duke Huan. After a turtle-divination is performed by the father of the diviner[85] Cuiqiu, a stalk-divination is also undertaken, presumably by the same man. He encountered $Da^4 you^3$ changing to $Qian^2$-- if this is the *Zhouyi*, that means, Hexagram 14 changing to Hexagram 1, thus making 14/5 be the sign selected. In the account we have, there is no setting forth of the line statement that would have been involved, and what the diviner goes on to say-- apparently his interpretation of the meaning of the line statement in the present context-- has no obvious connection with the line statement of 14/5 in the *Zhouyi* For what he says is simply: "the same again to his father, respected as if he had the lord's place." While this rhymed couplet may reflect an anticipation of something that did happen to the son-- at one time he fled to Chen, then returned and eventually became Duke Xi-- its grounding in any line statement, let alone in any other aspects of the sign, is omitted in the exposition.

If the *Zhouyi* was being employed here, then that line statement would have been $jue^2 fu^2 jiao^1$-$ru^2 wei^1$-ru^2; originally that would have meant something like "their captives, tied up crosswise, looking terrified". If that was the sign and its meaning to this interpreter[86], then it makes sense that he did not voice the actual line image but instead introduced a rhymed couplet of the sort that a crack-diviner would use in the reading of cracks. Certainly that couplet voices a more appealing sentiment likely to be acceptable to the Duke.

However, is this couplet and its sentiment grounded in any way in the line statement? Was it developed through association with anything in the actual line statement? Or in this case, do we not have the *Zhouyi* being employed, but another text? Or, finally, do we have here a case where the interpreter is freely inventing the response because (say) the actual response was something he would prefer not to voice to the Duke?[87]

a2. 645

In the second example, in 645[88], we find stalk-divination being attempted in the context of the conflict of Jin and Qin. Earl Mu of Qin was about to undertake a punishment attack on Jin, and after the diviner (the crackmaker Tufu) undertook the divination, he interpreted: "Auspicious, if Qin fords the river, the Lord (of Jin's) chariots will suffer defeat". Asked by the Qin Earl about this, the diviner expanded a bit: "it is very auspicious, after three defeats, we are bound to catch the Jin ruler."

As to the line figure encountered, it was *Gu* [superscript *t*] (what would be Hexagram 18, if this were the *Zhouyi*); according to the diviner's account, this said: "A thousand chariots, three defeats; among what is left over after the three defeats, catch the male fox". As he interpreted it, the hexagram's fox was bound to be the ruler of Jin.

Nothing like this set of rhymed lines appears in the hexagram text of the *Zhouyi* Hexagram 18, indeed in any of the lines of that hexagram or any other hexagram in the *Zhouyi*. That may be understood, of course, in alternative ways: we may be dealing with variant texts, or we may be dealing with a line figure from another system, or we may be dealing with an interpretation grounded in the hexagram text rather than that text itself, or ....[89]

However that may be, the initial reading-- a mixture of image (fox) and literal meaning (defeats, three)-- points into the future and to specific matters which the unfolding of the present is anticipated to hold. The words referred to, then, are not simply used as illustrative of something auspicious, but are taken as pointing to a determinate future which is auspicious in the terms which that symbolic pointing makes clear. There will be three defeats, and then the capture of the Jin leader.

The diviner goes on to provide an analysis through the trigrams involved. The language used includes a pair of words (*zhen* [superscript *1*] and *hui* [superscript *3*]) which, in another context we have considered[90], referred to the first and second hexagrams of a set of two hexagrams. Here, the pair is used to refer to the lower and upper trigram of the single hexagram involved. According to the associations, the lower is the wind, the upper the mountains. The time of year is autumn (the basis for saying this is not indicated: is this simply a report of the season they find themselves in at the time of this divination?). Given these associations, the diviner then says: "We will make the fruit fall and take the timber, therefore we will prevail; for with fruits fallen and timber gone, is that not defeat? What are you waiting for?"

The grounds for what is said seem clear in part, since the lower trigram is not only associated with wind but also wood, and the upper not only with mountains but with fruits and seeds. Thus the interpretation takes the (Qin) wind, sweeping over the (Jin) mountains, to bring down the ripe fruit. But why these associations are put together in this specific configuration of action, and how the conclusion was drawn, is not clear.[91] Nonetheless, the use of the associations seems to be to confirm the implications of the line image concerning victory over Jin, but in quite different terms. Whether, and how, these associations point into the future in determinate fashion is also unclear (What are the 'fruits' and the 'timber'? What actions will be the 'making fall' and the 'taking' of the image?).

a3. 576

The third case, in 576[92], arises as Jin and Chu are drawing closer to battle. Speaking to the Jin ruler, someone advises a certain way of attacking Chu, and the Duke stalk-divines it.

The scribe says: "It is auspicious. The line figure encountered was *Fu*[93]. It says: 'Southern country was coerced, they shot its first-and-foremost king, hitting him in the eye.'" Nothing like this hexagram text appears in the *Zhouyi* Hexagram 24, but something like it does appear in 36/3: "A calling pheasant, wounded in the southern hunt; they got the big chief." It is possible that the *Zuozhuan* text is defective here, and should read: "As to the line figure, I encountered Hexagram 36 changing to Hexagram 24", supposing that it is the *Zhouyi* that is in fact involved here. This would make the line statement of 36/3 be the relevant sign. The hexagram text and the line statement are not identical, but they are probably close enough to think that they are variations on a theme, so to speak.

The scribe then offers his interpretation of the sign: "The country being coerced, the king injured, is that not a defeat? What are you waiting for?" The image, relating to the field of action which is at issue in the question, is taken not for its specific pointing to something that the future is anticipated to hold (some realization of "coercion of a country", "injury of a king"), but for the auspicious bearing of the image in general (the image is of a victory, that means for you also a victory: what are you waiting for?). In this, there is no use made of the hexagram title-name image, or of trigram associations. And the use of the imagery is relatively straightforward, almost as a picture which it is anticipated will be repeated in the future if the Jin ruler attacks.

b. *Zhouyi?*

The final example, in 656[94], involves a Duke of Jin who, seeking to take a certain woman as his wife, first shell-divined (but it was not auspicious), then stalk-divined (it was auspicious). Although his diviner urged him that turtle-divination was preferable to stalk-divination, he followed the latter. After the diviner urged shell-divining as preferable, he added ("moreover") certain "connected appended-words (*xi⁴ zhou⁴*)". These seem to be connected with the shell-divination, not the stalk-divination, for their implication is that "this is certainly not acceptable". About all that can be said about them is that they are a set of rhymed couplets. The second may be a generalized statement which could be traditional, even part of a manual for turtle-crack interpretation (classifying cracks and their significance). But the first is too directly addressed to the Duke's single-mindedness to *be* the words of a text, though they may represent the *implication* of some words which the diviner is drawing out pointedly in reference to the Duke.

Not only is there no mention of *Zhouyi*, but there is no reference at all to a hexagram, a title-name, a hexagram text, or a line statement. There is no way of telling whether or not the *Zhouyi* was involved here, only that some form of stalk-divination was. If it was the *Zhouyi*, it seems to have been used only for its power to determine the auspicious or inauspicious, not for anything related to its distinctive divinatory features.

5. Conclusions

We have now completed our step by step review of the historical records which give us the earliest glimpse of the *Zhouyi* in use. What we have seen is a work whose use is in process of change during the historical period covered by the records (early 7th to early 5th centuries). But looked at in a broader context, even the earliest record comes well after the time of the composition of this work (late 9th century). Did change begin only 150 years later? That is unlikely, particularly in view of the fact that fundamental political, social, and other shifts took place in this interval between composition and the use shown in our earliest records. Those shifts were such as would significantly have affected the use of this work. In order most fully to recognize what the historical records which we have been reviewing disclose to us about the *Zhouyi* and its changing use, we need to recall what is essential in this broader historical context. Then in the light of what such a recall brings to mind, we can consider and discuss what the records seem to show us, namely, a several-sided adaptation and evolution in the use of the *Zhouyi*, expressed in which is a sense of the nature and meaning of the act of divination which significantly departs from that sense which was embodied in the original work.

Because this divination work was originally conceived as having a certain function for the Zhou King in his effort to carry out the Mandate of Heaven, it is the final failure of the Zhou leadership to effectively embody the sense of that Mandate that forms the appropriate point of departure for our historical recall here.

When Zhou leaders were imbued with the sense of the Mandate of Heaven, governance took place in an ongoing present charged with the spiritualizing impact of a Mandate being received and responded to. Corresponding to the deepening of the present went the enlarging of the future to make it that realm into which, through responsible and effective engagement with the present, the current leader could extend the interplay with Heaven and expand the achievement of the end meant to be achieved with the crucial mediation of his governance. Corresponding to this deeper present and enlarged future, was a past made grand for its holding the previous outworking of this interplay of ultimate divine power and human King which the present leader is to continue.

When the *Zhouyi* was composed for use in the time of Zhou revival under King Xuan, its composer offered a version of divination which was fitted to engage a royal inquirer imbued with that sense and spirit of service and achievement. It was suited to engage him more deeply in his present situation as it was taken up with under that sense, and to strengthen the hold of that spirit as it worked to facilitate the King's responsible execution of governance in a present so charged.

With the lapse after King Xuan of effective commitment by the Zhou King to the Mandate of Heaven, divination according to the method envisioned by the composer of the *Zhouyi* lost the spiritual grounding it had had in King Xuan's court. And when the Western Zhou period ended and the Eastern Zhou was initiated, the dissociation of political leadership from the Mandate that took place meant further detachment of the use of the *Zhouyi* from its original spiritual grounds.

Some sort of central political leadership and action continued to be recognized as vital to the Chinese way of life, and as properly committed to something like the integrity of the 'civilized' world. Similarly, the religious reference of the way of life which political leadership is to secure was recognized as vital, and the Zhou, while no longer effective political leaders, were assigned to continue the religious task of mediating between Heaven and the civilized Chinese world. But the Mandate which the Zhou had long ago received had been for governing and governing with a civilizing end. This altered arrangement profoundly changed the type of tie of the religious and the political that had been embodied in the Mandate notion.

Accordingly, what effective political leadership emerged in Eastern Zhou times carried with it a different sense; it had different values animating it. It did not assert the claim of King Wen, that Heaven had transferred the Mandate from the Zhou to such new leadership. It did not even see itself as the facilitating heart of a broader spirituality, and thus as governing in some faithfulness to the aspiration of the early Zhou leaders and to that sense of governance which the revival during King Xuan's time had sought to restore. Indeed, such leadership was no longer a spiritual matter in any sense. Instead, it was power and control, and secure enjoyment of the goods of life, which leaders wanted and and which their governance pursued. The change in times, then, brought a loss of the sense of the drama of history taking place at the political and religious center of life, a divorce of the highest governance (indeed, any governance) from the Mandate of Heaven as a relevant imperative at the heart of real life, and the effective disappearance of such an embracing matrix for all lesser activities and strivings (political, religious, or whatever). Within the altered horizon for life that emerged in Eastern Zhou, within the changed outlook and set of values that now obtained at the religious and political heart of the Chinese world, the *Zhouyi* was bound to be adapted for use and to be used differently, or to drop out of use altogether as an anachronism belonging to an earlier time.

For whatever reasons, the *Zhouyi* survived, but in these early Eastern Zhou times, it survived under adaptation. It continued in use in the Zhou court, but no longer could that use proceed within the original spirit; no longer was this divination method employed in a spiritually creative act that assisted a King in effectively facilitating the civilizing advance of history under the guidance of the supreme divine power Heaven. But more importantly, the *Zhouyi* gradually gained expanded use beyond the immediate sphere of the Zhou King. In those other contexts its use was new and had no tradition behind it, to say nothing of a tradition which made its use be grounded in a specific spiritual base. Freed everywhere, then, to be given other senses and meanings than its original one, the *Zhouyi* became subject to evolution under the needs and purposes of whoever would employ the work now. Because no comparable spirituality emerged to reinstate for its use the kind of temporal context-- the vision of future and past and the inspiration of service to deeper spiritual aims-- within which it had been originally framed to function, the *Zhouyi* became subjected to a substantial adaptation and reshaping, the work of an inventiveness and cleverness of mind which did not simply reflect the variations in individual capacity and perspective but also reflected and in turn contributed to some of the broader intellectual movements which were taking place in the Eastern Zhou period.

In the examples we have reviewed, several things are apparent.

One thing is that the users-- the diviners and their clients (in the examples, these are aristocrats and rulers)-- take up with the work for purposes quite other than those we might conceive to have been meant to be served by the original work.

A second thing is that once the sign has been selected by some unknown procedure using milfoil stalks, it-- or those parts of it which the interpreter considers relevant-- is taken up with in quite varied ways. In good part these different ways express the creativity and individuality integral to the act of interpretation.

A third thing is that factors other than those appropriate to the use of the medium and its elements in a good faith effort to discern the future often enter into the use of the work. Sometimes it is political considerations that modify the use, other times moral or personal ones; in such cases, we find responses being phrased or interpreted in reflection not of the interpreter's best judgment about the disclosure being effected with the help of the sign, but of the pressures and demands of the situation of the divining itself, the personalities involved, the desires of the inquirer. These call forth distorted uses, even misuses, of the work.

When we look beyond the foreground in what the records show us, we can see something else happening in the diversity of ways of taking up with this divination work.

One thing concerns its function of addressing the future, and in particular, the character of its divinatory reach into the future as this is achieved in the employment of this work. The future is no longer imbued with depth in virtue of the Mandate to which the royal inquirer is responsive; within an attenuated present and a futural dimension equally lacking in depth, the nature of the outreaching into the future achieved by an inquirer in the use of the work alters, and with it, the sense and meaning of the various elements of the divinatory work itself.

A second thing concerns a condition that originally was to have been realized in the present, in the person of the inquirer as he employed this divinatory work. The present is no longer that of a King, the reality of whose responsive commitment to realizing the Mandate was reinforced by the ritual nature of the act of inquiry; thus it is no longer inherently marked by the presumption of the inquirer's moral commitment, not even one simply cognate to that in virtue of which the King's consultation through the divinatory medium is aligned with Heaven's will and fitted to receive the guidance being sought. As within such a present devoid of depth use of the work often enough became undertaken as if the moral condition of the inquirer were indifferent to the divinatory inquiry, a counter urge to reclaim the act of divination to the realm of the moral eventually shows itself and promotes a different way of taking up with the work.

A third thing concerns the past in relation to this work. The past involved in its divinatory use is no longer one pregnant for a King with a Mandate handed down by predecessors, thus with the call for continuity of an undertaking begun aforetime and needing to be brought to completion. Yet in relation to later generations, this work, as something created in earlier times, is taken by some as embodying a wisdom which may still be drawn on even if the work is not taken up for its efficacy as medium for receiving wise guidance from the spirits.

Is it simply fortuitous that the fundamental things which happen to the *Zhouyi* in these early Eastern Zhou times, the basic changes which it undergoes, can readily be framed by reference to the three dimensions of time, future, present and past?

However that may be, let us take up these basic changes one by one.

a. First basic change: the future

In the original *Zhouyi* what was to be facilitated by the verbal symbols that constituted its distinctive element was a fathoming of the present in its futural dimension. The images were to help accomplish this work in a present deepened in a religious vein: first, by the immanence of an acknowledged Mandate of Heaven received by a responsive King, and second, by the ritual involved in consultation. The future correlating with such a present was one enlarged by being the locus of the concrete outworking of that Mandate. In the divinatory inquiry it was such a future that was to be fathomed in regard to some matter at issue.

The image-symbols which come into play in the use of the *Zhouyi* are fitted to help such fathoming not simply in virtue of their enigmatic character and thereby their ability to be ever more fully and richly directive for attention to the concrete. They are fitted to help as well in virtue of their intending a dynamic in the situation involved, and intending this through an image which is definite enough to focus attention in a fruitful fashion. Embodying one variation on a theme, such an image points to the situation as harboring in its own concreteness another variation on that theme. This latter variation is to be found in the concrete as that potential outworking of the future-in-the-making character of the present to which the spirits are pointing through the image. Finally, the images are fitted to help not simply as guiding present attention to the present in its futural side but as pointing a participant in the emerging future into that dynamic he/she is currently involved in. The actual future will emerge as definite from out of the present in virtue of a making which involves both an interacting of diverse participants (including divine as well as human) and some measure of dependence of the "will be" on how the participants included in its own making take part. In the measure in which the inquirer-agent's taking part is inflected by the functioning of a cognizance whose anticipation is formed in him/her under the guidance of such symbols, the "growing together" (the concreteness, thought etymologically) that is the eventual issue of the participation of these diverse powers is one to which those symbols themselves contribute through their being acted upon.

Symbols functioning in such a present in such a way are concrescent symbols. As enigmatic pointers to the in-process concrete realization of a thematic meaning which is also bodied forth in the symbol's own particularity, and contributors to a realization whose bringing to pass includes (along with Heaven and the spirits) an inquirer-agent who in some measure and manner is entering responsibly into the making and coming to be of the future, they are symbols apt for a role in aiding the Zhou King to act responsibly.

In contrast, when *Zhouyi* divination appears before us under the basically different conditions of Eastern Zhou life, its employment involves its being brought into play in a present devoid of such depth as well as of the enlarged future correlative with that deepened present. Over time in the employment of the work by different inquirers for their different purposes, three things happen which reflect adaptations of it to a functioning in the altered temporal matrix. Together, these three things express and contribute to a change in the sense of what divination using this work is fitted to accomplish, and more particularly, to a diversion of the inquirer's attention away from the futural import of present things and a directing of it upon future events (what will be) as what are being foreseen (if only indirectly or hiddenly) in the images.

a(1). Reality and symbol

Divested of a spiritual matrix such as that provided by the Mandate of Heaven when the Zhou Kings were responsive to this, consultation with the spirits through divination no longer addresses concrete reality as in-the-making. It also no longer employs symbols which are both correlative in their disclosive functioning with such an in-the-making reality and which also contribute (through their being acted upon) to the shape of the coming together (con-crescing) whereby the future comes to be and be such as it is.[95] Instead, the concrete reality amidst which inquirers find themselves is now taken up with as a factual reality, as fact which is there, which is presently simply what it is, and which is also subject to change. To the extent that it is futural, the focus of the symbols is now future fact, what will be the case-- especially, what change will bring-- but such fact quite independently of how it comes to be out of the present.

In regard to fact (whether past fact, present fact, or future fact), one may speak clearly or obscurely. In the latter case, it may be that the speech is unclear in a way that can be cleared up, or it may be that it is irremediably unclear. Viewed from the standpoint of clarity concerning fact, a symbol which is enigmatic is irremediably unclear. But if such a symbol is regarded as a riddle which can be deciphered and whose intending of fact can be laid out clearly and straightforwardly, then it is obscure in the former sense.

Broadly speaking, what happens in early Eastern Zhou times does not involve replacing the original verbal symbols with new ones. Instead, the original image-symbols are taken up with in such way as to bring them to function differently from before. They are no longer enigmatic concrescent symbols with an attention-guiding function for a participant in the con-crete, but are now riddling vehicles for identifying and grasping aspects of a factual reality. The inventive mind at work in this change thereby has transformed the way the symbols function, even the way in which they are symbolic, without obvious change in the symbols themselves.

a(2). Non-verbal symbols

In that same spiritually barren present of divination, the symbols which the *Zhouyi* is conceived to provide as the ingredients for the response of the spirits to an inquiry are expanded beyond the verbally-conveyed images which have this role in the original work. The realm of functional symbol now includes the non-verbal line figure components (trigrams) to the extent that these are assigned meanings and can thus be seen to stand for this or for that.

The basic terms of the system of interpretation for the trigrams are not related to, let alone grounded in, those of the imagery. Instead, they form a separate system which is focused first and foremost on certain natural factors in the world situation of a human being. Whether these terms and their connected envisioning of the major natural factors human beings must confront were developed initially within the divinatory context, or whether they stemmed from and expressed a different development of thought outside divination, they are brought to function within the divinatory framework as additional to the verbal imagery, and initially as grounding it and perhaps to some extent also as amplifying it.

The basic associations given to the line figure symbols are intended in straightforward fashion: a certain set of lines stands for heaven, another for earth, and so on. As further associations are developed to give meaning to the line figures, the same connection of non-verbal figure with words intending reality in literal vein is sustained.

The meaning of these non-verbal symbols can be quite complex, in virtue of the variety of associated meanings which are introduced. Yet it is of a definite and limited sort in its *manner* of meaning. Nothing like the way the verbally-framed line images are disclosive from the start, as enigmatic pointers imbued with spiritual meaning, is involved in this new realm of symbols. Further, nothing like the way the line image symbols function, as elements in a narrative and disclosive in a dramatic vein, in a story-telling fashion, is involved. Only if and when heaven (say) would become in turn itself an enigmatic symbol, not just a literal reality symbolized by lines, would something like the way of meaning of the original verbal-image symbols be approached in this new realm of symbols. Instead of this happening, the straightforward relation in this realm-- of non-verbal symbol to meaning framed in literally-intended words-- reinforces the way of taking up with the line images as riddling symbols addressing fact instead of as enigmatic pointers into reality-in-the-making.

Thus while the development of this separate symbolism harbors the possibility of an enriching of the sign which the *Zhouyi* offers and opens up an independent way of pointing into the future, at the same time it brings with it a different cast of mind and a different way in which symbolism is at work for that cast of mind. Together these express and reinforce the tendency of mind expressed in the reading of the verbal images as riddling signs instead of as enigmatic pointers. As a result, what is becoming developed in the interpreter in this non-verbal realm of symbols-- not a sensitivity to the richness of an enigmatic symbol but a cleverness in the grasping of the regular and many-sided connections and associations of these representations of factual realities-- works to undermine the original address to symbols and to strengthen this newer mind which works with verbal symbols as riddling pointers. This happens all the more as line figure meanings are brought into connection with the verbally-conveyed images and the latter are thought of as expressing or being grounded in the former.

Eventually fascination with this new symbolism leads to the displacement of the focus of the diviner's concern for the symbolic components of the sign from the images conveyed verbally to the assigned meanings of the trigrams, to the combination of such meanings based on the relation of such figures in the hexagrams, and to an increasingly complex network of diverse categories and correlations being built up for apprehending the world as it shows itself in its involvement in change. It is with this complex network of symbols, much more so than with the verbally conveyed images, that the factual future is now being foreseen.

a(3). Symbol-derived foreknowledge of fact

Even in the spiritually barren present of Eastern Zhou times, there is concern for the future and the desire to employ divination to help anticipate that future. But the Zhou King, as responsive to the Mandate, had been concerned for how to carry it out concretely. The original *Zhouyi* had provided a divinatory vehicle that could guide his exploration of the present as holding the future-in-the-making and that could support his anticipation of how that making was currently tending toward an issue. As a result, divination using this work allowed him to participate more knowingly in the coming to pass of the future, and to enter as party into its making in a way facilitated by an anticipation grounded in that use.

In contrast, with the detachment of this mode of divination from that spiritual grounding, divination became concerned not with the futural significance of a charged present but with those future events that would in fact come forth in time from out of the present such as it is. In this regard, as the divinatory inquiry concerned a future state of affairs, the symbols which the *Zhouyi* offered-- originally, and in the expansion just discussed-- became simply signs of one or another fact marking the future to come, instead of pointers into the present in its futural dimension.

In divination understood in this different way, a means was opened up for sketching out future fact based mainly on the character of the symbolism itself and with minimal attention to anything else. True, the resources with which to read the meaning of those pointers would include a grasp of the present and some expectations concerning the future. But the signs meant future fact, however its coming to be might take place, and the work to which the resources were harnessed was the accurate deciphering of that disguised foreshadowing of what would come which the symbols represented. For this, there was no need to explore the reality of the present with a view to discerning the dynamic of the future-in-the-making that is inward to that present and to discovering what that meant for the actual unfolding of the future out of that present.

Under the pressure of the presumption that divination was simply a fore-seeing of future events and that its symbols were a disguised rendering whose decipherment would lay out in clear and straightforward language what those events will be, not only were the verbally-framed images and the meanings of the trigrams brought forward to be seen through in their point-ing. All of the elements of the divinatory medium become drawn on for their contribution to this sought-for foreknowledge, this desired predictive grasp of the future.

The original *Zhouyi* system contains facets which are not intended to serve the same purpose: line images have one function, action indicators an-other, occasion responses another, and so on. But under this pressure in this Eastern Zhou context the richness of elements functioning in diverse ways for diverse purposes in the system becomes turned into a diversity of sources for developing associations and connections that ultimately have one func-tion, to contribute to foreknowledge.

It may well be that, in changed circumstances, later generations lost touch with the original meanings of various characters employed in the *Zhouyi*--title-names, occasion responses, parts of the line images; it may be that they also lost the feel for the variety of functions of the parts of the original work. But in this context it also seems that meanings of terms become reconstrued, and original functions and significance become ignored and replaced by others-- perhaps at times without clear recognition and understanding of what was taking place, but more often consciously and deliberately, or at least with some measure and mixture of the witting and the unwitting.

b. Second basic change: the present

In its creation and original use the *Zhouyi* was fitted to serve a Zhou King responsive to the Mandate of Heaven. The governance of that King was called to embody a sense of responsibility and virtuous kindness, and these were presupposed in his employment of the *Zhouyi*. As the Mandate lost its practical reality (though not its nostalgic appeal for some) and the *Zhouyi* became taken up for use by others than the King for purposes other than those originally intended, no grounds remained or emerged which required anything like the moral character governing its employment that was part of the original use of the work.

In time, the moral nerve of life came forward for attention, pressed there in a variety of contexts by a variety of things. There was the assertiveness of political leaders governing in a different (amoral, if not immoral) vein, which accompanied and brought change into life overall, and often enough change that was disruptive, destructive, on a broad scale. There was the growing visibility of the limited class-reference of the aristocratic code whose validity nonetheless still had some power to constrain leaders toward relatively civilized conduct. There was the emerging class of *shi'* which embodied and attested a morality apt to human beings whose value was recognized more on the merits of their service than on their birth.

The central place of genuine morality in life eventually entered into the understanding of the employment of the *Zhouyi* as a divinatory work. But now it was not the King whose use was involved: many individuals quite beyond the Zhou ruler, even beyond the sphere of political leaders, were taking up with the work. What emerged was a claim that the appropriate and effective use of that work by anyone depended on the moral character of the inquirer, and this, in a sense of morality that was not tied to the role of a King. As a reinforcement of such emphasis on the inquirer's moral character, the content of the language of the work became understood in changed fashion, to lessen the sense of mere fortune as important in life and to stress the centrality of morality among the different ways of being engaged with affairs. Finally, when the subject of divinatory inquiry was actions, those the inquirer proposed to undertake or those to be carried out by others, the idea of what divination might disclose of the future of any such undertaking was conditioned by the sense that the course of affairs was at bottom aligned with morality.

c. Third basic change: the past

As the link of the *Zhouyi* with the King and the Mandate becomes severed irremediably in early Eastern Zhou times, and as the work becomes taken up with and employed in ways adapted to the new circumstances, we find not only a changing sense of the divination accomplished with its help and a re-emerging sense of how its employment should be subordinated to morality. We find a way of taking up with its verbally-conveyed images quite apart from the divinatory context, the first signs of its function as a kind of wisdom book.

The basic condition for this transformation was the eventual failure of the revival of the early Zhou spirit and its sense of history-in-the-making in King Xuan's time. This failure, and the irretrievable rupture expressed in the political shifts called to the mind by the phrase "Eastern Zhou period", meant growing distance from the early leaders who were decisive initiators in a collective movement forward from which the present had fallen away. Such loss did not mean the loss of the past as important, but rather an alteration in the way the past was felt to be related to the present and thus in the way it functioned in the present.

The past, now clearly gone and increasingly distant, is well on its way to becoming the sphere of the ideal which is no longer realized among us of the present. One may be nostalgic about that past, and urge its restitution; one may reconstrue it in any number of ways, including in such way as distances the present from the past as in fact a progress beyond it. But one way which gains hold and eventually leads to the transformation of the *Zhouyi* into a wisdom book, is to see in it the sources of wisdom, of the insight and skill which we still know as heritage and with which we wish now to reaffirm our connection, so as to bridge over the real discontinuity.[96] In this perspective, 'we owe our origins-- the origins of matters of significance to us-- to that past, but we who acknowledge this are not carrying forward a movement begun there and carrying it to new heights. Wisdom lies in the past. We need simply to acknowledge it and instruct ourselves in it, and as best we can secure our own present participation in that ancient wisdom'.[97]

d. The three changes together: ambivalence

We can sum up what has become apparent in our review of the earliest recorded examples of divination using the *Zhouyi* in one word: ambivalence. By that I mean: the work originated in King Xuan's time, as part of the revival of the early Zhou vision of leadership and history; when venture in keeping with that vision effectively ended and the Eastern Zhou period arose, a profoundly different spirit and setting entered into the employing of the *Zhouyi*. In this Eastern Zhou time of profound transition-- politically, socially, and in most other ways--, the mind at work seeking orientation and order proceeded in a different vein than the mind expressing itself in the Mandate of Heaven and in the original late Western Zhou *Zhouyi*. Working in an atmosphere of alienation from the vital moral and spiritual nerve of the early Zhou vision of humanity and in an absence of any alternative spirituality on the strength of which to engage with a world becoming increasingly fragmented and dangerous, that mind transformed the *Zhouyi*. For concern for the future was still important, perhaps even more important in the considerable uncertainty of the time.   In the transformation gradually being effected, some things attest an advance: they are the transforming work of an inventiveness and energy which exhibit significant mental and conceptual complexity, and of a thoughtfulness which would boldly defend the supremacy of the moral to mere chance. But at the same time others attest a retreat: they exhibit the defensiveness and cleverness of a shallowing spirituality. This ambivalence is nothing strange, nor should it be anything unexpected. But it does require of us who would understand the functioning of the *Zhouyi* in this Eastern Zhou context, that we seek to disentangle and understand the different sides of the matter. That is what the preceding discussion has attempted to do in an initial and limited way.

POSTSCRIPT

The appearance of the *Zhouyi* in the records of the *Zuozhuan* is not limited to its employment in divination. As the divination work becomes something which a wide audience is conversant with, it functions as a text able to be cited for other purposes. These references begin at the end of the 7th C, over two hundred years after its composition.

Thus under Xuan-6 (603 BC), there is record of a brief conversation in which, after a noble had spoken with the King's son about his desire to be minister, the latter is reported to have commented to someone else: "Covetous and without virtue-- it's in the *Zhouyi* at Feng's Li .... He will not get beyond that."   The reference is to Line 6 in Hexagram 56, which holds a lengthy line statement which is not, taken by itself, obviously connected to the characterization "covetous and without virtue". It reads: "Grand-and-full the roof, dark the home; peek in the door, desolate its being without anyone there; three years, not see face to face. Ominous." If one sees this line statement in its hexagram context, and sees Hexagram 56 in its connection with Hexagram 55, one can make sense of this reference. It is to Prince Hai, whose story as told in the series of lines of the two hexagrams presents him in a rather unfavorable light; this particular line image comes at the end of the first half of the story, when he has left home after actions which reflect a character of that type. Its ominousness, in terms of the whole story, is confirmed by the fate he eventually suffers: loss of his cattle, and death. Now as Smith[98] comments: the remark of the King's son "is meaningless unless his listener (and the *Zuo* readership) can bring to mind this line statement. This has led Sargent to infer correctly that the *Yi* text must have been widely known at this time." But familiarity with the line statement is not enough; it must be understood in its context, as part of a story-telling, and understood not simply on the surface. Then based on a likeness of the noble to Prince Hai, the "ominous" prognostication present in the line relating to Prince Hai seems to the King's son to be warranted in the noble's case as well.

A second record occurs under Xuan-12 (597 BC). While a debate was underway whether the Jin armies should attack the army of Chu, a Jin officer (Zhizi) takes matters into his own hand, leading his part of the army across the river to attack without waiting for orders. Another officer speaks out: "Zhizi's army is in great danger! The *Zhouyi* has it, in Shi's Lin [i.e. Hexagram 7, Line 1] ... it says: 'The army goes forth according to regulations; its not preserving them is ominous.'" [I translate as I think the speaker meant it.] The officer continues, explaining the line statement and applying it to the case at hand-- and this, in much the same way as if it were the response in a divinatory inquiry. Yet it is not, even though after his explanation he antici- pates that "as a result, an encounter (with the Chu army) is bound to mean defeat. Zhizi has arranged that! Even if he escapes and returns home, he certainly has a great fault." In this case, the *Zhouyi* is referred to for some insightful general words contained in its line statements these are interpreted and applied for their wisdom to the present situation, in their literal meaning, and are not used as symbols which are disclosive in a divinatory vein.

A third case-- recorded under Xiang-28 (543 BC)-- involves the report of a Zheng emissary on his return from Chu: "The Chu king is about to die; he is not cultivating his political virtue, but hoping for obscurity among the varied feudal lords so as to indulge his wishes, he wants to last long, is that possible? The *Zhouyi* has it, in Fu's Yi [Hexagram 24, Line 6] ... it says, 'De- luded return, ominous'. Is this what the Chu king means? He wants to re- cover his health, and yet he casts away his foundation, returning back to nowhere: this is called making a deluded return. Can that be other than ominous? ..." Here the *Zhouyi* is cited for the aptness of one of its phrases for characterizing a present condition.

In these first three cases the *Zhouyi* is drawn on for the relevance of the general wisdom formulated in some of its phrases to a current situation. Other citations have a different reason and character.

Thus a fourth case-- recorded under Zhao-1 (541 BC)-- involves a physi- cian's explanation of a term he had introduced in a rhymed set of lines used to explain the illness (a derangement due to sexual excess) which he had diagnosed as incurable. The term, which is the title-name of Hexagram 18, is explained first by reference to the cause of the phenomenon in question ("what is produced by the debauchery-disorder"), then by an analysis of the graph used in writing it ("a vessel and insects"), then by a reference to a natural phenomenon for which it stands ("the flight of grain": insects flying up out of rotting grain, as if they were the grain spontaneously regenerating as insects), and finally by reference to the trigram composition of Hexagram 18. As regards the latter, he says: "In the *Zhouyi* a woman deluding a man and the wind blowing down a mountain are called Gu." In this reference, it is simply the name, and some trigram associations, which are noted, as giving the meaning of the term used in this context.

A fifth case-- in Zhao-29 (513 BC)-- involves an appeal to a variety of lines in Hexagrams 1 and 2, for their reference to dragons. The point seems to be to show how observant the ancients were in this matter of dragons. The images here are not understood symbolically but literally.

Finally, a sixth case-- in Zhao-32 (510 BC)-- involves reference not to the verbal side of the *Zhouyi* but to the line figures. After the death of the Duke, in a discussion of the stability of government in Lu, citation of a passage from the *Book of Poetry* is followed by reference to one of the *Yi's* figures (*gua'*). "Among the figures in the *Changes*, 'thunder mounting vigorous activity' means Great Vigor [Hexagram 34] ..., the way of Heaven." The speaker then goes on to recount the long ago emergence of the Ji clan in Lu and its conflict with the ducal house over political power through the subsequent generations. Here the line figure is taken as an image of the duplicate power centers and their relation.

What all these cases have in common is a non-divinatory use of one or another component of the *Zhouyi*. Clearly these uses reflect the work's becoming widely known (at least in the upper circles of society) and seen as having a power to be illuminating even when not functioning in divinatory fashion. But the rather humble and straightforward forms of the recognition of this work as embodying wisdom caught in these citations, are still a far cry from the grand and 'philosophic' construal of the work as a wisdom work found later in (say) some of the Ten Wings. The story of that later development, however, is something for another time.

Notes for Part I

Chapter 1

1. E. L. Shaughnessy *(The composition of the "Zhouyi")* (later cited as *CZ)* concludes a long discussion (16-49) as follows: "its literary development and linguistic usage show the *Zhouyi* to be a product of the latter stage of the Western Zhou dynasty, and the historical context of this period suggests a composition date in the early years of King Xuan's reign: most probably, during the last two decades of the ninth century, B.C." Because it was the scribe who was the official responsible for milfoil divination at the Zhou court, Shaughnessy concludes also that "it is quite probable that it was the scribes who created the *Zhouyi*". (297-8) Except for the plural "scribes", I would agree with these claims.

2. In fact, the irregular presence of such accompanying elements is something of a puzzle, and may indicate some dissociation of these elements from the image-bearing verbal accompaniments to the lines and line-figures. It might be e.g. that the readings of inauspicious and auspicious relate to a different (and older) use of the lines and line-figures in the *Zhouyi* than that which emerges when such factors are simply part of the medium for evoking the images. Such a reading of the lines and line-figures would be more akin to that of the tortoise-shells and the bones whose cracks were read mainly for their significance as auspicious or inauspicious.

3. In keeping with the evidence, the dating is rough and approximate only. In recent discussion greater precision is being claimed, although exact dates (year, even month and day) are still a matter of dispute. The rough dating I use is in keeping generally with the discussion found in: D. Nivison, "The Dates of Western Chou" *(Harvard Journal of Asiatic Studies,* 1983) (later cited as *DWC); E.* Shaughnessy, *Sources of Western Zhou history: inscribed bronze vessels* (University of California Press, 1991) and "The 'Current' *Bamboo Annals* and the Date of the Zhou conquest of Shang" *(Early China* 11-12: 1985-87) (later cited as *SWZ* and *CBA,* respectively); D. Pankenier, "Astronomical Dates in Shang and Western Zhou" *(Early China* 7: 1981-82) and *"Mozi* and the Dates of Xia, Shang, and Zhou: a Research Note" *(Early China* 9-10, 1983-85).

4. See D. Keightley (*Sources of Shang History*, 7-8) (later cited as *SSH*) and H. Creel (*The Origins of Statecraft in China (Vol. I)*, 31) (later cited as *OSC*). According to Creel in *The Birth of China* (161-2 and 171-3 in particular) (later cited as *BC*), writing seems to have evolved among the Shang in some important and close connection with religion but also in a chronicling of the significant affairs of the King and kingdom. These, of course, are not really separate affairs, since the King was the religious leader intermediate between man and the highest divinity.

5. The above characterization draws heavily on K. C. Chang (*The Archaeology of Ancient China*) (later cited as *AAC*), Creel (*BC*), and Ping-ti Ho (*The Cradle of the East*) (later cited as *CE*): different sources for different elements.

6. That, at least, seems to be the universal testimony of the extant bone and shell records. Ho (in *CE*) argues that the absence of other names for the supreme deity is a reflection only of ritual standardization (329, also 314-16). Even if this were so, that the standardization took this form and not some other form is significant of a distinctive sense of the ultimate power, and one in which the Shang seems to be in some contrast with the Zhou. More on this later.

7. See Keightley, *SSH*, 5-6.

8. Where it is matters of the future that are at issue, it is generally the immediate future that is involved-- the coming night, the next day, the coming ten-day period. But occasionally it is more extended periods.

9. Apparently the response was obtained at times from only one crack in one hollow, but at times from a series of cracks in a series of hollows, not necessarily all on the same bone or shell. When sets of cracks were involved, they were numbered, and this suggests that perhaps their order might be significant as well as their determinate crack-character taken singly. Sometimes also the questions or charges were grouped, paired as positive and negative alternatives, for example.

10. In all of this discussion, I am drawing on Keightley's characterization in *SSH*.

11. Shaughnessy (*CZ*, 51). I draw heavily here on his account (51-57) of this development.

12. Shaughnessy (*CZ*, 56-57). He speaks of the shift as making divination into a means of controlling events; but what seems at issue is not control so much as persuasion and influence.

13. In the course of offering his own revised chronology based in important ways on the *Bamboo Annals* and astronomical data, Nivison (*DWC*) comments on events recorded under 1157, which is actually, according to his thesis, 1145 in the original *Annals*. "We find that under that year, in the reign of Wu Yi, the 'Old Duke' Tan Fu,

who had already moved from Pin ... to Ch'i Chou ..., was confirmed as 'Duke of Chou' by the Shang king, and confirmed also in possession of the city of Ch'i, which was to become an ancestral Chou site. Tan Fu, Wen Wang's grandfather, is the Chou ancestor whom Wen Wang later recognized retroactively as 'T'ai Wang'..., Great King, the first of the Chou line of kings. The date in the chronicle must originally have been 1145-- fictitious, but laden with meaning." (564) ["Laden with meaning" because the date is exactly 100 years before the date in the *Annals* for the Zhou conquest of Shang. "Fictitious" because, while probably roughly appropriate, the precise date was probably determined by later astronomically-and-numerically-framed visions "in which human events are prefigured in the stars and ordained in even centuries".] We do have earlier glimpses of the Zhou, both in Shang oracle bone records and in later poetry. See Xu Zhuoyun (*Xi-Zhou shi* [*Western Zhou History*], especially 61-67) (later cited as *XZS*). Bagley ("The Rise of the Western Zhou Dynasty", found in *The Great Bronze Age of China*) (later cited as *RWZ*) speaks of the Zhou having "moved to settle at Qishan only in the reign of the fourth-to-last Anyang king, apparently from somewhere to the north or northeast. In their earlier location they must already have come into conflict with the Shang ruler, for expeditions against a people called Zhou are mentioned several times in the oracle inscriptions of Wu Ding's reign. After his time, however, the Zhou cease to appear in the oracle records; perhaps they were driven temporarily out of range." (194) And in another vein, we have several poems in the *Book of Poetry* which recall early times. These are later accounts, of course, and following Sun Zuoyun's suggestions in *Shijing yu Zhoudai shehui yanjiu* (*A study of the 'Book of Poetry' and Zhou dynasty society*) (later cited as *SPZ*), we may date them to the late 9th century (King Xuan's time) and see them as poetic formulations that met religious ritual needs of that time. These poems (including 245 and 250, 237 and 241) reflect the way the late 9th century Zhou remembered their origins. As to the first pair: Poem 245 speaks of the Zhou "first ancestor" Hou Ji (Lord Millet), and frames the Zhou sense of themselves as having come into their own distinctive being when they became an agricultural people (in contrast, say, to themselves when they were in some earlier nomadic phase). This poem gives us (historically) only the symbolic referral of this establishing of themselves to some time prior to the time of Duke Liu, whom later tradition knows as the "great-grandson" of Lord Millet. Poem 250 takes up this Duke Liu, and portrays him as having led the Zhou in a move to a new area, in Shaanxi, whose center was the settlement at Bin which he constructed and made his capital. As to the second pair: Poem 237 speaks of the Ancient Duke Dan-fu (also known as King Tai), who moved his people and built for them a new capital on the plain of Zhou at the foot of Mount Qi (later tradition knows him as the descendant of Lord Millet in the twelfth generation). Poem 241 recalls not only King Tai but King Ji, followed then by King Wen. How elliptical, how symbolic, and how accurate historically, these highlight-sketches are, is difficult to say.

14. Bagley, noting that when the Zhou had made this move they had driven from the area another tribe (the Quan Rong) who had been allies of Shang in its wars against Zhou, comments that in this act of making the Zhou leader a duke, the Shang ruler

may simply have been yielding to a situation he was powerless to control. (*RWZ*, 194)

15. This is Creel's characterization (*OSC*, 63).

16. In retrospect, the Great King (the Ancient Duke Dan-fu) is remembered in the *Book of Poetry* as the first Zhou King to have expanded the Zhou realm at the expense of the Shang. At least, that would seem the natural meaning of the phrase "he began the clipping of Shang" in Poem 300.

17. King Wen apparently became ruler of Zhou at the beginning of the eleventh century (1099, according to Nivison [*DWC*, 517]), but it was not until 1056 that he claimed that his rule was not simply of the Zhou people but something which Heaven mandated, thus a rule which carried a larger meaning definitely threatening to the Shang state. He initially married a Shang princess; when that marriage produced no (male) offspring he married a lady of Shen, through whom he had the sons who became so important in his undertaking against Shang. (See Shaughnessy [*CZ*, 239-44] for a discussion of this matter in connection with interpreting the lines of Hexagram 54.) At some point during the first 40+ years of his rule of Zhou, he spent six years in captivity at the Shang court, after which he was reinstated by the Shang ruler as vassal, with the title 'Lord of the West'. (See Bagley [*RWZ*, 194], who points to the decisive confirmation of the traditional accounts to be found in oracle bone inscriptions.) He also founded a new capital, to the east of the old one and close to the borders of the Shang state. Then in the immediately succeeding years to 1056, he led a series of attacks on neighboring peoples and countries, the Quan Rong, the Mi-xu, the Qi-guo, Yu and Chong, before his death in 1050 (see Nivison [*DWC*, 568]).

18. According to Creel (OSC, 63): "The genuine text of the *Bamboo Books*, which is a relatively late source, says (Wang, *Ku Chu-shu*, 6a) that 'King Chi of Chou came to court' to the Shang, thus acknowledging their overlordship. It also says that King Chi was appointed to high office by the Shang ruler and was later put to death by him. It further records a Chou attack on Shang at a date which would correspond, according to the traditional chronology, with 1190 BC."

19. *Book of Poetry*, Poem 186. Bagley puts this matter in the context of a growing rivalry of Zhou and Shang, and speaking of how, from the time when Dan-fu established the Zhou under Mount Qi, the Shang kings must have been increasingly uneasy about the power of their western neighbor, he says: "Later texts mention that Danfu's son Jili received lavish gifts from the Shang king and even took a Shang noble lady to wife; they also record that, on a subsequent visit to the Shang court, he was detained and died. The pattern of bribes alternating with force-- or treachery-- is familiar enough from the dealings of later dynasties with barbarians." (*RWZ*, 194)

20. As noted above, this King Wen also initially took a wife from the Shang; therefore he was connected both by his mother and by his wife to that "great country".

21. See Creel (*BC*, 227). The idea in question is that of the Mandate of Heaven.

22. Creel (*BC*, 222) claims that the Zhou "took up Shang culture with the enthusiasm always shown by new converts, developed many of its aspects with the intellectual vigor often shown by 'barbarian' peoples, and spread it abroad with their wide conquests."

23. It is significant that while King Wu actually effected the conquest and ruled as first King in the new dynasty, King Wen was by far the more honored by later generations and was even thought of as the founder of the dynasty despite his having died before it started. The picture of King Wen which evolved may have elements of idealization in it, but it provides a clue to the nature of the Zhou dynasty and Zhou cast of mind. Thus he was praised for the virtue he exhibited, for his pious and filial respect for the deities and spirits and for his ancestors, for his modesty and caution, for his care and concern to protect and bring peace to the people he ruled, and also for his ability to foster harmony among the persons under him. His intelligence, his · far-sightedness, his competence in planning and building, in organizing and forming alliances, was highly praised. In contrast, King Wu is praised mainly for his martial bearing and achievements. See Creel (*OSC*, 65-69) for particulars and for reference to original sources and materials.

24. For example, there are repeated claims concerning the degeneracy of the last Shang King, perhaps exaggerated claims but perhaps also reflecting some actual disintegration of Shang leadership and character in important places.

25. Nivison (*DWC*, 517, 532) and Shaughnessy (*CBA*, 36-38) point out that this number is figured under King Wen's 'Mandate' calendar; the latter died in his 7th year as Mandate-holding ruler, so the 9th year for King Wu is actually the 2nd year of his personal rule as successor to King Wen, and the 11th, the 4th.

26. See Note 32, below.

27. The reasons for the disaffection are variously described; perhaps it was fear that the Duke of Zhou was going to usurp the throne himself, perhaps it was jealousy over his power. It is not really clear what was the case, although the portrait which Shaughnessy develops ("The Duke of Zhou's Retirement in the East and the Beginnings of the Ministerial-Monarch Debate in Chinese Political Philosophy") makes the usurpation-fear plausible.

28. See Nivison (*DWC*, 546), and Shaughnessy (*SWZ*, 241).

29. Found in the *Shujing* (*Book of Historical Documents*) or the *Shang Shu* (*Ancient Historical Documents*). See, among others, the documents entitled *Kang gao*, *Jun Shi*, *Da gao*, and *Duo shi*. When considering the documents which formulate this vision, one should keep in mind that, as with any historical document, there may be

some disparity between what was actually involved historically and what is presented in these records as having happened. Still, that these records were kept in the center of government and that, as records, they had that relative fixity which writing provides, means that they themselves provided a continuously available reference-point through which succeeding generations could call back the matters recorded to mind. Thus in their own right they were important forces for the subsequent making of history in the peoples of this tradition. This is subject, of course, to their relative fixity; that is, to the conditions of their own enduring. The fixity of writing depends (a) on the materials used, and (b) where these are perishable, on the character of the transmission, thus (c) on the absence of copy errors (mistakes, omissions, additions) and deliberate forgeries, (d) on the continued understanding of the meanings of the early language, and (e) on the continued understanding of the actual historical context of the original writing and thus of that on the basis of which the implicit assumptions, references and allusions, and the like, can be grasped. Bagley notes how early inscriptions on bronzes express in language and content this same sense of things. Speaking of an inscription from a *zun* from the early years of King Cheng, he points to "the tone of the inscription, with its repeated invocations of the will of Heaven. Implicit in these references is the assertion that the Zhou rulers were commanded by Heaven to overthrow the Shang.... The statement that Wen Wang 'accepted' Heaven's command, while Wu Wang carried it to fulfillment, accords perfectly with later accounts, in which Wen Wang somehow figures as the author of the conquest and is more to be admired than Wu Wang, who carried it out at the unavoidable but nonetheless deplorable cost of war and regicide.... The moralistic tenor of the inscription is consistent with the style of certain speeches attributed to Cheng Wang and the Duke of Zhou in later texts. Transmitted texts and bronze inscriptions alike give the impression that the early Zhou rulers were deeply conscious that they had usurped the throne, and they were much exercised to justify themselves." (*RWZ*, 198) Distinguishing the Zhou from the Shang, he notes: "The Zhou rationale for imperial legitimacy, which was central to Chinese thought in later times, clearly implies that the right to rule is dependent on the moral quality of the ruling house-- a claim that it would not have occurred to the Shang king to make. It is extremely interesting to find that this notion of the right to rule bestowed by Heaven is no projection into the past by a later generation of dynastic apologists, but is clearly in evidence from the earliest years of the Zhou dynasty. Inscriptions like that of (this) *zun* ..., by providing a touchstone to authenticate the spirit of later texts, encourage us to have confidence in the substance as well, even when the texts supply information that is not explicitly confirmed by the bronze inscriptions." (199)

30. Bagley argues in an interesting fashion that the Shang did not have such a vision, which he understands as framed to provide legitimacy to the Zhou usurpation. He notes that the oracle bone inscriptions from Anyang give no sign that the Shang kings were ever concerned to assert their legitimacy. Indeed, the question could hardly arise, because the principal deities were the spirits of the deceased Shang kings, and the living king could trace his line of descent from the supreme deity, Shang Di. "One might almost say that the Shang king was related by blood to the natural order."

(*RWZ*, 198-99) In contrast, while the Zhou were deeply concerned with the ancestral (and respected the Shang royal ancestors as enduring powers also), they referred to the supreme divine power as Heaven, not Shang Di, and they asserted that Heaven had chosen to withdraw its protection from the Shang and shift it to the Zhou because the Shang kings had declined in virtue. "Thus, when the Zhou kings began referring to themselves as Tian Zi, Son of Heaven, the relationship they claim is, quite literally, adoptive." (199)

31. In "The Archaic Royal Jou Religion" (236-7, Toung Pao, XLVI, 1958), Homer Dubs claims that this vision originated with King Wen, the first of the Zhou said to have received the mandate. This seems likely, but regardless, the vision animated all three of the important early leaders. This means that it is the vision of the royal family; while it gives a place to others, and others may have accepted it, it held most forceful sway among the leaders in this hierarchically ordered society.

32. As we have seen above, the Zhou pre-conquest relation to the Shang was complex, but two important threads in it were long time connections of allegiance and of marriage among the leading families. Some witness to such connections is found among the divination scraps discovered in a Fengzhucun hoard from pre-dynastic Zhou days. There the Zhou King is recorded apparently sacrificing to Shang Kings, from the early founder of the Shang dynasty down to the father of King Wen's first wife (see Xu Zhouyun's discussion in *XZS*, 61-64). Whatever else one may make of this, the Zhou leaders here and elsewhere show a relation to the Shang religiosity which makes it not surprising that the terms for the ultimate divine power as worshiped by the Shang could on occasion be used within the Zhou religiosity as well. And this, quite apart from uses which might only reflect the effort to speak and appeal to the Shang leaders in their own terms, not genuinely in terms inherent within the Zhou religiosity.

33. However it may be in the case of other religious visions, in the Zhou there was no incompatibility between the extensive use of the human mind and the working of the divine. Indeed, Heaven demanded human effort: a human being had no religiously-acceptable alternative of simply leaving things up to God, of laying claim to the blessing of the divine without exerting him-/herself morally. Included in the demand for moral effort and responsibility-taking on the human being's part was encouragement to enlarge human access to sources of insight, both via religious ritual directed back to the hidden governing and intelligent forces (as in divination) and via the careful and disciplined exertion of the unaided human mind. If one looks at the matter on a large enough historical scale, one may read the history of the Western Zhou and early Eastern Zhou as exhibiting a momentum that built up within that interplay of divine (Heaven) and human (Zhou) and led over time to the liberation and development of a broad range of human capacities under this divinely-supported aspiration toward civilized existence. Even as the course of events in the 9th C called into question the simple-- even simplistic-- initial conception of a moral deity and cast human beings back upon themselves in the midst of considerable questioning,

even as that course also called into question the Zhou as fit to be the continuing political center of collective civilized existence, the encouragement to respond by venturing and taking responsibility continued to reverberate and to be heeded. A whole complex of different responses that enriched and transformed the strands of tradition being woven together in the movement into the future arose in Springs-and-Autumns times. The social, political, economic and artistic strands all became enriched and altered even as that very religious sense and framework within which the impetus toward achievement had been nurtured became less credible, less effective, as guide for the energies being released. Among the different responses that eventually emerged was philosophy. Interestingly enough, a similar religious nurturing and self-overcoming lies in the background of the beginnings of philosophy in Greece; and in that regard, the Homeric poems that transformed the bardic tradition of the Greeks have a comparable (but also more significant) place and function in the Greek development to that of the *Zhouyi* in the Chinese.

34. In the immediate evidence there is nothing that would seem to warrant the view that the Shang sense of the divine and human contained anything like this sense of the ultimate divine power as universal, as one and as the one all human beings are to reach back to. See Bagley's comments in Note 30 above. See also the discussion by Xu Zhouyun (*XZS*, 95-97, 99) on the matter of the Shang conception of Shang-di, in contrast with the Zhou concept of Heaven and with the Shang-di meant by the Zhou, that is, with the Shang-di transformed from an ancestral spirit with a particular nature relating to the Shang and transformed into a power with a universal nature.

35. There likely was some sense among the Shang of their centrality and superiority, but as previous discussion makes clear, it would not have been conceived in the terms that frame the vision of the Mandate of Heaven. One may see here, as elsewhere, the Zhou leaders not simply developing ideas that move beyond the traditional Zhou view of Heaven and the Zhou people, but doing this in such way as also grasps something which might have been acknowledged and been a part of the Shang culture and tradition and gives it their own meaning. Perhaps this also involved seeing a significance in things that the Shang did not find significant in their own history and culture. In the face of the Zhou acknowledgement of Shang cultural superiority and the Zhou placing their conquest of the Shang in the context of the Shang conquest of the Xia, a cynic or 'realist' might suspect the Zhou leaders of mere propaganda. But that seems belied by the tenor of the documents as a whole. To bring forth elements in a vision that would be helpful politically and to use them for persuasion, is scarcely the same thing as fabricating claims that are not sincerely believed by the speakers and using them in order to manipulate the persons spoken to and to subject them to the will of the speakers.

36. The merely functional status of King and Kingdom are absolutely crucial. It is never birth and heredity simply, not even if this involves descent from a god, that qualifies a human being to be King; similarly it is never simply belonging directly in the continuation of certain traditional ways and/or of a certain group of people, that

qualifies a culture or a people to be the Kingdom.

37. It is the work of the divine to seek and point out the human being who can perform this role; indeed, in a poem such as No. 241 in the *Book of Poetry*, it almost seems that Heaven works to foster the needed qualities in the leaders and people to be selected. In this connection, one might compare and contrast the notion Krsna formulates in the *Bhagavad Gītā*, to the effect that when the world is threatened with the prevalence of evil and the decay of order, the divine descends in incarnation to undertake the task of renewing *dharma*. (See Chapter 4, verses 7/8.)

38. That is, now peacefully at rest.

39. That is, the ancestors who are pointing through the oracles, giving him guidance from the dead about the work ahead for the living.

40. I mostly follow Shaughnessy (*CZ*, 57-60) in the following discussion.

41. Shaughnessy (*CZ*, 59).

42. Zhang's thoughts are expressed in an article entitled "*Shishi Zhou chu qingtongqi mingwen zhong de Yi gua*" (*Kaogu xuebao*, 1980.4, 403-415); this (with emendations by the author) has been translated into English in *Early China*, 6 (1980-81), 80-96, under the title "An Interpretation of the Divinatory Inscriptions on Early Chou Bronzes". (Later cited as *IDI*.) Further examples of the type of inscription in question are provided by Chen Quanfang in an article entitled *Zhou-yuan xinchu bujia yanjiu* (305-7 in the collection entitled *Xi-Zhou shi yanjiu* [published in 1984]).

43. See the article entitled "*Cong Shang-Zhou bagua shuzi fuhao tan shifa de jige wenti*" (*Kaogu* 1981.2: 155-63, 154), which is translated by Edward Shaughnessy in *Early China*, 7 (1981-82), 46-55, under the title "Some Observations about Milfoil Divination Based on Shang and Zhou *bagua* Numerical Symbols". (Later cited as *OMD*.)

44. Indeed, the number symbols are to be found on bone and horn spoons as well as on antler ends, at a site which belongs to the Neolithic culture of the Yangzi basin. (See Zhang Zhenglang, [*IDI*, 93-94 (EC version)]; Shaughnessy [*CZ*, 314].)

45. Creel (*OSC*, 427-8) comments that, during the first seventy years of the dynasty "the Chou cause was served by a whole series of very remarkable men-- not only Kings but also ministers, generals, and a host of more humble men whose capacities may not have been more than normal but who became caught up in the sense that they were making history-- as indeed they were. It may seem improbable that a concentration of particularly able men should occur in one time and place, but it is not impossible. The most remarkable example of this is, no doubt, Greece in the 'age of Pericles'. The persons of note who spent all or part of their lives in the single city

of Athens during the fifth century B.C. included among many others: Aeschylus, Alcibiades, Anaxagoras, Aristophanes, Aspasia, Euripides, Gorgias, Herodotus, Hippocrates, Pericles, Phidias, Pindar, Plato, Protagoras, Socrates, Sophocles, Thucydides, and Xenophon. Such things can happen."

46. In this characterization, and through much of what immediately follows in this section, I draw upon the judicious reconstruction of these matters presented by Creel in *OSC*.

47. The preceding discussion centers on the political dimension, and that seems to have been of primary significance to the Zhou not simply at the beginning but enduringly. But the Zhou were active in other dimensions, for example, in the artistic, where we find the Zhou developing and transforming the Shang bronze-working tradition. And if the period of consolidation of power and initial development did not involve much increase in the size of their domain, it did involve trade and peaceful intercourse with peoples of more distant places, and new cultural directions opened up by the initial conquest itself and by the further currents entering into the Zhou world from beyond.

48. See the *Shujing*, and passages from various parts of it which include warnings against complacency and self-indulgence (loss of earnestness and zeal for the work to be done).

49. These are Creel's translations from the *Shiji* (*OSC*, 427 and 429).

50. Shaughnessy (*SWZ*, 166), discussing the failed attempt to extend the Zhou colonial expansion into southern China, in the course of which King Zhao (r. 977/75-957), King Mu's father, was killed and his armies decimated, thinks it "most likely" that the catastrophic military setback that Zhou suffered caused a general retreat to the capital area. This contraction in the territory under effective Zhou control led in turn to increased pressure and competition for the limited land available in the capital region. The setback then helps explain what at present is the marked contraction in the archaeological distribution of inscribed bronzes beginning about the time of King Mu (181). It also helps us understand how it was that in subsequent times we have the first appearance of inscriptions that describe legal cases involving land tenure disputes. But if Shaughnessy can plausibly urge that the death of King Zhao marked an "important turning point" in the fortunes of the Zhou ruling house, which thereafter "must have slipped into a long decline" before its final demise, in the west, in 771 BC, still that turning point is not in any straightforward sense the beginning of decline. Even simply at the level of governance, while at the start of King Mu's reign the vast areas of eastern China to which the Zhou kings once claimed title were no longer under their control (181), the retreat was reversed by the end of that reign. And as Shaughnessy himself notes (see the next Note), the reign of King Mu was also one of cultural innovation.

51. Nivison (*DWC*, 48-49) offers a brief but vigorous defense of King Mu, claiming the latter has been "treated shabbily" by historians.

52. Shaughnessy (*CZ*, 43) also offers a positive assessment of King Mu, or at least of the times under his rule: To his mind, the reign of King Mu marked a period of political expansion and cultural innovation. This can be seen in the incidence of campaigns reported in a large number of bronze inscriptions from that period, in certain new court rituals, and in a dynamic new style of decor on the vessels themselves. (The new court rituals he refers to concern the entrance of an official into the 'central hall' of the king, and the king's entrance into the ancestral temple (39). These, he claims, were associated with the developing use of the appellation 'Son of Heaven' which seems to date from the reign of King Mu.)

53. In an article entitled "Western Chou History Reconstructed from Bronze Inscriptions" (later cited as *WCH*), Nivison, based on his readings of certain inscriptions (in particular, the *Yu ting*: he dates this to 891), sees the revolt of the Marquis of E, documented in that inscription, as belonging to the early part of the reign of King Yì and as a factor in making it evident that King Yì was not competent. Of the inscription, he says: "It records a revolt of one Yu-fang, Marquis of E, leading the southern and eastern non-Chinese peoples-- mounting just the kind of threat that Ch'u and Hsu had posed earlier. (Other inscriptions show that this Yu-fang had previously been the main ally of the throne in the south. 'Yu-fang' may be a title, 'Defender of the borders.') The royal western and eastern armies proved helpless. The revolt was finally put down by the author of the inscription, commanding the chariots and foot soldiers of his own lord, who came to the aid of the king." (49)

54. *Shiji* (4.140) says: "During the time of King Yì, the royal house thereupon declined and poets composed satires."

55. See Nivison (*DWC*, 546-56; *WCH*, 49-50) and Shaughnessy (*SWZ*, 265-6) for brief but generally persuasive proposals on how to understand the situation, given the relatively limited evidence available.

56. See Creel, *OSC*, 429-30. Creel says of these events: "...(I)t is quite clear that some unusual maneuvering went on, for the *Historical Records* says that 'the feudal lords again set up the heir of King I... this was King I.' This is the first recorded instance in which the succession in the Chou house was determined, not by its members, but by its vassals. Whether King I conspired with those who placed him on the throne we do not know, but the *Records on Ritual* says that he was the first King to mingle in undue familiarity with the feudal lords in the court.... In fact, we are told, 'in the time of King I' the royal house was so weak that the feudal lords sometimes did not come to court, and fought among themselves.'" Nivison (*DWC*, 551) also refers to the *Shiji* suggestion of the irregularity of the Xiao reign, and proposes that some sort of power struggle may have ensued at Xiao's death, in which the ruler of Wei gave help to the King Yi faction and received some sort of payoff, including a

top court position for the Earl He of Gong.

57. Thus the old dynasty ended without a renewal of spirit in a new dynasty, and the utter failure of spirit masked itself as a continuation of the Zhou past. The Zhou King now served, in virtue of his religious standing, as a figure-head rallying-point for a non-spiritual future.

58. Nivison (*WCH*, 49) says: with King Yì "we enter a period when the royal institution is ceasing to work, and one different attempt after another is made by home area lords (who are close to the throne and so are dependent on it) to keep it going. Each of these attempts is ultimately unsuccessful."

59. Given the character and paucity of the evidence, even the most judicious accounts of the dates and events of King Li's reign diverge in significant ways. For example, Nivison (*WCH*, 49) claims Li succeeded to the throne in 859, came of age (at twenty: born 864) in 845, ruled in his own name from 844 till 842, and in 841 was sent into exile but remained nominal king until his death in 828. In his reading of events the Earl He of the state of Gong acted as regent not only in the years 841-828 while Li was in exile, but also in 859-845 when he was nominally King but still a minor. Nivison further observes: "Li Wang, it seems to me, has obviously been treated rather unfairly by the historians. They rate him proverbially as one of the worst kings in Chinese history. But Li Wang was not on stage long enough to justify any such judgment. He was a functioning king for only three or four years. He was probably a spoiled child, and may have been overreacting to feelings of insecurity. But it is not impossible that his ouster was the consequence of the Wei faction seeing power slipping from its hands: The confirmation of Shih Tui's position in the third-year Shih Tui *kuei*-- it was previously only an acting one-- may have been a thrust at Kung Ho." (51) In some contrast, Shaughnessy (*SWZ*, 272-86) urges a succession date of 857, coming of age in 853 (when he was fourteen), and then (in agreement with Nivison) rule in his own name until 842, with exile from 841 till his death in 828. Only in the exile period is Earl He of Gong regent.

60. Earl He of Gong, who later became regent when King Li went into exile, had come to be part of the royal court at the time when King Yì ascended to the throne. Nivison (*DWC*, 551) suggests that "perhaps some kind of power struggle ensued at Hsiao's death". Explaining an entry in *Shiji*, to the effect that "the lord of the Wei state 'bribed' Yi Wang to raise his status from *po* to *hou*" (551), he says: "It appears to me likely that in succession maneuvering in the Chou court in 867-66 Wei gave the Yi Wang faction valuable support. Some kind of advance in status for the Wei ruler may have been part of the payoff. Another part of the arrangement, apparently, was a top court position for a Wei prince, who is none other than Kung Ho, later Wei Wu Kung...." (551) As part of the supporting evidence for his idea of a regency for Earl He in the time of King Li's minority, Nivison (551-2) recalls that "the Mao Preface to the *Shih ching* identifies Wu Kung [i.e. He of Gong] as the author of the ode 'Yi'..., 256." He goes on to say: "This ode may well have been written by Kung

Ho, for its author reveals himself as an older man having a fatherly relation to a young and wayward king, who is Li Wang, according to the Mao Preface. And this must have been Kung Ho's relationship to Li Wang...." (552) In some contrast, Sun Zuoyun (*SPZ*, 385) dates this poem considerably later, in the time of the reign of King You.

61. Nivison, *WCH*, 51.

62. What that course of action was is not altogether clear from our records. One particular understanding of the provocative royal actions is presented by Sun Zuoyun in *SPZ* (in a chapter entitled "First great serf uprising in our country's history", 204-238). There, Sun urges that the rebellion was provoked by an effort on the part of King Li to change the land tenure system, in particular, to exploit through additional taxation the harvest on serf-land that in the traditional ways had been reserved for the livelihood of the serfs. This effort at exploitation, Sun sees as a reflection of King Li's covetousness. He further sees that one of King Xuan's achievements was to undo this act of King Li and to institute a more acceptable change in the land tenure system, in particular, to initiate a land-lord system that was able to revive the economy and to form a flourishing economic underpinning for the revival for which King Xuan is known.

63. These facets of King Li's character are reported by Sima Qian as follows: "When King Yí died, his son King Li, named Hu, was established. King Li reigned thirty years, liking profit and being close to Duke Yi of Rong. The great minister Rui Liangfu remonstrated with King Li.... King Li did not listen and in the end made the Duke of Rong his counselor, who therewith served. The king's actions were cruel and arrogant, and the people of the country criticized the King. The Duke of Shao remonstrated.... The King became more oppressive and none of the people of the country dared to speak, expressing (their feelings) on the road with their eyes. King Li was happy and announced to the Duke of Shao: 'I have been able to stop the criticism; now no one dares to speak.' ... (In) three years, then (the people) joined together and revolted, attacking King Li. King Li fled into exile at Zhi." (Translation by Shaughnessy, *SWZ*, 273.)

64. He had remonstrated with King Li earlier, about his ways; a poem which is traditionally attributed to him is preserved in the *Book of Poetry* collection (as Poem 253). His action in this case, to save the son of such a King at the expense of his own son, expresses a sense of loyalty to the royal family that is extreme.

65. As quoted in Sun (*SPZ*, 374). Sun quotes the Mao Preface to the *Book of Poetry* as follows: "King Xuan returned to the ancients. He was capable of inward cultivation and of administering affairs; outwardly he resisted the Yi and Di, and restored the original land of Kings Wen and Wu; he repaired the carts and horses, and prepared equipment and tools; and he again convened the feudal lords at the eastern capital, and carried on hunting, selecting the carts and companions for it." (*SPZ*, 378).

66. *OSC*, 437-8.

67. I do this only for this one point of focus; such material is very important in numbers of ways: for example, in helping us date the vessels, and in confirming or adding to our knowledge of historical events.

68. Rawson also notes other phenomena appearing in the ritual arena and showing the same sign of purposeful change which is in part discontinuous with the immediate past and not a matter of gradual evolution. These include calligraphic style changes that suggest a reform of the script used for bronze inscriptions, and the incorporation of certain types of bell into ritual sets.

69. As he sets them forth, they are Poems 245, 250, 237, 235, 241, 242, 240, 236, 243 and 244. (See 347-8.) The occasion for the overhaul of sacrificial ritual, Sun sees as provided by the fact that the Zhou palace and ancestral temple had been burned in the uprising against King Li fifteen or so years previously. With the building of a new palace and a new temple, would readily come the creation of new ritual for use at the ancestral sacrifice.

Chapter 2

1. Even the phrase "three *yi*" suggests a priority and independence for the *Zhouyi* in relation to the other two-- it was the only *yi*, if one judges by title-names.

2. For the citation, see Note 42, in Chapter 1. My page-references are to the English translation.

3. See the citation in Note 43, in Chapter 1.

4. "*Bagua qiyuan*" (*Kaogu*, 1976.4 [242-255]).

5. In notes at the end of the article, he adds four more examples.

6. Despite the differences in the materials on which the numbers are inscribed, the time and place of the creation of the artifacts involved, the location of the discovery of the materials, etc.

7. In fact, however, as Zhang notes in an added set of notes at the end of the article, all of these numbers appear in other examples, from different time periods-- the 2, 3, and 4, for example, from very primitive times, and the 9 from pre-dynastic Zhou times.

8. Within the *Zhouyi* text, of course, the numbers 7 and 8 do not appear, only 6 and 9. But later tradition provides a context of explanation which Zhang and other interpreters plausibly use to introduce reference to the numbers 7 and 8.

9. In his reading of his examples, Zhang presumes that the *Zhouyi* method's use of "moving lines" is to be found in whatever method was involved in the use of the number-sets he is studying. But there is no direct evidence of that in the inscriptions, only the presumption on his part that writing number sets side by side indicates one set was derived from the other by such a process. And in fact, as he acknowledges for the paired sets he lists, there is no such connection in the manner of the *Zhouyi*: that is, taking certain numbers as standing for moving lines, others for unmoving, and seeing the second hexagram as derived from the first by the changes in the moving lines. "In our materials, however, 1, 5, 6, 7, 8 can all change, while there are no unchanging lines." (*IDI*, 86) This suggests that the analysis that reads the inscriptional material as signifying a transformation of one set into the other might be a misreading of material which instead represents two independent efforts to determine an answer to the same question. The side-by-side location of the written representations would signify simply that they are separate results of divination addressing the same matter at issue.

10. Zhang (*IDI*, 94) cites bamboo chips in a Warring States period burial, which are like the *Zhouyi* (as ordinarily interpreted) in using only four numerals. In this case the numbers are 1, 6, 8, and 9.

11. This seems a case of reading back into the earlier what is found later, and ignoring other alternatives. In particular, it is much too hasty to interpret the third case in the manner done, even if it may be possible in the first two cases to think of the single character as a number-set title.

12. Zhang Zhenglang, *IDI*, 86.

13. This reflects the close-- but unfortunate-- assimilation of stalk-divining with divination through shells/bones. A footnote in Zhang and Liu (*OMD*, 54) reads as follows: "A passage in the *Zuozhuan*, 15th year of Duke Xi, reads: 'The turtle [gives] the image and the milfoil the number.' This shows that in turtle-shell divination, what is auspicious and inauspicious appears in the images formed by the cracks in the shell, while divining by milfoil, what is auspicious and inauspicious appears in the numbers obtained from the milfoil-formed hexagrams...."

14. Not only the *Zhouyi* needs such an address, but the subsequent tradition as well. In the Appendix to this work, I make a start on such a rehearsal of the developments in the use of the *Zhouyi* in later tradition.

15. The divination whose anticipatory insight is into a future whose shaping is currently underway *with* the agent and is dependent in some measure on *how* that agent takes part, is prophetic in nature and function. Prophecy here is a pointing to the future which is addressed to beings who can themselves change and act differently depending on their knowledge and will, and whose change and action can 'falsify' the prophecy as an anticipatory affair.

Chapter 3

1. In the preceding discussion and in what follows, I am offering an interpretation of the *Zhouyi* in its original divinatory character and functioning. With the collapse of the Zhou dynasty in the early 8th century, we find that, in keeping with the changing times and the altering sense of those later generations about many aspects of their world, the *Zhouyi* was subject to further development and reinterpretation. Its history in that regard shows three sides. (1) There was a continuation and development which managed to some degree to keep faith with the character of the *Zhouyi* as such a divinatory work as I have pointed to. (2) There was a development of the work which altered its character, keeping it in mind as a divinatory vehicle but often bringing back the horizon of the auspicious and inauspicious as ultimate and focusing attention on the line-figures instead of the verbal images as the most fundamental sign-vehicles. (3) There was a development both parallel and divergent from the second, in which the work was gradually dismissed as a divination work and reconstituted as a wisdom book, as it becomes for the most part in the Appendices of the *Yijing*. These matters, I discuss briefly in the Appendix to this work.

2. Edward Shaughnessy has recently provided us with a translation of this version, under the title *I Ching: the Classic of Changes* (Ballantine, New York: 1997).

3. In our previous discussion, especially concerning pre-*Zhouyi* stalk-divination, we have encountered some suggestions about how line figures might have come to enter into divination and similar such things. In reality, our ignorance is considerable concerning the source of the two line-types as divinatory elements, and any meanings which they might have had in divination prior to their appearance in the hexagrams of the *Zhouyi*-- to say nothing of the source of the six-line figures as divinatory elements, and whether or not they were, say, a development from lesser line-sets (for example, from trigrams or three-line figures). [We do know that, if the number-sets of three and six found inscribed on Shang and early Zhou materials are related somehow to line-sets of three and six, both types are of long-standing and any derivation-relation of one to the other is without direct evidence.] Our concern is with how these factors functioned in the *Zhouyi* system. The most crucial ignorance, then, is of how, in the original 9th century working of the *Zhouyi* system, the hexagrams were brought into play and the signs selected. There are clues, and some later accounts, but not a lot to go on.

4. An increasingly complex way of taking the line-figures as having their own determinate meanings quite beyond what meanings the words introduce, develops in the course of the tradition of use and interpretation of the *Zhouyi*. Thus later tradition seeks to fix the reference of the figures more definitely, taking the trigrams to have definite meanings, taking each of the six different lines to have specific senses and functions, taking the lower two/middle two/upper two lines to have specific significance, and so on. There is no sufficient reason to think that any of that was part of the 9th century BC functioning of the figures.

5. The situational character of the reference would be something that includes the inquirer as participating in that situation, as agent who might have some impact on the issue through how he/she takes part in the unfolding of the present into the future and influences the factors whereby the issue is reached. What else is included, will differ from inquiry to inquiry; the essential indeterminateness to the reference of the line-figures simply means that 'the relevant situation is composed of an ordered multiplicity of forces at work in a way relevant to the future under inquiry'. The inquirer's thoughtful work of appropriation of the sign as 'response', as 'oracular message', includes determining the actual scope of the situation relevant in the inquiry at hand. As noted above, it is only in a later age that this indeterminateness is somewhat modified in the tradition of interpretation and use.

6. Although this normally is placed first in the textual exposition of the hexagram, on occasion the copying through which the text was transmitted through a series of perishable versions collapsed the title-name with the first words of the hexagram text. But normatively, it is a distinctive and separate element in the structure of a hexagram.

7. Forty-eight of the sixty-four hexagrams have one or both portions of this element present, but sixteen have no trace of it, whether due to loss in the course of copy-transmission or because there never was any such element belonging to them, or .... It might be that here the lack of such an element is a sign in itself: the situation does not call for a sacrifice, or the occasion is a-beneficial, so to speak (that is: it is neither beneficial nor not beneficial but indifferent altogether in this regard). In any case, there is no negative correlating to the positive in either case.

8. This is an optional part, apparently, for one or more elements of it appear in only twenty-eight of the sixty-four hexagrams.

9. The phrases reflect the use of the *Zhouyi* within the general horizon of the auspicious and inauspicious. However, unlike in the case of occasion responses where there is a question posed to which such responses are the direct answer, these phrases presuppose the distinctive use of the *Zhouyi* and merely address additional facets of the situation beyond its bearing on the matter being inquired into. Such phrases move generally within the horizon of the beneficial, and address an agent concerning opportunities for actions, or the lack of opportunity, which mark the situation in question.

10. This seems to be another optional part; one or more elements of it appear in only twenty-six of the sixty-four hexagrams.

11. Here, too, the phrases reflect the use of the *Zhouyi* within the general horizon of the auspicious and inauspicious. And as in the case of action indicators, in contrast with the occasion responses, these phrases presuppose the distinctive use of the *Zhouyi* and merely address additional facets of the situation beyond its bearing on the

matter being inquired into.

12. Found in only nine Hexagrams, namely: 8, 9, 20, 35, 43, 45, 48, 51 and 59.

13. In the case of Hexagrams 1 and 2, there is an added title, indicating the case when all of the lines in the hexagram in question are either 9's (Hexagram 1) or 6's (Hexagram 2). These seem likely to be later additions, perhaps introduced when the line titles were added.

14. Of the 386 lines, there are 377 lines with an image, 8 lines without any image, and 1 with only a partial image. It is clearly an essential component.

15. None of the components of the divinatory system-- neither the line figures and lines, nor the images-- function in the divinatory act as pictures or literal representations; they are vehicles for symbolic meaning, they are symbolic pointers. It is important, then, to distinguish five things. There is (for example) the word "well"; there are the realities (actual wells) meant literally by that word, those for which it is a sign. There is such a reality-- an actual well-- taken as a symbol and not simply as something represented literally in the word as significant sound; and together with this, there is the meaning which the symbolic reality embodies and which is being conveyed for interpretative application to the realities of the situation of inquiry. And finally, there are those latter realities. A question posed about a military matter might find as its response a verbally-conveyed image-- a mountain goat going lickety-split down the middle of the road; what is conveyed in this as symbol is a meaning applicable to the realities of the military situation, one embodied in the image when taken symbolically. It points to the dynamic of the military situation as to be attended to guided by this image-- by the sense that it is marked by a wild and quick forward movement, say. What is required for the appropriate 'application' of such a symbol, however, is not simply the drawing out of *some* meaning which *we* might claim to be harbored in it and finding how that meaning could find purchase in the facets of the world as we know it. For the images, as they are given in the work, are those images as they would have been intelligible and meaningful within the early Zhou tradition. If we would use *that* system and 'apply' it in accord with the images as originally intended, we would have to enter fully enough into the tradition to get the sense of their symbolic meaning as that would appear for someone steeped in that tradition. That is very difficult, at least with any fulness.

16. The image, however, can be much more complex and rich in its signifying.

17. The hexagram that results from the change in Line 1 of Hexagram 50.

18. This is evidently an optional part: of the 386 lines, only 54 have such an element.

19. Of the 386 lines, 293 have such a prognosticatory element. Despite its absence in numbers of lines, it seems to be an essential element in the verbal component

accompanying a line. The absence is probably due to its being an easy element to omit in copying: it often consists of one character or two, whose absence would not readily be noticed because it is independent, not such as would make sentences or phrases before or after it hard to understand.

20. Note that it is the upper trigram which is decisive here, even though the hexagrams are formed from the bottom.

21. There are no exactly comparable companions to the last or thirty-second pair in terms of their inner structure of two trigrams. But if we take the constituent trigrams of 63 and of 64, they are in each case the converse of each other. The hexagrams with a comparable relation of constituent trigrams are 31, 32, 41, and 42, and an inverse relation holds between the two pairs 31/32 and 41/42 in each case. We shall note their role in the discussion of Group C below.

22. The other two pairs, 53/54 and 61/62, occur in connection with the other two pairs of double-trigram hexagrams, namely, 51/52 and 57/58. They do not figure in the present grouping. Exhibited visually the four pairs in question here are:

27 and 28   31 and 32   17 and 18   41 and 42

23. The four pairs in question involve the following trigram-components:

In contrast, the hexagram pairs 1/2 and 63/64 involve the following trigram-components:

24. Thus in three of the four paired pairs, a visible expression of their linking is provided by the presence of an identical trigram in each of the four hexagrams of such a paired pair: the solid-broken-solid trigram in 21/22 and 37/38, the broken-broken-broken trigram in 23/24 and 35/36, and the solid-solid-solid trigram in 25/26 and 33/34. Only the paired pairs 19/20 and 39/40 have no such visible expression of their connectedness.

25. Except to the extent that allusion to the ritual reform of the late 9th century is part of the realization of the connectedness of increase and decrease, and this specific allusion is important in the ordering.

26. For examples, Hexagrams 13 and 14, 55 and 56, in addition to Hexagrams 1 and 2 (as mentioned earlier) .

27. Hexagrams 57 and 58.

28. Hexagrams 63 and 64.

29. Hexagrams 9 and 10 both tell stories, but the story-telling does not carry over continuously from 9 to 10 as it does in Hexagrams 1 and 2. Each story is self-contained, a separate vehicle for adumbrating the theme of its hexagram whole. Hexagram 43 is a tragic-comic story, linked with an ordered set of variations on a theme of enclosure and entanglement in Hexagram 44.

30. As in Hexagram 45.

31. See Hexagrams 36 and 54.

32. As in Hexagrams 3, 4, 22.

33. Hexagram 9.

34. One of the things which happens to the *Zhouyi* in the course of time is that this sense of its symbolic intending of the dynamic of change becomes reconceived; aided by focus on the line figures and the introduction of meanings to these and eventually of concepts such as *yin/yang* and the *wu xing*, not only does the nature of its divinatory functioning alter but the work eventually becomes a wisdom book embodying a categorial grasp of the intelligibility and order of the universe.

Chapter 4

1. In this case, the person might seek to understand afterward how and why the method worked. If in that subsequent reflective examination such a person was not able to provide plausible reasons accounting for what happened, at least he/she would have experienced the practical fruitfulness of the method.

2. One version of these two methods is sketched out in Chapter 4 of the explanatory chapters of John Blofeld's *I Ching: The Book of Change* (Dutton, 1968). See also Kerson and Rosemary Huang's *I Ching* (Workman, 1985: 61-68) [later cited as IC].

3. The two cases in which there is an unspecialized prognosticatory phrase seem likely to be cases of displaced text.

Notes for Part II

Prefatory Textual Note

1. I borrow the characterization from H. Roth; it is to be found in his article "Text and Edition in Early Chinese Philosophical Literature" (*Journal of the American Oriental Society*: Vol. 113.2, April-June 1993, 227).

2. In the traditional texts, there are several lines which begin with the action or prognostication words, and place the image after these. 15/4, 31/4, 34/3, 34/4, 38/5, 41/2, 46/5, 49/3, 49/4, 57/4, 62/4, 64/4, and 64/5 are examples. There are a number of lines where this might be the case, but there are either only action and prognostication words (no image) or only an image (no action or prognostication words), so one cannot tell. Examples of the former: 2/Extra, 4/3, 6/5 (?), 16/5, 25/4, 26/1, 32/2, 34/2, 35/5, 38/1, 40/1, 42/1, 45/2, 45/4, 57/5, 59/1, 64/3 (?). [The two question-mark cases are instances where the line is composed of the hexagram title-name and some action/ prognostication words.] Examples where there is only an image are fairly numerous.

3. When E. Shaughnessy speaks of them as a late accretion to the text, presumably dating no earlier than the mid to late Warring States period (*CZ*, 136), he voices a generally held view. The "presumably", however, might better be "perhaps".

4. See also 17/6 ('9' for '6'), 28/5 ('6' for '9'), 28/6 ('9' for '6'), 35/1 ('9' for '6'), 42/2 ('9' for '6'), 44/5 ('5' for '9'), 54/4 ('6' for '9'), 58/3 ('9' for '6'), 59/4 ('9' for '6'), 63/1 ('6' for '9'). In the case of 28/5 and /6, there seems to be a reversal of the number appropriate to the two lines; does that mean anything for the way the text from which the copying was made was itself written out? Such a double mistake could happen under any circumstances, but are there other clues that suggest the text being copied from was written in a certain way and that that facilitated such a copy error?

5. For example, Hexagram 8, Line 3; Hexagram 56, Line 2.

6. See Hexagram 31, Lines 2, 3, and 5: this involves repetition of the start of a line, and because the whole is not repeated, the connection of line and number is not disrupted. But such repetition shows one way by which the repetition which starts Hexagram 19 (in Lines 1 and 2) could have arisen.

7. These are characters which have the same sound, and one is used to stand for the other, even though their meanings may have nothing to do with each other. If one does not recognize this is occurring, and tries to read the loan-character in its own proper meaning(s), one will probably find it makes little sense and in any case will misunderstand what is being said.

8. The title-names of Hexagrams 58 and 43 are examples of this; both are proto-graphs for characters, the first with the heart radical added, the second with the foot radical added.

9. Another device-- the substitution of one character for another on the basis of their equivalence of meaning in the context-- can also become occasion for confusion. For example, the use of *wang²* instead of *sang⁴* (in the Hexagram Text of Hexagram 2, for one place); or the use of *pu²* instead of *chen²*, as in Line 6 of Hexagram 41.

10. For example, 8/1, 42/5, 57/6.

11. For example, 10/4 and the Hexagram Judgment in 10; 60/6 and the Hexagram Judgment in 60. Retention of a nearly identical line occurs in the case of 51/1 and the Hexagram Judgment in 51.

12. There are nineteen cases where this seems to have happened. They are: 2/3, 2/4, 3/2, 6/3, 7/5, 10/2, 10/3, 11/2, 12/6, 17/4, 24/6, 28/HJ, 31/2, 35/1, 41/1, 48/4, 52/6, 59/3, and 59/6.

13. Hexagram 62, Line 1. I take the phrase *shi wei zai sheng* to be a late commen-tary addition at the end of Line 6 of that Hexagram. The note in question refers to the text between the beginning of Line 1 and the end of Line 6; it says: "'Flying birds' on to 'ominous'." This means that the first line began with the phrase which in the traditional and Mawangdui texts is found in the Hexagram Judgment (it starts with `flying birds'); and the note refers for some copy purpose, I presume, to the text from there on to the `ominous' at the end of Line 6.

14. This is 23/3.

Hexagrams 1-8

1. The *yong⁴* (用) which I here translate "act" means to busy or apply oneself, to employ one's energies, thus to act or to do something, to take some definite initiative. In other contexts it means "to use", but to receive a sign included in which is the in-junction not to use it (that is, not to act on it) makes no sense.

2. In the world from which the images are drawn, "big man" could mean the King, or some nobleman, or the chief diviner for the King, in short, someone with con-siderable status. The "seeing" in question is a visiting to resolve something or to achieve something with the big man's help. See R. Kunst, in his *The Original "Yi-jing": a Text, Phonetic Transcription, Translation, and Indexes, with Sample Glosses*, for comments on the possible meanings of the phrase (393, also 395-6). (Later cited as *OY*.)

3. *CZ*, 166-67; see also 267-78, for a more extended and detailed account of this

matter.

4. It is difficult for the ordinary urban dweller to imagine how deeply agricultural people are imbued with a sense of timing and the timely when it comes to the land, the needs of growing things, and small but crucial changes in the weather that can have a profound impact on whether or not there is a crop at all, let alone on what kind of harvest may ensue. I know from early youth the voice, the gestures, and the concern of my grandfather, a southern Illinois farmer, addressed to what could happen overnight at this crucial time of planting. Indeed, I remember times when we worked through the night to get the corn or soybeans planted in timely fashion, pressed by his apprehensiveness about changing weather conditions.

5. Despite Kunst's attempts at refutation (*OY*, 411-16), Shaughnessy (*CZ*, 272) seems right in reading "necked (dragon)".

6. Hexagrams 1 and 2 are anomalous as having an extra notation, signifying not a separate line but all six lines taken together. (It may well be that these two notations are also later additions, and not part of the original *Zhouyi*.) If one takes the notation here as part of the story-telling despite its anomalous status, this would not involve implicit reference to some other time than the mid-August of the Line 6 image, but it could be taken to represent this same time of ripening in a particular respect. That would be as a time when the forces that have been at work at each step along the way are now working in consolidated fashion, to effect in the last concerted surge of vigorous activity a final ripening of the fruit of plants which by now have reached their full form. In contrast with the focus of Line 6 on the 'throat', the extra notation focuses on the 'head': crowds (because all the lines are changing) of headless dragons are visible.

7. For another use of this phrase, in connection with another pattern, see Hexagram 44, Line 5: "Using purple willow to wrap melons: a cherished pattern, something fallen from Heaven".

8. The lines of Hexagram 3 also importantly show human life as relating to animal life-- to deer (hunting) and horses (riding). Such a reference is expanded in the correlative pair to this one, namely, Hexagrams 15 and 16, whose title-names refer to animal life. For further thoughts on that, see under those Hexagrams.

9. Notice how the circling imagery, conveyed in the refrain of Lines 2, 4, and 6, is strengthened by the contrast of firm stability (Line 1), of potential for dispersion (Line 3), and of collection and concentration (Line 5), which enter into the movement imagery of the other three lines. One might see this hexagram as expanding the focus on the seasonal circle effected in Hexagrams 1 and 2; whereas they brought heaven and earth forward in connection with the agricultural rhythm of life, Hexagram 3 brings forward not simply another side to the continuation of human life (through the generations, the outcome of marriage: again involving ceremony)

but also the inclusion into ongoing earthly life of non-agricultural animal forms (horses, deer). In this light, the pair to Hexagram 3 (Hexagram 4) introduces plant life into the ongoing and circling.

10. See Li Jingchi in *Zhouyi tongyi* (4 of the Introduction, and 9 of the main text). (Later cited as *ZTong*.)

11. Hexagram 22, Line 4 has a similar structure, but seems to require a quite different way of interpreting the function of the elements.

12. *Fa¹* (發) has a number of senses which seem appropriate here: not only "dislodge" but also "uncover, find", even "clear away". I include two of these in the translation of this one term.

13. Is a 'metal'-husband a military-man (with bronze weapons) (see Li Jingchi, *ZTong*, 12)? a money-man (with much goods) (see Gao, *ZGJ*, 19)? or a 'statuette'? or ...?

14. Liu Baimin (*Zhouyi Shili Tongyi*) suggests that what is involved is a *qi⁴* (棄) (discarding, rejecting); if this involves a taking the best and rejecting and discarding what is not the best, this would be appropriate, and account for such a L-A as is given here.

15. The *heng*-ritual is, according to Waley (*Analects*, 177, 249), a ritual for "stabilizing, perpetuating the power of good omens and auspicious actions".

16. The opening phrase may also mean, "(he) offers captives in sacrifice".

17. Or, if one understands the opening phrase in its alternative sense (see the preceding Note): the sacrifice of frightened captives may succeed in creating a certain favorable state of things for a while, but eventually ....

18. Note that in terms of internal order, Hexagrams 7 and 8 have a parallel pattern with 5 and 6 (in each pair, one is a set of variations on a theme, the other a story).

19. Shaughnessy's account of the narrative exposition in these lines (*CZ*, 237-8) is on the whole excellent.

20. Or, "are made to come". See Hexagram 58, Line 3, for such a usage.

21. Presumably, those without a chief or leader, a "head" in that sense.

22. K. and R. Huang (*IC,* 12 and 86) treat this image as a recall of a historical event. The event involves Yu, founder of the Xia Dynasty and conqueror of the Great Deluge; "when a particularly uppity chieftain, Fang Feng, came late to a summoned

meeting, Yu used that as the pretext to have him executed". Gao (*ZGJ*, 30-31) cites a number of uses of the phrase involved here, including the reference in the *Bamboo Annals* to this incident which the Huangs cite.

23. An alternative understanding of the incident being alluded to is offered by the Huangs (*IC*, 86-87). They translate: "Deed of a famed counselor: the King lost the game after three chases, but the townsfolk were spared his wrath. Good omen." They interpret: "This appears to be a fragment from a long-lost tale recounting the helpful act of a famed imperial advisor who, through his tact and discretion, managed to prevent a frustrated king from venting his wrath on some innocent townsfolk." Gao (*ZGJ*, 33) also understands this as probably a story from ancient times, of much the same character. But whichever way it be understood, what is being imaged here is the kind of solidarity between King and people, the kind of character in the King and supportiveness in his relation to the people, that is called for in the Mandate of Heaven.

Hexagrams 9-16

1. Li (*ZTong*, 22) interprets the "paths" as those between the fields, and the image as of a return from the fields along those paths. Gao (*ZGJ*, 34) cites a *Shuo-wen* definition of *fu⁴* (read as 复) as "traveling the old established ways" (*xing² gu⁴ dao⁴*: 行故道).

2. Shaughnessy (*CZ*, 122) also notes the displaced status of this phrase, but thinks it is either an intrusion from line statement 10/3 or else is a separate line statement that has been displaced.

3. Gao follows a variant reading (*er²*: 而 , for *neng²*: 能), interpreting the phrase to speak of those without the ability who can nonetheless do the thing.

4. In Hexagram 54/Line 5, however, it is noted that she was upstaged at the wedding by her niece, who eventually replaced her as wife of King Wen and became the mother of his sons, including King Wu and the Duke of Zhou.

5. Or: "a wrapped steamed-meat offering".

6. The Huangs (*IC*, 94) claim that the inauspiciousness for the big man is because such an offering violates ritual, a proper bronze vessel should be used for an offering of ceremonial meat. Gao (*ZGJ*, 47) argues similarly, to the effect also that the wrapped offering is appropriate for the little man, suiting his circumstance and resources.

7. The Huangs (*IC*, 95) suggest that while wrapping meat offerings is inappropriate for a formal occasion, as a cooking technique it is appropriate for everyday meals. The absence of any prognostication words makes it difficult to know whether that is

relevant here, however.

8. The image in this line is dual. If the first is the original and only image, and the second a later addition, then the image here is simply of the obstruction ceasing. But if the two images belong in the original, then the overall sign involves a cessation of obstruction which is colored in the specific way pointed to through the rhyming couplet. According to that way, the petty obstruction which has brought one to the point of perishing will itself cease in function of one's having tied oneself to the solid (here, the bushy mulberry).

9. Both Gao (*ZGJ*, 50) and Li (*ZTong*, 29) cite a *Zhou-li* passage to the effect that the myriad people are brought to the royal gates when the country has a major affair pending. Li (31) speaks of the set of lines as a whole as addressing in orderly fashion pre-war preparations, war conditions, and post-war withdrawal of the army.

10. Gao (*ZGJ*, 52) discusses the sacrificial nature of the event alluded to here. Presumably the people are gathered here to offer gratitude and reverence to the spirits and to Heaven.

11. Or: "blame".

12. This is a sacrifice made at the side of the temple gate; but what it was more than that, and why this denial is made, is not clear.

13. One which (as Gao notes: *ZGJ*, 53) is fit for "carrying what is heavy and conveying it over distances".

14. Hexagrams 3 and 4 correspond to Hexagrams 15 and 16, as the outer pairs in a grouping centered around Hexagrams 9 and 10. The first pair introduce non-human life forms in connection with human life and life-ceremonies (see the commentary relating to the two hexagrams). In contrast, the pair presently being considered introduce non-human life forms (the hamster and the elephant) as having lives of their own, as being nature (in animal form) in independence of the human even though also impinging upon the latter.

15. Or, "strengthening, making sturdy", making the protective barrier greater by adding rocks.

Hexagrams 17-24

1. The term translated "virtuous power" here is one generally used for the beneficent power of the one King who holds and lives up to the Mandate of Heaven.

2. Shaughnessy (*CZ*, 232-5) also interprets the hexagram lines as telling a story. His cautious characterization: the lines present "a general scenario" with little basis for

tying the story to a specific historical event. Yet it has both historical and literary interest in the way it develops the pursuit, capture, and eventual sacrifice by the king himself of some person or persons. The identity of these persons is never specified beyond 'little boy' and 'man', but "the nature of the Topics in these lines ... combined with the emphatic insistence that their (re-)capture is the result of a pursuit or chase ..., leads one to suspect that this hexagram is concerned with run-away slaves, or other persons under the bondage of higher authorities."

3. The *jia*-stem day is the first day of a calendrical period such as the week is in our calendrical division.

4. Does this mean, "the likes of leaders" ('big men'), who would be looked up to in other circumstances?

5. Li (*ZTong*, 45-46) suggests that a marriage custom preserved from primitive society by the Ewenki nationality can throw light on the wedding reception set forth in this hexagram's lines.

6. In general, I follow Li (*ZTong*, 46) here and in Lines 2-4.

7. Li (*ZTong*, 46) takes this to refer to those who have run on ahead and whose running has brought them to greatly perspire over their whole body.

Hexagrams 25-32

1. Shaughnessy (*CZ*, 196-201) also takes the lines as telling a story, and understands it much as I do. Taking the title-name as standing for a disease and for the spirit which causes it, and taking Lines 1 and 6 as describing the active operation and the departure of this pestilential agent, he suggests that the lines in their traditional form may have somehow been interchanged. Looking at the lines in rearranged order, he sees them as exhibiting "a definite logic" of progressive development. "The bottom line would then announce the pestilence, the second line would describe its ravages, the third the people's attempt to eradicate it, the fifth their success in that attempt, and finally the top line would climactically announce the departure of the pestilence" (201).

2. Shaughnessy (*CZ*, 198-99) speaks of this line as a description of the condition of an agricultural community plagued by a pestilence. He translates: "Not planting or harvesting, not in the first or second year of cultivation", explains the meaning of the terms, and concludes that the image evokes severe damage as having been done by the pestilence. As a result of it, agricultural work was not done during a several year period.

3. Or: "good horses pursue". Perhaps even: "good (men) on horse pursue."

4. See Gao, *ZGJ*, 96; also Li, *ZTong*, 56.

5. The time when hunting was the primary mode of existence, before settled agricultural life became primary, may underlie this as well; but hunting persisted into the time of settled existence as an important element in life, especially in the life of the upper classes and royalty, even when its meaning was not to provide the main foodstuff for existence.

6. Kunst (*OY*, 14) says: "While the majority of hexagram-chapters have at least one mention of a sacrificial rite, some hexagrams have an overriding concern, such as Hexagrams 19, 31, 52, or 59. Many of the sacrifices involve a step-by-step procedure, such as a careful dismemberment of the victim, which might be either animal or human." And yet there is nothing explicit in the text that requires that the dismembering be for a sacrificial ritual and not simply for food.

7. Only in this Line does a second image appear; its relevance is unclear to me.

Hexagrams 33-40

1. Or: "a piglet worthy of the celebration".

2. To himself and/or others.

3. This line seems to allude to the story of Yin King Hai; for that story, see the discussion of Hexagrams 55 and 56.

4. For example, Li (*ZTong*, 68-69) sees it as alluding to an incident between the Zhou and the barbarians, at the time when the former moved from Bin down to the area of Mt. Qi.

5. Feng, the next to the youngest of the sons of King Wen, became enfeoffed eventually as the lord of Kang. This happened after the death of King Wu, who had finally achieved the Zhou victory over the Shang, and in connection with the suppression of a revolt, following which the Shang people were forcibly removed from the original homelands.

6. This suggests that his journey was as leader of a military foray. His success contrasts with the experience of the pheasant, who knows the other end of one bowman's "bagging" his bird.

7. Uncle of Shang King Zhou[4] (紂: the last of the Shang line), he was also Prime Minister and much admired for his courage and wisdom. Thrown into prison when he admonished Zhou[4] on his excesses, he escaped execution only by feigning madness. When released from prison by the conquering Zhou[1] (周), he did not want to serve under the Zhou rule, but migrated and founded what eventually became

Korea.

8. The phrase concerning wife and children has inadvertently been copied to intrude into and divide the three-character prognostication word set that belongs with it. I have restored the order by treating the *ji²* (吉) as belonging with *zhong¹ lin⁴* (終吝), not with the *hui³ li⁴* (悔厲) which immediately precedes it in the traditional and Mawangdui versions.

9. See Li (*ZTong*, 73-75) for a slightly different account of the theme of the whole hexagram and of the various lines.

10. Li (*ZTong*, 74) seems right in taking *jia¹* (家) as *jia¹ miao⁴* (家廟) (family temple or shrine), and in referring for this to Hexagrams 45 and 59, with their phrases *wang² jia¹ you³ miao⁴* (王假有廟). The difference in phrasing, he explains: "Because this hexagram speaks of the house (*jia¹ ting²*: 家庭), the word here is *jia¹*, not *miao⁴*, the place of ancestral worship. ... The ancestors are an inseparable component of the house, if one does not have ancestors one does not have a house. That is the ancient view of the family."

11. The Chinese (*zhu³*: 主) could mean a variety of things: 'master', 'lord', 'chief or leader', 'host'; and if it were being intended elliptically, it could stand for 'the one who officiates at or presides over or is in charge of ...' (a ceremony, ritual; or a committee, an office, an undertaking). Presumably in this context it refers to the main man in this matter of a marriage, thus the head of a family. Who else is involved in the meeting, is not clear, but presumably it would be someone representing the other family involved.

12. I base my reading of these on Shaughnessy, *CZ*, 212-220, and his "unabashedly speculative" interpretations of the imagery in a celestial reference. In his concluding comments (220) Shaughnessy asserts that his interpretations-- both possible and plausible-- depict a society of sky-watchers who invested the night-time luminaries with earthly qualities. If I may take this comment in a slightly different direction than he does: the early Chinese linked the celestial sky and the conditions and affairs of humans on earth not simply in the calendrical and seasonal fashion of Hexagrams 1 and 2, but in the even more intimate connection which includes decisive human affairs that were not grounded in the natural rhythms in the way raising food-crops is. Marriage is simply one instance of that. But short of knowing much more than I currently do about the Chinese vision of the night sky and other aspects of late Western Zhou social conventions and affairs, I do not offer my reading of the lines with much assurance as to their particular sense. That there is coherence to be found here, however, and something like the interweaving of celestial and human that I have sought to elicit, I would affirm much more confidently.

13. Since this constellation is the paranatellon of the "Heavenly Swine", Lines 1 and 6 are linked by the imagery. In general, when celestial phenomena are given earthly

meanings, as in this case and in other lines, the image becomes very complex. For there is not only what is involved in the happening as a celestial affair; there is a dimension to the meaning of celestial which is introduced by the earthly figures and events (here, horses). Thus while the basic symbol here is a constellation and its movement in the night sky, the meaning of that sign includes (earthly) horses and their behavior.

14. Or: "their bodies are".

15. Or: "hobbling backward".

16. There is no image in Line 1, so the start of the story is lacking.

Hexagrams 41-48

1. Li (*ZTong*, 81-85, esp. 81, 83, 85) has his own suggestive way of making a kindred point about the two hexagrams. He claims that they are organized as opposites which explain the antithetical transformatory principles involved in matters of increase and decrease. These are 'either/or', or 'one has the other in itself'. More specifically, the two hexagrams show pure dialectical thought, with Decrease exhibiting this in miscellaneous affairs and stressing the principles of increase/decrease as reflected in concrete conditions, while Increase takes historical material as evidence, stressing the shifts up and down of the Zhou House (from increase to decrease).

2. Given that in the line-figure drawings of these two hexagrams these two lines are the 'same' line in reversed position, such a copying of the corresponding Line 2 in Hexagram 42 as if it were Line 5 in 41 is not unintelligible. For a similar case of miscopying, see Hexagram 44/Line 3 and Hexagram 43/ Line 4.

3. Cowrie shells are used like money as a measure of value; a 10-cowry turtle is fairly valuable.

4. Or: "to do a big deed or major work".

5. The name of the King's diviner. He divines concerning the captives, and announces the results to the King.

6. I follow Li (*ZTong*, 84) in understanding this to mean: he carries out a sacrificial act involving offering some of the captives as sacrifical animals.

7. Or: "he is unable to walk".

8. Or: "is hobbled and faltering in its walk".

9. This is translated by Kunst as ...: "they lock their horns."

10. One could also take Lines to be related differently: for example, 1 and 6, 2 and 5, 3 and 4, link with each other in certain regards; and then again, 1 and 5, 2 and 6, and 3 and 4, link with each other in other regards.

11. There is a dispute about what this sacrifice is and involves, whether it is a summer sacrifice or a spring sacrifice (cf. Gao, 154). See also 46/2 and 63/5.

12. Or: "forward[b] in ascent".

13. See Hexagram 45/ Line 2, and the Note there.

14. Or: "ascent in the darkness".

15. The very etymology of the title-name, which shows the natural (a tree) circumscribed (surrounded by an enclosure), suggests the basic sense here, that of a being hedged in, being frustrated or inhibited, being oppressed or beset and besieged.

16. That is, overwhelmed and oppressed.

17. The identity of the border-state in question is not clear.

18. The identity of the border-state people in question is not clear. Presumably it is different from that state alluded to in Line 2; at least the Chinese characters for 'vermillion' and 'red' are different, and that difference is probably significant.

19. Li (*ZTong*, 95) fills out the meaning of this image a bit differently.

Hexagrams 49-56

1. The title-name *ge²* (革) has the more concrete meaning of "a hide whose hair has been removed; leather" and the more general meaning of a "change, transformation", particularly a change which involves removing, getting rid of, eliminating, renovating, making into something new.

2. That is, changed their countenances.

3. Or is it: their faces were leather-like and showed nothing of their own attitudes?

4. One should keep in mind what Kunst remarks on (*OY*, 422), that the cauldron is a bronze sacrificial vessel type, with three or four legs, whose function in sacrifice forms the background for its occurrence in the *Zhouyi* "with the differing ways in which it was used, differing styles, and extraordinary events involving the cauldron all affecting the effectiveness of the sacrificial ritual." Nonetheless, the Lines do not seem to pertain to the cauldron in any sacrificial use.

5. Shaughnessy (*CZ*, 116, 204-210 [esp. 207 and 208], 332-33 [n44]) makes numerous suggestive observations about thunder, the seasons, and the stirring of life and growth, as the ancient Chinese felt and conceptualized these matters. We should keep in mind here that in north China winter (beginning in the 10th month) is the dry season, and that spring (beginning in the 2nd month) brings thunder and its attendant rains. This also is the time of the thawing of winter's frozen ground and the beginning of agricultural work again. Thunder's role in 'arousing' the countryside was institutionalized in the agricultural almanac by naming the period of thunder's first sounding as 'arousing the hibernating'. Before work in the fields began, ceremonies were held to celebrate the survival through the winter and ritually to ensure the fertility of the soil for the coming growing season. Thunder played an initiating role in these spring festivals.

6. As Shaughnessy (*CZ*, 202) indicates, the characters here signify a looking around anxiously.

7. Or: "trunk of the body".

8. Xun-zi, for example, speaks of feathers being used as ornaments in the Peace Dance (see 樂論, lines 28-29 in the Harvard-Yenching Institute Sinological Index Series version of his works).

9. Cf. Shaughnessy, *CZ*, 194-5, and more broadly, his analysis of the lines of the hexagram (189-195).

10. This is capable of different interpretations. For example, Kunst (*OY*, 347) understands "younger sisters as secondary wives"; Shaughnessy (*CZ*, 241) says that the principal wife was regularly accompanied by younger members of her generation.

11. That is, has married later than normal, at an older age. Shaughnessy (*CZ*, 239) translates: "misses her time".

12. The Shang ruler who gave his daughter in marriage to King Wen of the Zhou. The marriage was unsuccessful, at least in that the mother of King Wu and the other brothers who led the Zhou in their conquest of the Shang later was a different woman.

13. The acts here are ritual, and their unsuccessful character is symbolic.

14. Shaughnessy (*CZ*, 239-44) makes a very good case for this being the story being told in the Hexagram lines.

15. The title-name has the sense of "big, large, great", but with particular reference to the "grand looks of anything".

16. There is no clarification of the "it" here, but in other phrases of the same type the entry is into the royal temple or the royal home (as a place of worship). *Wang* could mean "King" or "Prince" here.

17. That is, Prince Hai, the member of the royal family in early Shang dynasty times who seems to be the subject of the story being told in Hexagrams 55 and 56.

18. As David Hawkes (*Songs of the South*, 52) characterizes him, Prince Hai, son of Ji, was the first herdsman. He committed adultery with the wife of Mian-chen, lord of You Yi, where he was pasturing his flocks and herds. He was killed by Mian-chen in revenge. Hawkes cites and translates a *Tian Wen* passage which alludes to him, as follows: "Hai inherited Chi's prowess. His father was a goodly man. Why did he end by losing his herdsmen and his oxen and sheep in Yu I? When he danced with shield and plumes, why did she yearn for him? How did her smooth sides and lovely skin get so fat? Why did the herdsmen of Yu I come to meet them? When they struck the bed he had already gone out. How did he meet his fate? Heng inherited Chi's prowess. How did he get back those oxherds and oxen? How did he go about there dispensing his gifts and not return back emptyhanded?..." K. and R. Huang (*IC*, 14-15) provide a more sanitized characterization of Prince Hai as "a clever, enterprising, and restless man who left his home to travel to the Kingdom of Yi to raise cattle and seek his fortune .... There Prince Hai encountered mysterious conspiracies against him. He had a flourishing flock of sheep, but somehow lost it.... He then raised oxen and invented the ox yoke to put them to work in the field. There was an attempt to burn him to death in his house, from which he was able to escape only because a mysterious rap on his bed roused him.... His luck did not hold out for long, however. The local King, Mianshen, who may have been behind all the conspiracies, finally killed him and took his oxen .... Prince Hai's death was eventually avenged by his son Wei, who, with the assistance of a neighboring state, attacked Yi and killed Mianshen." Hexagram 55 tells the story of Prince Hai as a youth before he left home, showing something of his character (his restlessness and his adulterous tendencies) and what would move him to the acts of self-destruction and wandering that appear in Hexagram 56.

19. Or: "into small bits".

Hexagrams 57-64

1. In the calendrical use of the terms, this stem-day is the seventh in a ten day cycle.

2. That is, coin shaped like an axe.

3. The image in this line could itself have to do with religious ceremony, but what seems a pattern in the grouping of lines suggests that it rather has to do with an indecisive military conflict. It is concerning this that the sacrificial religious ritual is called for in the next line, and repeatedly called for in the third line.

4. The lack of image does not let one know whether the hunting theme is continued or whether the religious ritual becomes thematic again, now as celebratory (the prognostication words suggest this). It would seem, in any case, a time of peace and tranquility.

5. Li (*ZTong*, 219-221) suggests that the lines set forth a story of conflicts (country with country, clan with clan) and show a dramatic movement in the series of joys being enumerated. What is at issue is "problem solving and attaining happiness and well-being". I have not followed this suggestion, though it is appealing, but have treated the lines as more analytical in character.

6. This is a sacrifice of repose, offered on the day of the funeral to appease the spirits.

7. The use of bird imagery to link the hexagram pair of 61 and 62 involves four lines. In the present hexagram, the calling crane (Line 2) and the whirring sound of wings (Line 6) bring in intimate connection and departure. In Hexagram 62, the fitness of flying birds leaving behind their sounds to descend to earth (Line 1), and the shooting and netting of a wounded bird (Line 6) bring in the joy of arrival (ready to descend) and the act of violence and entanglement by which a human being ends a bird's life.

8. Or: "It is not fitting for the flying birds, leaving behind their sounds, to rise, it is fitting for them to descend".

9. Gao (*ZGJ*, 214) seems right in taking "meet" in the sense of "welcome and stop someone"; it refers to a coming to recognize and acknowledge, to have something to do with, another person, to receive and be received each into the other's being so that the parties really meet each other.

10. Kunst (*OY*, 363) translates: "He does not pass them. They prevent him. Someone following him injures him. Ominous."

11. See Note 7, above.

12. The Shang King, Wuding.

13. See Shaughnessy (*CZ*, 257-65) for a good discussion of these two hexagrams (63 and 64) in their connection with each other.

14. See Shaughnessy, *CZ*, 263.

15. See the Note to Hexagram 45/ Line 2.

16. That is, the pre-dynastic Zhou leader Ji Li. Shaughnessy (*CZ*, 263-4) notes that

it was under Ji Li that the Zhou first appeared as a major military and political force. The emoluments granted him by the Shang ruler seem to represent the first formal recognition of the Zhou state's status. "Ji Li ... marked the beginning of the rise of Zhou."

17. That is, the Shang.

18. See Note 13 above.

SELECTED BIBLIOGRAPHY

Collections or Reference Volumes

A Concordance to Shih Ching. Harvard-Yenching Institute Sinological Index Series, Supplement No. 9. Reprint, 1974.

A Concordance to Yi Ching. Harvard-Yenching Institute Sinological Index Series, Supplement No. 10. Reprint, 1973, Taipei.

Shang Shu tong-jian. Edited by Gu Jiegang et al. Harvard-Yenching Institute, 1936.

The Beginning of the Use of Metals and Alloys. Editor: Robert Maddin. Cambridge (MA): MIT Press, 1988.
    Rawson, Jessica. "A Bronze-Casting Revolution in the Western Zhou and Its Impact on Provincial Industries". 228-238.

The Great Bronze Age of China. Editor: George Kuwayama. Los Angeles County Museum of Art, 1983.
    Bagley, Robert W. "The High Yinxu Phase (Anyang Period)". 177-182.
    ———. "The Rise of the Western Zhou Dynasty". 193-202.
    ———. "Transformation of the Bronze Art in Later Western Zhou". 241-244.
    Kuwayama, George. "The Cultural Renaissance of Late Zhou". 56-57.
    Ma Chengyuan. "The Splendor of Ancient Chinese Bronzes". 1-19.
    Nivison, David S. "Western Chou History Reconstructed from Bronze Inscriptions". 44-55.

Xi-Zhou shi yanjiu. Renwen zazhi congkan, No. 2. Xianshi weidangxiao yinshuahu: 1984.
    Chen Quanfang. "Zhou-yuan xinchu bujia yanjiu". 294-307.
    Liu Baocai and Zhou Suping. "Xizhou shiliao shuyao". 359-393.
    Meng Shikai. "Jiaguwen zhong suojian Shang Zhou guanxi zai tantao". 255-261.
    Wang Mingge. "Cong jinwen zhong Xi-Zhou tudi wangquan suoyouzhi de bianhua". 67-70.

General

Blofeld, John. *I Ching: the Book of Change.* New York: Dutton, 1968.

Chang, K. C. *The Archaeology of Ancient China.* New Haven and London: Yale University Press, 1968.

Chen, Shih-chuan. "How to form a hexagram and consult the *I Ching*". *Journal of the American Oriental Society*, Volume 92, Number 2, April-June 1972. 237-249.

Creel, H. *The Origins of Statecraft in China* (Vol. I). Chicago: University of Chicago Press, 1970.
___ . *The Birth of China.* New York: Ungar, 1937.

Ding, Shouchang. *Du Yi Hui-tong.* Taibei: He-luo tushu chubanshe, 1975.

Dubs, Homer. "The Archaic Royal Jou Religion". *Toung Pao*, XLVI, 1958. 236-7.

Falkenhausen, Lothar von. "Issues in Western Zhou Studies: A Review Article". *Early China* 18, 1993. 139-226. [A review of books by Shaughnessy and Rawson].

Gao Heng. *Zhouyi gu-jing jin-zhu.* Taibei: Le-tian chubanshe, 1974.
___ . *Zhouyi gujing tongshuo.* Beijing: Zhonghua shuju, 1958.
___ . *Zhouyi zalun.* Jinan: Shandong Renmin chubanshe, 1962.

Gu Jiegang. "*Zhouyi* guayaoci zhong de gushi". An article in *Gushibian*, Vol. 3. Beijing: 1931. 1-44.

Hawkes, David. *Songs of the South.* Oxford: Clarendon Press, 1959.

Ho Ping-ti. *The Cradle of the East.* Chicago: University of Chicago Press, 1975.

Huang, Kerson and Rosemary Huang. *I Ching.* Workman, 1985.

Huang Peirong. "Xianqin shishu kao". *Shumu jikan*, 17.3: December 1983. 80-87.

Huang Shengzhang. "Wei *he, ding* zhong 'zhu' yu 'zhu tian' ji qi qianshe de XiZhou tianzhi wenti". *Wen Wu*: 1981. 9. 79-82.

Karlgren, Bernhard. *The Book of Documents.* Stockholm: Museum of Far Eastern Antiquities, 1950.
___ . *The Book of Odes.* Stockholm: Museum of Far Eastern Antiquities, 1950.
___ . *Grammata Serica Recensa.* Stockholm: Museum of Far Eastern Antiquities,

1964.

___ . "New Studies on Chinese Bronzes". Stockholm: Museum of Far Eastern Antiquities, Bulletin No. 9, 1937. 9-117.

___ . "Yin and Chou in Chinese Bronzes". Stockholm: Museum of Far Eastern Antiquities, Bulletin No. 8, 1936. 9-154.

Keightley, D. *Sources of Shang History.* Berkeley: University of California Press, 1978.

Kunst, R. *The Original "Yijing": a Text, Phonetic Transcription, Translation, and Indexes, with Sample Glosses.* Doctoral dissertation, University of California (Berkeley), 1985.

Li Dingzuo. *Zhouyi ji-jie.* Taibei: Taiwan xuesheng shu-ju, 1976 reprint of a Tang dynasty compilation.

Li Jingchi. *Zhouyi tong-yi.* Beijing: Zhonghua Shuju, 1981.

___ . *Zhouyi Tan-yuan.* Beijing: Zhonghua Shuju, 1978; reprinted, with corrections and new publisher's note, 1982.

Li Ling. "Xi Zhou jinwenzhong de tudi zhidu". *Xueren* 2. Nanjing: Jiangsu Wenyi, 1992. 224-256.

Liu Baimin. *Zhouyi Shili tongyi.* Taibei: Yuan-dong tushu gong-si, 1965.

Liu Dajun. *Zhouyi gailun.* Jinan: Qilu shushe, 1986.

Lu Deming. *Jingdian shiwen.* Taibei: Ding-wen shuju, 1975.

Nan Huaijin and Xu Chinting. *Zhouyi jin-zhu jin-yi.* Taibei: Taiwan Shang-wu yinshuguan, 1979.

Nivison, D. "The Dates of Western Chou". *Harvard Journal of Asiatic Studies*, 43 (2), 1983. 481-580.

Overmyer, Daniel L., with David Keightley, Edward Shaughnessy, Constance Cook, and Donald Harper. "Chinese Religions-- The State of the Field. Part I. Early Religious Traditions: The Neolithic Period through the Han Dynasty (ca. 4000 B.C.E to 220 C.E.)". *The Journal of Asian Studies,* 54, no. 1 (February 1995). 124-160.

Pankenier, D. "Astronomical Dates in Shang and Western Zhou". *Early China* 7: 1981-82. 2-37.

___ . "*Mozi* and the Dates of the Xia, Shang, and Zhou: a Research Note". *Early China* 9-10, 1983-85. 175-183.

Rawson, Jessica *Western Zhou Ritual Bronzes from the Arthur M. Sackler Collec tions.* Washington [DC] and Cambridge [MA]: Arthur M. Sackler Foundation & Arthur M. Sackler Museum, Harvard University, 1990 (Vol. IIa).
___ . "Ancient Chinese Ritual Bronzes: The Evidence from Tombs and Hoards of the Shang (c. 1500-1050 B.C.) and the Western Zhou (c. 1050-771 B.C.) Periods". *Antiquity,* 67.257, 1993. 805-823.

Roth, H. "Text and Edition in Early Chinese Philosophical Literature". *Journal of the American Oriental Society,* Vol. 113.2, April-June 1993. 214-227.

Shaughnessy, E.L. "A First Reading of the Mawangdui *Yijing* Manuscript". *Early China* 19, 1994. 47-73.
___ . *I Ching: the Classic of Changes.* New York: Ballantine, 1997.
___ . "Marriage, Divorce, and Revolution: Reading between the Lines of the *Book of Changes".* *Journal of Asian Studies,* 51. 3, August 1992. 587-599.
___ . "On the Authenticity of the Bamboo Annals". *Harvard Journal of Asiatic Studies,* 46 (1). 149-180.
___ . "The 'Current' *Bamboo Annals* and the Date of the Zhou conquest of Shang". *Early China* 11-12, 1985-87. 33-60.
___ . *The composition of the "Zhouyi".* Doctoral dissertation, Stanford University, 1983.
___ . "The Duke of Zhou's Retirement in the East and the Beginnings of the Minister- ial-Monarch Debate in Chinese Political Philosophy". *Early China* 18, 1993. 41-72.
___ . "The Origin of an *Yijing* Line Statement". *Early China* 20, 1995. 223-240.
___ . *Sources of Western Zhou history: inscribed bronze vessels.* University of California Press, 1991.

Smith, Kidder Jr. "*Zhouyi* Interpretation from Accounts in the *Zuozhuan".* *Harvard Journal of Asiatic Studies,* 49.2, 1989. 421-463.
___ . "The Difficulty of the *Yijing".* *Chinese Literature: Essays, Articles, Reviews,* 15, 1993. 1-15.

Smith, Richard J. *Fortune-tellers and Philosophers.* Boulder, San Francisco, Oxford: Westview Press, 1991.

Song Zuoyin. *Zhouyi Xinlun.* Changsha: Hunan jiaoyu chubanshe, 1982.

Sun Zuoyun. *Shijing yu Zhoudai shehui yanjiu (A study of the 'Book of Poetry' and Zhou dynasty society).* Beijing: Zhonghua Shuju, 1966.

Tang Lan. "Shaanxi Sheng Qishan Xian Dongjiacun xinchu Xi Zhou zhongyao tongqi mingci de yiwen he zhushi". *Wen Wu,* 1976.5. 55-59,63.

Waley, Arthur. *The Analects of Confucius.* London: Allen and Unwin, 1938.

___ . "The Book of Changes". Stockholm: Bulletin of the Museum of Far Eastern Antiquities (Vol. 5), 1933. 121-142.

___ . "The Eclipse Poem and its Group". *T'ien Hsia Monthly*, October 1936. 245-248.

Wang, C. H. *The Bell and the Drum.* Berkeley: University of California Press, 1974.

Wang Ningsheng. "Bagua qiyuan". *Kaogu*, 1976.4. 242-245.

Xu Qinting. *Zhouyi yiwen kao.* Taibei: Wu-zhou chubanshe, 1975.

Xu Zhuoyun. *Xi-Zhou shi.* Taibei: Lianjing chuban gongsi, 1984.

Ye Daxiong. *XiZhou zhengzhi shi yanjiu.* Taibei: Mingwen shuju, 1982.

Yu Yongliang. "Yi guayaoci di shidai ji qi zuozhe". An article in *Gushibian*, Vol. 3. Beijing: 1931. 143-170.

Zhang Liwen. *Zhouyi sixiang yanjiu.* Wuhan: Hubei renmin chubanshe,1980.

Zhang Zhenglang. "Shishi Zhou chu qingtongqi mingwen zhong de Yi gua". *Kaogu xuebao*, 1980.4. 403-415. This (with emendations by the author) has been translated into English in *Early China*, 6 (1980-81), 80-96, under the title "An Interpretation of the Divinatory Inscriptions on Early Chou Bronzes".

Zhang Yachu and Liu Yu. "Cong Shang-Zhou bagua shuzi fuhao tan shifa de jige wenti". *Kaogu*, 1981.2. 155-63, 154. This has been translated into English in *Early China*, 7 (1981-82), 46-55, under the title "Some Observations about Milfoil Divination Based on Shang and Zhou *bagua* Numerical Symbols".

INDEX

DATE DUE

Demco, Inc 38-293